POETIC FORM AND
BRITISH ROMANTICISM

D0217951

Poetic Form and
British Romanticism

STUART CURRAN

OXFORD UNIVERSITY PRESS
New York   Oxford

PR
590
.C8
1986

Oxford University Press

Oxford   New York   Toronto
Delhi   Bombay   Calcutta   Madras   Karachi
Petaling Jaya   Singapore   Hong Kong   Tokyo
Nairobi   Dar es Salaam   Cape Town
Melbourne   Auckland

and associated companies in
Berlin   Ibadan

Copyright © 1986 by Oxford University Press, Inc.

First published in 1986 by Oxford University Press, Inc.,
200 Madison Avenue, New York, New York 10016

First issued as an Oxford University Press paperback, 1989

Oxford is a registered trademark of Oxford University Press

All rights reserved. No part of this publication may be reproduced,
stored in a retrieval system, or transmitted, in any form or by any means,
electronic, mechanical, photocopying, recording, or otherwise,
without the prior permission of Oxford University Press, Inc.

Library of Congress Cataloging-in-Publication Data
Curran, Stuart.
Poetic form and British romanticism.
Bibliography: p.
Includes index.
1. English poetry—19th century—History and criticism.
2. Romanticism—England.
I. Title. PR590.C8   1986   821'.7'09145   85-28436
ISBN 0-19-504019-8
ISBN 0-19-506072-5 (PBK)

2 4 6 8 10 9 7 5 3 1

Printed in the United States of America

For
JOSEPH WITTREICH
as constant in intellect as in affection—
with whom this conversation began and continues

. . . we will sit and talk of time and change
As the world ebbs and flows, ourselves unchanged.

CONCORDIA UNIVERSITY LIBRARY
2811 NE HOLMAN ST.
PORTLAND, OR 97211-6099

Preface

This book is a history of British Romantic poetry, even though its subject may initially appear intractable to such an ambition. The argument that form, rather than being generally dismissed in the period, is a significant key to its character is embodied in the ensuing chapters. Yet, in the abstract, the supposition that every major poem of the period, and dozens of minor ones as well, can be treated profitably under such a rubric does testify to the importance of a subject generally disregarded in criticism of the British Romantics. And that, as the last chapter attempts to suggest, it may also be a key to the achievements of European Romanticism as a whole indicates the scope this study wishes to assume.

Although the critical approach is deliberately pluralistic and the vocabulary is unspecialized, the study undoubtedly is engaged in the methodology of genre and reception theory and in what we now call contextuality. In recent years we have come to read the inner complexity of Romantic poetry with increasing delicacy and sophistication, and all critics of the period have profited as well from major studies of the historical conditions and intellectual inheritance impinging on the poets. But we know surprisingly little—or, perhaps, have forgotten too much—about the actual literary conditions of the time. Hence we tend to read the poetry as a centering of psychological stresses or of historical and philosophical forces, ignoring much that is crucial to any poet as practitioner of a craft. This study certainly does not itself wish to ignore either personal or social dynamics, but instead hopes to right the balance by placing them within the specific cultural conditions that spawned and nurtured Romanticism. If in the process many accepted readings are questioned or at least focused within a new perspective, this will testify to the dimensions of the cultural ferment within which the poetry was created, as well as the multiplicity of contexts in which its art can be viewed. This late in human history there is no such thing as creation *ex nihilo*, and to pretend otherwise (which is, to be sure, what the Romantics themselves sometimes did) inevitably leads to distortion.

Aside from its aim of provoking a new dialogue about the nature of Romanticism, this book also hopes to suggest ways in which the formal elements in all literature influence ideological perspective and, if not wholly cautionary in its motives, would wish at least to encourage open eyes as a preliminary to broad conclusions.

This subject first began to engage my attention during a fellowship from the John Simon Guggenheim Foundation a decade ago, was pursued during a sabbatical leave from the University of Pennsylvania and, in the writing stage, was greatly facilitated by a summer grant at the Henry E. Huntington Library and a fellowship from the National Endowment for the Humanities, which the University of Pennsylvania also generously subvened. I have been contemplating this subject, discussing it, teaching it, and in truth burdening friends and colleagues with it for so many years that it is impossible to record all the debts I have accrued, the valuable suggestions and equally important challenges, that have led me this far. It is easier to acknowledge debts to institutions, but even then difficult to honor so abstractly the extent to which every page of this book depends on the resources and staffs of major libraries: the British Library and Bodleian Library of Oxford University, in Great Britain; and in the United States, the Library of Congress, Folger Shakespeare Library, Huntington Library, Houghton Library of Harvard University, and Van Pelt Library of the University of Pennsylvania. I have been materially helped by the advice of friends who have read the manuscript in whole or in part: Frank Paul Bowman, Celeste Langan, Annabel Patterson, Arkady Plotnitsky, and Joseph Wittreich. And I do think the debt I owe to the ingenuity of the unadvertising David Kay should be recognized: his Kay-Pro was, for me, the most liberating intellectual enabler of my experience, especially as it was watched over by the knowing, patient guidance of its magus, Hollister Moore.

For all quotations I have used standard editions. For the major Romantic poets these are cited, with appropriate abbreviations, in the text. Page references are to the following editions:

- William Blake: *The Poetry and Prose of William Blake*, ed. David V. Erdman (New York: Doubleday, 1965).
- Lord Byron: early poems are quoted from *The Poetical Works of Lord Byron*, Vols. 1-3, ed. Jerome J. McGann (Oxford: Clarendon Press, 1980-1982; "The Blues" is quoted from Vol. 4 of the Ernest Hartley Coleridge edition (London: John Murray, 1901); and *Don Juan* from Leslie Marchand's edition (Boston: Houghton Mifflin, 1958); *Byron's Letters and Journals*, ed. Leslie Marchand (Cambridge: Harvard University Press, 1973-1981): (*L&J*).
- Samuel Taylor Coleridge: *Poems of Samuel Taylor Coleridge* (London: Oxford University Press, 1912); *Collected Letters of Samuel Taylor Coleridge*, ed. Earl Leslie Griggs (Oxford: Clarendon Press, 1956-1966): (*LSTC*); *Biographia Literaria*, ed. J. Shawcross (London: Ox-

ford University Press, 1905): (*BL*); *Shakespearean Criticism*, ed. T. M. Raysor (Cambridge: Harvard University Press, 1930): (*SC*).

- John Keats: *The Poems of John Keats*, ed. Jack Stillinger (Cambridge: Harvard University Press, 1978); *The Letters of John Keats, 1814–1821*, ed. Hyder E. Rollins (Cambridge: Harvard University Press, 1958).
- Percy Bysshe Shelley: *Shelley's Poetry and Prose*, ed. Donald H. Reiman and Sharon B. Powers (New York: Norton, 1977); the text for *Rosalind and Helen* is taken from *Poetical Works*, ed. Thomas Hutchinson (London: Oxford University Press, 1905); *Letters of Percy Bysshe Shelley*, ed. Frederick L. Jones (Oxford: Clarendon Press, 1956).
- William Wordsworth: *Wordsworth's Poetical Works*, ed. Ernest de Selincourt and Helen Darbishire (Oxford: Clarendon Press, 1952–1959): (*WPW*); *The Prelude*, ed. Ernest de Selincourt and Helen Darbishire (Oxford: Clarendon Press, 1965); *The Letters of William and Dorothy Wordsworth*, ed. Ernest de Selincourt, Chester Shaver, Mary Moorman, and Alan Hill (Oxford: Clarendon Press, 1967–1970), The Early Years (*WLEY*), The Middle Years (*WLMY*), The Later Years (*WLLY*); *The Prose of William Wordsworth*, ed. W. J. B. Owen and Jane Smyser (Oxford: Clarendon Press, 1974): (*Prose*).

April 1986   S. C.
Philadelphia, Pennsylvania

Prolegomenon:
A PRIMER ON SUBTITLES IN BRITISH ROMANTIC POETRY

Adonais, An Elegy on the Death of John Keats (Shelley)

The Blues, A Literary Eclogue (Byron)

Childe Harold's Pilgrimage, A Romaunt (Byron)

Dejection: An Ode (Coleridge)

Endymion: A Poetical Romance (Keats)

The Fall of Hyperion: A Dream (Keats)

The Giaour. A Fragment of a Turkish Tale (Byron)

Hellas, A Lyrical Drama (Shelley)

The Idle Shepherd-Boys, a Pastoral (Wordsworth)

Joan of Arc. An Epic Poem (Southey)

Kubla Khan: A Vision in a Dream. A Fragment (Coleridge)

Lalla Rookh, An Oriental Romance (Moore)

Michael: A Pastoral Poem (Wordsworth)

The Nightingale, A Conversational Poem (Coleridge)

The Oak and the Broom, A Pastoral (Wordsworth)

Perspiration, A Travelling Eclogue (Coleridge)

Queen Mab, A Philosophical Poem (Shelley)

Rosalind and Helen, A Modern Eclogue (Shelley)

The Spirit of Discovery: A Descriptive and Historical Poem (Bowles)

The Two Foscari, An Historical Tragedy (Byron)

Upon the Plain, A Ballad (Clare)

Venice. An Ode (Byron)

Waltz: An Apostrophic Hymn (Byron)

Ximalpoca, A Monodrama (Southey)

Ye Mariners of England: A Naval Ode (Campbell)

Zapolya: A Christmas Tale (Coleridge)

Contents

POETIC FORM AND
BRITISH ROMANTICISM

CHAPTER ONE

Of Form and Genre

[A] person of genius is beyond ordinary criticism, and may set common rules at defiance: let him then be a law to himself. In the very act of spurning the inferior rules of critics, he is obedient (let not the expression offend) to the superior laws of reason: he may, perhaps, soar higher, and see further, than ordinary critics; but he must not pass the bounds of fitness: would he pass the *flammantia moenia mundi* [Lucretius], those flaming walls, that are the boundaries of the world? He cannot perceive propriety amid want of proportion. The man who transgresses these bounds, and sees such visions, loses himself in clouds, or buries himself in the darkness beneath. He may like Swedenborg soar above the heavens, and think to set angels right, or with Cervantes' hero fight and dispute with windmills; but he is out of the right way, and by his act of defiance against that order which harmonizes the universe, gives proof that he is neither a philosopher nor a poet, whatever he may think of himself as a genius. But no! the highest flights of fancy are not mere castles in the air: they have a foundation in nature; otherwise they could not be pronounced excellent. And the superior genius who revolts at the perpetuity of art, at the monotony of rules, is but trying new associations; plunging, if the expression may be allowed, into a mighty ocean; where, though the varieties are endless, yet symmetry and order prevail in every direction.

> George Dyer, "On Poetical Genius and its
> Subjection to Rules," *Poetics* (1812), II, 29-30

I

CONCEPTUAL STRUCTURES haunt the human mind, and their syntax takes many forms. On the grandest scale mythologies, synchronizing independent legend and history into enfolding structures, resonate through all art, subdividing into encoding systems, each of which will ultimately possess an independent integrity. Thus the symbolic referentiality of Christian iconography underpins the medieval world over many centuries, self-evidently so in painting, often more subtly in literature, but ingeniously nuanced even in the structures of music. Well into the eighteenth century, and still lingering into the nineteenth, the traditional shorthand of Old Testament typology constantly insinuates itself through every pathway of European art. Yet more compressed by abstraction, cosmographical emblems, designed to figure the inherent harmony of human, natural, and divine spheres, likewise furnish conceptual frameworks for artistic experimentation. Even the principles of scientific classification, if they do not themselves issue as metaphors, are easily appropriated to metaphorical purposes: the familiar tropes of Donne's "A Valediction Forbidding Mourning," so apparently random and violently yoked together, are all unified by the alchemical symbol for gold, a circle with a dot in its center, on whose structure the poem forms an intricate and profound meditation. Though numerology, with its allowance of opposite conclusions drawn from the same evidence, has provoked some derision among scholars of the Renaissance, the fact remains that it informs the culture and some of its greatest art. Along this spectrum of conceptual syntax, ranging between myth and mathematics, could be enumerated manifold other structural systems without altering the truth underlying them all, that wherever the human mind conceives a system for organizing reality, the artist is bound to appropriate it, sometimes certainly as a principle of belief, almost always as a realm for conceptual play. But to emphasize only the incorporation of extrinsic structural elements into literature is severely to limit the ingenuity of human thought and artistic organization. The intricate geometric ring structure that Cedric Whitman and other classical scholars have identified in *The Iliad* and *The Odyssey*, though admittedly an insight of our own time, was glimpsed for centuries by those critics who extolled the unity of Homer's fable as an example for all subsequent literature. Or, to revert to microscopic structures, metrical and rhyme schemes, as John Hollander has been the latest and perhaps the cleverest critic to remind us, carry implicit tonalities and gradations of aesthetic affect, all those subtle values that plump literary decorum into its full ripeness of what we call taste.[1]

The continuity of such conceptual patterning perhaps testifies less to an instinctive rage for order in humanity than it does to the primary imperative of every artist to structure experience. And yet, even to the internal balances of Homer's narrative that testify to mnemonic devices, all of the foregoing principles of structure, though sometimes spanning centuries, are culturally determined and culturally limited. And the same conditions apply to what is ultimately the most consistent conceptual syntax informing literature, that of genre. Beyond any other motive force, beyond even the sense of artistic belatedness, the fear of there being little left to say, that has been present at least since Homer, it is the driving principle of literary history—of all literary history. It is because of this that Tzvetan Todorov can proclaim with uncompromising simplicity, and with an authority that only the French language seems any longer to command: "La poésie c'est les genres, la poétique, la théorie des genres." On the other hand, Todorov has also sharply posed the problem that this book confronts, an entrenched belief that Romanticism was inherently suspicious of, even hostile to, traditional literary forms, thus divorcing itself from history, from the continuities of Western literature, and from the conceptual syntax that encodes them: "The Romantics and their present-day descendants," he asserts, "have refused not only to conform to the rules of the genres, which was their privilege, but also to recognize the very existence of such a notion."[2] We have inherited the myth of a radical generic breakdown in European Romanticism that in fact never happened, but that with its own logic of cultural determinism has essentially distorted our perceptions of both Romantic literature and culture. To explore how very deeply generic conceptions penetrate the particular culture of British Romanticism, and why they do so, is the purpose of this book.

If we begin with the premise that genres underlie, motivate, and organize all literary discourse, still we must immediately acknowledge that their function is dependent on their formulation; and criticism has never been able to set precise lines of definition and demarcation. For many students of literature genre simply means Aristotle's tripartite division of literary discourse, according to the dictates of voice and setting, into narrative, dramatic, and lyric forms, whose natures are so inherently distinct as to exclude combination. Yet from the first, choral odes and expository messenger speeches intruded upon classical drama, complicating its singularity of mode, and so it has been ever after. The sugared lyricism of *Romeo and Juliet* only reinforces generically the practical wisdom of its plot, that a prescribed separation into antithetical families generally encourages the young to intermarry. As the British Romantics were not the first to conceive of hybrids like lyrical ballads and lyrical dramas, so it is certain they were not the last. Now we incorporate film into stage representations, and the players are discovered to be the audience. The objective narrative voice plunges into a lyric stream of consciousness at one moment, and in the next is as likely to disrupt the supposed integrity of the narrative by pointedly reminding the reader of authorial manipulations. The effect of such experiments is, however, not a confusion of values, but a paradoxical reinforcement of them, reminding us sharply of the very aesthetic distances they subvert.[3]

In normal parlance genre refers to a subdivision of these large families of literature into species with common characteristics: epic, pastoral, tragedy, comedy, and so on. But leaving to later chapters the ways in which these distinct kinds also inevitably intermarry, we must immediately acknowledge that none is susceptible to an exact definition. Even if we can discern that the European epic has a common basis in oral poetry, for example, the cultural differences subsisting between the Mediterranean and Baltic basins, in climate no less than polity, profoundly influence the poem that results. Even the characteristic verse form, the brevity and intensity of the alliterative line in *Beowulf* as opposed to the spacious extendability of Homer's dactylic hexameter, enforces a different literary effect. And the dynamics of any single culture impose upon what may be supposed the common inheritance of them all, at least common to the Western tradition. We know immediately, without stopping to compare notes, that French pastoral and British pastoral will be distinct from one another, and both again from the Alexandrian pastoral from which both stem, even though we may also assume that sheep stray through all three. Language, culture, norms of education, availability of models, religion, climate, commercial centrality or isolation, relative peace or vulnerability to warfare, not to ignore the ever-present practical necessities of any literary marketplace—such are the elements that continually temper the inherited values of literary kinds.[4]

And yet, once we alert ourselves to variables of this dimension, we must also honor the extent, particularly in the advancement of literary culture, to which they can dissolve before what appears to be a version of the kind less contaminated by the parochial concerns of a poet's culture. At any moment and in any city—always a city—the vernacular ease and spontaneity of Theocritean pastoral can arise to propose a legitimate challenge to accumulated artifice. Indeed, it could be argued that this is in encapsulated form the history of post-Virgilian pastoral. The sudden recovery of lost literatures toward the end of the fifteenth century and again three hundred years later had in both instances an extraordinary impact on generic development. Suddenly, to cite but one case, in each culture there were new examples of the romance, and though in the first instance they were Hellenistic and in the second medieval, they became conspicuous testing-grounds for the received generic paradigms. In effect, the Greek romances of the Renaissance sophisticated the shopworn marvels of the British tradition, which returned three centuries later with a rough vitality to crack the veneer of neoclassical niceties.[5]

Recovery of this type is much more common than the actual discovery of a new genre, at least in respect to poetry. (In prose, as the single example of journalism is sufficient to indicate, there are genres that Homer left to others to invent.) Importations from Eastern cultures, notwithstanding Ezra Pound's ideograms and the sudden shower of haiku that emanated from San Francisco in the 1950s, have had no substantial impact on Western poetry, being rather assimilated into established forms than retaining a foreign independence. And yet, as the history of beating Shelley about the head with "The Indian Serenade" (now restored to the title of "The Indian Girl's Song") should caution us, not to recognize a generic import at the dock can result in observing a decorum alien to its nature. In this case, criticism has yet, after a century and a half, to pay the full custom's duty. Needless to say, for a critic to lack the poet's working sense of generic decorum is always a threat to artistic integrity. We would find more comfort in Francis Jeffrey's woeful ignorance of Wordsworth's generic experimentation were it not repeated, on a higher plane, everywhere around us. Indeed, the process that Wordsworth is constantly engaged in is approximately what Claudio Guillén has defined in the exemplary case in Western literature, Cervantes' establishment of the novel against the standards of Spanish romance, as a countergenre.[6] In a countergenre the received generic tradition is subjected to such a radical deconstruction that the result constitutes virtually a new form, its attributes soon claiming the integrity of generic conventions for subsequent writers. And yet this collision of literary sensibilities

is not quite the rare and historically charged dramatic event that Guillén's example would lead us to believe. To some extent or other, the
dynamics are in place whenever convention subsides into cliché and dead
metaphors cling to a genre like leaves on winter branches. One estimable
critic has gone so far as to argue persuasively that every major epic poem
in the Western tradition, beginning with *The Odyssey*, has been created
as a countergenre.[7] And if that is true, then we confront a radical example
of the complexities of generic inheritance, forcing the critic to weigh with
all the delicate precision possible the comparative pressure exerted by
multiple, antithetical influences on examples late in the history of the
form.

And inasmuch as our concern here centers late in the history of every
poetic form that we will explore, another, more relative critical principle
must be invoked from the start. The particularized generic histories of
modern criticism are unlikely to guide us very far in a culture lacking our
knowledge or generic priorities that have generally magnified the place
of prose fiction. Much modern generic criticism has directed its efforts at
understanding—probably a hopeless task—just what it is that makes a
novel.[8] Yet the modern British novel was invented in 1814 by Walter Scott
(or, if we like to think there are two modern British novels, Jane Austen
published the other in 1811), and the anachronistic application of later
developments to an era ignorant of them must of necessity falsify reality,
even if only on the level of expecting of poetry standards conditioned by
prose. This is a particular problem for criticism stemming from the
Marxist tradition, for it is always wont, so to speak, to read georgic where
the poet meant only pastoral.[9] And yet, even as we advance the claims of a
received generic propriety, we must be aware that peculiarities of the
culture of the Romantic period, from the insularity of British culture on
the one hand to the character of its neo-Hellenism on the other, from its
Protestantism to its native epistemology, from its surprising ignorances
(not Herbert, not Donne, but William Drummond of Hawthornden was
considered the major metaphysical poet in its tradition) to its unanticipated erudition, ranging from Indian mythology to Druid lore—all such
matters have an impact on how genres are conceived and employed. Some
genres have an ancient heritage whose components, like the pastoral and
epic, are taught in all the schools; but the inheritance of romance is being
counted out only as the period unfolds. In either case distortion is
possible. For though we must necessarily compensate for the conditions
of the culture, we incur the risk of overcompensating. Let us once assume
that the period could never know all we comprehend under the rubric of
medieval romance, and suddenly we will confront Byron's astonishing
prescience, or intuition, in regard to structuring principles identified by
modern scholarship. If, on the other hand, we recognize that Virgil's
Eclogues were almost universally misread—and the evidence for that is
abundant—it does not mean that a mind of comparable delicacy, a
Wordsworth or a Shelley, could not discern the deep strain of melancholy

that counters his pastoral ease. However extensive the generic line or obvious its pressure, the poetic genres are never mere abstractions: they are always individually recreated in a particularized time and place, and to discuss that recreation attentively requires both immersion in its historical setting and sensitivity to the ways in which great literature spans time.

Such complexes of caveats, in recognition of the difficulties that attend a generic criticism, go far to explain why it has been comparatively easy to wish it away in Romantic literature. The hegemony of neoclassical rules, with their simpleminded and impossible clarity, broke down in the eighteenth century and with it a facile means of taxonomy. But genres have never depended on prescribed rules per se, but rather on a conceptual syntax derived from earlier examples and applied to modern conditions. And over time they create their parameters not by simple imitation but by a competition of values, a subversion of precursors, all the paraphernalia of revision that Harold Bloom has offered as the dynamics of literary anxiety but that in this context constitute merely the ways in which poets accommodate the past in the present.[10] If Bloom's revisionary categories are transported out of the enclosed psychological arena in which he relentlessly employs them into the everyday world in which poets work—that is to say, employ a craft—and occasionally play—Byron turning Southey upside down to imagine what he might look like standing on his head—they provide in the aggregate a forceful counter to any simple model of artistic influence or transmission.

The modern history of generic criticism, inaugurated by Ferdinand Brunetière in 1890, began with its own historical conditioning, confusing art with a Darwinian nature. Though genres do admit to natural selection—there is no room at 10 Downing Street to stage a masque and no inclination in the White House—and cultural change is both heralded by and productive of shifts in artistic values, to speak of a simple evolutionary development in a genre is to slight the continuing presentness of the past and the variety subsumed by the genus, even by any exemplary text within it. Imitation of Virgilian pastoral in the Restoration is likely to be politically reactionary in its motives, whereas in the Romantic period it is just as likely to pose questions to the authority of church and state.

As there are no simple rules for genre nor any unambiguous pattern of progressive development, so there is no rigid methodology for generic criticism. The manifest result is a confusion of apples and oranges, of rabbits and ducks, in its history. The most useful models of etiquette have, not surprisingly, come from scholars of the Renaissance such as Rosalie Colie, Alastair Fowler, and Barbara Lewalski.[11] Eighteenth-century studies have been so dominated by the history of generic criticism, which is decidedly different from the history undergone by its genres, that we find ourselves with a compendious comparative anatomy of pastoral and epic, while looking far and wide for the actual corpus.[12] The rapid development of prose fiction in the nineteenth century has eclipsed the

comparable complexity of the poetic genres. Thus, any generic criticism
that is specifically set within the British tradition will be conditioned by
what we learn from Renaissance generic studies. And these, compensating for the signal differences in cultures, nonetheless instruct us that
rules, however they organize priorities or indicate cultural norms, are no
substitute for the richness of literature itself, that the myriad ways in
which authors may give what Fowler has called a "generic signal"
require of the modern critic an educated sensitivity to the signs of specific
times, and that the cross-currents of the culture are mirrored in the
dialectic among and within both genres and their critics.

II

So to discriminate is undoubtedly useful. But, in what terms? Aside from
the complexities that arise from or within generic transmission, there are
problems and confusions in the very vocabulary used for critical analysis.
In French (*genre*), Italian (*genera*), and German (*Gattung*), the central
term carries connotations of gender that simply do not arise in English.
Especially in a period like ours where consciousness of gender has become central to the operations of criticism, the disparity between connotations separates the scholarly communities. If one is not certain that
Alastair Fowler and Jacques Derrida are discussing the same cultural
principle, it is because, in sober truth, they are not. It is at least plausible
to infer that the entire history of generic development and of critical
response has been subtly infiltrated by this disparity, to the extent that
there is a fundamental difference of value on both counts between the
European continent on the one hand and Great Britain and North America on the other.

Since our concern is with those British traditions, we may safely revert
to what is the almost unsolvable problem of English synonyms. Genre,
kind, mode, and form are terms often used interchangeably by critics
simply as an instrument of rhetorical variety, though they can clearly be
distinguished in meaning and purpose. In a puristic application of
terminology, genre would stand for the three divisions of literary discourse into master categories (narrative, drama, lyric), kind for the species
of literature, mode for a more generalized orientation within the kind
(Hardy's pastoral novels, or—and here the complexity is obvious—
Spenser's pastoral romance), and form for a fixed structural principle (the
structure of a sonnet). And yet the Renaissance "kind," though it can still
be found as a term of reference among the Romantics, must be reclaimed
as a scholarly anachronism in our own day, where the associations of the
word have in general parlance been transferred to "genre." Where there is
no common agreement about usage, critical discourse inevitably continues to stumble over terminology. At times, of course, it is of crucial
importance to distinguish these words precisely.

In particular, form operating as a structural principle and genre conceived as a nexus of conventions and a frame of reference exercise distinct constraints on a poet. Although obviously interconnected, the one is an abstracted arena of logic, the other of connotative meaning. The sonnet presents an exemplary instance of how different are the pressures. The poet who sets out to write a sonnet in the Italian form has one overriding imperative, which is how to turn the form (the technical term is "volta") from octave into sestet. The rhyme scheme of the octave, with its two *abba* patterns, also exerts a pressure for return and doubling. The logical result of these formal pressures is an assertion first made, then reaffirmed or extended, and finally turned or countered: "yes—yes, indeed—but." The abstract pattern of such a logic is polarity between the octave and sestet. As we might expect, the conventional subject matter of the Italian sonnet is therefore naturally polarized; but the elaboration of the Petrarchan tradition into separated lovers or the breach between human and divine, however dependent on an initial logical assumption, creates a complex of associations upon that premise rich enough to impel several centuries of poets across disparate cultures and even forms. Eventually, that complex suggests new possibilities for logical arrangement, and Shakespeare subjects the entire tradition to its fullest critique and extension by forcing the sonnet through a different abstract grid, one consisting of three quatrains and a couplet. As Rosalie Colie has shown, the pressure toward epigram in the concluding couplet draws in another generic tradition, with its distinctively social tonalities, to confront and challenge the inherited Petrarchan polarities.[13] Even from so condensed a synopsis of this lengthy historical development, we can see how formal logic at once creates a genre and remains independent of it.

At the same time, the example insists on the primacy, the inescapability, of logic within fixed formal patterns. The logic of the volta establishes contrast, polarity, as both instrument and subject matter of the Italian sonnet. Even if a poet were to write a sonnet in which the polarity was somehow avoided, the very absence would call itself to the educated reader's attention, establishing a spectral presence in the void. All such fixed forms are invested with the logic of their structure. When a poet sets out to write a villanelle or an ode, no less than a sonnet, the first question is not one of subject matter but of the logic inherent in the form. To turn that proposition around so as to reveal its full implications, the formal structuring principle in large part predetermines ideological orientation.

In this respect, genre is form writ large. Let us assume—and the opening stanzas do reinforce the hypothesis—that Byron from the very first conceived of *Childe Harold's Pilgrimage*, even while uncertain whether to call the hero Biron or by some more distanced name, as "A Romaunt," the subtitle appended to the poem. What will immediately occur to this Byron, hypothetical as he is for the purposes of illustration, are the examples he knows within this genre, the conventions they share, the place of the genre within received critical categories, the cultural priorities assumed by the genre. What may not at this point occur to the

poet involved in such a series of reflections is what the genre excludes—
for instance, a romance is not an epic; but as our fictive Byron mulls over
what he is going to write, he has by his generic orientation already,
without thinking about the matter, excluded those elements distinguishing epic from romance. Before pen is put to page the poet will have cast
himself into a particular mental framework that limits human options
and prizes certain values above others. Obviously, Byron's own tastes,
needs, even obsessions, will intrude upon this framework as he begins to
write, so that it becomes his romance and not that of Spenser or Keats.
But the generic choice has already committed him to what, in the ensuing
pages, will be called a mode of apprehension. It is an ideological con-
struct, and it may be in place, forcing choices, before a word is written—or
the subject matter is even conceived. Let us, shifting our viewpoint, now
assume the kinds of ideological (as well as biographical) conclusions that
might be drawn from the poem in its finished form: that Byron is
antisocial, or that he is an escapist involved in a continual displacement
of reality, or that he is instinctively attracted to the ritualized order of
Roman Catholicism. Since such conclusions—and others of the same
ilk—*have* been derived from this poem, the issue is not as fanciful as it
might first seem. An inherited generic order is confused with an author's
own values; and Byron's refined sense of social nicety (he moved in circles
in which most of his critics would not know how to behave), his intense
political commitments, and his religious skepticism are all inverted because of a confusion over what is art and what life.

Every time that a work of art is taken as a key to its author's system of
belief, there is a dangerous confusion in the principles ordering reality.
And where the imperatives of genre for a period are systematically denied,
the danger is all the more acute. Let Shelley write a hymn, and he
becomes a theist. Let him write a tragedy, and something like original sin
is added to the mix. Let him write a pastoral elegy in line with the
conventional requirements of the form and—so much for "The Necessity
of Atheism"—he is a transcendental Christian of a Neoplatonic stamp. And
yet his contemporary critics saw in all three works—the "Hymn to Intellectual Beauty," *The Cenci*, and *Adonais*—the same dangerous, antireligious
skepticism, and, though often themselves guilty in the aggregate of over-
reading the surface of literature, in Shelley's case were scarcely to be fooled
by the arbitrary constraints of genre.[14] That we are, more than a century and
a half after the period is over and at the end of a generation of intense
theoretical self-analysis, still constantly beguiled into confusing the contexts of art with the lineaments of belief or the necessities of existence or the
psychological anxieties of influence, testifies in a perverse way to the
modern critic's faith in an abstract lyrical moment, itself a spurious distillation from Romanticism, and consequent distrust for the artifice that makes
art. Making is not the same as living, though often it will structure the
chaos of a poet's life and sometimes, as Wilde was fond of reminding us, it
is much better. Geoffrey Chaucer, whom we like to think of as a repository

of all things natural at the dawn of modern British poetry, is granted a rare vision by the muse because of his veneration for poetic authority and thus begins "The Parliament of Fowles" by distinguishing with a sigh between "The lyf so short [and] the craft so long to lerne."

Craft, most assuredly, is not synonymous with rules, as neoclassicism proved with a vengeance. But if the eighteenth century responded to the hegemony of rules by celebrating unfettered genius, and Wordsworth followed in kind by defining poetry as "the spontaneous overflow of powerful feelings," which Hazlitt reduced to abstract passion and Shelley even further to the emblem of burning coal, we should pause before such a continuum and realize that here too is a conceptual syntax spanning centuries, the one that first identified Apollo, mover of the sun, with poetry.[15] Wordsworth and Shelley are also, on a more practical level, concerned with creating poetry, and, though the one was peripatetic and the other sedentary, both had to be aware of the imperatives of their craft. For both of these master defenders of poetry, what inspires a poem is a mystery of obscure and almost divine import; but that art emerges from what at once constricts and empowers it, as practicing poets, they were fully aware. There is no such thing as automatic writing in the making of a poem. A meter, perhaps a rhyme scheme, thus a form, then likely as not a genre: each step adds to a tendentious process that fulfills itself in closure, even if an indeterminate one. Each step constricts the process further in the interests of that closure, and each is in some measure an ideological constraint—or, to be sure, an enabling mechanism for the imagination that plays best when it knows the dimensions of the sand-box. Shelley's remark in the preface to *Prometheus Unbound* that "nothing can be equally well expressed in prose that is not tedious and supererogatory in verse" honors the distinction between exposition and creation, the marshalling of fact and the determined artifact, the intrinsic center of contexts, which is a poem.

The ensuing chapters concentrate on how major forms of earlier poetry are resuscitated and transformed in the Romanticism of Great Britain. Each chapter could have been elaborated into a book-length argument, though perhaps only by taxing the reader through accumulating examples. Since, even so, this exploration is scarcely brief, some important generic lines have been excluded or only tangentially drawn into the discussion. The ballad revival is one such, but it has been so ably treated in modern criticism that it stands as one form whose impact we have adequately understood. The song is omitted, partly because the form tends to be amorphous, partly because its nature is often dictated by its musical setting, but also because the consideration might require lengthy forays into ornithology; and also because, from Wordsworth's "The Solitary Reaper" to Shelley's "To Constantia" (written to a Mozart aria), songs about the nature of singing are apt to seem redundant.

A more serious omission is that of satire, which, as will be noted immediately in the next chapter, is an extremely vital mode in British Romanticism, one whose full dimensions have never been addressed in criticism. But a genre whose constituents have never even been catalogued, where the customary anonymity of authorship necessitates detective work to establish identities, and where extended quotation from original sources must compensate for a nearly universal lack of familiarity must await a different forum for elucidation from this one. Drama is similarly a special case, though it is richly informed and just as deeply troubled by the Renaissance revival to which we immediately turn. Numerous minor genres persist from the previous age or are recovered from earlier times, but to notice at any length the surprising continuity of loco-descriptive poems in praise of country estates would quickly dissipate the element of surprise; epigrams, inscriptions, and epitaphs abound in rather the proportions of the previous century; and epistles in this period lend themselves more valuably to stylistic than generic analysis.

What remains is certainly enough to merit detailed attention, the principal fixed forms and genres of British Romantic poetry, both lyric and narrative: the sonnet, the hymn, the ode, pastoral, romance, and epic, as well as experiments in generic combination. In their development can be discerned the outlines of a simultaneous recovery and transformation of major proportions.

CHAPTER TWO

The Second Renaissance

We maintain that the poets, who have flourished during the reign of
George the third, have produced as great a quantity of lasting poetry, as
those who flourished during the reign of Elizabeth, or during any other half
century of the British annals.

*The Annual Review: and History of
Literature for 1806*, 4 (1807), 563

. . . we have raised up, as it were, from the tomb, a spirit that was only lying
asleep, and that now, from the dust and the darkness, walks abroad among
us, in the renovation of all its strength and beauty.

"On the Revival of a Taste for our Ancient
Literature," *Blackwood's*, 4 (1818), 266

I

THE ADVENT of British Romantic poetry in the 1790s coincides with a
decade of unparalleled intellectual tumult fostered by a strange, jostling
mix of the new industrialism, religious enthusiasm, middle-class education, and political instability of a kind not witnessed for a century, all of
it hovered over by the revolution in France. The colonial failures of the
1780s—a successful war for independence in America, corruption in
India, and a slave empire in the West Indies—had fomented national self-
questioning, turning an expansionist culture back on itself. Thus, the
explosion in France initially had a salutary effect, consolidating a national sense of values and allowing the British once again to represent
themselves as a model to other nations in Europe. It was not long,
however, before the collective pride collapsed before the stresses of involvement in the war against the French, the attendant political repression, and commercial isolation. By the end of the century it might well
appear that only the threat of Napoleon's invasion and a nearly universal
sense that the revolution had been betrayed gave a defensive cohesion to
British society. For another fifteen years the nation doggedly honored its
commitment to a war it hated for an end it could not foresee. In the end it
was the longest experience of continuing warfare in modern history,
enveloping an entire generation.

Conventional literary history has tended to concentrate on the psychological, social, and economic dislocations caused by such a prolonged
and retrograde national mission. And obviously, with the British nation
fundamentally altered by the experience of the Napoleonic Wars, this
ongoing scholarly emphasis is of essential importance to a comprehen-

sion of later history and literature.[1] But traditional historical analysis does not begin to explain the artistic revolution caused by Fuseli, Turner, Constable, Blake, and Martin, the architecture of Nash and Soane, the splendors of Regency style in the decorative arts, the music of John Field, the supremacy of the London stage, or the sudden efflorescence of the periodical press. Especially does it not account for the most eccentric feature of this entire culture, that it was simply mad for poetry. What does encompass the phenomenon of the arts in this age is the other side of the historical equation, Britain's isolation and inward turning toward self-discovery. As is only to be expected, the result in the arts is often unreflecting patriotism and sanctimonious piety, transparent fictions of national destiny that cover troubling instabilities, a taste for superficial finery, and a generous quantity of self-congratulation by the second-rate. And yet, the ferment is undeniable. It justifies, for instance, the stirring peroration of Shelley's *Defence of Poetry*, whose enthusiasm is hard for a later culture to grasp, but which represents the actual state of British culture at the end of the Regency:

> In spite of the low-thoughted envy which would undervalue contemporary merit, our own will be a memorable age in intellectual achievements, and we live among such philosophers and poets as surpass beyond comparison any who have appeared since the last national struggle for civil and religious liberty. The most unfailing herald, companion, and follower of the awakening of a great people to work a beneficial change in opinion or institution, is Poetry. At such periods there is an accumulation of the power of communicating and receiving intense and impassioned conceptions respecting man and nature. The persons in whom this power resides, may often, as far as regards many portions of their nature, have little apparent correspondence with that spirit of good of which they are the ministers. But even whilst they deny and abjure, they are yet compelled to serve, the Power which is seated upon the throne of their own soul . . . for it is less their spirit than the spirit of the age. (p. 508)

Such a cohesive national self-confidence is the paradoxical end of the defensiveness and troubling doubt experienced by the British over nearly half a century.

The simple truth is that the age of British Romanticism constitutes one of the greatest ages for poetry in the nation's history. A magazine like *Blackwood's* in its first years, whether celebrating the genius of the Rev. George Croly and Shelley in the same breath, lecturing Byron month after month, or violently excoriating the Cockneys, has almost no other subject but poetry. The naiveté of its enthusiasm sets *Blackwood's* apart from later imitation or emulation, and its immediate rise to the pinnacle of subscriptions suggests that it had an audience no less infatuated than it was.[2] Something of the same spirited energy drives the outpouring of literary satire in the Romantic period, the boisterous swan song for this genre in English verse, mirroring the experience of an exact century before in the intensity and volume, if not the greatness, of its productions. In the dozens and dozens of poetic satires on poetry, of which only the *Poetry of the Anti-Jacobin* and *English Bards and Scotch Reviewers* retain any notice, are the ephemeral records of an incomparable literary passion. Like most passion, that for poetry was oblivious to common sense, even perhaps transcendently so. There is, for instance, a strain of bemused admiration in George Daniel's portrait of one Crambo, a representative spirit of the age discovered inebriated and dead to the world by bailiffs in the fourth poem of his *Virgil in London; or, Town Eclogues* (1814):

> His pockets next they rummag'd, but the duns
> Found naught but scraps of epigrams and puns,
> Flat, fulsome, panegyrics, stiff in stays,
> Remnants of farce, and fragments of new plays;
> Love-sonnets, form'd the appetite to glut,
> With interlarded sentiment and smut;
> An ode to riches, an address to morn,
> With duplicates of sundry things in pawn;
> Satires to give the ministers a trimming,
> Dull elegies, and sermons for old women;
> Smooth verses, full of groves and tinkling rills;
> "The Spirit of the Book," and alehouse bills,
> A Scotch romance in namby-pamby verse,
> Three speeches of a tragedy in Erse. . . . (pp. 39–40)

Bemoaning the literary profligacy of an age, such satires nonetheless contribute to the momentum, happily riding upon wheels whose revolutions they would ostensibly stop. George Daniel clearly had talent and in the Regency made his literary mark, and presumably some small fortune, in applying his lash to the carriage as well as its passengers. Francis Hodgson, though writing anonymously over three decades, is another such. His description of the later Romantic literary scene is shrewd in recognizing its origins and its distinguishing character.

> Sound Mother-Wit, that knows her proper sphere,
> Ne'er with her betters dares to break a spear;
> Leaves not her counting-house for verse, nor tries
> On waddling duck legs to usurp the skies—
> —While, 'mid the maddening sons of Church or Kirk,
> Broad frames and odes throw thousands out of work;
> While every "calling for this idle trade"
> Is left, and each commandment disobey'd;
> Sad she invokes those times of nobler note,
> When few, but gentlemen and scholars, wrote—
> When none, but Nature's licensed minstrels, sung—
> Ere Cowper taught the tame colloquial tongue
> In awkward measurements of verse to crawl,
> Like limber willows trained against a wall.[3]

Hodgson's vision of a democratic melée of poets, rushing to the market-place in search of the fame and fortune to be accorded by an ever-expanding publishing industry, testifies to a wholesale shift in cultural values. Its economic underpinnings are observed by others as well. Here, for instance, is the Rev. Charles Colton on the same subject:

> Drawn up in columns dense, our Land can boast
> Of Epic, and Heroic Bards, an Host;
> High rolls th' o'erwhelming tide of copious song!
> Printers drive Critics, Critics bards along![4]

But to concentrate on voices that would stem a tidal wave is to obscure the energetic delight, the sense of power and imaginative capacity, of those who rode upon it. Never before or after has literature witnessed its like. Two adolescents at Oxford, Southey and Landor, writing epic poems (one principally in Latin). A later adolescent, Shelley, creating in *Queen Mab* a virtual manual for nineteenth-century revolutions, off-handedly noting that "The Past, the Present, & the Future are [its] grand & comprehensive topics" (*Letters*, I, 324). Another youth, Joseph Cottle, collecting in faraway Bristol the best poetic talents of the 1790s, publishing their ventures (until London firms came calling), then, with time to spare, writing and publishing his own epics. An entire school of bards and essayists assembling a new Mecca in the farthest reaches of England and starting a tourist industry among its lakes. The haughty Byron, told to retire to the House of Lords and leave poetry for those with talent for it, synoptically shellacking every poet of note in the land. Keats, obsessed with poetic fame, just twenty-one and a spokesman for his culture: "Great spirits now on earth are sojourning. . . . Listen awhile ye nations, and be dumb." Shelley in Italy, publishing six volumes of poetry in the space of two years, with several others held in reserve by his English representatives for fear of prosecution. William Hayley, who lived a life of heroic couplets, within a single decade the patron successively of Charlotte Smith, William Cowper, and William Blake. Women poets everywhere—writing sonnets, writing epics. The market for sermons dwindling, and the clergy—the Rev. Mr. Beloe, the Rev. Mr. Boyd, the Rev. Mr. Bowles, the Rev. Mr. Crabbe, the Rev. Mr. Croly, not to ignore the Rev. Mr. C. Colton (and many further along the alphabet)—trading their clerical caps for laurel.

In 1822, the year after Shelley's *Defence of Poetry*, historical inevitabil-ity made a poet, George Canning, foreign secretary and leader of the House of Commons, an acknowledged legislator of the world. In 1823 he published his collected *Poems* with one hand and with the other severed Britain's support for the reactionary Holy Alliance of continental mon-archs. The long war against revolution was over, and with it, by strange coincidence, the great flowering of British Romanticism.

II

There are, it should be obvious, more predictable evidences of historical inevitability in this period than Canning's reversing the course of the ship of state, even if perhaps none is quite equal in consummate poetic justice. Those that concern us here are more narrowly literary, but of immense consequence nonetheless. The elderly Bishop of Dromore, Thomas Percy, was still alive in 1810 to witness the logical culmination of his efforts of fifty years earlier, the publication of Alexander Chalmers's monumental twenty-one volume edition, *Works of the British Poets*. Between 1765, when Percy first put to press his *Reliques of Ancient English Poetry*, and 1810 Great Britain recovered its national literature. The process was prolonged and difficult, requiring the concerted labors of successive generations of scholars, and even at the start of the Regency it was as yet incomplete. Thus although Harold Bloom was entirely accurate, he was also perhaps overly honorific, when he observed some years ago: "That English Romanticism, as opposed to Continental, was a renaissance of the Renaissance, is happily now a critical commonplace."[5] Even Chalmers, after half a century, did not have it all: his signal omissions, for instance, immediately prompted selections from Carew and Herrick to be printed. The latter, undertaken by Dr. J. Nott, earned a notice from the *Quarterly Review* that is worth quoting briefly to suggest the conditions of a time when the canon of British literature could not be taken for granted nor its masters adequately acknowledged:

> Herrick, a more exquisite poet than Carew, whom Mr. Headley ranks above Waller, had nearly buried for ever all his feeling and fancy beneath the conceit, the pruriency, and the obscenity, with which his volume (of more than fourteen hundred poems) abounds, when a writer in the Gentleman's Magazine for 1796 first informed the public, that in the scarce volume called Robert Herrick's Hesperides, which had been flippantly passed over by Phillips in his Theatrum Poetarum, and by Grainger after him, there was much true poetry; and Mr. Ellis, in the second edition of his "Specimens," raked four beautiful pearls from the dunghill: Dr. Drake, in the third volume of his "Literary Hours," noticed the poet's beauties more at large, collected his biography, and furnished an essay on his genius and writings, with a recommendation that a hundred of his poems should "be chosen by the hand of taste," and formed "into an elegant little volume."[6]

The condescension and insecure ignorance that yet pertained in 1810 throw into sharp relief Percy's achievement and the even greater accomplishment of Thomas Warton's *History of English Poetry*, the three volumes (1774, 1778, 1781) of which are among the finest fruits of the British Enlightenment—truly of seminal importance for the age of poetry that followed.

Until Warton there was simply no firm historical basis for understanding the development of British literature. That he never reached beyond the sixteenth century (nor, in truth, even fully covered its ground) suggests the magnitude of what still remained for his successors to accomplish.[7] Warton and Percy were in continual consultation over their respective labors, and their contribution to the recovery of medieval texts and vernacular literature has been universally honored, even where their methods have aroused serious question. Between them they spawned the ballad and romance revivals whose impact will be observed in Chapter 6. But ballad scholarship has so accustomed us to hear in the *Reliques of Ancient English Poetry* only "native wood-notes wild," somewhat domesticated by Percy's tinkerings with texts, that conventional wisdom distorts the full dimensions of his efforts, and, indeed, Warton's too. Percy's *Reliques* resembles a primitive version of Palgrave's *Golden Treasury*: a number of now well-known poems of the sixteenth century, like Marlowe's "Passionate Shepherd to His Love" and Raleigh's "Nymph's Reply," are included. So are Sir John Suckling's "To Althea from Prison" and "Why so pale and wan, fond lover." "Ancient English Poetry," it appears in Percy's conception, becomes modern sometime around the middle of the seventeenth century, or about the time that the edition of English verse for which Samuel Johnson provided biographical and critical introductions would begin its coverage. After Johnson, the next effort to represent the span of British poetry is Robert Anderson's *Works of the British Poets* in thirteen volumes (1792–1795). Even here, Restoration poetry begins with the sixth volume, testimony to how much of cultural bias (and ignorance) remains. That the annotations of Wordsworth, Coleridge, and Southey are copiously intermingled in the first five volumes of the Folger Library set is its own eloquent affirmation of the true significance of Anderson's edition.[8]

A fundamental paradox underlies the conflict of cultures by which we discriminate the literary shifts that separate Romantic poetry from that of the preceding age, increasingly called the age of Johnson after earlier nomenclature fell from favor. We are accustomed to viewing Samuel Johnson as conservative in his values and a traditionalist in literature. His own poetry certainly reflects a neoclassical taste; yet at the same time he encouraged Percy in his ballad research and is said to have preferred earlier poets than those for whom he wrote his celebrated lives. His catholicity is sometimes surprising, but then so is his unanticipated narrowness. There are venerable literary traditions, for instance, that he seems neither to have respected nor found of much interest. In particular, he regarded the customary forms of Renaissance poetry as worn by time and overuse and as irrelevant to modern literature:

> Wheresoe'er I turn my view,
> All is strange, yet nothing new;
> Endless labour all along,
> Endless labour to be wrong;
> Phrase that time has flung away,
> Uncouth words in disarray;
> Trickt in antique ruff and bonnet,
> Ode and elegy and sonnet.

So in 1777 Johnson greeted the publication of Thomas Warton's *Poems*. A personal animus of long standing is undoubtedly present in this squib, but so is scorn for Warton's almost instinctive taste for the old-fashioned. Literary revival is antiquarian labor, not to intrude upon a true creativity for which the past is past. Rather, Johnson the eighteenth-century modernist prizes taste and common sense—not neoclassical rule, and not the forms for which those rules were set. Though he seems not to have worried much about imitative satire, writing his own best poetry in the mode, his aversion to imitative pastoral is a commonplace. In decrying it as unrealistic and artificial, Johnson actually did much to prepare the climate for the resurgence of pastoral late in the century. As a critic, it is safe to conclude, he was averse to the formalistic except insofar as it could be accommodated to his inherent concern for delicacy of expression.

Yet, Warton's *Poems* of 1777 point British literature in a new direction—not that they are particularly "pre-Romantic" in theme or style (unless fustian is thought an attribute of the type). Nor by any means are they throwbacks, for the pronounced urge to resuscitate older poetic forms that Johnson detected in Warton's poems is their surest key to a changing taste. Forty years later, *Blackwood's* would use not Johnson's realism but Hume's, in reference to Spenser, as a basis from which to discuss what is to the writer "the great fact in literary history":

> The feelings with which our ancient poetry was generally regarded at the beginning and at the close of the last century, were essentially different. In our Augustan age, we see the mind of the country tending with determined force *from* that ancient literature; and in these later days we have seen it returning upon the treasure of those older times, with an almost passionate admiration. . . . [W]e cannot help observing, in passing, that the just estimate and passionate feeling of poetry do really appear to have declined and revived amongst us, in point of time at least, in correspondence with the temporary neglect and returning love of our ancient records.[9]

It was the fortune of Samuel Johnson, in one of the great ironies of literary history, to codify for his succeeding age the poets they could safely neglect, referred to contemptuously by Wordsworth as "reputed Magnates—metrical writers utterly worthless and useless, except . . . when their productions are referred to as evidence what a small quantity of brain is necessary to procure a considerable stock of admiration, provided the aspirant will accommodate himself to the likings and fashions of his day." For Wordsworth, writing his "Essay, Supplementary to the Preface" of 1815 only a generation after the Johnson edition, it had with few exceptions omitted the entire national heritage:

> What is become of the morning-star of English Poetry? Where is the bright Elizabethan constellation? Or, if names be more acceptable than images, where is the ever-to-be-honoured Chaucer? where is Spenser? where Sidney? and lastly, where he, whose rights as a poet, contradistinguished from those which he is universally allowed to possess as a dramatist, we have vindi-

cated,—where Shakspeare?—These, and a multitude of others not un-
worthy to be placed near them, their contemporaries and successors, we have
not. (Prose, III, 79)

So accustomed is the mature Wordsworth to seeing the Renaissance as the
central repository of British poetry that he does not reflect that it had
become so only during his lifetime as a poet.

To place this shift in its largest perspective, Johnson's own denigration
of the neoclassical precept (in which he is joined by the best critical
minds of the later eighteenth century) prepared the way for a rejection of
what was written to its dictates. In the late Enlightenment the absolute-
ness of neoclassical models lost its cultural hold, to be replaced by a linear
history of literature within whose constructions we still customarily
think. Although a pan-European phenomenon, its effect in Great Britain
is of a different kind from that in France or Germany. Walter Jackson
Bate has remarked with admirable clarity where the distinction lay:

> The comparative restraint of English romanticism . . . was partly due to an
> acute if occasionally confined awareness of English poetic tradition. And,
> more than any other European people, the English possessed a large body of
> creative literature which had been written before neo-classic rationalism
> became extensively reflected in European art; and this literature, in addition
> to its other attributes, had been characterized by an imaginative strength and
> an emotional spontaneity which were at once congenial to romanticism and
> which at the same time had been channeled to either a religious, formal, or
> objectively dramatic end.[10]

The potential vacuum left by the large shift in literary models was averted
for British culture by the poets simultaneously being recovered by antiquarian scholars. A revolution in poetry was the simple effect.

The liberating nature of this rediscovery of a poetic tradition probably
results as much from its initial freedom from scholarly strictures as from
the national genius it embodied. More precisely, scholarship and discovery went hand in hand; when the critics were not poets themselves, they
were never distant from circles of writers. Whether it is Scott unwittingly
preparing for his later career through research on Renaissance ballads
and medieval romances or Coleridge translating his subtle creative gifts
into critical paradigms, the bridge is essential and constantly being
crossed. And yet, modern criticism has tended to view the age as through
the partial eyes of one of the few critical arbiters who did not cross that
bridge, William Hazlitt. Hazlitt became a critic after failing as a painter,
and what immediately engages him is color and finish rather than intrinsic design. He characterized the Lake School as if it had been founded by
Friedrich Schlegel, as having "its origin in the French revolution" and
rising immediately "to the utmost pitch of singularity and paradox. . . .
According to the prevailing notions, all was to be natural and new.
Nothing that was established was to be tolerated."[11] As hyperbolic and
distancing rhetoric, Hazlitt's critique has stylistic integrity, but as to fact

(beyond the recognition of a prevailing democratic impulse) it is simply wrong. Wordsworth, Coleridge, and Southey looked to Percy's *Reliques* for inspiration, to the early volumes of Anderson's *British Poets* for examples, amassing (at least the latter two) a prodigious learning in earlier literature. But the absence of authority did allow such poets to make what use of it they might. It was a vital national tradition without codified rules.

Hazlitt's curious strictures may well say more about him, Napoleon's defender to the bitter end, than about the practices of the Lake poets. He is the prime exponent of gusto, sheer intensity, as the mark of great literature, and he characteristically begins his *Lectures* with a leveling, expressionist maxim: "Poetry is the language of the imagination and the passions. It relates to whatever gives immediate pleasure or pain to the human mind." The anticlassical and revolutionary force of his remarks becomes even more extreme in subsequent paragraphs: "Poetry puts a spirit of life and motion into the universe. It describes the flowing, not the fixed" (*Works*, V, 1, 3). Yet, as a historian of the national literature Hazlitt is much more precise and, though not believing literature to be progressive and thus explainable by "what is mechanical, reducible to rule, or capable of demonstration" (V, 44), he must resort to some means of comparison or of taxonomy to rise above an impressionistic citation of beauties. The initial lecture, stressing literary mobility, ends without a note of incongruity by distinguishing high tragedy from its subgenre, domestic tragedy. Later, Hazlitt compares Dryden and Pope on the likely grounds of their claims as satirists, enumerates the qualities of an ode, and remarks on the dearth of pastorals in British poetry. It never occurs to him to make the leap that Friedrich Schlegel and the Jena school felt to be an immediate logical necessity for a comparable aesthetic of liberation, freedom from the constraints of genre. It is not that Hazlitt is stupid; he simply has too great a veneration for Renaissance poetry. And he is of a piece with his age, which undoubtedly sought to revivify its literature, but never sought the escape from tradition exemplified by such monuments of the previous century as *Night Thoughts* and *The Task*. The paradox of British Romanticism is that its revolution came about through an intense and largely isolated engagement with its own past.

III

When Henry Headley published the key instrument in the Renaissance revival, *Select Beauties of Ancient English Poetry. with remarks* (London: T. Cadell, 1787), he gave virtually every entry a fanciful title. The absence of scholarly purity is one indication of the time; another is his method of arrangement. Whatever the original context—and some of his selections are taken from drama—he arranged them according to contemporary generic categories: Descriptive Pieces, Pathetic Pieces, Didactic and Moral Pieces, Elegies and Epitaphs, Miscellaneous Pieces, Sonnets,

Speeches. In his introduction he actually compounded this generic organization by making a table of principal sixteenth-century poets, dividing
them according to an implicit hierarchy of modes in which they made
their chief contribution: epic, philosophical and metaphysical, dramatic,
historical, satyrical, pastoral, amatory and miscellaneous, and translation
(p. xv). In contrasting these poets with those of the present day, Headley
criticized the "lifelessness of modern poetry, which too often resembles an
artificial nosegay . . . while that of a century and half back, appears as a
garland fresh from the gardens of nature, and still moist and glittering
with the dews of the morning" (p. xxv). The contrast between the artificial and natural is a familiar Romantic dictum, one that later is increasingly centered on Pope in the strictures of Bowles, Hunt, or Keats. But as
we have observed in the case of Hazlitt, Headley sees no contradiction
between arranging his poems and poets by generic category and arguing
for naturalness as a literary priority.

Nor, on a much more sophisticated conceptual plane, does the greatest
critical mind of the Romantic period, Coleridge (who by the end of 1796
had written at least twenty poems he designated odes and over forty
sonnets). Unquestionably, Coleridge is an eloquent opponent of writing
according to rule, of mechanical art; his notion of organic form is
probably his best-known and most influential contribution to critical
discourse. And were one to take the term only within the sentence where
it is initially defined, organic form might well seem to be opposed to any
generic construction honored by tradition: it "is innate; it shapes as it
develops itself from within, and the fullness of its development is one and
the same with the perfection of its outward form" (*SC*, I, 198). In his essay
"On Poesy or Art" Coleridge contrasts an organic and mechanical formal
principle as "the difference between form as proceeding, and shape as
superinduced;—the latter is either the death or the imprisonment of the
thing;—the former is its self-witnessing and self-effected sphere of
agency."[12] As this finely articulated phrasing suggests, Coleridge is not
propounding a rhapsodic theory of poetry in his emphasis on organic
form. Indeed, it is exactly otherwise, for the emphasis of Coleridge's term
falls equally on the substantive and its modifying adjective. The context
for his initial definition in the Shakespeare lectures of 1811–1812 is an
eloquent defense of the inseparability of form and content, of function
and essence, in literature:

> The spirit of poetry, like all other living powers, must of necessity circum-
> scribe itself by rules, were it only to unite power with beauty. It must embody
> in order to reveal itself; but a living body is of necessity an organized one,—
> and what is organization, but the connection of parts to a whole, so that each
> part is at once end and means! This is no discovery of criticism; it is a
> necessity of the human mind. (*SC*, I, 197)

What Coleridge opposes is the use of an exterior shell without relation to
its interior substance. True form is intellectually congruent with and

empowering of its content. Not only does Coleridge emphasize a formal imperative in art, but his very metaphor assumes the centrality of genre, of genus and species within the multitudinous organization of the natural world. The organism that fulfills itself out of its own nature is an affirmation of the inherent individuation possible within its kind. So John Payne Collier noted of Coleridge's distinction between "mechanic and organic regularity" in the ninth lecture: "He illustrated this distinction by referring to the growth of Trees, which from peculiar circumstances of soil, air, or position, differed in shape even from trees of the same kind, but every man was able to decide at first sight which was an oak, an ash, or a poplar."[13] A kind that is "self-witnessing and self-effected" will also of necessity be self-contemplating, not imitating conventions merely because they are an aspect of the literary heritage, but reconceiving their organic relationship with a genre, how in the first place they came to be associated with it, their ideological implications, their relationship with other conventions of the kind. Though Coleridge's reflections on organic form occur relatively late in the development of British Romanticism (and borrow heavily from German thinking), they accentuate the preoccupation of the period with the nature and function of artistic form. And that scrutiny is itself the clearest symptom of a culture turned in upon itself to forge its national identity, to become at once "self-witnessing and self-effected" in history as in art.

But for such a national enterprise, grand theoretical notions about the nature of artistic form must revert to mundane ground. And there the late eighteenth century encountered some problems. The most acute was that not every one could still tell the difference between an oak, an ash, and a poplar. The Linnaeus of literary forms for the Renaissance, Julius Caesar Scaliger, no longer held authority and, indeed, was known only to the most erudite. Poetic practice since the Restoration had considerably narrowed the range of poetic forms (though it is only fair to observe that within that range there was a sharp sense of subgenres). Satire and epistle, pastoral and loco-descriptive verse, odes and epics were common enough, but when poets and critics of the later eighteenth century moved beyond the standard forms of the age, they lacked an assurance of how to discriminate genus from species and even the proper nomenclature to use in the process. Henry Headley's main divisions of the genres into descriptive, pathetic, and didactic/moral, and of fixed forms into elegies and epitaphs, sonnets, and speeches, suggest both a paucity of knowledge and a willingness to obscure minor distinctions in favor of larger areas of common rhetorical value.

The constriction of potential forms can quickly be measured by a comparison of the brief survey of poetic kinds in the preface to Joshua Poole's *English Parnassus* (1657), the *vade mecum* for versifiers of the mid-seventeenth century, with the inaugural lectures of the Oxford Chair of Poetry, given by Joseph Trapp and published as *Lectures on Poetry* in

1742. Though Poole's survey occupies but three pages, it breaks down each of the main poetic genres into a multitude of subspecies. Under Lyrick are congregated "*Madigrals, Sonnets, Hymnes, Ballets, Odes,* whereof some are *amorous,* some *rural,* some *military,* some *jovial,* made for *drollery* and *drinking* . . . To these may be added, *Epithalamiums,* written upon occasion of Nuptials, *Epinicions,* of Victories, *Genethliacks* of *Nativities, Congratulatories,* &c." (a4–a4[1]). Trapp, on the other hand, devotes fully twenty lectures to just eight genres: epigrams, elegies (on death and love), pastorals, didactic or praeceptive poetry, lyric (that is, the ode), satire, drama (comedy and tragedy), and epic, simply setting the traditional subject matter of each kind and then enumerating authors and works. A similar organization can be found in Charles Batteux's *A Course of Belles Lettres,* translated into English by John Miller in 1761. *The Art of Poetry,* John Newbery's handbook of 1762, finds Trapp's generic categories inadequate and therefore adds epitaph, epistle, the descriptive poem, tales and fables, and allegory.[14] It is only after Percy's and Warton's researches begin to take cultural effect that romance enters the lists with a formal lecture by Hugh Blair devoted to it in his *Lectures on Rhetoric and Belles Lettres* (1783). The sonnet similarly reappears, characteristically aligned with the elegy, in Nathan Drake's *Literary Hours* of 1798, after elegiac sonnets had become the rage of British poetry. The examples of Akenside and Southey also bring Drake to examine the formal decorum of inscriptions. Such a survey of generic categories in later eighteenth-century criticism could be extended without adding any substantial new integer to it. The dual conclusions are self-evident, that generic distinctions are in no way eroded through the century—indeed, they are beginning to recover ground by its end—and that those commonly accepted are wholly insufficient to characterize the full range of European poetry. Furthermore, as we move late in the century, with exemplary figures like Blair and Drake (not to neglect Johnson), the sense that generic imitation by rule has emptied forms of their vitality becomes increasingly explicit.

It is thus against something of a sense of crisis that the revival of Renaissance and medieval poetry occurs. And it is within the same context that the celebration of vernacular poetry, whether in old ballads or in contemporary Scottish songs, links up with the "naturalness" of Renaissance verse. The fame of Percy's *Reliques* obscures the importance of other antiquarian recoveries of vernacular poetry. John Aikin's *Essays on Song-Writing: With a Collection of such English Songs as are most eminent for Poetical Merit* (London: Joseph Johnson, 1772; rev. 1774) classifies by subspecies three types of song corresponding to the stages of societal development, defends and encourages vernacular ease in composition, and in its examples combines numerous poems from Percy with a generous sample of Restoration and earlier eighteenth-century song. Aikin was followed in 1783 by Joseph Ritson's three-volume set, *A Select*

Collection of English Songs, also published by Joseph Johnson, preceded by a customarily learned and opinionated "Historical Essay on the Origin and Progress of National Song" of over seventy pages, and embellished with plates by a young engraver whose secondary interest in poetry resulted in his first publication of verse that same year, William Blake.[15] The vogue for Burns, along with that for Chatterton, was in many respects a culmination of the Enlightenment celebration of spontaneous genius; but with Aikin and Ritson classifying and subclassifying song, the spontaneous was scarcely to be separated from the artful in any mind.

Nor was the past to be sequestered from the present. When the *Gentlemen's Magazine* began at the end of the 1780s to publish modern and Renaissance poems together in its monthly selection of verse, it signaled the course of the future. In the three decades that followed, the significance of Renaissance literature wholly altered, so much so that by 1819 there was in place a journal calling itself the *Retrospective Review* that was to last a dozen years and to constitute what would appear to be the first British periodical devoted to literary scholarship. Its principal interest was in the sixteenth and seventeenth centuries, and it included lengthy critical articles on the poets recovered in recent times. But it also became, without so designing, historically retrospective on British Romanticism. Quoting the first stanza of Donne's "The Blossom," the author is moved to observe, "The admirer of Wordsworth's style of language and versification will see, at once, that it is, at its best, nothing more than a *return* to this." An article on William Browne's *Pastorals* remarks on the poet's "extraordinary command over his native tongue" and the resulting liberty of linguistic invention in his verses, then turns to what might initially appear a surprising parallel in contemporary poetry:

> This peculiar freedom of expression and propriety of phrase, is by no means uncommon in many of the poets of the present day, who are, in reality, of the old school revived. In truth, that which has been termed unbounded license, and even vulgarity, in the poems of Leigh Hunt and others, is frequently neither more nor less than a free imitation of the Old English masters of the art, whose spirit they have imbibed, with the addition of the ease and point of modern versification.[16]

So independent a critical perspective throws into relief the familiar biases of the major periodicals of the age, though not necessarily as they are usually conceived. We tend to spread them along a political or religious spectrum of ideological adherence, both of which aspects are undoubtedly present. But to reduce all critical judgments to a journal's power base, or the assumed biases of its class of readers, blurs exactly what is most problematic, their standards of literary decorum. These, as we should expect, mirror the conflict of taste and of literary cultures accompanying and even enabling the recovery of Renaissance and to a lesser extent medieval poetry. The pillar of Tory respectability, the

Gentleman's Magazine, might be thought a most unlikely candidate to agitate for Renaissance verse. The liberal Whig spokesman Francis Jeffrey ought to have been open to its influence on contemporary writing, but he is much less so than the Oxford graduates who founded the arch-conservative *Blackwood's*, priding itself on a general catholicity of taste. Jeffrey reflects the standards of the late eighteenth century's landed gentry who subscribed to Johnson's *Poets* thinking them the models of literary propriety, and he is uncomfortable with both the very new and the very old. Yet, we would seriously misconstrue the situation were we to associate the recovery of earlier literature with ideological reaction. The most politically radical of established journalists, Leigh Hunt, became the champion of early Italian poetry during the Regency and undoubtedly was a major conduit of Spenser for the young poets, Shelley, Keats, and Reynolds, whom he celebrated in the columns of the *Examiner*. There is no consistency in the critical press during the entire period, except perhaps that its wonderful exuberance masks the extent to which it is conditioned by an absence of absolute standards and increasingly pressured by the growing popularity of a literature that casts in doubt the reliability of normative judgment.

This complexity, and even at times confusion, of values accounts for both the coexistence of antithetical standards and poetics during the Romantic period and the mode of its artistic development. The critical press was vociferous, but it had surprisingly little influence on literary creation, and where it did it was probably deleterious. Poets were free to follow their noses, with potential influences from earlier writing proliferating around them. From the perspective of literary form, the absence of authority, or the multiplicity of possible authorities, translates into a continuity with certain eighteenth-century norms of verse, particularly the ode and satire, the reassimilation of older forms, such as the ballad and romance, recovered through antiquarian scholarship, and curious (though characteristic) phenomena such as the sonnet revival beginning its career as a vehicle for eighteenth-century sensibility and increasingly becoming reconceived according to Renaissance practice. In an atmosphere at once so liberating and so intimidating it is perhaps inevitable that poetry be continually self-conscious about the traditions it invokes and how it uses them—self-conscious, too, about the freedoms it asserts. Where the standard measure of the natural is two centuries older, the resulting cultural and stylistic distance enforces a novel if rich tradition, but, having done so, it immediately demands a problematic reconciliation with modern conditions. The one certainty, that there was no longer a prescription for winning the laurel, both enjoined experimentation and impelled the search into the past for guidance. The peculiar intensity of the British Romantic period in literature is thus strangely congruent with the entire national experience during these years. The ambivalence of a culture that proclaimed itself the one bastion of liberty in Europe and embraced the Holy Alliance might be bluntly characterized as two-faced. But, if the literary endeavors are more salutary as manifestations of a national identity, they too are Janus-visaged. The cultural isolation of Britain during the long years of warfare coincides with a scrutiny of the past as a means to secure the uncertain present and to determine the future as a reflection of that all-but-mythological past grandeur.

CHAPTER THREE

The Sonnet

Bruin-Bear!
Now could I sonnetize thy piteous plight,
And prove how much my sympathetic heart
Even for the miseries of a beast can feel,
In fourteen lines of sensibility.

Robert Southey, "The Dancing Bear.
Recommended to the Advocates of the Slave-Trade" (1799)

We have been at some pains to take a census of the Sonnets now in London and the suburbs, and we find them to amount to the unprecedented number of 27,695,780. Last year the births and the deaths were about equal. So that almost all the Sonnets now surviving, must have been born since the 1st of January 1821, and we offer a bet of a rump and a dozen, that before the 1st of January, 1822, of the 27,695,780 returned by the late census, not more than five or six thousand will be above ground.

Blackwood's, 10 (December 1821), 580

I

THAT THE SONNET virtually disappeared from the British shores in the century after Milton's death is an oddity that could not be obfuscated by blandly defining it as "not very suitable to the English language."[1] On the contrary, it is a symptom of the cultural distance the eighteenth century imposed between itself and the Elizabethans, who were commonly understood to have been barbaric, their example effaced by subsequent refinements of language, literary conception, and versification. The omission of the sonnets from eighteenth-century editions of Shakespeare is a measure of the time, an interdiction justified at least as much on literary as on moral grounds.[2] Even at the beginning of the nineteenth century, in the midst of the resurgence of interest in the form, Renaissance sonnets still appear foreign to a refined taste. However strange seem the observations of George Henderson, writing in 1803, he represents the mainstream of opinion:

> . . . our early Sonnets abound with sentiments so extravagantly and uncouthly drawn, as must necessarily render them disgusting to any but a rude and uncultivated taste. . . . [U]ntil the time of DRUMMOND, (of Hawthornden,) whose Sonnets first appeared about the year 1616, we can advance slender claim to any degree of elegance in this species of versification.
>
> Immediately after DRUMMOND, there does not appear to have been any writer of the sonnet of considerable consequence except Milton.[3]

29

Certainly, there were those in the eighteenth century who knew some-thing about sonnets. Thomas Warton caused a stir when he published a modest series of sonnets in his *Poems* of 1777, but his *History of English Poetry* breaks off just as he was to begin the first full discrimination of Renaissance sonnet traditions. The great sonnet of the English Enlight-enment was not published until 1775, four years after the death of its author, Thomas Gray. That scholarly antiquary was one person who knew his literary heritage and wrote consciously in reference to it. No stranger to elegies, he wrote his lapidary "Sonnet on the Death of Mr. Richard West" in the encoded tradition of Renaissance love sonnets, suppressing the record of his emotional life until after its cessation. It is some measure of where knowledge of the British tradition in the sonnet stood that as late as 1800, in the preface to *Lyrical Ballads*, Wordsworth, himself soon to make a signal contribution to the repertory, could so blatantly misperceive the dynamics of Gray's sonnet. But also he took it on so directly because in the previous quarter century it had been placed on a pedestal where few lyric poems, let alone sonnets, have ever rested. An early issue of the *Edinburgh Review* typically observes that of all those attempting to write English sonnets, it is "Milton and Gray who have cultivated it with most success."⁴ Gray's elegiac sonnet, the sup-pressed record of his unfulfilled secret life, is the motive force underlying the entire Romantic revival of the sonnet, a model for hundreds of poets who, whether or not they had a secret life of their own, brought invention to the rescue. Where the Renaissance had played its variations on the ecstasies of love and religion, the later eighteenth century reared its monument to unavailing sorrow.

Sonnets of sensibility flooded forth like tears. Starting in the 1780s and continuing for some four decades of rediscovery, this most exacting small form of the British tradition was bent, stretched, reshaped, rethought. Its rebirth coincides with the rise of a definable woman's literary movement and with the beginnings of Romanticism. The palm in both cases should go to Charlotte Turner Smith, whom Wordsworth a generation after her death accurately described as "a lady to whom English verse is under greater obligations than are likely to be either acknowledged or remem-bered."⁵ Her *Elegiac Sonnets*, which first appeared in 1784 and by 1800 had reached their ninth edition, established the mode of the new sonnet in pensive contemplation, mostly sorrowful, at times lachrymose. The initial preface justified her generic decorum by claiming that she had approached each poem "as no improper vehicle for a single sentiment," that is, as a sonnet revealing the author's sensibility.⁶ Yet the evocation of a momentary emotional state may have its fictive extension as well, and such a perspective governs many of her sonnets. Whether deliberately or not, Smith prepared for her subsequent career as a novelist by capturing moments of emotional intensity within the sonnet. Her first edition contained five sonnets "Supposed to be written by Werter"; by the sixth edition she had incorporated another five-sonnet sequence from her own novel, *Celestina*. Even Smith's supposedly personal sonnets share in the tincture of novelistic emotions, shorn of the impedimenta of character, plot, and exposition. Doubtless her literary strategy entails a sacrifice of sharpness in language, conception, and actual personality, but on the other hand Smith's singular achievement is to free established poetic discourse from its reliance on polished couplets, formal diction, and public utterances, and through centering on internal states of mind to realize an expressive and conversational intensity.

Or at least to seem to. The rebirth of the sonnet, however little later centuries have attended to its growing pains, was no mere indulgence in raw nerves and emotional excess but was a genuine artistic movement with much of the fervor, the aggressive creation and dismantling of conventions, even the proliferation of coteries that accompanied its predecessor in the sixteenth century. Charlotte Smith found herself surrounded by admirers, followers, and detractors. Of the latter perhaps chief was Anna Seward, who, for apparently no good reason but a sense of professional threat to her eminence, upbraided Smith for her formal lapses.[7] Anne Bannerman wrote her own series of ten "Sonnets from Werter," later adding sonnets from Petrarch and even Ossian. One John Armstrong produced a series of forty-two "Sonnets from Shakespeare," all drawing on moments of lyric intensity in the plays with *Romeo and Juliet* predictably accentuated. In the 1790s the most elaborate sequence, both in numbers, complexity, and elegance of appearance, was the work of one of the most popular of the novelists of sensibility, Mary Robinson's *Sappho and Phaon, in a Series of Legitimate Sonnets,* which recast Ovid's epistle from the classic exemplar of a betrayed lover through a self-dramatization that loosely concealed the author's experience as "Perdita," rejected mistress first of the Prince Regent and then of Colonel Banastre Tarleton who is the prototype of her Phaon. And yet it is significant that such a publication would be prefaced by "Thoughts on Poetical Subjects," largely a spirited defense of her "legitimate" sonnets against the formal anarchy she perceived around her:

> . . . for every rhapsody of rhyme, from six lines to sixty [so] comes under that denomination, that the eye frequently turns from this species of poems with disgust. Every school-boy, every romantic scribbler, thinks a sonnet a task of little difficulty. From this ignorance in some, and vanity in others, we see the monthly and diurnal publications abounding with ballads, odes, elegies, epitaphs, and allegories, the non-descript ephemera from the heated brains of self-important poetasters, all ushered into notice under the appellation of SONNET![8]

Charlotte Smith had good reason to express an undiscriminating sorrow (and good reason as well to suppress the discriminated facts): a wastrel husband whom she left in debtors' prison and from whom she subsequently separated, a large brood of children for whom she undertook whole responsibility, the vicissitudes of earning a living in these circumstances, and the cruel fact that her spouse had legal claim, which he exercised for over twenty years, on the money she earned by her pen. It is thus a true irony that the most successful of her followers, William Lisle Bowles, lay claim to public adulation—the original *Fourteen Sonnets, written chiefly on Picturesque Spots during a Tour* (1789), like Smith's *Elegiac Sonnets*, gradually expanding through nine editions in the subsequent fifteen years—on the grounds of an actual, nonfictional sorrow. Yet his, it is clear, was only a higher fiction. The pretense to sincerity and spontaneous emotion, however, was honored by Bowles's readers as it was insisted on by him: "melancholy poetry," he remarks in the preface to his ninth edition (1805), "has been very often gravely composed, when possibly the heart of the writer has very little share in the distress he chose to describe."[9] In the same preface he at last gave his readers a reason for the grief he had attenuated over a period of fifteen years, the death of a young woman with whom he was passionately in love. If that seems a curious confession from the vicar of Bremhill (and future canon of Salisbury Cathedral), it does suggest how widely accepted was the language and literature of sensibility. And it almost goes without saying that the young woman, a niece of Sir Samuel Romilly, was not dead; she had simply rejected an offer of marriage from Bowles, a refusal that, as George Gilfillan nicely puts it, "first stung him into rhyme and rambling."[10] But Bowles's readers were distracted by neither such nurtured grief nor the symmetry of his travels, accepting on faith the immediacy and directness of his charged emotions as he represented his personal record of loss and tentative renewal. In placing his sonnets within the framework of travel, Bowles wed the sonnet of sensibility to the eighteenth-century prospect poem and on a broader spectrum unwittingly created one of the paradigmatic modes of Romantic thought, most thoroughly developed not in his fragmented miniatures but in the infinitely distendable meditative romance of his later polemical antagonist, *Childe Harold's Pilgrimage*.

For all their effect on the young Coleridge, an effect that even he had difficulty explaining to himself in his celebration of Bowles in the *Biographia Literaria*, these sonnets are not sophisticated in subject or form. They are largely written to formula—five of the twenty-one are addressed to rivers, another four juxtapose cliffs and the ocean pounding their base—and the sentiments are generally predictable. Basically structured to a Shakespearean scheme, the sonnets actually divide along the conventional lines of the Italian form: if a happy past is recalled in the octave, it will necessitate a sorrowful present in the sestet; similarly, a pastoral retreat in one part must be balanced by the world's harsh realities in the other. Yet, the predictability of situation should not blind us to the significance of Bowles's accomplishment. If he did not invent those formulae, he certainly codified them for a generation. And in placing the meditative mind in a natural scene that offsets its introverted solitude, Bowles marked the boundaries in which his contemporaries, especially Wordsworth and Coleridge, would formulate distinctive visions.

Bowles's one influential innovation was in loosely structuring the sequence of his poems around two journeys: the one up the east coast of England into Scotland, the other across the North Sea to Ostend and from there up the Rhine before a return to England. In each case, the farthest point of travel—Clydesdale, the Rhine—is celebrated for its variegated beauty, but cannot provide the traveler with a home, only with a field for the frustrations of memory. To live with such indelible memories can taint the present: Bowles artfully balances his tribute to Clydesdale as a source for happy memories in the future (No. 8) with a return to the river Itchin associated with his youth, whose beauty only augments his sense of isolation and deprivation (No. 9). Other such oppositions between adjoining sonnets (for instance, Nos. 3 and 4—"As slow I climb the cliff's ascending side" and "Ye holy tow'rs that shade the wave-torn steep"—or 11 and 12—"On these white cliffs, that calm above the flood" and "The orient beam illumes the parting oar") complicate the formulaic simplicity, reinforcing the reader's sense that the melancholic poet is beyond easy comfort. If he flees England to escape sad memories, in the end they constitute the one stable referent to which he inevitably must return. The abiding continuity amid such disjunctions is his sheer emotional unrest; nothing but his acute sensibility is consistent. Yet, unable as he is to exert rational control over his own mind, the poet projects himself as its victim.

What makes Bowles something more than an emotional exhibitionist or mere sentimentalist is the extremity of the case he poses—that and the curious formal propriety with which he invests it. It is not just that his mental reaction to the scenes through which he travels is our focus throughout these poems, but that mental reaction is their only point. Inconsistent, even contradictory, the mind nonetheless subdues the otherness of its environs into a true objective correlative, however many cliffs and castles offer a specious image of stability and fortitude. The division between self and other on which these sonnets are structured cannot be sustained within such a grinding mill. Repeatedly, the formulaic—a natural object evoking a contemplative response—is engulfed by the mind's power to absorb, and the octave and sestet split not between self and other, but within the mind itself. If the aim of Bowles's sonnet sequence is to represent self-division, his use of the form is perfectly congruent with his ends. Beneath the gothic trappings of the following sonnet, one singled out by Coleridge for praise, is a truly remarkable rhetorical structure, one that continually folds in on itself and exhausts its alternatives in lightning shifts of perspective, denying the resolution it seems so forcefully to posit.

> Thou, whose stern spirit loves the awful storm,
>> That borne on terror's desolating wings
>> Shakes the deep forest, or remorseless flings
> The shiver'd surge; when bitter griefs deform
> Thy peaceful breast, oh! hie thee to the steep

That beetles o'er the rude and raving tide;
And when thou hear'st distress careering wide,
Think in a world of woe what thousands weep.
But if the kindred prospect fail to arm
            Thy patient breast; if hope, long since forgot,
            Be fled, like the wild blast that hears thee not;
Seek not in nature's fairer scenes a charm,
            But shroud thee in the mantle of distress,
            And tell they poor heart "This is happiness."[11]

Few of Bowles's sonnets are so extreme, but as a group they appear to aspire to turning themselves inside out through self-division. That is perhaps the logical end of sensibility itself, but the tendency to reversal seems endemic to the form when its dramatic properties are accentuated, as any number of Renaissance sonnets—for instance, Drayton's "Since there's no help, come let us kiss and part" or Donne's "Batter my heart, three-person'd God"—attest.

Still, the sonnet of sensibility did not, like an avatar of the Werther it continually returned to, commit suicide in Bowles's hands; nor does the inherent self-division in his sonnets explain their influence on Coleridge. On the contrary, Coleridge praised Bowles, as Mill was later to celebrate Wordsworth, for the wholesome spontaneity of his emotion; and in his own sonnets of the 1790's, unlike his experiments with the ode, Coleridge never used the form to cancel its own statements. But there is no question that Bowles inspired Coleridge's interest in the sonnet, no question either that it soon became a passion. We might conjecture that his enthusiasm was contagious, for by the mid-1790s Coleridge was at the center of a new school of poets, and every one of them—with that innocence so characteristic of the revolutionary decade—was out to make a name through writing sonnets.

In the several years after he penned his "Sonnet to the River Otter," the most directly indebted to Bowles, in 1793 Coleridge himself wrote a score of sonnets, published seventeen in the first edition of his *Poems*, drew thirty-seven sonnets by himself, Charles Lamb, and Charles Lloyd into the second edition, and gathered another twenty-eight, the majority his own and those of his friends, into an ephemeral pamphlet to be bound with the sonnets of Bowles.[12] In both editions of his own poetry Coleridge introduces his sonnets with a sonnet to Bowles and pays lavish prefatory tribute to him (as Bowles had nodded in the direction of Charlotte Smith and she toward William Hayley). In fact, in his first edition he would not call his poems sonnets from fear of comparison with Bowles, but substituted "effusions" as more in the character of poems "lacking that *oneness* of thought which I deem indispensible in a Sonnet."[13] More self-assured a year later, Coleridge not only placed these poems under the rubric of "Sonnets, Attempted in the Manner of the Rev. W. L. Bowles," but prefaced them (and those of Lamb and Lloyd as well) with an "Introduction to the Sonnets" in which he defined the form in terms of its encouraging *"Totality"* (p. 71). Fervent as is this admiration for Bowles, Coleridge conceals the extent to which he and his friends have altered their inheritance, expanding the accepted range of possibilities with crucial implications for its future development.

In particular, Coleridge's "Sonnets on Eminent Characters," twelve poems he published in the *Morning Chronicle* during December of 1794 and January of 1795, return the sonnet to its assumption of public and polemical responsibility, an area conspicuously identified in the British tradition with the achievement of Milton, though to be discerned, as Milton had, among numerous Italian poets of the Renaissance. Coleridge's poems of panegyric, like Milton's, divide among artistic, intellectual, political, and military exemplars, and the models seem deliberately kept in mind. Milton's celebration of Henry Lawes (sonnet 13) provides the pattern for the sonnets to Bowles, Sarah Siddons, and (yet a minor) Robert Southey; the military virtues of a Lord General Fairfax (sonnet 15) are replicated not among modern British warriors but in Lafayette and Koskiusko [*sic*], heroes of universal liberty; and the statesmanship of Cromwell (sonnet 16) and Sir Henry Vane (sonnet 17) is to be rediscovered in the libertarian Whigs Sir Thomas Erskine and Richard Brinsley Sheridan. Most remarkable in this series, both for its rhetoric and its political daring, is the sonnet on Prime Minister Pitt. Suddenly appearing halfway through the series, two days before Christmas in 1794, it recaptures accents that had not, perhaps, been heard in this form since Milton's "On the New Forcers of Conscience" a century and a half before; nor did even Milton, for all his intensity, stretch his metaphors to such virulence:

> Yon dark Scowler view,
> Who with proud words of dear-lov'd Freedom came—
> More blasting than the mildew from the South!
> And kiss'd his country with Iscariot mouth
> (Ah! foul apostate from his Father's fame!)
> Then fix'd her on the Cross of deep distress,
> And at safe distance marks the thirsty Lance
> Pierce her big side! (4-11)

Its bombast notwithstanding, this poem by itself marks the restoration of the sonnet to a central place in English literature, aspiring to the clarion voice that Wordsworth would utter a decade later. Given the battery of repressive laws that Pitt was marshaling, it is surprising that its publication did not have serious consequences for Coleridge or his publishers.[14]

Coleridge's passion for the sonnet was as yet undiminished. His untitled pamphlet collection is a striking collaborative effort, an early manifestation of his penchant for assimilating and reprocessing writings he admired.[15] What is most remarkable, however, is Coleridge's evident determination to re-present Bowles as well. In drawing together the twenty-eight sonnets (bound in different versions with twenty-one or

twenty-seven of Bowles's, in either case a neat numerological completion), Coleridge appears deliberately to have recreated and then enlarged
Bowles's focus. Starting with Bowles's initial sonnet, he follows it with a
Southey prospect poem (which, in its view behind and before, exactly
replicates the perspective of Bowles's second sonnet), then adds two by
Charles Lloyd presenting Scotland through its pastoral solitude and its
ruined grandeur, then prints his own sonnet "To the River Otter," so
reminiscent of Bowles's river sonnets.[16]

Yet, if one reads in this strange assembly the attempt to draw all
contemporary sonneteers into a circumference already defined by Bowles,
as the sequence continues there is an equal impulse to enlarge the
intellectual and political circle in which Bowles's sonnets exist. Charles
Lamb is tapped for several poems about a young woman cut off in her
prime, whose name is Anna but could as well be the Lucy soon to be
lamented by Wordsworth; and Robert Southey, who in the 1790s had the
most radical sympathies in the circle, rings in with stirring pieces on
Isabel (who poisoned herself and her unborn, illegitimate child) and on
"The Negro Slave." Coleridge's sequence turns almost imperceptibly
from Bowles's solitary figure, divorced from innocence but unable to
cope with maturity, to the experiential world he must grow into, one
where the presence of mortality is everywhere felt. In this world the
equivalent to the solitary is the social outcast—unwed mother, slave,
beggar, urchin—the survey of whom elicits a group of sonnets suggesting
the consolation of a wise philanthropy. At last the various forms of
pastoral harmony in the early poems realize their complement in imaginative projections by which the sublime—whether of sea storms or of
Schiller—assumes its place. More than a mere anthology, Coleridge
builds, from the emotional plane he found established by Bowles, a
virtual manifesto of early Romanticism. The sophistication is yet a few, a
very few, years off, but the claims—for the sensibility isolated through
sorrow, love, social oppression, or imaginative vision—are already present in this collective effort. In an anthology never technically published
Coleridge has assimilated a school.

That it is a school isolated from tradition is, given the aversion of the
age to Renaissance traditions of the sonnet, not surprising (though to
find Coleridge flaunting his ignorance is). In his "Introduction to the
Sonnets" he confesses himself unable "to discover either sense, nature, or
poetic fancy in Petrarch's poems; they appear to me all one cold glitter of
heavy conceits and metaphysical abstractions" (p. 71).[17] Rather than revert to the traditional bases of the sonnet, Coleridge proceeds to define it
by the example of its two major contemporary writers, Charlotte Smith
and William Lisle Bowles. The laws thus derived are loose and disarm-
ingly simple: "The Sonnet then is a small poem, in which some lonely
feeling is developed." Aspiring to an enclosed wholeness, the best examples are those "in which moral Sentiments, Affections, or Feelings, are
deduced from, and associated with, the scenery of Nature. . . . They create

a sweet and indissoluble union between the intellectual and the material world" (pp. 71-72). The later Coleridge would lodge these concepts in more sophisticated terms, but the true mark of his mind is nevertheless obvious. The sonnet is by nature a ruminative form, one conducive but not limited to introspection, in which the natural world supplies counters, context, balance to the mind. In the largest sense that balance will be achieved through linking or even merging the individual and universal, the ideal and real, conception and perception, mind and matter. To derive all of this from the achievement of William Lisle Bowles would seem incongruous or merely amusing if we did not hear in Coleridge's language the unmistakeable resonance of the Preface to the *Lyrical Ballads* (1800) and, more, the program and practice of William Wordsworth, whom Coleridge had met within the year of this pronouncement. But also, the "sweet and indissoluble union between the intellectual and the material world" contains the polarities around which Petrarchan conventions are organized and through which they aspire to subsume the large within the small, multitudes within a compressed intellectual center.

In the "Introduction to the Sonnets" Coleridge is as cavalier about form as about tradition. The fourteen lines are merely customary; the number and pattern of rhymes should depend on the poet's mood and convenience; a rhymeless sonnet is perfectly acceptable.[18] On the other hand, there is a serious undercurrent to what at first appear to be breezy dismissals of authority. Coleridge defines a sonnet by attending to a characteristic mode of thought rather than a set of formal rules; in other words, as a genre, not merely a form. Formal decorum may mark the sonnets of Thomas Warton, but in Coleridge's view they are largely not true sonnets but rather epigrams on the Greek model. Such a distinction is seldom encountered in contemporary writing on the sonnet. Capel Lofft, for instance, whose immense collection—*Laura, or an Anthology of Sonnets (on the Petrarcan Model,) and Elegiac Quatuorzains*—turns on the idiosyncratic distinction marked in the title between Italian and Shakespearean forms, denies the latter claim to legitimacy.[19] In a similar vein, William Herbert complains:

> Some of our old sonneteers introduced, from the worst Italian writers, a spurious form, in which a detached quatrain, followed by a couplet, was substituted for the tercets [comprising the sestet]. Encouraged by this example, some of our later writers have presented the public (under the name of a sonnet) with three elegiac stanzas, concluded by a solitary couplet.

Herbert goes on to offer a definition succinct enough to be quoted as authority by subsequent writers: "The subject should, according to the strictest division, be set forth in the first, and illustrated in the second quatrain; confirmed by the first tercet, and concluded in the last."[20] Robert Housman, who nearly four decades later quotes this definition with approval, recognizes the folly of numbering every streak in an entire bed of tulips—"Mr. Lofft . . . enumerates no fewer than fifty-two species of the Legitimate, and fifty-four of the Irregular Sonnet''—and even of an overreliance on formal rules:

> Undeviating obedience to such rules, though a very important requisite, is not the *only* test and criterion of a sonnet. If it were, the productions of Shakespeare, and Bowles, and Coleridge, would be supplanted by the polished triflings of Hayley, the laborious common-places of Capel Lofft, and the mawkish effusions of Mrs. Mary Robinson and Mrs. Charlotte Smith.[21]

As these remarks forcefully remind us, for all Coleridge's fascination with Bowles or with the sonnet, neither he nor his exemplar was a paragon of obedience to the rules. None of the twenty-one sonnets of Bowles's second edition corresponds to an exact Italian or Shakespearean model: and of the forty or so sonnets written by Coleridge up to the end of the 1790s when he essentially lost interest in the form, there are only two in a strict Italian form, neither of which was published among his poems during his lifetime, and only four Shakespearean sonnets, of which only one, "To Earl Stanhope," the last of the Miltonic "Sonnets on Eminent Characters," has genuine poetic merit.[22] Generally, Coleridge follows Bowles's example in adapting the Italian form to introduce new rhymes in the second quatrain. He does so purposefully, he explains, because poetic forms should be accommodated to the language one writes in, and English allows greater variety in sound than Italian: "surely it is ridiculous to make the *defect* of a foreign language a reason for not availing ourselves of one of the marked excellencies of our own."[23]

By 1797 Coleridge had taken considerable pains, it would appear, to seize control of the burgeoning sonnet industry of the British Isles. Suddenly, he divested himself, and in such a way as to implicate his co-authors, Lamb and Lloyd, the latter of whom felt compromised, even betrayed. The three "Sonnets attempted in the Manner of Contemporary Writers" by Nehemiah Higgenbottom were printed in the *Monthly Magazine* for November 1797, so close upon the heels of the second edition of the *Poems* (with the "Introduction to the Sonnets" and some forty pages of examples) as to constitute a review. The parodies, making their point through italics about stock postures and hackneyed diction, might suggest not an ill use of Coleridge's friends (though the future record of his life would compound this example many times) but healthy self-criticism—perhaps, as well, a retrospective sense of the fictionality of the putative sincerity that for fifteen years the sonnet had been made to represent. In a relatively short time the revitalized form had lost intellectual and poetic vigor, more and more prey to the decadence—in diction, preciosity of thought, and inanity of subject—that marked the contemporary school of rococo emotionality called Della-Cruscan. Reared on a modest island in the flowing waters of self-regard, the sonnet of sensibility had little further ground to exploit. From this point on Coleridge raised his sights and his ambitions, deprecating the waste of talent on such trifles, even—ironically—when undertaken by the poet who singlehandedly transported the sonnet of sensibility to the mainland of British art.

II

To give Wordsworth his due, he sat by while every bard of his acquaintance was hatching sonnets, thinking the results, or so he recalled much later, "egregiously absurd" (*WLLY*, I, 71). His belated entry into the field is all the more remarkable for its having been deserted by every one of its previous champions. By the end of the first decade of the nineteenth century, shortly after Wordsworth's first sonnets were published, the sonnet had regained the low esteem it had held through most of the eighteenth century, its recent history being held by more than one critic a key to a vitiated public taste:

> Formerly (we speak not of the times of Elizabeth and James) few attempted it, and still fewer succeeded. But the present race of poetasters have made ample amends for this blank in our literature. Attracted by its brevity and supposed facility, and probably not a little dazzled by the meretricious ornament of which it has been found to be susceptible, every rhyming schoolboy and love-sick girl now give their crude effusions to the public under the denomination of sonnets. The press teems with volumes of this description, and unless another Censor shall "sweep the swarm away," in all probability the evil will progressively increase until it become a real disgrace to British Literature.[24]

Against this swarm, or perhaps in Olympian disregard of it, Wordsworth wrote and published his sonnets. The forty-seven "Miscellaneous Sonnets" and "Sonnets Dedicated to Liberty," published in the *Poems, in Two Volumes* of 1807, represent the most significant recasting of the form since Milton.

And yet, when Wordsworth turned to the form in 1802 to begin an involvement that is unparalleled in English literature, however independent of the school of the 1790s he held himself, was it possible for him not to have recalled Coleridge's ventures, whether for his friend's excesses or his limited achievements? This supposition is materially strengthened when it is recognized that virtually all the sonnets printed in the *Poems, in Two Volumes*, already separated into two parts, were transcribed early in 1804 for the notebook that Coleridge was to take with him on his excursion to Malta. One of those sonnets, the thirteenth of the "Sonnets Dedicated to Liberty" ("O Friend! I know not which way I must look"), was originally addressed to Coleridge and would have extended the personal frame of reference already established by the partial manuscript of *The Prelude* that was also prepared for the notebook.[25]

Two writings in Coleridge's career as author of sonnets are of particular interest for Wordsworth's later endeavors: the "Sonnets on Eminent Characters" and the "Introduction to the Sonnets." Whatever their lapses in an ultimate scale of value, the "Sonnets on Eminent Characters" stand out from the thousands of sonnets published in the closing decade of the eighteenth century for their creation of a sustained public posture and unified cultural vision. Wordsworth's address to Coleridge in the thirteenth of the "Sonnets Dedicated to Liberty" is more than a gesture of friendship, more even than an echo of Coleridge's addresses to Bowles and Southey: it is as well an implicit acknowledgement of obligation to his example. As for the "Introduction to the Sonnets," Wordsworth clearly would have seen its horizons as parochial, but even where his tones are most stentorian, the sonnets of the *Poems, in Two Volumes* uniformly attain to power out of a self-consciousness intensified by formal enclosure, a highly sophisticated version of the "lonely feeling" that Coleridge saw inherent in the sonnet. As he began his tutelage with the sonnet, Wordsworth stressed the element of confinement, "crowding into narrow room more of the combined effect of rhyme and blank verse than can be done by any other form of verse I know of" (*WLEY*, 379). Many years later, reflecting on his mastery of the form, he elaborated this figure, celebrating the "pervading sense of intense Unity in which the excellence of the Sonnet has always seemed to me mainly to consist. Instead of looking at this composition as a piece of architecture, making a whole out of three parts, I have been much in the habit of preferring the image of an orbicular body,—a sphere,—or a dew-drop" (*WLLY*, II, 604-605). It may be that "'twas pastime to be bound / Within the Sonnet's scanty plot of ground," as Wordsworth testifies in the "Prefatory Sonnet" of the 1807 edition (lines 10-11), but the sense of isolation, of "some lonely feeling," however refined the emotion or privileged the experience, underlies all the great sonnets of Wordsworth's maturity.[26]

A number of the poems in both sequences adopt the mode of the prospect sonnet popularized by Bowles and frequently indulged in by Coleridge and Southey. The ninth of the "Miscellaneous Sonnets," the first of Wordsworth's many sonnets "To the River Duddon" ("O mountain Stream! the Shepherd and his Cot"), is the closest in kind to these, reminiscent of Bowles's "To the River Itchin" and Coleridge's "To the River Otter." But the type appears in less obvious situations: in the two sonnets addressed from an immense distance to ships moving through the ocean (nos. 2 and 8), in the linked sonnets on cloud formations in the evening sky (nos. 3 and 4), or in two of the most famous in this group, the Westminster Bridge sonnet (no. 14) and "It is a beauteous Evening, calm and free" (no. 19), which again reverts to the ocean for its energy. Indeed, aside from the closing tribute to Raisley Calvert (no. 20), and the triplets "To Sleep" (nos. 5 through 7) and "From the Italian of Michelangelo" (nos. 10 through 12), all of the "Miscellaneous Sonnets" in some pointed way invoke this central type of the sonnet of sensibility. But it is not confined simply to the "Miscellaneous Sonnets." The "Sonnets Dedicated to Liberty," beginning with the very first—"Composed by the Seaside, near Calais, August, 1802" ("Fair Star of Evening, Splendor of the West")—continually surprise the reader either by enforcing immense

distances that link nations and cultures or by a sudden reversion to saving
particularities like "those Boys that in yon meadow-ground / In white
sleev'd shirts are playing by the score" (lines 3–4), which he celebrates in
the tenth, "Composed in the Valley, near Dover, On the Day of landing."
As the entire sequence of "Sonnets Dedicated to Liberty" suggests, to
Wordsworth's mind prospect rightly viewed must become vision. What
both sequences also and even more subtly suggest is that "some lonely
feeling" is in constant definition, self-contemplating and self-creating on
the axis of its visionary extension.

For something like four years Wordsworth contemplated these sonnet
sequences, originally as one unit and then split by subject matter into
two. Many years later, he recalled the singular episode that spurred his
career as a master of the sonnet:

> In the cottage of Town End, one afternoon in 1801 [actually May 1802], my
> Sister read to me the Sonnets of Milton. I had long been well acquainted
> with them, but I was particularly struck on that occasion by the dignified
> simplicity and majestic harmony that runs through most of them,—in
> character so different from the Italian, and still more so from Shakespeare's
> fine Sonnets. I took fire, if I may be allowed to say so, and produced three
> Sonnets the same afternoon, the first I ever wrote except an irregular one at
> school. Of these three, the only one I distinctly remember is "I grieved for
> Buonaparté."[27]

In other words, Wordsworth began his enterprise in the attempt to
recapture the tone and ethos of the Miltonic sonnet. It was natural
enough that he do so, although, notwithstanding Milton's contemporary
reputation as the foremost writer of sonnets in English, only Coleridge
among his fellow poets had dared so openly to risk the comparison. The
careful dating of the "Sonnets Dedicated to Liberty"—the earliest of
which (the first) specifies "August, 1802" as the point of composition—
testifies to how quickly and thoroughly Wordsworth engaged himself in
the attempt to rival, or equal, Milton.

The boldness of the undertaking and the integrity of the achievement
alike depend on Wordsworth's unwillingness to fall back on mere imitation. But also the numerous signals that alert the reader to a Miltonic
context seem deliberately placed, creating a complex interplay between a
generic tradition and a modern sensibility conditioned by past history
and past literature. To view the "Miscellaneous Sonnets" from the immediate perspective of the "Sonnets Dedicated to Liberty" is to be aware of
an anomaly, or at least a curiosity. Amid the many prospect poems are six
sonnets emphasized by being uniquely grouped in triplets and seeming of
a wholly different cast from the rest: three "To Sleep" (nos. 5 through 7)
and another three "From the Italian of Michelangelo" (nos. 10 through
12). Moreover, were these six poems removed from the sequence, a surprisingly coherent pattern would emerge among the sonnets preceding
the last few in which the tone deepens. The two sonnets in which ships
are perceived at a distance (nos. 2 and 8) have an obvious corollary in the

sonnets in which cloud shapes spur the imagination (nos. 3 and 4): these poems, as it were, surround and condition our response to the sonnets "To Sleep." Likewise, the translations from Michelangelo are surrounded by sonnets linked by their rusticity and their connections with the poet's past, "To the River Duddon" (no. 9) and "Written in very early youth" (no. 13). Further indication of this pattern is provided by the sonnet of nostalgic return, "'Beloved Vale!' I said, 'when I shall con'" (no. 15), which stands between two poems in which life seems or is suspended, with the sleeping city of the Westminster Bridge sonnet (no. 14) and the dead child glimpsed in a dream—sleep once more intruding upon the sequence in both—in no. 16, "Methought I saw the footsteps of a throne." The interweaving of theme and subject is as apparent as the interconnections are at first obscure: Wordsworth goes out of his way to indicate that he is practicing upon the reader, but forces our active intelligence to engage his in the process of discovery.

Perhaps it were wise if we brought our learning to bear as well. The significance of translating Michelangelo's poetry at this stage in England's knowledge of Italian literature—Cary's first complete rendering of *The Divine Comedy*, for instance, was yet a dozen years from publication—might have been lost on Wordsworth's countrymen.[28] But the traditional religious subject is readily apparent. And a reader would have truly had to be ignorant not to recognize the context of the triplet "To Sleep" in the familiar tropes of Renaissance sonnets. Yet, the undisguised Catholicism of the Michelangelo translations is as unexpected as the humorous deflation of the conventions of the sonnet on sleep. At once Wordsworth defines a context and distances himself from it. However puzzled a contemporary might be by his aims, the context is as obvious as it is initially odd. Wordsworth's "Miscellaneous Sonnets" are a sequence in the Petrarchan mode as surely as the "Sonnets Dedicated to Liberty" derive from the Miltonic.

Although the three translations were understandably not included in the manuscript intended for Coleridge's trip to Malta, they probably reflect his influence, at least negatively. Wordsworth resurrects the Petrarchan tradition dismissed by Coleridge as irrelevant to a modern sensibility, demanding that we see its affinities with his own far more radical departure from the customary grounds of the sonnet. At the same time, in an intricate balancing act, he deflates both the hyperbole lodged in tradition, especially in the humorous central poem of the "Sleep" group ("A flock of sheep that leisurely pass by"), and the posturing of his own sensibility, at which he actually records himself laughing in the last of the lighter sonnets, no. 15.

The first two of the Michelangelo sonnets reassure the poet that his love is not a mere capitulation to the things of this earth but through them aspires to an eternal ideal; the last testifies that God animates what is otherwise the "barren clay" of the poet's "unassisted heart" (12.3), thereby inspiring his verse. Together the three express conventional sentiments of the Renaissance sonnet and reinforce its focus as mediator between this world and an idealized conception of it in order to confirm that the intelligence that is properly schooled and disciplined "breathes on earth the air of paradise," as the final line of the first affirms. And yet, it is because of this "air of paradise"—or something very like it—that "Nuns fret not at their Convent's narrow room; / And Hermits are contented with their Cells; / And Students with their pensive Citadels." Everywhere in the "Miscellaneous Sonnets" are recorded moments of wonder—distant ships, a distant city, shifting cloud formations, the sea as a "mighty Being [that] is awake" (19.7). Even as one laughs at how one's imagination recasts treasured memories, it recurs:

> To see the Trees, which I had thought so tall,
> Mere dwarfs; the Brooks so narrow, Fields so small.
> A Juggler's Balls old Time about him toss'd;
> I looked, I stared, I smiled, I laughed; and all
> The weight of sadness was in wonder lost. (15.10-14)

The Michelangelo sonnets provide Wordsworth with a traditional focus for two pervasive modes of thought in the "Miscellaneous Sonnets": the moments of wonder all harbor a recognition of how the small and local can intimate the grand and universal; and the connection of the two produces a motivating force, a movement out and back, which, almost abstract, seems truly unmotivated, spontaneous, essential. The "Miscellaneous Sonnets" are entirely free of the "cold glitter" Coleridge associated with Petrarch, but they retain in a remarkable transformation the "heavy conceits and metaphysical abstractions" of the Renaissance sonnet tradition. The modes of thought Wordsworth explores are not the ostensible subject of his sonnets, as they are in the strictly philosophical elaboration of those he translates from Michelangelo. They are instead implicit, universally felt impulses within the mind—indeed, the primary means by which we recognize the workings of the imagination in all its "miscellaneous" guises.[29]

"How sweet it is, when mother Fancy rocks / The wayward brain, to saunter through a wood!" (1.1-2). Exclamation point to the side, the group of sonnets begins in such an offhand manner that the reader scarcely realizes that Wordsworth has announced the unifying theme of the sequence. It becomes even clearer as the sestet opens out into its predictable complementarity: "Verily I think, / Such place to me is sometimes like a dream / Or map of the whole world" (1.9-11). Thus the imagination stretches to escape what confines it; and yet, even here the second process, ebb succeeding upon flow, is simultaneously at work, as the continuing lines demonstrate:

> thoughts, link by link,
> Enter through ears and eyesight, with such gleam
> Of all things, that at last in fear I shrink,
> And leap at once from the delicious stream. (1.11-14)

The imagination in transcending its confinement draws the mind beyond its capacity to hold the center stable, until finally the centering impulse must reassert its control and reinstate mundane reality.

This simple pattern is present everywhere, but often in oblique ways that surprise the reader with their extensions. It is implicit in the combined urge for identification and awareness of difference that create the tensions of the second sonnet. "Where lies the Land to which yon Ship must go? . . . / Yet still I ask, what Haven is her mark?" (2.1,9). But the ship eludes the poet's stationary perspective and is only truly at home without referents: "a beaten way / Ever before her, and a wind to blow" (2.7–8). The same kind of relationship is juxtaposed in the succeeding dual sonnets, "Composed after a Journey across the Hamilton Hills, Yorkshire." In these, "Ere we had reach'd the wish'd-for place, night fell" (3.1), and, denied the prospect they had longed to see, the visitors create another one, sublime and with happily incompatible elements, in the cloud formations still suffused with light. The two sonnets balance the evanescent and substantial: even as the former are elevated almost to the terms of Michelangelo—the cloud formations representing "A contrast and reproach to gross delight, / And life's unspiritual pleasures" (4.3–4)—the poet's principle of reality reasserts itself, demanding his share of the flowers of paradise in the here-and-now: "The immortal Mind craves objects that endure" (4.12). And yet, no sooner is this principle laid down as an enduring premise than the poet yearns to break it, even if in an essentially comic way: the ensuing triplet of sonnets "To Sleep," deflated into the protestations of an insomniac, depict a mind whose source of irritation is its very inability to leave the realm of the sensible.

As usual with Wordsworth at this point in his career, there is nothing doctrinaire about his employment of a universal rhythm except his assertion of its universal applicability. Even the moral outcry of "The world is too much with us" (no. 18) traces its lineage to this aesthetic rhythm whose perversion is everywhere evident: "late and soon, / Getting and spending, we lay waste our powers" (18.1–2)—powers of imaginative growth and renewal, connecting singular and universal, the palpable and ineffable, not to be reduced to materialistic contracts without being destroyed. The poem does not merely inveigh against such perversions: it enacts through its intrinsic rhythm the necessary antidote, moving from the chill moralism of its opening to a pagan remythologizing of the world with Proteus and Triton envisioned arising from the sea at its end. The effect is scarcely isolated, but joins with the Westminster Bridge sonnet and its own surrounding poems—"Lady! the songs of Spring were in the grove" (no. 17) and "It is a beauteous Evening, calm and free" (no. 19)—in a reinforced sense of the sublimity attending the internalization of the rhythm already subtly marked. Each begins in the local and mundane yet discovers there a locus for the infinite, discovers beyond the fixed and known—like the ship embarking for an open ocean—an incarnate potentiality. The sonnets virtually explode from their access to power: a sleeping city is discovered to be animated by a "mighty heart" (14.14); a dormant winter garden is seized by "all the mighty ravishment of Spring" (17.14); the ocean beside which the poet and innocent child walk is both a "mighty Being" and "awake" (19.6). The repeated adjective acknowledges dynamic force underlying all experience. These sonnets testify—but in fact so do all the "Miscellaneous Sonnets"—to Wordsworth's ringing assertion as he recalls crossing the Simplon Pass: "Our destiny, our being's heart and home, / Is with infinitude" (*Prelude*, VI.604–605). However preoccupied with the things of this world, we are continually drawn forth to touch the infinite, reverting, as we must, to solid ground again. The Petrarchan system has been transfigured, its principles discovered to be those not of cosmology but of psychology. Of course, that had always been true, as Coleridge, before denigrating Petrarch, especially ought to have realized.

Wordsworth not only reestablishes the underlying mode of Petrarchan thought within the sonnet, but does so by eschewing the romantic and divine subjects by which that mode was conventionally expressed. If only by example, he suggests the innumerable ways in which the earthly and universal intersect, the infinite capacity of the mind to charge the mundane with spiritual import. The achievement is as brilliant on the one hand as it is vernacularly conceived on the other, the two poles of conception and execution in terms of their art wonderfully recreating the reach between the spiritually charged and the mundane. Yet, there is an even subtler aspect of this achievement, one directly related to the inner dynamics of the form Wordsworth employs. The Petrarchan sonnet, reduced to abstract principle, balances, as the Michelangelo sonnets so clearly demonstrate, here and there, finite and infinite, micro- and macrocosm. The tension existing between these poles empowers Wordsworth's series of "Miscellaneous Sonnets": invariably, octave and sestet turn on some variation of this division. Whatever Coleridge in a momentary lapse of self-recognition may have thought improper about a sonnet's harboring "metaphysical abstractions," Wordsworth shows an extraordinary capacity to conceive the Petrarchan form with the eye of a geometrician, first reducing it to its abstract relations before imagining it anew.

Having become sensitive to the structural intricacies of the "Miscellaneous Sonnets," we should expect of the "Sonnets Dedicated to Liberty" a comparable richness of effect in the Miltonic mode. Unlike the variations on an abstract theme that motivate the earlier series, these sonnets are organized in a narrative sequence; yet, if we try to pursue a simple line of plot through them, we immediately recognize their affinities with the *Lyrical Ballads* and *The Prelude*. For the true narrative is internalized, events serving as markers for the mental and imaginative growth discerned in the narrative voice. As with the "Miscellaneous Sonnets," the prospect sonnet accentuates perspective. Wordsworth, whether deliberately or not, recapitulates the pattern that Bowles had popularized, extending his sonnet sequence as travelogue into a public and political realm, so insistently forcing moral questions to the center of the observing consciousness that it becomes a conscience for its times. In the process, throughout the twenty-six poem sequence that constituted the original "Sonnets Dedicated to Liberty," Wordsworth recaptures the tone and moral grandeur of Milton with an almost unerring touch, one inspired as much by past example as by present urgency. It is small wonder that it could not be sustained when, later, he expanded the series to document the ensuing course of the Napoleonic Wars, for they are only the immediate occasion, not the underlying cause, of this sonnet sequence.

With powerful effect Wordsworth incorporates the mixed emotions of his countrymen into the quandaries of the sequence. Written, except for the last poem, between May 1802 and October 1803 and insisting on this temporal framework through conspicuous dating, the poems reflect the general public ambivalence that accompanied the Peace of Amiens (25 March 1802 to 18 May 1803). After ten years of war England was financially strapped, physically exhausted, and morally dispirited; and yet, the Peace settled nothing. If anything, it threw into sharp relief the futility of the war abroad and the ignominy of an English state where financial speculation made fortunes for some while others were deprived of what had long been assumed to be constitutional rights. Relief over the cessation of war was antithetically combined with disgust over the means of peace.

Wordsworth supplies no answers but rather confronts directly what in a rigorous analysis might be said to distinguish England from France. The evening star that shines over his homeland as he stands on the Calais beach in the first sonnet is greeted with patriotic emotion: "Fair Star of Evening, Splendor of the West, / Star of my Country!" (1.1–2). Yet, the subtle shift of syntax that follows presages the course of the ensuing sequence: "Thou, I think, / Should'st be my Country's emblem" (1.6–7). By the middle of the sequence the star no longer represents his country, nor is it even perceived as participating in the times, but is set apart in the distant memory of John Milton: "Thy soul was like a Star and dwelt apart" (14.9). As Lee Johnson has perceptively observed, the star of sonnet 1 is portrayed in nuptial terms, that of sonnet 14—"London, 1802"—is conceived elegiacally.[30] In the opening sonnet Wordsworth finds himself isolated in France "with many a fear / For my dear Country, many heartfelt sighs, / Among Men who do not love her" (1.12–14). The sense of separation intensifies as he looks upon Napoleon's election as First Consul with a disgust wholly opposite the jubilation he felt a decade before in witnessing the birth of the Republic. But rather than dissipating upon his return to England, his alienation only increases, as does his fear for his country, now reconceived as "a fen / Of stagnant waters" (14.2–3). "London, 1802," at the center of the sequence, records a nadir of despair. Paradoxically, this most famous of the "Sonnets Dedicated to Liberty" is not the independent statement about the nature of English society it is customarily perceived to be, but a momentary and partial denunciation in the midst of a psychological progression. Indeed, it justifies its crucial point midway through the sequence by serving as a fulcrum from which the demoralized poet allows himself tentatively to assert a sober optimism about the future state of Europe.

The ostentation of riches, the cynical accumulation of wealth through the marketing of warfare, the moral indifference appall the traveller who has returned from a corrupt state to celebrate Britain as the bastion of freedom, of "Plain living and high thinking" (13.11), as he expresses it in the sonnet preceding "London, 1802." Yet, in the one that follows it Wordsworth recovers his voice through distinguishing the idea of England from its current degenerate state:

> Great Men have been among us; hands that penn'd
> And tongues that utter'd wisdom, better none:
> The later Sydney, Marvel, Harrington.
> Young Vane, and others who call'd Milton Friend. (15.1-4)[31]

Milton is a continuing presence in the culture of England: it is not just that he should be, but that he is, "living at this hour" (14.1), if only within the consciousness of the dispirited successor who calls upon his memory. The sonnet that marks that despair remarks as well its antidote. The second half of the sonnet sequence recovers motive force through the incorporation of Milton as abiding genius within it. The sequence does not simply pay tribute to Milton: it regains its sense of purpose and integrity, both cultural perspective and inner assurance, through incorporating Milton's voice and vision. If it is true that "by the Soul / Only the Nations shall be great and free" (11.13-14), Wordsworth discovers his country's soul not in venal speculators who look to momentary advantage but in a consciousness that presides over the past and prefigures the future. Moreover, exactly what Milton allows Wordsworth is the perspective by which to free himself from his own trap in the momentary. The early group of poems that look beyond the particular confrontation of the French and English—"On the Extinction of the Venetian Republic," "The King of Sweden," and "To Toussaint L'Ouverture" (nos. 6 through 8)—implicitly affirm that civilized, humane values are superior to the vicissitudes of time. Venice can be oppressed but can never lose its force as a model of civilization; and, if failure is evident in this instance, new successes can be observed at the opposite extreme of Europe: the Swedish king "stands *above* / All consequences: work he hath begun / Of fortitude, and piety, and love" (7.10-12). Thus, as the succeeding poem argues, it makes no ultimate difference what will be the precise fate of Toussaint L'Ouverture, revolutionary leader of the newly independent Haiti now ironically languishing in a French prison. He, too, is "*above*

all consequences," elevated to the realm where Milton will also be found
to exist, among "exultations, agonies, / And love, and Man's unconquerable
mind" (8.13–14).

Though the last of the "Sonnets Dedicated to Liberty" appear to fall
off from this grandeur, as fears of French invasion prompt from Wordsworth
conventional tributes to the yeomanry of England, those tributes
are themselves the testaments to a regained faith in his countrymen and
bring the sequence, except for its 1806 postscript, back around to the
patriotic fears with which it began in the first sonnet. The spherical
sonnet emulated by Wordsworth is thus translated into the structure of
the sequence. But not utterly: the shift of syntax that was discernible in
the opening sonnet is recapitulated in the structure as a whole. The final
sonnet not only brings the sequence into rough contemporaneity with
the point of publication, but through its sense of England's isolation in
the Napoleonic Wars demands that the true mettle of his culture show
itself. The sestet balances the alternatives on the fulcrum of a conditional
clause, an enabling possibility, but only if Miltonic virtues can be incorporated
by a resolute people:

> We shall exult, if They who rule the land
> Be Men who hold its many blessings dear,
> Wise, upright, valiant; not a venal Band,
> Who are to judge of danger which they fear,
> And honour which they do not understand. (26.10–14)

The final line, with its unresolved ambivalence poised on a razor-thin
edge, exactly mirrors the moral and intellectual construction of the entire
sequence of "Sonnets Dedicated to Liberty."

These are public statements, but they are also notably self-reflexive.
Infused with the power of his mentor, Wordsworth discovers himself and
his vision renewed in the process. The sonnets record the process of their
own creation, a coming to vision by discovering the mental preconceptions
necessary to utter the Miltonic voice, to write a Miltonic sonnet. No
less than the "Miscellaneous Sonnets" are the Miltonic "Sonnets Dedicated
to Liberty" psychological in their orientation. What begins as a
simple, if extreme, polarization of France and England soon prompts an
inner division—one between the temptation to despair and the duty to
hope, between the issue of the moment and the liberty not subject to time,
between the alienated poet and the mentor whom he projects from himself
and who speaks for the highest ideals of his culture. Wordsworth
creates the greatest of neo-Miltonic sonnet sequences through the profound
imagining of what Milton would have required of the poet who
would emulate him.

And yet the same might be said of Wordsworth's sense of the more
distant Petrarch. And, once we distinguish the styles and characteristic
conceptions Wordsworth inherits from the two poets, we should recognize
the remarkable extent to which, however distinct the two tradi-

tions—the one emphasizing links between the mundane and supernal, the other between individual and cultural values—they share common features that themselves make the two sonnet sequences aspects of one great and revitalizing whole subsuming them within its commanding mental structure. The imaginative rhythm of the "Miscellaneous Sonnets" is in its essential drive the same urge that motivates the "Sonnets Dedicated to Liberty."

III

With the publication of the *Poems, in Two Volumes*, the sonnet's revival was assured. Elsewhere in the collection Wordsworth's trifling with butterflies and daffodils dismayed his conservative critics, but even the harshest of them recognized the high plateau of art attained in the sonnets.[32] At the same time, such an achievement left to his emulators, not to mention himself, the problem of succession. His reception encouraged Wordsworth to continue his formal exploration of the sonnet: first, by the expansion of the political unit into "Poems Dedicated to National Independence and Liberty," the preponderance of which were sonnets, and then in his concerted redirection of the Bowles prospect sonnet within sequences once again conceived as single poems: *The River Duddon* and *Ecclesiastical Sonnets* of 1820 and 1822.[33] Yet the former, even though individual sonnets retain the stamp of Wordsworth's inimitable compression, is constrained by the obviousness of the programmatic metaphor— the enlarging river figuring the passage of life—and the latter soon loses its congregational independence in the institutional exigencies of ecclesiastical history. By the time that Wordsworth steered the sonnet into conservative polemics, in the "Sonnets on the Punishment of Death" of 1839, he leaves the perverse impression of having pursued across the arc of his career an almost undeviating course away from the internal debates and epiphanies by which he had redefined the form for his culture.[34]

But in whose hands, if not Wordsworth's, would the sonnet find a new champion? Literally hundreds vied. The quarterly, monthly, weekly, and diurnal journals, whose numbers continually increased with the size of the potential readership, overflowed with sonnets, all now truly fugitive from the fame the poets sought.[35] Even Byron, who had once vowed never to write a sonnet, entered the fray, as if to prove himself indisputable lord of every last inch of the poetic terrain.[36] His "Sonnet on Chillon" has in typical fashion served the contradictory purposes both of elocutionary platitude and interpretive ambiguity (since it appears wholly to diverge in its sentiments from *The Prisoner of Chillon*, which it prefaces). Perhaps, however, it is most perceptively read as the best manifestation of how well Shelley "dosed" Byron with Wordsworth in the summer of 1816 when it was written.[37] For the Miltonic timbre of the sonnet seems filtered through Wordsworth, as its noble rhetoric invokes the ideals of an isolated humanity against tyrannies that thrive in its despite.

Having proved that he could paint bold strokes with a small brush, Byron reverted to the more expansive forms, primarily the romance and epic, that were natural to a genius who spurned being "crowd[ed] into narrow room," leaving the emulation of Wordsworth to others. One poet who was eager, having surrounded himself with a school of talent (albeit one that contained none of the Cockneys by which it was characterized) and having in the preface to *The Story of Rimini* already defined his style and poetic conceptions as derived from Wordsworth, was Leigh Hunt. The modern critical sensibility, schooled in a literature of bourgeois values, has been strangely ungenerous to their exemplar in British Romantic poetry, who in fact was the first truly to experiment with their compatibility to serious art. We tend, like Hunt's detractors in *Blackwood's*, to find *kitsch* where he earnestly sought artistic purpose and thus have blinded ourselves to how thoroughly he conceived himself as persevering in Wordsworth's program to modernize poetry and, in particular, to revitalize the sonnet for a contemporary taste. Bowles may visit half a dozen picturesque rivers for local effect and emotional afflatus, but Hunt is content to remain at home, heading the twenty sonnets of his *Foliage* in 1818 with a "Description of Hampstead." The village is celebrated not for its romantic qualities but for its very lack of them. Its balance between London to the south and open nature to the north represents an equilibrium between poles. Life in Hampstead is easy, pleasant, by no means uncommitted politically or culturally, yet calm, eschewing austerity or intensity. The first pre-Raphaelite, devoted to the early Italian Renaissance, Hunt transports Petrarch (as he did Dante and Tasso) to his suburban village, where he also relocates the by now conventional subjects of the Romantic sonnet. To peruse this sequence of sonnets is to be surprised by their modernity, though one, like all professed modernity, that must appear quaint to a later time. The brave Kosciusko reappears in this comfortable environment wholly transformed from Coleridge's martial hero, as one who, faced with swearing allegiance to Napoleon or the Holy Alliance, forswears both, substitutes rhymes (spade for blade), and heroically tends to his garden: both warrior and nature are quietly methodized. Hunt likewise revises the customary tribute to the energizing artist, here Raphael, portrayed neither as towering intellect nor isolated visionary but as a happy youth attracted to the beauties of the earth: "How sweetly sure he looks! how unforlorn!" ("Written under the Engraving of a Portrait of Raphael, Painted by Himself when He was Young," l. 9). Milton's legacy is joined to Wordsworth's in the double sonnet "To Percy Bysshe Shelley, on the Degrading Notions of Deity" (a curious reduction of or response to the "Hymn to Intellectual Beauty," which Hunt had published in *The Examiner* on 19 January 1817), and, with intentional irony, in the triple sonnet "To — —, M. D. on his Giving me a Lock of Milton's Hair," where the constancy of Milton's values is contrasted with Wordsworth's apostasy.

Yet, the true influence of Milton comes from his later sonnets, where, as Mary Ann Radzinowicz succinctly represents them, Milton "turn[s] from public movements back to the private individual as the source of public hope."[38] Perhaps such a retreat is natural, since the Regency writes in an atmosphere of political disillusionment, if not dismay, similar to what is encountered in Milton's late verse. Whatever the case, like Milton's sonnets to Henry Lawrence and Cyriack Skinner, Leigh Hunt's sonnets center on his household, the friends who visit, the art and politics they discuss. Fifteen of the twenty sonnets are addressed to such friends not as public figures but as genial associates within a protected domestic circle. They participate in a free, unconstrained speech, culture, and affection that, as the twenty sonnets gather, transcribe a circle representative of the Miltonic community as Hunt reconceives it. What is principally to be honored in such a community is not great public achievement or political purpose or private vision, but rather the community's simple, irreducible, dependable humanity. Though he is programmatic in domesticating the sonnet, Hunt is nonetheless making a determined political statement, one directed at the poet whom he follows. In his symbolic Vale of Health are preserved the household virtues singled out by Wordsworth in that earliest of his great sonnets:

> Wisdom doth live with children round her knees:
> Books, leisure, perfect freedom, and the talk
> Man holds with week-day man in the hourly walk
> Of the mind's business: these are the degrees
> By which true Sway doth mount; this is the stalk
> True Power doth grow on; and her rights are these.
> ("I griev'd for Buonaparte," 9–14)

Hunt's portrayal of Wordsworth, in the first of the three sonnets on receiving a lock of Milton's hair, as the poet who had once deserved such an honor but who had resigned his title to it, is thus a generic signal. Hunt, in fact, is claiming not only the honor of the Miltonic succession, which Wordsworth has abdicated, but also to represent the Wordsworthian vision with an accuracy and thoroughness never adumbrated by the older poet. That, objectively viewed, Wordsworth's troubled confrontations in the "Sonnets Dedicated to Liberty" are more complex than what can be encompassed by Hunt's rosy optimism is somewhat beside the point. To Hunt's mind, he and his friends reconsecrate a faith abandoned by its founder.

One way they do so is by writing sonnets. That is why the title "On the Nile" appears among the poetical works of Hunt, Keats, and Shelley alike, the result of a quarter-hour sonnet-writing contest among the three friends in Hunt's parlor, and why so many of the sonnets in Keats's 1817 *Poems* share titles with those in Hunt's *Foliage*.[39] The latter fact, confirming his tutelage, did not accrue to Keat's advantage among reviewers. His early sonnets, while they exceed Hunt in all categories of Cockneyism—erotic coyness, adolescent fantasy, a leveling informality, and studied neologisms—cannot claim anything comparable to the intellectual vision implicit in the sonnets of *Foliage*. Five of the early sonnets are, in fact, "thank-you" notes. One commemorates his brother Tom's birthday; several are conventional exercises in amorous gallantry; and as late as January 1818, the thirty-seventh sonnet in chronological sequence, Keats was still capable of the strained wit of "To Mrs. Reynolds's Cat." Fully half of his sixty-two sonnets bear the indelible imprint of Hunt in style and treatment: they are primarily exercises, bagatelles. And it must be remembered that these derivative sonnets are those by which Keats was judged for many years; not until mid-century could his actual achievement be fairly measured. The ironic result is that, after Wordsworth, probably the most influential writer of sonnets for the subsequent generation of poets was not Keats but Leigh Hunt. Yet there is another, far-reaching aspect to Keats's literary exercise outside a prescribed program. Constrained neither by Milton's, Wordsworth's, nor finally Hunt's conception of decorum in subject, Keats slowly came to an independent perspective on the form. He did so largely by returning to traditions that were only starting to accord with contemporary cultural tastes. In Regency England Keats had the legacy of Renaissance sonnets, especially those of Shakespeare, largely to himself.

No English Romantic spent more time writing about writing than Keats. He discovered very early how well the sonnet's inherent polarity suited his interests—so early, indeed, that initially it is likely he had little thought for generic propriety. The sonnets on Byron and Chatterton date from the winter of 1814-1815 when he was completing his eighteenth year, and their conventional tonalities appear as late as "On the Story of Rimini" (March 1817) and "Spenser, a jealous honorer of thine" (February 1818). But the use of the sonnet to record, or enact, an artistic experience, beginning with "On First Looking into Chapman's Homer," took Keats far beyond the conventional in response: the sonnets on *King Lear*, on Homer, on Robert Burns realize an intensity of presence and response—even an anxiety—as Keats contemplates what at once excites, troubles, and mocks him. He may have begun by composing elegantly phrased, encapsulated book reviews, but he soon transforms his mere assessment of writing into a revelation of the psychology of aesthetic experience. In many ways this is the characteristic drive of nearly all the great sonnets: what he discovers in *King Lear* is also manifest in the Elgin Marbles, in natural features like the sea, and most disturbingly in that unfathomable other whom he both desired and feared, Fanny Brawne.

Virtually all of Keat's mature sonnets center on psychological confrontation in which he is simultaneously drawn forth in attraction or admiration and repelled by his sense of the limitations and constraints of his existence. Wordsworth plays over such materials so as to comprehend a dialectical rhythm within his unifying sensibility, not so much absorbing them into the egotistical sublime as realizing the objective intensities of what Keats called negative capability; but Keats's major sonnets assert a raw tension between their contraries. The characteristic rhetorical effect that results from these impasses is a structure of paradoxes. The Byron sonnet begins with a "sweetly sad . . . melody" and ends with a "tale of pleasing woe," but by 1818 the interchangeability of terms carries enormous ethical and existential weight. It can be suggestive of good coming out of evil, as in "O thou whose face hath felt the winter's wind" or "To Homer":

> Aye on the shores of darkness there is light,
>> And precipices show untrodden green,
> There is a budding morrow in midnight,
>> There is a triple sight in blindness keen. (9-12)

On the other hand, the essential paradox of human life may be a universal cancellation of value, including that in life itself, as Keats suggests in "Why did I laugh tonight? No voice will tell" and in the "Sonnet to Sleep," with its reversal of Renaissance conventions, "O soft embalmer of the still midnight." More directly than the ode, the sonnet presupposes division, but, as with that other form, Keats's characteristic urge is to question, if not collapse, the distinctions he confronts. The most obvious formal result is a resort to catalogs that subsume opposites, a union of polarities. The process is set forth, both as psychological reality and as aesthetic experience, in the sestet of "On Seeing the Elgin Marbles," where the sonnet's contraries, seen to be irresolvable, are left in their manifest integrity.

> Such dim-conceived glories of the brain
>> Bring round the heart an undescribable feud;
> So do these wonders a most dizzy pain,
>> That mingles Grecian grandeur with the rude
> Wasting of old time—with a billowy main—
>> A sun—a shadow of a magnitude. (9-14)

This technique, which appears in several early sonnets, becomes especially prominent in the late experiments in the form, in which Keats's artistic control is assured.[40] His last sonnet is also his most audacious experiment, a poem not easily conceived merely in terms of its art, but also one that carefully invokes its multiple traditions.

> I cry your mercy—pity—love!—aye, love,
>> Merciful love that tantalizes not,
> One-thoughted, never wand'ring, guileless, love,
>> Unmask'd, and being seen—without a blot!
> O, let me have thee whole,—all,—all—be mine!
>> That shape, that fairness, that sweet minor zest
> Of love, your kiss, those hands, those eyes divine,
>> That warm, white, lucent, million-pleasured breast,—

> Yourself—your soul—in pity give me all,
>   Withold no atom's atom or I die,
> Or living on perhaps, your wretched thrall,
>   Forget, in the mist of idle misery,
> Life's purposes,—the palate of my mind
> Losing its gust, and my ambition blind.

In its opening diction and its subject, as well as its markedly Shakespearean fourth line, this sonnet resurrects the conventional lover's complaint of the Renaissance sonnet, but in the sheer intensity of its expression and its psychological revelation it is an extreme form of the sonnet of sensibility. The atomization of the catalog is essential, reaching toward the "atom's atom," with syntax, logic, conjunctive language all displaced, as if integers of "Life's purposes," by the poet's craving. Yet, the apparent plenum of the octave collapses of its own weight into inanition, a vacuum that swallows every element of the catalog in a dying fall suggestive of Wordsworth's practice. Keats's condensation of uncontrollable passion is paradoxically achieved through a breathtaking technical mastery. At the same time that he could pride himself on having created out of two sonnet traditions an example like nothing ever written in English before, he must have realized that he had gone far beyond the fine excess he saw as the hallmark of great art, creating a virtuoso display as an end in itself, incapable of repetition. Such a polished representation of frenzy, in which the polarities of plentitude and emptiness are discovered to be the same, strains the sonnet form to the utmost and bears intimations of decadence.

Still, if this is not the calm, reserved power that Wordsworth could extract from a sleeping city or a dormant garden, its intensity of effect derives from Wordsworth and testifies to a similar ability to compress explosive elements within a just-encompassing form. Undoubtedly, these two are the masters of the Romantic sonnet. That being the case, it is perhaps surprising to realize the truth of François Yost's observation: "In English literature the prize for prosodic variety in sonnet composition undoubtedly goes to Shelley, if we restrict the competition to major poets up to his time. . . . He never used the same [rhyme scheme] twice."[41] One reason that Shelley is not usually thought of in this light is that he does not pursue the programmatic endeavors of Bowles or Wordsworth, Hunt or Keats. But from that most famous sonnet excursion into the Romantic sublime, "Ozymandias," to the austere Petrarchan moralism of "Lift not the painted veil which those who live / Call Life," to the ambivalence of representation in "To Wordsworth," to the five terza rima sonnets from which he constructs his "Ode to the West Wind," Shelley is always conscious of the traditions against which his sonnets resonate and masterful in his use of form. His greatest sonnet—"England in 1819"—is deeply indebted in rhetoric and even eschatology to Milton, but, like "I cry your mercy," relies on a minutely discriminated catalog for its intensity of effect.

An old, mad, blind, despised, and dying King;
Princes, the dregs of their dull race, who flow
Through public scorn,—mud from a muddy spring;
Rulers who neither see nor feel nor know,
But leechlike to their fainting country cling
Till they drop, blind in blood, without a blow.
A people starved and stabbed in th'untilled field;
An army, whom liberticide and prey
Makes as a two-edged sword to all who wield;
Golden and sanguine laws which tempt and slay;
Religion Christless, Godless—a book sealed;
A senate, Time's worst statute, unrepealed—
Are graves from which a glorious Phantom may
Burst, to illumine our tempestuous day.

Shelley's balancing of his pointillist survey with a heavily constraining scheme of but four rhymes is replicated in the sudden enjambment of the final couplet, with its ambiguous modal auxiliary—"may"—throwing the accumulated weight of the single-sentence catalog onto the active, explosive verb so long awaited. The melding of form and content appears seamless. Yet ultimately the appearance is a paradox, for the informing idea of this marriage is an impossibility: the subject, as Shelley conceives it, is pitted against the form itself. If small reveals large, if the limitations of this world intimate manifold perfections of an ideal, then the sonnet always has had an apocalyptic thrust implicit in its form. Yet, there is the counterurge that Wordsworth demonstrates, to contain, to retreat to solid ground. Shelley pivots his poem on a syntactic potentiality—"may"— that yields to the bursting of its formal bonds in a movement parallel to the revolutionary explosion that will invert the anti-forms repressing contemporary society. The form symbolically consumes itself, as surely as does the society it catalogs.

"England in 1819" is as singular an achievement as "I cry your mercy," both poems deliberately turning themselves inside out with a sophistication that Bowles scarcely intimated in his similar endeavor thirty years before. And yet no sequence could grow, nor could followers branch out, from such ironic seed.[42] Though written within the year, the poems influenced neither each other nor any contemporary. Shelley's apocalyptic sonnet was withheld from publication until 1839; Keats's cry of passion did not appear until 1848. Both sonnets, if only through the self-conscious brilliance of their technical manipulation, testify to a fully realized art: the Romantic revival of the sonnet is complete. By the time intervening decades had allowed the achievements of Keats and Shelley to be justly discriminated, the potentiality of the smallest and most constraining, and thus most challenging, of traditional forms was once again being independently explored by Tennyson and the Rossettis, then by Meredith and Hopkins. And this time it did not have to be rediscovered as well.

CHAPTER FOUR

The Hymn and Ode

Hail, Liberty, fair goddess of this isle!
Deign on my verses, and on me, to smile;
Like them, unfetter'd by the bonds of sense,
   Permit us to enjoy life's transient dream,
To live, and write, without the least pretence
   To method, order, meaning, plan, or scheme:
And shield us safe beneath thy guardian wings,
From law, religion, ministers, and kings.

Soame Jenyns, "An Ode" (1780)

I

SONNETS by the logic of their form inhabit a world that in conceptual, intellectual, and emotional terms is a polarity. A necessary discontinuity intervenes between the speaking voice and the external object it desires to assimilate, creating tensions between here and there, now and then, self and other, and magnifying their consequences. The spaces between microcosm and macrocosm are essential to the sonnet as genre, which is why it so naturally adopts the timbres of a complaint. Conventionally, the poet protests to the contrary, but were those spaces not assumed to be an insuperable barrier, the sonnet, notwithstanding the arbitrary constrictions of its length, would melt into the hymn. Yet, we are never, on the simple level of expectation, unsure of the distinction between these forms, even when confronted with religious sonnets of personal address and convincing sincerity. There is a fundamental difference between the implicit suppositions of "Batter my heart, three-person'd God" and "A Hymn to God, my God, in my Sickness." The dynamic of the first poem lies in Donne's recognition that God is revealed through the very absence of his presence; of the second poem in the assumption that his presence can be touched, that the space between can close. Division is essential to the "Holy Sonnets," even to the less personalized and rhetorically more unified "La Corona" series, as it is in the nineteenth century to the anxious devotional sonnets of Christina Rossetti and, in starkest detail, the "Terrible Sonnets" of Hopkins.

There are, of course, other distinguishing attributes of a hymn—at least in a popular generic conception. It is construed as a series of like stanzas suited by their uniformity to a repeated musical setting and addressed to a divine, an immortal being, in whose efficacy, on both cosmic and personal planes, one has the certainty of belief. The speaking voice is presumed both sincere, admitting no intrusion of irony, and devout, insisting on the veritable existence of the being called upon. Hymns are likewise communal, implicitly acknowledging the underlying and mutually binding faith of a congregation. Such would be a conservative and seemingly universal list of assumed elements. In practice, however, as is frequently the case with any absolute generic prescription, the exceptions to these rules are almost as numerous as the verses exemplifying them.

Precisely because the hymn, unlike the sonnet and the Pindaric ode, is not a fixed form, it is susceptible to the range of generic possibilities one associates with the more capacious literary modes. The congregational assumptions of the hymn, for instance, are controverted by the intense privacy of most literary hymns in the English tradition and by the tendency of Protestant sects to emphasize the solitary, individualistic nature of religious experience.[1] John Henry Newman's intellectual gravitation to the ritualized order of Roman Catholicism cannot temper the sense of spiritual isolation so powerfully evoked in his early poem, "The Pillar of the Cloud," which is probably the greatest English hymn of the nineteenth century:

> Lead, Kindly Light, amid the encircling gloom,
>   Lead Thou me on!
> The night is dark, and I am far from home—
>   Lead Thou me on!
> Keep Thou my feet; I do not ask to see
> The distant scene—one step enough for me. (1-6)

By the time of the English Romantics, indeed, hymn writing was all but identified in the popular mind with Protestant Dissent. The accents of the Wesleys, Isaac Watts, and finally William Cowper came to dominate religious song in the eighteenth century.[2]

Like the congregational motive, the imperatives and apostrophes associated with hymnody are similarly dispensable. Indeed, when the community is centrally evoked, it is often itself the subject of the hymn, called upon in a range of attitudes from the participatory to the admonitory: "Stand up, stand up for Jesus," "Onward, Christian soldiers," (or, in the distinctive accents of John Wesley) "Sinners, turn, why will ye die?" Along with exhortations to the congregation, Protestant hymnody emphasizes individual testimony of religious experience: "Jesus loves me; that I know." The presumptive list of attributes is, then, quickly exposed as too restrictive, perhaps as too decorously pious, better suited to the devout intensity of the "Veni, creator spiritus" or the communal rejoicing of "Adeste fideles" than to the troubled and solitary walk with God or the raucous marching bands in the vanguard of his army.

Nor, in truth, is this tentatively broadened definition wholly appropriate to the nature and ends of hymnody in the eighteenth century. The more the enthusiasts burst into song, it would appear, the more the upper class divorced its hymns from conventional Christian subjects. Among, for instance, the representative poets of the late seventeenth and the eighteenth centuries gathered together in Chalmers's *Works of the English Poets* (1810), few who essay the form limit themselves to Christian subjects. Hymned abstractions abound, exemplified originally by such a poem as Cowley's "Hymn to the Light" but tracing a progressive secularization. Mark Akenside's celebration of pastoral England, "Hymn to the Naiads," is typical of another sort of hymn, its neoclassical paganism being sustained by fastidiously learned footnotes. By late century Britain might have been expected to have produced an Enlightenment savant capable not only of distinguishing to public satisfaction a Turkish from a Persian ode, but of investing with local color and inimitable learning a series of hymns to Indian divinities. Among these curiosities from the pen of Sir William Jones, what is most remarkable about a poem like his "Hymn to Durga," composed in nine three-part sections, is the way it testifies to a combined awareness of religious connotations of the triad (both Christian and Indian) and of the symmetry appropriate to the Pindaric ode.[3]

The English Romantics inherited this Enlightenment tradition of learned and retrospective hymnody, and it influenced their assumptions and practices perhaps far more than did an Isaac Watts. In the early 1790s the precocious and as yet unpious Robert Southey composed and showed considerable partiality to a "Hymn to the Penates" celebrating his family home. A similar resuscitation of classical values and attitudes marks Keats's fine set-piece, the "Hymn to Pan"—"a Very pretty piece of Paganism," exclaimed Wordsworth—around which he organizes the opening scene of *Endymion*.[4] But it is not just the classical pantheon that is susceptible to invocation. William Lisle Bowles, who was usually deferred to as "the Reverend Mr. Bowles," troubled his conscience as little over publishing a "Hymn to Woden" as he had over advertising his broken heart; while Byron, to prove himself a proper match for his conventionally devout bride, versified several psalms in *Hebrew Melodies* without a thought about how such a title befit a lord of the Anglican realm. Coleridge, who wrote the only significant literary hymn of a Christian persuasion during this entire period, also proposed a set of hymns on the subjects of "Sun, Moon, Elements, Man & God."[5] The best of the Romantic poems bearing this generic designation—Shelley's "Hymn to Intellectual Beauty"—in title looks back to Spenser and in subject responds antithetically to Coleridge's "Hymn Before Sunrise." (Shelley also translated a group of the Homeric *Hymns* to classical deities, which are hardly hymns at all but were poems of which he was greatly fond.) His friend Leigh Hunt, who later proposed a "religion of the heart" to resolve Victorian religious crises within undogmatic sentiment, did as an adolescent publish four smoothly conventional "Hymns for the Seasons." He was shortly followed by the even more precocious

Felicia Browne, later to become Mrs. Hemans, who similarly demonstrated her youthful piety for the subscribers.[6] Yet, any society whose hymns are written by its children may have become too consciously sophisticated to be serious about the devout. With children hastening into print there is the contrast of adults who seem not to have intended to. The signal contribution to the Anglican hymnal in this period, the hymns of Reginald Heber, were written in 1811 for use by his parish but published posthumously by his widow only in 1827. An even more extreme deferral envelops the only hymn by a major Romantic poet adopted in the standard repertory, rather by accident and a century late: the prefatory stanzas to Blake's *Milton*—"And did those feet in ancient time"—which Sir Hubert Parry set as a battle-cry for a feminist conference in 1918 and which thereafter has had a remarkable, self-sustaining life in British culture.

The hymns of British Romanticism are literary, often dramatic in conception, self-conscious, self-reflective. How these elements infuse the generic conception can be readily observed in the two slight pieces that the older Wordsworth denominated hymns. The tenth poem in his *Memorials of a Tour of the Continent* (1820), a series that by its very notion distances us from the present inner life of the poet, is called "Hymn for the Boatmen, as they approach the Rapids under the Castle of Heidelberg."

> JESU! bless our slender Boat,
>   By the current swept along;
> Loud its threatenings—let them not
>   Drown the music of a song
> Breathed thy mercy to implore,
> Where these troubled waters roar! (1–6)

In like vein, the hymn continues through three further stanzas, ending thus:

> Where the whirlpool frets and raves
>   Let Thy love its anger soothe:
> All our hope is placed in Thee;
>   *Misere Domine!*

Whatever alterations Wordsworth's religious convictions underwent, the habits of mind exhibited in this poem recall the much earlier poet. The focus of these verses is not Jesus but the boatmen who continually hazard their lives in dangerous waters. Not only is it not a hymn that Wordsworth himself would utter, but its very terms suggest a psychological profile of its singers. The quality of the piece to the side, it is—to recall the language of the 1800 Preface—"a selection of the real language of men in a state of vivid sensation," and it certainly serves to illustrate "the manner in which we associate ideas in a state of excitement" (*Prose*, I, 118, 122, 124). If in this hymn Wordsworth reveals himself more interested in adducing a collective persona than in celebrating a divinity, his second such venture, "The Labourer's Noon-Day Hymn" of 1834, devotes three-quarters of its length to a poetic disquisition on the nature and purposes of hymns. Characteristically self-reflexive, this hymn is likewise written, though with patronizing class-consciousness, to the requirements of its personae. As the laborers contemplate the universal applicability of hymning, they are drawn to their own hymn, which occupies the last two of the eight stanzas. Wordsworth, as usual, is less interested in the after-thought than in the process of mind leading to it, a process he conceives as universally shared by humanity.

Neither embarrassment nor a recoil from religious enthusiasm leads Wordsworth so to filter hymnody through the representation of its psychological impulse. It is rather entirely characteristic of British Romanticism, setting it off from its European counterpart, where, as with Novalis, the spontaneous welling up of hymns is at once enacted and celebrated. But it is not simply the interest in psychological motivation that reveals the fundamentally Protestant culture of the British Isles. Self-justification is inherent as well, and the result is a hymn that usually begins or ends by questioning its reason for existence. Even the best of the hymns written from an orthodox perspective, Coleridge's "Hymn Before Sun-Rise, in the Vale of Chamouni," is not straightforward. Far from it; it is a prototype of the hymn that begins in an interrogative mode: "Hast thou a charm to stay the morning-star / In his steep course?" (1–2). Since the Book of Revelation promises that exactly such a charm will be uttered by the disembodied voice of God, the question immediately raises doubts about the quality and extent of the speaker's faith. And rather than being dispelled, the doubts are increased, as we learn in the succeeding line that the apostrophe is not directed to God but to the mountain presumed to figure his presence: idolatry, after all, is a primitive form of symbolism. Not until line 28, marking off the first third of the poem, does the hymn transcend the physical features of Mont Blanc to confront a spiritual presence revealed by them. This is all, even in the opening confusion, carefully plotted, so much so that the modern reader is likely to find the actual hymn, in which Coleridge resorts to boisterous ventriloquism on behalf of natural features, far less compelling than the process by which one comes to hymn documented in the first third. There can be little doubt that this was Coleridge's own interest: the later exclamations echo with a flat sameness before the mysteriously stratified lodes in which symbols reveal what sustains them. Years later Coleridge recalled Wordsworth's condemning the poem "as a specimen of the Mock Sublime," then proceeded to analyze his hymn as representing his *"Idiosyncratic"* habits of mind: "I have been accustomed to *abstract* and as it were unrealize whatever of more than common interest my eyes dwelt on; and then by a sort of transfusion and transmission of my consciousness to identify myself with the Object." Such a process he acknowledges leads inevitably to a poetic of self-allegorization.[7]

That, one might safely say, is Shelley's point in the two poems he wrote in the summer of 1816, with Coleridge's "Hymn" so sharply in mind that both—the one in subject, the other in genre—appear a direct refutation of his theistic inferences from the mountain. It seems unlikely that Shelley could have read the note Coleridge attached to early versions of the "Hymn" that claimed, "Who *would* be, who *could* be an Atheist in this valley of wonders!"[8] It was, however, near here that Shelley wrote in the inn register *"demokratikos philanthropatatos kai atheos"*—democrat, great lover of humanity, and atheist—after his name. "Mont Blanc" and the "Hymn to Intellectual Beauty" develop the ramifications of that declaration, with one eye on the mountain and the other on Coleridge's text. "Mont Blanc" reverts to the first third of the Coleridge "Hymn," mediating upon the nature of symbols and the mind's capacity to create and react to them.[9] Shelley's "Hymn" turns inward to explore its own impulse.

The ingenious nuances of argument in "Mont Blanc" reinforce the pervasive skepticism of the poem, making it and "The everlasting universe of things" (1) it treats an endless puzzle that can be organized but never solved. One reason for that is its generic mode, for the impulse to hymn continually runs against the urge to understand the nature of hymning. The more the poet seeks identity with what he confronts, the more urgently insistent becomes the separation requisite to both analysis and poetic creation. The poem begins with an objective epistemological premise—"The everlasting universe of things / Flows through the mind" (1-2)—that is subsumed almost immediately within apostrophe: "Thus thou, Ravine of Avre—dark, deep Ravine . . ." (12). Yet, by a process so natural that it conceals the artfulness of design, the urge toward identity in the apostrophe is almost too successful, forcing the reassertion of difference:

> Thou art pervaded with that ceaseless motion,
> Thou art the path of that unresting sound—
> Dizzy Ravine! and when I gaze on thee
> I seem as in a trance sublime and strange
> To muse on my own separate phantasy,
> My own, my human mind. . . . (32-37)

Shelley implicates signifier and signified, the symbol and the subtle operations it shadows forth, only to recognize the "separate" nature of his mind from its object of identity. The closer he draws to the symbol, the closer he comes not to what it symbolizes—mental formulation in general—but to what in the first place has designated its symbolic quality—"My own, my human mind."

The mind has reverted to its separateness, contemplating an ultimate other, an other whose essence can safely be defined as nonhuman, a presumptive criterion of divinity. Yet, with the conclusion of the third section of the poem, the impulse to apostrophe reasserts itself: "Thou hast a voice, great Mountain . . ." (80). Even though the entire fourth section reverts to the contemplation of Power as something separate from human agency, the poem has implicitly established its final paradox. For in identifying with the mountain, the poet defines a voice that can only be a version of his own, uttering, in Coleridge's words, a charm from the poet's own magical lore. Only at the conclusion of "Mont Blanc" does the hymnic apostrophe recur, yet it does so in such a way as to establish the irreducible identity of symbolizer, symbol, and symbolized earlier glimpsed in the Ravine of Arve. And even as it claims identity, the mind asserts its analytical separateness through an unexpungeable question mark:

> The secret strength of things
> Which governs thought, and to the infinite dome
> Of heaven is as a law, inhabits thee!
> And what were thou, and earth, and stars, and sea,
> If to the human mind's imaginings
> Silence and solitude were vacancy? (139–144)

Shelley's concluding question is subtler in its extensions, but otherwise is essentially the same as that with which Coleridge began his hymn. Both mountains and morning-stars are accorded their charms by poets' imaginations.

Even more directly than "Mont Blanc," the "Hymn to Intellectual Beauty" contemplates its own mode of discourse. Again, apostrophe is a key to its nature, as the poem calls for yet resists the poet's identity with intellectual beauty. As if to forewarn us, the first stanza devotes itself to the activities of "The awful shadow of some unseen Power" (1) in a human sphere, and the strangely doubled abstraction is analytically described through continually multiplied, and thus ironically distancing, analogies. The more infinite the force appears, the more finite seems its perceiver. The "Spirit of BEAUTY" (13) is directly invoked at the beginning of the second stanza, yet immediately is represented as an absence: "where art thou gone?" (15). Again, this absence is rendered through multiplied analogies. The entire poem proceeds within the same rhythm: "Beauty" is invoked, only to have the apostrophe disintegrate in an elaboration of its effects in the world and on the poet's life, which stirs the poet to a renewed invocation, as if absence could be inverted into presence by simple intensity of desire. Shelley's balance ably represents the "inconstant glance" (6) characterized as fundamental to the operations of intellectual beauty in the initial stanza, but it also embodies it. The curious tension between self as thinking analyst and as inspired bard is never resolved by Shelley's "Hymn" because it is not meant to be resolved. To be absorbed by pure beauty is to lose the capacity of discernment, to become one with the cause and unconscious of its effects. To paraphrase Yeats's gnomic valediction, a poet cannot both know and embody the force of inspiration. Yet it is equally true, and exactly the balance Shelley enforces on his hymn throughout, that neither knowledge nor inspiration, however opposed their natures, can stand alone in the mixed economy of the human mind. Shelley's "Hymn to Intellectual Beauty" thus presents us with an essential generic crux, one exactly congruous with the poet's self-profession as atheist. The poem ostensibly desires the constant presence of the power it invokes, but in its employment of the form and underlying awareness of the value of absence, it draws back from the identity it claims to embrace a middle ground that is defined only by what it is not. The "Hymn to Intellectual Beauty" implicitly subscribes to the dialectical condition of humanity it pleads to escape. Tenuously mediating between thesis and antithesis, purely ironic in subverting the form it invokes, Shelley's poem adopts a logic leading unswervingly toward a countergenre. The major hymn of British Romanticism is, in fact, an ode.[10]

II

The argument advanced by Kurt Schlüter that odes derive from hymns is probably accurate but assuredly academic, the result of a scholar's natural urge to ascertain immutable truth rather than welter in historical tides. The odes of Pindar clearly are related to communal celebrations and even consecrations, but the moral contemplations of Horace are just as decidedly solitary. The odes of Anacreon or Alcaeus are, in the main, drinking songs, whereas the few examples attributed to Sappho celebrate love and marriage. The problem of classification is exacerbated in the early Renaissance: little unites the Italian *canzoni* and the odes emanating from the Pléiade except the fact that they are poems. The paradoxical truth about the history of the ode is that it had little history, though many examples, until comparatively recent times. Indeed, if Horace's designation, *carmina*, had not been rendered into a Greek generic term covering a very different repertory of verse, centuries of confusion might have been avoided.[11]

Nonetheless, the confusion is fundamental to later Western literature, to be joined in the progress of the ages by others, like Cowley's notion of Pindarick poetry as stylized hyperbole, or the Enlightenment's concerted attempt to subsume the Psalms of David within this poetic category. Because the notion and therefore the nature of the ode alters with each succeeding epoch, it is all but impossible to write a normal history of the form (though that, of course, has not inhibited the attempts of a number of respected critics to do so).[12] But there is a contrary paradox as well: the point in British literary history when the sense of the traditional uses and conventions of the ode coalesces so that a body of poets can reasonably be charged with the fullness of that knowledge is the late eighteenth century. The Romantic ode owes much of its greatness to its bearing the burden of that collective history, whose accumulated weight may safely be said to impinge—and inspirit—everywhere.

The introduction of the ode as a major literary form in England comes surprisingly late but in auspicious circumstances, and it can be dated almost exactly. In 1629 both the acknowledged reigning monarch of English poetry and his then obscure heir apparent—Ben Jonson and John Milton—composed masterpieces in the form that, tapping different traditions, identified common elements that became endemic to its subsequent development. "On the Morning of Christ's Nativity" is the first of Milton's poems to reveal his unique architectonic genius, in this case a poem erected upon the opposing stresses of hymn and ode, of a hymn to the recreated godhead and an ode celebrating his human incarnation. From this tension other oppositions multiply: the new dispensation and the pagan superstitions overthrown by it, the historical Jesus on his actual natal day and the atemporal idea recovered through celebrating his anniversary 1629 years later, heaven and earth, and even, at the center of the ode, a sudden conflation of genesis and apocalypse. The brilliant disruption of anticipated verb tenses in the four-stanza introduction mirrors both the oppositions and their collapse within the oneness of God's creation. But the incarnation is also mirrored—and centered. The driving force to contain the polarities is the imaginative sympathy of the poet, who is personalized to the extent that he presents himself as fulcrum and mediator for the ode's dialectical claims.

Milton's Nativity poem is Horatian in its meditative, progressive structure, psalm-like in its solemnity and sweeping temporal urgency. Ben Jonson's "To the Immortal Memory and Friendship of That Noble Pair, Sir Lucius Cary and Sir H. Morison" is the first true Pindaric ode in English, with its structural terms anglicized in such a way—"The Turn," "The Counter-Turn," "The Stand"—as also to remind a reader of their extension in the choral odes of Athenian drama. Here again time, as defined by the conjunctive phrase beginning the title, is problematic, leading through Jonson's meditations to ever subtler interconnections between life and death. These contraries, though painfully opposed, are never allowed to collide, but through their psychological tension enforce a continual renegotiation of an uneasy equilibrium. The final balance draws the dead Sir Henry and living Sir Lucius into a whole, each a portion of the other, linked only through the intellectual straining of their mutual friend and celebrant, who divides his name across stanzas (lines 84–85) as across the boundary between states of being. It is he who in his verse guarantees an "immortal memory," who creates in his art a vital calm from yet active contraries pulsing beneath its polished surface. As with Milton's "Nativity Ode," the implied subject of Jonson's masterpiece is himself.

If literary history were written to the dictates of a retrospective simplicity, the subsequent development of the English ode would be inherent in these two poems. But Abraham Cowley intervened and, with much less Greek than either Milton or Jonson, reinvented Pindar, necessitating the tactful correction of Congreve and other successors, who nonetheless pursued a similarly spurious classicism.[13] Part of their problem was, indeed, that Greek was much less known than Latin.[14] The first English edition of Pindar's Greek was not published until 1697, and the first English translation of a large number (but by no means all) of his odes came to print a full century after Cowley emerged on the scene, with Gilbert West's 1749 volumes of poetry. Conversely, Horace was a staple of the educational system. Whatever in matter and style Horace was not, it would seem, the Cowleyan Pindarick came to be. As Norman Maclean astutely remarks, "the Great Ode was 'the free verse' of the neoclassical period" (p. 424). Although Maclean's impressive survey of the eighteenth-century ode harbors familiar prejudices, his recognition that the Cowleyan Pindarick was gradually replaced by a more puristically defined form is important:

> . . . the proportion of odes written in the irregular stanzas of Cowley declined during the eighteenth century, a number were written in triadic structure, and the majority were written in a stanza, however varied internally, that was repeated throughout the poem. Anyone wishing to interpret these facts as a sign that the neoclassical period placed regularity, reason, and conformity above the powers of the imagination, even in lyric poetry, should at the same time explain why approximately these same facts are true of the odes written by the Romantics. (pp. 425–426)

Part of the explanation Maclean calls for lies in the raw data of literary history: the simple fact is that the first full translation of Pindar's odes into English occurred in 1810.[15]

However, general agreement on Cowley's faulty scholarship, his transliteration of Pindar's notorious difficulty into enforced obscurity, and his sheer love of bombast cannot alter his immense influence on subsequent odes. Earthbound he may have been, but through him the ode became the principal lyric vehicle for the sublime. The Horatian rumination retired into elegiac stanzas, leaving behind only the solitary voice of its speaker and its progressive mode for assimilation with the Pindaric reach for the infinite. For the other elements that were to become conventional to the English ode, its dramatic quality and its preoccupation with its own lyricism, history—ever delighted in how great things spring from small— must acknowledge that the London Musical Society was responsible. Its decision in 1683 to sponsor an annual celebration of the power of music on St. Cecilia's Day inevitably created a special and highly visible category of ode whose nature thereafter continued to resonate even when the subject seemed far removed from the original institutional purposes.

The cause for this may be even simpler, the effect of what immediately upon its publication was accorded the status of a classic: John Dryden's "Alexander's Feast; or, the Power of Musique," the St. Cecilia's Day Ode for 1697. Dryden's virtuoso piece plays cleverly on the notion of power, as Alexander's servant Timotheus demonstrates his control over the master of the earth. Public issues of the greatest moment are rooted in private passions, as they are aroused or subdued by art. But even Timotheus is then a servant of another power, the divine idea represented by St. Cecilia in the *deus ex machina* of Dryden's last stanza: "He raised a mortal to the skies; / She drew an Angel down" (169–170). Behind the draperies of this grandly staged drama is, of course, its author and director, who himself knew something about how to accommodate and influence power and who, as surely as Milton or Jonson, places himself as mediating presence at the center of his dramatic ode, between power and art, his patrons and his craft, the earthly endeavors of art and the transcendental perfections they shadow forth. The formal balance between these overarching contraries is at the same time the motivating principle of the ode's development, as Maclean ably observes it:

> . . . with one exception, each stanza is connected to the next by the principle of psychological contrariety; that is, the set of passions aroused in Alexander by a given song is the opposite to the set of passions aroused in him by the preceding or following stanza, and thus the emotional progression is startling in its variety and suggests, after a time, a completeness of emotional effect (a succession of opposites having the quality of suggesting all-inclusiveness).[16]

To be sure, a progression by polar opposites affords Dryden (and a successor such as Pope in his version of "Alexander's Feast") maximum rhetorical effect, yet rhetoric here directly serves function and form. Baldly stated, "Alexander's Feast" offers us a dialectic of the passions created through the dialectical possibilities of human art, presented ironically against a dialectic composed of public action and retiring art which mirrors the largest perspective of the ode, a dialectic between human necessities and transcendent yearning. The structure of Dryden's ode is a nest of Chinese boxes: at its center, its essential subject, is itself.[17]

Throughout the eighteenth century the ode of public celebration that Cowley transposed from Pindar continually reverts to the poet himself as centering force. The private complexities of this role increasingly become the focal point, as the servants of established power observe how dependent it is upon their empowering rhetoric and as the musician surrogate fades into the reality of the self-dramatizing poet. The radical internalization of the public ode by which Collins and Gray realign the traditional form and which attains its fullest development among the Romantics does not so much alter the nature of the ode as explore implications present since it had been drawn into English literary traditions by Jonson and Milton. By the time the history of the ode embarks on the century in which it was to become synonymous with lyric poetry, its greatest examples had already made conventional its nature as a dramatic, self-reflexive, and dialectical form.

These are, recognizably, conventions that inform the British Romantic ode, and they are in place a full century before its earliest examples.[18] If large errors in our historical conceptions have tended to oversimplify the complexity of the ode in its early development in England, it is just as true that ignoring the traditions associated with it, so central is this form to the literary efforts of the eighteenth century, can have enormously distorting consequences for literary history. In particular, the odes of Collins and Gray have been used to portray an age of poetic anxiety, paralyzed before its ancestry and the future alike, with little subject beyond its own inanition.[19] It is probably true that characteristic temperaments can be discerned in the odes of both writers: the intense, mercurial poetry of Collins certainly hints at the madness that would abridge his brief career, and Gray's chronic self-effacement is the mark of a scholar as well as, in the eighteenth century, the destiny of a homosexual. But more than temperament and certainly far more than *Zeitgeist*, what principally distinguishes the odes of both poets is their traditional knowledge and formal invention.

It is hard to see, on the very face of it, how Collin's *Odes on Several Descriptive and Allegorical Subjects* of 1746 could be construed, except through a retrospective awareness of the ensuing madness, as representing anything other than a radiant self-confidence. The volume begins with externalized self-contemplation, as Collins anatomizes his passions upon the table of world literature, and ends, after assimilating both immediate historical subjects and the grand progression of Whig history (the "Ode on the Poetical Character" and "Ode to Liberty" are intimately allied, as later for Shelley, in subject), with a just, though intricate, balance between public obligations ("The Manners") and private resources ("The Passions"). As a first volume of adult poetry, Collins's *Odes* publicly announce a coming of age, audaciously assert for their author a claim to major rank, and in subject and range constitute a remarkable essay on the nature of the ode. Moreover, not only does Collins continually dramatize himself in his allegorical confrontations and initiations, but the entire volume is organized, as Eric Rothstein pointedly attests, around a dialectical progression of opposites that lead this fledgling poet from the insecurities of pity and fear to assured mastery, at least as he projects himself, over history, literature, and the inner life.[20]

In other words, the entire volume of Collins's *Odes*, mediating between its private and public voices and continually invoking a spectral pantheon of past poets, is a single ode. But there is a significant shift in the nature of the self-reflexiveness in this volume. If the St. Cecilia Day celebrations encouraged odes about odes, or at least if one discerns that subject in the "Alexander's Feast" poems of two acknowledged masters, the youthful and obscure Collins forces his way to attention by writing odes about writing odes. That is to say, as he shapes his odes, so he shapes himself. The same process on a smaller scale is evident a year earlier, as the similarly unknown Mark Akenside introduces himself to the public in his *Odes on Various Subjects* (1745), which beings with an "Allusion to Horace" and ends, after weaving contraries together symmetrically through eight intervening odes, with "On Lyric Poetry," celebrating

Greek writers of odes.[21] Such volumes undoubtedly make fragile edifices: at some point presumably a poet is at last shaped and must find a further subject besides himself and his poetry. And yet, of course, the examples of Wordsworth and especially Keats suggest that the motivating forces among the new poets of the 1740s were far from played out by their odes, even if they were uncertain how to proceed.

The early odes of Thomas Gray share in this dynamic, if only by their inversion of it. The "Ode to Spring" and "Ode on a Distant Prospect of Eton College" attain their remarkable power by simply unshaping their author. The latter poem in particular, with its complex interlaying of spatial and temporal axes on which the poetic voice is centered and acutely isolated, allows its dialectical forces such intensity that all "prospect" disintegrates in irony. But, as was suggested earlier, rather than psychoanalyze the author or convert his prospect into that of his age, we might instead honor the fact that at any point in which the formal properties of an art attain a general sophistication, inversion and parody will inevitably follow. Indeed, their inversion has a magnetic attraction for a poet like Gray, who wrote little and exceedingly well and polished the results to brilliance.

In this respect Gray's most influential ode is certainly "The Bard," which distances and dramatizes its subject so as to create a truly archetypal figure of the visionary poet scorned by his time. Gray's bard grandly plunges to his death as another of the poet's projections of self-effacement, but his is the irony of martyrdom, for his death creates the history he has prophesied and through which his vision will triumph. This is a stage primed for melodrama, but it is self-evidently the one on which Dryden's Timotheus bowed sixty years before and on which Collins's spectral passions had stalked in the previous decade. The power of poetry and its inherent relationship with the public realm are as central to Gray's exercise in dramatic self-reflexiveness as to those earlier odes. The effect of the bard's rhapsodic anathema, redoubled in the grandeur of the Welsh scenery and the obscurities of past time, gave Gray his contemporary reputation as master of the sublime; but perhaps the ultimate irony of this poem is that its barbaric wildness derives from Gray's arcane learning and his skillful manipulation of the traditional propensities and structure of the ode.[22] Reduced to its essentials, Gray's subject is the inspired freedom attributed to this mode of poetry.

There are unquestionably thousands of odes in the eighteenth century that do not reflect the formal character discernible in the odes of Dryden, Collins, and Gray but rather revert to the stentorian tones and public bombast associated with Cowley.[23] Nonetheless, major poets obviously carry their influence across time, and great peaks dominate and define a mountainous wilderness. But, leaving to the side the self-reflexive character of the ode, there is a further influence tending to reinforce its conception as dramatically staged and dialectical in progression: the conflation of the conditions of the Pindaric ode with those operative for the choral odes of Greek drama, which were resurrected from Greek scholiasts and widely repeated. Pindaric odes, in this view, were thought to have been sung by a chorus, moving to the left during the first strophe, to the right during the antistrophe, and standing still in the epode. It would appear that Jonson anglicized the terms of the Pindaric ode ("Turn," "Counter-turn," "Stand") from this same comprehension. Congreve's "Discourse on the Pindaric Ode," describing these danced movements, suggests their rationale:

> Some have thought, that, by the contrariety of the strophe and antistrophe, they intended to represent the contrarotation of the primum mobile, in respect of the secunda mobilia; and that, by their standing still at the epode, they meant to signify the stability of the Earth. Others ascribe the institution to Theseus, who thereby expressed the windings and turnings of the laby-rinth, in celebrating his return from thence.[24]

This was all nonsense, according to John Brown's view of the matter in 1764, as he easily transposed the supposed practice of Pindar to the Athenian stage: "Much Labour cannot be necessary for the confutation of these Refinements, as the Practice arose so evidently from the Dictates of Nature: It was a natural and sensible Improvement; for the plain Reason of *preventing Giddiness*, which ariseth from running around in the same Circle."[25] Brown's practical skepticism had no effect on the grand design seen to be figured through the choral movements, as the notion is re-peated by the poet laureate, Henry James Pye, in 1792 and by Leigh Hunt in the first decade of the nineteenth century.[26] Thus, both the choral movement and its neoplatonic meanings were again questioned by Regi-nald Heber in his review of Girdlestone's Pindar translation of 1810. Since the Pindaric odes were sung by a chorus escorting the Olympic victor to his lodging, "it is evident that such evolutions . . . would not only be very inconvenient in the narrow and crowded streets of a Grecian city, but, as they consisted in merely dancing backwards and forwards, must have been inconsistent with any progress at all."[27] With such common sense we can undoubtedly leave this much-vexed issue, whose pedantic silliness served to remind readers well into the Romantic period of the inherently dramatic character of the ode.[28] The connection with Greek tragic choruses was also enhanced by the critical commentary that arose around the writings of Collins and Gray. Since it largely consisted of pointing out sources, the echoes of Aeschylus, Sophocles, and Euri-pides that were regularly noted served to substantiate the direct link between lyric and dramatic poetry.[29]

An incidental result of the constant linkage between Pindaric and dramatic odes was an increasing agreement on the constituents of formal propriety. Though lip service continued to be paid to a rhapsodic free-dom from constraint, elaborate formal symmetries distinguish the true Pindaric from the irregular ode popularized by Cowley. Indeed, the Cowleyan model itself was transmuted, its true genesis being discovered in classical dithyrambs and particularly in the Psalms of the Old Testament. But far from merely assimilating the hymn to the ode, this redefinition was so historically distanced that the tendency was just the opposite. The enthusiastic nature of the ancient Hebrews, the ever-present sense of divine revelation that imbues their psalms, was, in Bishop Lowth's influential perspective, a distinguishing mark of both a nonmodern culture and of a widely shared poetic. His *Lectures on the Sacred Poetry of the Hebrews* of 1753, a watershed in the study of Biblical hermeneutics, discriminated three forms of ode in the Old Testament: the hymn of gratitude, the sublime apprehension of the divine, and a mixed style combining attributes of these two.[30] The adjustment in literary history is almost instantaneous. For instance, the widely disseminated primer published by John Newbery in 1762, *The Art of Poetry on a New Plan*, gives priority to the divine ode in its account of the form:

> The ode . . . is very ancient, and was probably the first species of poetry. It had its source, we may suppose from the heart, and was employed to express, with becoming fervor and dignity, the grateful sense man entertained of the blessing which daily flowed from god the fountain of all goodness: Hence their harvest hymns, and other devotional compositions of that kind.
>
> But in process of time it was employed, not only to praise the Almighty for bounties received, but to sollicit his aid in time of trouble; as is plain from the odes written by King *David* and others, and collected by the *Jewish Sanhedrim* into the book of *Psalms*, to be sung at their fasts, festivals, and on other solemn occasions. . . .
>
> It is reasonable to suppose that the awful purpose to which the ode was applied, gave rise among the ancients to the custom of invoking the muses; and that the poets, in order to raise their sentiments and language, so as to be acceptable to their deities, thought it expedient to sollicit some divine assistance. Hence poets are said to be inspired, and hence an unbounded liberty has been given to the ode; for the lyric poet, fired, as it were, with his subject, and borne away on the wings of gratitude, disdains grammatical niceties, and common modes of speech, and often soars above rule, tho' not above reason.[31]

The sacred ode, its history and traditions thus recovered by Enlightenment antiquarianism, was sanctioned by this Christian culture as the first of lyric modes; and King David, at least among institutional apologists in the later eighteenth century, replaced Pindar as the foremost of inspired bards. Both Charles Batteux, in his *Course of the Belles Lettres* (1761), and Hugh Blair, in his *Lectures on Rhetoric and Belles Lettres* (1783), place the sacred ode first in the hierarchy of lyric modes, followed by the heroic ode, derived from Pindar, the moral or philosophical ode, mainly associated with Horace (and the principal type in modern poetry), and the festive, amorous, or joyful ode, this latter deriving from Anacreon and barely distinguishable from a song.[32] By the end of the century shifts in the established hierarchy are discernible. John Bell's "classical" categories are apostrophe (which assimilates odes to personified abstractions and sacred odes); philosophical and contemplative odes; sublime odes, dealing with mythological subjects and natural law; odes on places or on general subjects; occasional and light lyrics; and political odes. Less constrained by the need for an inclusive and retrospective taxonomy, Nathan Drake adopts terms that appear particularly bound to the practices of early Romanticism, arranging lyric poetry into four classes: "the *Sublime*, the *Pathetic*, the *Descriptive*, and the *Amatory*."[33] That the hierarchies alter through the last decades of the eighteenth century is probably of much less moment than that they continue thus to dominate literary thought.

Yet, to compare the perspective on lyric poetry at the end of this century with that common a hundred years before is to recognize simply how much more is known about its nature, its differing cultural strains, its constraints, and with them its possibilities. The ode, as it enters British Romantic poetry, has been codified by a fully realized literary history. Hymns, as noted earlier, had become the preoccupation of Dissenters; but the sacred ode, with all its antiquated enthusiasm, is a type to be resuscitated by a Coleridge or a Shelley with a sense of modernist revival. The sublime, worried over for the preceding half century and increasingly transposed from object to subject, similarly offered an age fascinated with psychology an arena for experimentation. And, by the mid-1790s, with all of Europe at war, there existed an urgent dialectical pressure—indeed, what would appear to be universal contraries—against which to test the mind brave enough to internalize its tensions.

III

The intrinsic paradox of the English ode, as traced in this brief survey of its fortunes, is that, almost from the first, a Horatian voice was invested in a Pindaric form. To reduce that complex to its logical components, the Horatian meditative presence, its contemplations built through a sequential and associational logic, becomes a mediating presence standing above sequence, forced to impose, or to create within itself, a synthesizing order—an epode—upon the universal strophe and antistrophe of experience. In the 1790s this was no easy task. The problems were compounded by the accumulated clichés that naturally followed upon a century and a half of unremitting popularity and the massive investment of the previous generation in historical recovery.[34] All in all, the ode represented a daunting field for youthful poets to test their originality in. In such a context the odes of Coleridge and Wordsworth are all the more remarkable, for they are sophisticated occasions for a pitched battle—at times violent, at other times the attrition of the trenches—out of which the poet endeavors to find (to unsheathe Wordsworth's honed and double-edged sword) recompense.

The young Coleridge practiced upon the ode as diligently as upon the sonnet. His "Ode to the Departing Year" of 1796, which is the first to reveal his mature course, is actually the twentieth English poem he designated as an ode; and, in addition, as an undergraduate at Cambridge he had won a prize for a Greek ode.[35] The most interesting of the adolescent odes is a minor tour de force suggestive of the future direction of the author's "abstruse research." In the poem he originally titled "Prospectus and Specimen of a Translation of Euclid in a series of Pindaric Odes," Coleridge literally abstracts the nature of the Pindaric ode to conceptualize an equilateral triangle:

> . . . in mutual affiance
> None attempting to soar
> Above another,
> The unanimous three
> C. A. and B. C. and A. B.
> All are equal, each to his brother.
> Preserving the balance of power. . . . (48–53)

It is a long way from this intellectual exercise to the apocalyptic tonalities of the "Ode to the Departing Year" or "France: An Ode," and yet the political odes are no less implicated with a Pindaric logic, no less concerned, either in formal or political terms, with "the balance of power." Yet, finding and maintaining it seems all but hopeless. "France: An Ode," written in mid-1798, a year and a half after the "Ode to the Departing Year," marks a considerable stylistic advance; but even so, and even with its being originally entitled "The Recantation" and thus marking Coleridge's political about-face, it ultimately resorts to the same questionable ground as the earlier ode for its conclusion. As these poems develop their opposite political visions, there appears to be no other ground for a "Stand," which adds to the sense of moral desperation both convey.

The first, the "Ode to the Departing Year," begins with an appeal to the eternal providence governing time and thus history, the second to the liberty universally manifested in nature. These are contrasted with the time-bound, the self-manacled, in human society, an element that in "France: An Ode" is enlarged to include the entire French nation, which in reducing the free Swiss had placed itself on the level of Europe's reactionary monarchies. France is carefully excluded from the earlier "Ode to the Departing Year," which engages its dialectical motion along the axis of England's own potentiality for good and evil. The latter clearly predominates as the poem concludes, with Coleridge able only to claim the satisfaction of having testified honestly. The poem ends with his arising from the slough of history where "Woes" and "young-eyed Joys advance" (22) alike, where the centering consciousness is constrained both to "Weep and rejoice" (32), at last reasserting his allegiance to a transcendent truth that, if it is uncontaminated by time, seems also to have no effect upon it. The "Ode to the Departing Year" bears frustrated witness against history. "France: An Ode" ends with Coleridge, again in solitude, reexpressing his commitment to Liberty as the soul of nature. Neither poem basks in the glow of its righteousness; yet there is nothing else for the isolated bardic visionary to fall back upon. The situation of both odes is self-evidently that of Gray's frustrated Bard, but there is no prophetic imposition of design upon history, nor can the poet precipitate his own apocalyptic redemption from the "sea-cliff's verge" (99) where he is stranded at the end of "France: An Ode." It is his responsibility to bear the weight of a dialectic over which he can have no effectual control. The external political universe forces its tensions upon him and, internalized whether or not he wills, impresses a moral dialectic beyond his solution. In both odes the concluding epode cannot resolve the conflict except by appeal to a commanding, extrahuman authority for whom the poet testifies. Self-fashioned as witness, the poet can create for himself only a burdened solitude.

It is by no means odd that two odes, conflating traditions of the prospect and political ode and written early in the maelstrom of the Napoleonic Wars, should thus issue in indecision and frustration. But it is odd, or at least curious, that Coleridge's mature, nonpolitical odes should so insistently repeat, then deflect, this pattern. Perhaps it is simply characteristic of Coleridge to portray himself with finely shaded self-pity as an isolated figure attempting to assume personal responsibility for universal conflicts he cannot control. Nonetheless, the stance exemplified in his odes of 1796 and 1798 recurs in the political odes of Byron and especially Shelley, suggesting more than the quirks of Coleridge's temperament at work. And when the stance is repeated by Coleridge himself, in personal odes enriched by the complexities of self-analysis, critics would appear rather hasty in attributing the continuity to neurotic compulsion. That, of course, Coleridge had in ample measure, but to discern it unmediated, as if the poet were everywhere engaged in spontaneous free association, ignores the extent to which poets' lives, especially as recorded in the history of the English ode, are shaped according to the dictates of art. Such self-fashioning, which is evident throughout the early odes, continues unchanged but for intensification in "Dejection: An Ode" and "To William Wordsworth," where the specter of self-paralysis has at least as much to do with Coleridge's recreation of his literary heritage as with his reading in abstruse philosophy.

"Dejection: An Ode" is a classic case of interpretive vexation: the numerous problems it raises can be compressed into a single large one, which is that a poem of such range, power, and artistic success should register a defeat and issue in a paralysis essentially unchanged from that with which it began. But, if the poem is considered in relation to Coleridge's earlier odes and to those of his predecessors, then the frustration of expectations that Coleridge achieved would appear no accident but his intention, repeating on a higher level of sophistication the pattern elaborated in the early odes.[36] However apparently confessional the discourse,

Coleridge's great ode was rewritten again and again, constantly being shaped to a further refinement of its art. That it came about from a powerful sense of personal inadequacy is probably true, but the pride with which Coleridge transcribed so supposedly personal a poem for William Sotheby or included extracts in letters to Southey and Thomas Wedgwood does not suggest an unremitting anxiety, nor does his first publishing the ode in the *Morning Post* six months after composing the initial version show much reticence in publicly advertising his failure.[37] Indeed, Coleridge seems from this record to have been inordinately pleased with it, as well he should have been: Gray's Bard, he would have recognized, also had succeeded through failure.

The form of the poem, so immediate and dramatic, has been justified on the sensible grounds that a crisis worthy of the name cannot be resolved in a short poem and retain its claim to authenticity.[38] In the largest sense, however, it is not just a dramatic decorum that must be preserved, but a fitting sense of the irreducible complexity of human experience as well. It may all be represented through recognizable patterns—the strophe and antistrophe of universal contrariety—but, though the poem may subsume them, it does not thereby synthesize them, even as one's life must tolerate their conflict but cannot derive sustaining force from their interaction. And yet such a construction as this may still be too facile, slighting the actual experience of the poem: whatever the poet as self-dramatized center of his ode may understand, it is the universal estimate of posterity that the poem *does* synthesize its contrarieties into the dynamic force of great art. Moreover, within the ode itself there is also the pointed recognition, though it never attains the personal internalization that Shelley will create from a like situation in his "Ode to the West Wind," that human beings can be similarly charged through what Coleridge calls a "mountain-birth" (129). Yet, that final hope, deflected originally upon Sara Hutchinson, then upon Wordsworth, and finally and most tellingly on the unnamed lady who represents an almost abstracted human linkage, is both asserted and suspended at the same moment—"Joy lift her spirit, joy attune her voice / . . . Thus *mayest* thou ever, evermore rejoice" (134, 139, italics added)—creating at the end what every other aspect of the poem points to, a middle ground between potentiality and its realization. Coleridge's deliberately balanced ambiguousness is finely represented by the way in which he transmutes the centrally recurrent pattern of the ode.

"Dejection: An Ode" does not have strict stanzaic regularity like the three sets of three stanzas marking the eighteenth-century odic formulation of the "Ode to the Departing Year." Indeed, if one wishes to represent its formal structure, it might be best in terms like those of Collins's "Ode to Liberty," with an introductory epode added to his sequence of strophe, epode, antistrophe, epode. The structure is thus balanced in this fashion: the strophic contemplation of the poet's inertia is juxtaposed against the antistrophe of the great storm, with the vernacular humor of the beginning—"Well! If the Bard was weather-wise"—modulating into the paean to joy at the center, which yet again modulates into the deflected prayer for the lady at the end. These three epodes, as thus identified, share figures of synthesizing power against Coleridge's inversion of the conventional odic formula, the unmoving negation of the strophic inertia and the violent positive of the antistrophe. They represent variations on the idea of Joy, which becomes the central value of the ode. The importance of Joy, as it is celebrated in the fifth stanza, is in "wedding Nature to us" (68) with a force that recreates and reconciles the contraries of the transcendent and mundane and that thus "gives in dower / A new Earth and new Heaven" (68–69). This Joy transfigures all it touches, and its synthesizing touch is universal. So the poet in the final stanza conceives its effect on the lady who will be set amid a natural vitality whose "life" is described as "the eddying of her living soul" (136). For her the violent storm presages that "mountain-birth" (129) which is the progeny of the wedding imaged earlier. And yet, the promise of the introductory epode, if alike in kind, is exactly opposite in effect. The new moon as yet unseparated from the old does, indeed, represent a union, but one just preliminary to a birth that will be a cataclysmic sundering. The very imagery of the central celebration of Joy contains the opposites that exist, though differently directed, in the first and last stanzas, for it is drawn from John's vision of the lamb descending for the marriage supper in the Book of Revelation:

> And I saw a new heaven and new earth: for the first heaven and the first earth were passed away; and there was no more sea. And I John saw the holy city, new Jerusalem, coming down from God out of heaven, prepared as a bride adorned for her husband. (Rev. 21: 1-2)

The storm may indeed produce a new birth, but its existence is conditional on an apocalyptic death.

The utter ambiguity of this fused symbolic core, the dynamic force for good or ill, is surrounded and reinforced by a matrix of dialectical oppositions: enervation and power, the passive and the active, lifeless void and natural effulgence, the internal and external, the temporal and eternal, past and present, present and future, winter and spring. The ode is structured deliberately to hold its balance of contraries in exact proportion, with the poet apparently unredeemed by the storm and the lady hopefully reborn from it serving as the extended outrigging of the central structure. A curious precision thus underlies the conversational and confessional tone of "Dejection: An Ode"; it is a complex and sophisticated elaboration of that "Prospectus and Specimen of a Translation of Euclid in a series of Pindaric Odes" authored by the adolescent Coleridge.

And the "series" continues, it could be argued, in "To William Wordsworth,'" the epistolary ode written after recitation of *The Prelude*, which restores the tension between Coleridge and Wordsworth that "Dejection" in its earlier version depicted and which reverts to the same religious imagery to place its author in the process of conversion at its end: "And when I rose, I found myself in prayer" (112). Yet, precisely what is important is that we and Coleridge are left in this suspension, with the dialectic in motion, moving toward revivifying union but as yet unresolved by it. It is surely part of Coleridge's purpose to underscore the progressive, vital nature of Wordsworth's poem and the irreducible potentiality embodied within it. At the same time, he leaves himself in ambiguous process at the end, perhaps himself engaged in a mountain-birth or perhaps simply once again testifying in the central stanza of this ode, as he had in his odes of the 1790s, to his unremitting admiration for the creative spirit he can never adequately embody—all these verses being "but flowers / Strewed on my corse, and borne upon my bier / In the same coffin, for the self-same grave" (73-75). Though drawn by the inspired verse, Coleridge cannot help but, as he says, "wander back on such unhealthful road" (79). His morbid perversity can be ascribed to a streak of willful self-destructiveness in him, once more publicly advertised. Again, however, it accords perfectly with the dialectical universe inherent in the ode and fundamental to Coleridge's earlier conceptions of the form.

Wordsworth's early odes, from a somewhat more optimistic prospect, survey essentially the same landscape. The technique of displacement, which in "Dejection: An Ode" survives Coleridge's several attempts to determine a single object for it, first occurs in Wordsworth. Given how richly complementary their early relationship was, it is no simple matter to attribute the invention of a particular literary strategy to one or the other. Nonetheless, this displacement is but one of several devices in "Lines Written a Few Miles above Tintern Abbey" that link the poem to Coleridge's practice in the ode. In 1800 Wordsworth added this note to "Tintern Abbey": "I have not ventured to call this Poem an Ode; but it was written with a hope that in the transitions, and the impassioned music of the versification would be found the principal requisites of that species of composition." Wordsworth's hesitation, one would surmise, pertains to the style and diction of the poem. At least with the "Intimations Ode" he created a much more formal, ritualized style in which to embody his vision. "Tintern Abbey," however, lies fully within the grounds of the Horatian ode, and, in respect to its immediate traditions, shares the meditative structure of loco-descriptive poetry with the heightened language and moral issues of that species of ode called by Nathan Drake "the *Descriptive*."[39] What most surely ties "Tintern Abbey" to the main pattern of the Coleridgean ode is implicit in Wordsworth's regard for its "transitions," which means the accentuation of a dialectical rhythm in the poem.

The transitions of "Tintern Abbey" are sudden, sharp, self-advertising. They call attention—which, notwithstanding, has too seldom been gained—to the continuing reversal, both in the main argument and in its subterranean layers, that is experienced in the poem. "If this / Be but a vain belief . . . (50–51) begins one verse paragraph, undercutting the "harmony" and "joy" with which "we see into the life of things" (49–50) in the preceding line. "Nor, perchance, / If I were not thus taught, should I the more / Suffer my genial spirits to decay" (112–114): the accent returns after Wordsworth has summoned his childhood memories and mature intimations of spiritual harmony to account for a beneficent oneness that he thus immediately fragments. All the verse paragraphs of "Tintern Abbey" begin with a recognition of shifting ground, either of time or of mental stability. These large demarcations of dialectical transition merely codify formally what is otherwise apparent in the basic course of argument. Just as the world we experience is a combination of "both what [the senses] half-create / And what perceive" (107–108), so no movement in the poem is without counterflow. Even its great statements of belief—"Nature never did betray / The heart that loved her" (122–123)—admit betrayals, dashed hopes, nagging doubts as being fundamental to human life. Every element defined as a good in "Tintern Abbey" is threatened, if not directly taken away. What justifies the rhetoric and open play for emotional power in the poem is the bravery of its irrevocably dialectical vision. Everything Wordsworth celebrates must be eroded, either by the temporal process so insistent in its intrusions on the poem or by the mind's inability to discover a singular perspective to which it can honestly adhere and through which it can render this contention into harmony.

The incessant rhythm will not endure abridgement, which is why Wordsworth must displace his synthesizing epode so that Dorothy, her perspective itself conceived in dialectical relation to his, can recreate the harmonious whole he can recall from his past but cannot project into the future. Whether the shift to Dorothy confesses his inadequacy or intuitively recognizes that the love essential to a harmonious society is a fundamentally dialectical emotion is for rival interpreters to argue from the same insufficient evidence. That is not to detract from Wordsworth's achievement, only to honor its generic purity. Again, the poem is alive with drama and incapable of resolution within any simple formula. "Tintern Abbey" is the paradoxical record of the mind's desire for relief from contraries—"a repose which ever is the same" is the apt phrase of the "Ode to Duty"—within a genre that emphasizes them and that, in this particular case, reveals a structure that is incesssantly, uncompromisingly dialectical.

Wordsworth's other two significant odes, the "Ode to Duty" and the "Intimations Ode," show something of the same paradoxical impulse. The "Ode to Duty" is a rumination specifically modelled on Gray's "Hymn to Adversity." It relies heavily on Horatian precept but cannot thereby escape its own tensions. As Paul Fry has shrewdly observed, the nostalgia with which Wordsworth glimpses his past freedom "effects the disruption of his poem."[40] Fry, however, appears to think this an unintentioned accident. Although one does sense in this poem of 1805 that the later Wordsworth is coming to the fore, at the same time perhaps the poet should be given the benefit of the doubt concerning his own nostalgia, which he lived with intensely for most of his eighty years. This resistant nostalgia actually rights the dialectical balance threatened by too strictly conceived an adherence to Duty; and Wordsworth certainly had precedent in Gray's poem, whose praise for adversity is characteristically ironic and at best reluctant.

If the "Ode to Duty" is too slight a poem to vie with "Tintern Abbey" for the perfection of its art, perhaps the "Intimations Ode" is too grand a poem for comparison. It is, in form and style, the one ode of English Romanticism that reverts to the irregular Pindaric of the Cowleyan tradition for animating spirit. It is, however, hardly the impetuous rhapsody to which that tradition alleged to aspire, composed as it is in a recognizable triad of stanzas 1 through 4, 5 through 9, and 10 and 11. The first section simply renders the familiar pressure of contraries: the vibrancy of spring evokes what has been lost everywhere in nature and, with intermittent spasms of pain, within the mind's contemplation of experience. The antistrophic movement attempts to place the personal sense of mixed loss and resurgence within a universal perspective. That perspective is complex, if not representing contradictory elements, at least allowing the juxtaposition of opposite impulses without forcing their merger. Nature is both prison-house and unending repository of imagery, seducing us away from our spiritual essence and providing a continual means of rediscovering it. This translates into the ongoing discovery of the self through the elemental friction of the dialectic, which is what the concluding epode celebrates in "the philosophic mind." Unlike "Tintern Abbey," where contrary rhythms arise almost by chance into a complex pattern of ambivalence, or the "Ode to Duty," where the balance is direct yet perhaps conceals unplumbed depths of psychic commitment, the "Intimations Ode" has a grandiose simplicity to its array of forces. Legions of frustrated interpreters have attempted to resolve the open questions or contradictions seen in the work. But that is to miss the fundamental generic point, which is that once again and on his grandest scale Wordsworth has created a work with open dramatic tensions that it can encompass without collapsing. No clever formula will eradicate tensions that are integral to human life, universal, resistant to resolution or a false synthesis. The epode finds its resting point in an open and undifferentiated sympathy, suppressing its urge to break down antimonies, discovering a virtue in its own frustration, content with a dialectic that reveals the mind to itself, and treasuring both the joy and the pain that result.

Through the labors of Coleridge and Wordsworth, then, the first generation of English Romantics evolved, or reinforced, a recognizable conception of the ode as an inherently dramatic form in which the poet risks the stability of his synthesizing consciousness before universally contrary pressures. Not only does the poem render those pressures unmediated by prior choice, but it pretends to enact a crisis demanding firm choice only to undercut the value and even the possibility of such an outcome. The more impulsive Coleridge accentuates the extremity of his case, conceiving himself, in both political and personal odes, as paralyzed exactly where the power of his will requires exertion. His representation of an unavoidable, however detested, inertia contrasts with Wordsworth's subtler portrayal of himself as unaccommodated man, responsive to all impulses, confident that his ability to center them will ultimately prevail yet perplexed that the effort must be so continually renewed, so psychologically enervating. Both Wordsworth and Coleridge, if only by inference, acknowledge the cost to a mind of being so conscious of its own vulnerability. The ode they bequeath to their fellow poets and successors is thus self-contemplating and self-reflexive. No sooner does the poet determine an external agent to celebrate or vilify or an objective antithesis to be balanced against his consciousness than he finds himself drawn within, where the tensions are both complementary and primary. The logic of the genre reinforces and is reinforced by the logic of internal debate. The result is a dramatic confrontation that is self-consciously staged, perhaps before a mirror.

The odes of the younger Romantics, fully conscious of the achievement of Wordsworth and Coleridge, tend to take the impulses evident in their earlier odes to an extreme, converting their antitheses into paradox, their paradoxes into self-cancelling irony. Extremes meet: strophe and antistrophe become almost indistinguishable. The collapse of antithetical distinctions in Byron's political odes—the "Ode to Napoleon Buonaparte" and "Venice. An Ode"—is universal in application. His representative man is Napoleon; his all-too-human community is Venice: both embody an unrelieved irony. Napoleon is described as

> The Desolator desolate!
> The Victor overthrown!
> The Arbiter of other's fate
> A Suppliant for his own! (37–40)

In the collapse of oppositions the very notion of heroism is brought down to the undifferentiated ground of "vulgar clay" (101). Venice is similar in its fortunes, a spectacle become spectrous:

> Thirteen hundred years
> Of wealth and glory turn'd to dust and tears;
> And every monument the stranger meets,
> Church, palace, pillar, as a mourner greets. (15–18)

Only in its ongoing death does Venice continue to live. Its history presages all history: "The everlasting *to be* which *hath been*" (59). Formally speaking, both odes threaten the integrity of the traditional progress piece, the Whig political ode exemplified in Collins's "Ode to Liberty." Even more extreme than Coleridge two decades before, Byron transports the conventions of the type to reaffirm its morality but question its conclusion. The history of Venice is not an ascendency but a progressive deterioration, so that its past becomes the ironic counterpart to its abject present. In both odes only in the voice of the poet can one discern the reality of an opposition between virtue and vice, honor and shame, freedom and tyranny, strophe and antistrophe. Both poems effect the same strategy, levelling all distinctions until the very last moment, when Byron adopts the tactic of Wordsworth and Coleridge to displace this sad reality with a renewal of potentiality, setting a heroic Washington against Napoleon and America against a moribund Europe.[41]

Against this context provided by Byron and Coleridge, Shelley writes his political odes. Fittingly, it was to Byron that Shelley lavished praise on "France: An Ode."[42] His "Ode to Liberty" and "Ode to Naples" present alternative variations on the Coleridgean model, balancing between the contest of liberty with tyranny, on the one hand, and the consciousness of a poet who must reproduce the epic struggle within his own mind, on the other. Shelley inflates the formal rhetoric of these political odes, wielding the ornate and ritualized high style with greater authority than the Coleridge of the 1790s—the "Ode to Naples," indeed, may be the most consummately crafted of all English odes—but he is no more sanguine in his expectations than was his predecessor and, if anything, sees the political struggle in more urgent terms. But from the isolation of bardic necessity, he attempts to wrest a virtue that Coleridge either did not see or would not grasp.

Alone among the English Romantics, Shelley reverts to the rhapsodic element that the previous century had claimed a distinguishing mark of the ode. But he ties it organically to theme and ideology in a way that is not true, for instance, of Collins. Both the "Ode to Liberty" and the "Ode to Naples" begin by representing their author as empowered by vision, and both poems explicitly relate imaginative vision to political liberty as singular to plural, individual to community. The ode, in its exercise of sublime flight, is thus by any standard of literary decorum the proper medium for celebrating freedom from arbitrary constraint, as Soame Jenyns recognized with witty irony. But Shelley is deeply serious in his conceptual understanding of the ode. For him, the influx of visionary inspiration corresponds to the gradual exfoliation of liberty through time or across contemporary Europe.

And yet there is also an obverse aspect to this correspondence, one not so much revealed to Shelley in the course of the poems as embedded in their very conception. The vision of the "Ode to Liberty" reaches a climax of urgency—"have not the wise and free / Wept tears, and blood like tears?" (269–270)—beyond which there is only an abyss. The last stanza reverts to the precarious state of the poet, whose vision has been "suddenly withdrawn" (272) and who in five varied, actually contradictory, similes suggests a range of possible reasons, each with large implications for the public issues of the ode. So multiple an uncertainty compounds the vulnerability of the inspired and the liberated. The "Ode to Naples" ends with the southern onslaught of the Austrian army, which Shelley depicts in an even more disturbing simile: "The Anarchs of the North lead forth their legions / Like Chaos o'er creation, uncreating" (137–138). The force of analogy has elevated the correspondence of liberty and imaginative vision to a cosmic level, where creation and uncreation form stark and irreconcilable antitheses. Shelley represents this opposition in balanced strophes, but no dialectical progression is possible from so Manichaean a contention. Thus the notion of polarized conflict itself becomes a pole against which the poet's consciousness pits itself. As the rhapsodic frame of these odes implicitly reminds us, the result is both creative, with inspiration energized by its correspondence with liberation, and purgatorial, for the mind testifies to its impotence to sustain either its own inspiration or, on a large scale, the besieged forces of freedom.[43]

The complexity of the accrued paradoxes is bewildering, but it need not, as with Coleridge, lead to inanition, or, as with Byron, to self-cancelling irony. Indeed, it is the genius of Shelley's greatest ode, the "Ode to the West Wind," that without compromising or simplifying the multiplied dialectical force, it can testify to its essentially creative impact on the mind. As Coleridge's political odes supply an illuminating context for those of Shelley, so, though there is not the same certainty of actual influence, "Dejection: An Ode" provides interesting parallels for the "Ode to the West Wind." Both poems start from the same perceived discrepancy between the elemental forces of nature and the speaker's powerlessness and lack of will. Coleridge is more specific in tracing the causes of his inertia, but for both it is a state concomitant with reflective adulthood. Yet where Coleridge, longing for marriage, can find only a universal bill of divorcement, Shelley's ode gradually erases the sense of division it predicates. Or, more precisely, by acceding to and internalizing the dialectical rhythm everywhere evident in nature, Shelley is able to identify himself with the elemental force he invokes, becoming in the final stanza both spokesman for and aspect of its vital power. To do that, however, he must, like Wordsworth, accept the inevitability of decay and death in the universal scheme. Throughout the ode the forces of destruction and preservation are so independent as ultimately to be twin aspects of one reality. The balance is equally true, whether in autumnal seedbeds, the hearth of political liberation with its intermingled ashes and sparks, or the creativity quickened by the thorns of private anguish. Of all the Romantic odes, the "Ode to the West Wind" most fully adopts the ideological preconceptions implicit in the form, insisting throughout on the mind's gathering synthesis of a universal contention.

Like Shelley, Keats invests his odes with a fundamental dialectic, but they discover synthesis almost by default, even against the poet's will. In effect, Keats completely reverses the Coleridgean formula for the ode. Looking for distinctions and divorces, he instead confronts enigmatic samenesses, marriages that should never have been sanctified, but, however tenuous and quarrelsome they appear, are unending. Among the distinctions blurred are not only those between art and reality, the ideal and real, and joy and sorrow, but even the concomitant distinctions between the mind and the independent world perceived by it. "Do I wake or sleep?" is an unanswerable question.

That phrase, the resolution of the "Ode to a Nightingale," is wholly ironic, an irresolution that perfectly represents the incomprehensible dissolution of opposites that has occurred through the progress of the poem. The synthesis, though familiar, is here rendered strange and distasteful, even threatening. How is it possible that the more we seek to escape the pains of mortality graphically detailed in the third stanza of the ode, to "fade away into the forest dim" (20) where the nightingale's rapture constitutes a sole intensity, the more we find ourselves confronting the very death we flee? How can Keats divide "here" and "there" so insistently in the poem, only to find not simply their interdependence but their actual superimposition on the same ground? Even simple diction in the "Ode to a Nightingale" conceals a double meaning of synthesizing force. The poet reiterates his desire to "fade away . . . / Fade far away" (20-21), only to confront the same process in the "youth [who] grows pale, and spectre-thin, and dies" (26) and in the "Beauty [who] cannot keep her lustrous eyes" (29). When in the final stanza the bird's "plaintive anthem fades" (75), it merely recapitulates, with a total ironic effect, how the poet, drawn by the bird's life-destroying rapture, would "To [its] high requiem become a sod" (60)! Doubtless, there are homilies to be extracted from these ironies, but underlying them all is the sheer formal logic of the ode, as Keats transposes the familiar contrary principles into a dramatic confrontation between alternate states of desire.

The "winding mossy ways" (40) of the "Ode to a Nightingale" are those of a maze, all of which promise a false egress and lead inexorably back to the same center. It is a place of dynamic force, intense, palpable, a fusion of polar impulses. The "Ode on Melancholy" and "Ode on a Grecian Urn" explore the center itself, with all dialectical impulses synthesized into oxymorons, the union of contradictory elements. Melancholy

> dwells with Beauty—Beauty that must die;
>   And Joy, whose hand is ever at his lips
> Bidding adieu; and aching Pleasure nigh,
>   Turning to poison while the bee-mouth sips:
> Ay, in the very temple of Delight
>   Veil'd Melancholy has her sovran shrine. (21-26)

The same double nature is discovered in every aspect of the urn that Keats explores as an enigma no more truly known at the end than at the beginning. The urn is an impossible presence, drawing together a myriad of opposite qualities, never quite what it seems to be: the "bride" of the first line is "unravish'd," which is to say, not truly a bride, as "silence and slow time" of the second line are not the true parents of their "foster-child." The "Cold Pastoral" of the last stanza is a contradiction in terms. And yet, the urn is a presence precisely because its terms cancel one another even as it remains. And because it is so tangibly able to "tease us out of thought" (44), it is strangely intangible—"tease us out of thought / As doth eternity." There is no way to fix this artifact within the field of a dialectical physics except by recognizing the urn as a kind of energy, drawing us out of ourselves, constantly in the process of redefinition and so agent in the self-definition of those it teases out of themselves. The ink spilled on the last two lines is—with poetic justice—evidence of the continuing energy within this field defined by observer and artifact. The urn enigmatically pronounces what in any conventional sense we know to be untrue, as it has pronounced itself through every line of the poem: truth is to beauty what the "nevers" of the second stanza are to the "forevers" of the third. The presence contains multitudes and is without fixity itself.

The polar revision of the second stanza by the third—strophe and antistrophe constructed from the same elements—is likewise a strategy in the "Ode to Psyche." The field of energy is also curiously the same, though we may observe a determined shift of intellectual axis. Here, the fused and defining center is not an external object but the sanctuary of the imagination itself, its energy being the product of intercourse between love and spirit. The "pleasant pain" (52) of the poet's thought testifies to the same oxymoronic nature of experience, but here it is all collapsed within a mental formulation, is wholly self-reflexive. Through its meta-phorical structure, to be sure, the ode implies continuities between ancient and modern life as between mental and natural prospects. But the dialectical relationship between inner and outer in the "Ode to Psyche" rests only on metaphor. The poem deliberately invokes a world of public responsibility—the high and solemn obligation of a priest to his community—only to internalize all its functions into a wholly private commitment. But, the ubiquitous art of these odes would suggest that this is a knowing, deliberate reversal of generic expectations. Keats would surely have been surprised to think such a reversal could be transmuted through Freud into a suspicion of narcissism.

And yet, to worry over narcissism in the "Ode to Psyche" and then honor "To Autumn" as a healthier poem is at least to recognize that the poems are mirror opposites, though it moralizes the results of artistic experimentation. As the reader's metaphorical extrapolation introduces a public realm into the private recesses of the "Ode to Psyche," it also constrains the richly externalized world of "To Autumn." "Where are the songs of Spring? Ay, where are they?" (23): surely the proper answer is that they are in the multivolume collections of English poetry antholog-ized for the Romantic period by Robert Anderson, John Bell, and Alexander Chalmers, in Burns's ribald parody as yet not collected into *The Merry Muses of Caledonia*, even in Gray's autumnal "Ode to Spring."

Readers in Keats's day could be assumed to know the properties of an ode to spring by heart. By withdrawing personality from the most urgent of human dialectical conflations, that of life and death, in "To Autumn" Keats creates what many think a perfect poem by undermining—or counterbalancing—the expectations of an ode. In essence, he omits the crucial polarity in the firm expectation that the mortal reader will supply it from both literary tradition and personal experience, will thus internalize the poetic details and thereby establish the dynamic interchange—simply a new version of the familiar one between the public and the private—that is the vital principle of the genre. "To Autumn," viewed from such a perspective, constitutes the logical culmination of a poetic of self-reflexiveness and of the characteristic displacement of the Romantic ode, forcing the self-reflexive principle from the author and onto each reader of the poem.

Undoubtedly, the skeptical spirit of the age underpins the dialectical modes of thought revealed in all these odes. Still, such mental processes are accentuated by the inherent logic embedded in the form and in its characteristic national traditions. In reanimating that logic within a fresh context, or in discerning strange intricacies within the customary design, or in superimposing one version of the design upon another to see what symmetries or asymmetries result, the Romantic poets join a literary continuum of long standing. If modern criticism has sometimes drawn unwarranted conclusions from their imaginative play within circumscribed boundaries, perhaps it is simply because their odes are so matchless in wedding necessity with that liberty of invention that looks so very like rapture.

CHAPTER FIVE

The Pastoral

. . . of all Poems, the most meagre commonly in the subject, and the least diversified in the strain, is the Pastoral. From the first lines, we can, generally, guess at all that is to follow. It is either a Shepherd who sits down solitary by a brook, to lament the absence, or cruelty of his mistress, and to tell us how the trees wither, and the flowers droop, now that she is gone; or we have two Shepherds who challenge one another to sing, rehearsing alternate verses, which have little either of meaning or subject, till the Judge rewards one with a studded crook, and another with a beechen bowl. . . . I much question, however, whether this insipidity be not owing to the fault of the Poets, and to their barren and slavish imitation of the antient pastoral topics, rather than to the confined nature of the subject. For why may not Pastoral poetry take a wider range? Human nature, and human passions, are much the same in every rank of life; and wherever these passions operate on objects that are within the rural sphere, there may be a proper subject for Pastoral.

Hugh Blair, *Lectures on Rhetoric and Belles-Lettres* (1783), II, 345–346

We have few good pastorals in the language. Our manners are not Arcadian; our climate is not an eternal spring; our age is not the age of gold.

William Hazlitt, *Lectures on the English Poets* (1818), V

I

NOTHING BETTER EXEMPLIFIES the intractability of generic definition than pastoral. As literary currency, the term predates and traverses the boundaries of most nations of the Western world; and yet its value fluctuates from one culture to another, demanding continual adjustment to the local economy. And it goes without saying that in most cases the economy is an urban one where sheep may not safely graze. The one certainty is that the literary kind that celebrates simplicity is far from simple in either practice or critical taxonomy.

First of all, it is the only kind that regularly ignores the standard generic distinctions between narrative, drama, and lyric.[1] The story is seldom more than a slice of life, a vignette, and it will invariably be incomplete, and yet the concerns it expresses—the good life, human fellowship, success or failure in love—are universal. The eclogue, sometimes glorified by the term Amoebean pastoral, is a dialogue, often rudimentary in characterization, whose denouement is likely to be anticlimactic; and yet it is undeniably dramatic in form and progression. But

85

if the end attained by the continual resort to anticlimax or the stress on poetic creation, song, is a dialectical suspension, even the eclogue shows affinities with the lyric mode.[2] Indeed, that high noon of pastoral pleasance, whose celebration is an enduring aim of pastoral poetry, seems the essence of the lyrical in its translation of momentary delight into an untramelled mode of existence withdrawn from temporal concerns, temporal costs.[3]

The necessary consequence of its protean character is that pastoral has migrated far from the original relatively brief exercises in Greek hexameters created by Theocritus. With Guarini's celebrated *Il Pastor Fido*, it emerged from the embryonic and ritualistic trappings of medieval religious mysteries (as in the *Second Shepherds' Play* of the Wakefield cycle) into full-scale dramatic representation. Although pastoral drama itself has never amounted to more than a literary curiosity—it is difficult, for instance, to understand, let alone justify, the deference paid to Allen Ramsay's *Gentle Shepherd* by his eighteenth-century contemporaries— its infusion into *As You Like It* or *The Winter's Tale* suggests its enduring power.[4] Likewise, as early as the *Daphnis and Chloe* of Longus the pastoral entered the arena of prose fiction, where, assimilated with other, and often antithetical, elements, it may paradoxically test the civilized values of a sophisticated reader against the claims of the natural and innocent, as in Goldsmith's *Vicar of Wakefield*, or invert the focus, as in Hardy's novels, to acknowledge the incompatibility of human nature with its pastoral ideals. In Britain, especially, with its deep cultural ties to the land, pastoral elements are everywhere in the history of its fiction.

Even within the province of poetry, however, pastoral cannot readily be defined. Again, it naturally assimilates itself to larger forms. Its inherent animism and closeness to folk traditions make it particularly congenial to the romance, as in *The Faerie Queene* or *Endymion*, or, on a more limited scale (but one of special significance in the eighteenth century), the ballad. Its evocation of a natural order that nurtures human freedom continually tempts it to transform itself into its opposite, the epic, or into a subsuming moral vision such as Thomson essayed in *The Seasons*.[5] Virgil's paradigmatic canon, from the *Eclogues* to the *Georgics* to *The Aeneid*, is not only immensely influential for all Western poetry but testifies to the necessary relationship between ideals of well-being and of community, the labor required to constitute them, and the cultural structures that foster or inhibit them. But it could be argued that the labor came first, that Hesiod's *Works and Days* establishes the realistic context from which Theocritus creates the pastoral retreat of his *Idylls*. Whatever may be the chains of influence in an all but irrecoverable past, the relationship between pastoral and georgic, as between shepherd and farmer, is intimately linked: Virgil subtly acknowledges the fact by repeating the first line of his *Eclogues* as the last line of his *Georgics*; and Pope follows him, with an educated sense of the complexity of the relationship, by returning in the last line of *Windsor Forest*, a poem not usually considered within the georgic tradition, to the opening of his *Pastorals*. Although the history of attempts to build walls between pastoral and georgic is long and distinguished both by names and the reiteration of academic arguments, it is inevitably distorting. Also, of course, it never lasts.

But is there an essence to this Proteus beyond a capacity for seemingly infinite transformation? Rapin, exemplifying neoclassical exactitude, nicely begs the question in defining pastoral: *"It is the imitation of the Action of a Sheapherd, or of one taken under that Character."*[6] Precisely because of its removal from the everyday world of its readers, the pastoral retreat is inevitably a locus for allegory, for synechdoche or litotes, or for simple irony. A world characterized by simplicity will necessarily become cryptic to the civilized, as its oral spontaneity is transmitted into written fictions. However many versions of pastoral we detect (and Empson somewhat diminishes the impact of his survey in *Some Versions of Pastoral* by concentrating so heavily on those which appear superficially most unpastoral), they share one ironic feature, which is that they are written for, and usually in, the city.[7] Theocritus sets the standard: he may invoke Sicilian muses and recreate Coan landscapes, but his audience was in Hellenistic Alexandria and his patron a Ptolemy presiding over the most polished court of the Mediterranean world. Indeed, what is surely among the greatest of his *Idylls*, the Fifteenth (once known as "The Syracusan Gossips"), is one of the most vivid enactments of city life in all classical literature. Scholars systematically exclude it from Theocritean pastoral, though it shares the same vital detail, the emphasis on comradeship, and even the vulgarity of the earlier idylls. Its main characters, notably, are all women—shepherds, so to speak, of the domicile. It is at least questionable that Theocritus made the kinds of generic distinctions that developed in his wake.

Even more so is this the case with Virgil's *Eclogues*, recently characterized by Paul Alpers, with becoming hyperbole, as "probably the single most important document in the history of poetry."[8] Important it is, to be sure, for codifying a tradition until that point only implicit in the corpus of minor Hellenistic poets; but important, as well, for constituting the *locus classicus* of pastoral poetry among Virgil's numerous followers, whether poets or readers. The *Eclogues* were a standard feature of the educational curriculum for centuries—certainly as late as the nineteenth century and even, as Chaucer may wryly be suggesting, for budding prioresses in fourteenth-century convent schools.[9] Their rich texture, which has prompted one of the truly remarkable critical revivals of recent years, is complex enough as it resonates through later literature.[10] Yet, the complexity is exacerbated by our being forced to recognize the many kinds of distortions these poems were wont to suffer through the various epochs interpreting them. We are all properly thankful that the supposed Christian foreshadowings of the Fourth *Eclogue* got Virgil out of limbo

and as far as Dante's purgatory, but the misapprehension directly trace-
able to Rapin's imposition upon the world of the *Eclogues* and thereafter
repeated without question for at least a century—that pastoral treats of
the golden age—is the major reason for the decline of significant pastoral
in the eighteenth century.[11]

Leaving aside for the moment the continual paradox of the misprision
practiced by the second Augustan age as it professedly imitated the former
one, we should revert to the question of what constitutes a definable
essence for so protean a form as the pastoral. As Alpers suggests in
placing his accent on a suspension of contraries, and as the previous
comments have implied in recognizing the fluency with which pastoral
migrates into other forms, the enduring feature of pastoral is its double
vision. It may enact a retreat, but it brings its civilized auditors with it,
guaranteeing a tension of values. Similarly, its celebration of simplicity is
predicated on our comprehension of complexities; its *otium* presumes
our *negotium*; its noontide allegro our midnight penseroso. Moreover, of
course, it is not simply that we cannot slough off our everyday worries
when we enter a timeless bower: those worries are continually present, in
microcosmic form, within the pastoral itself. Gilbert Lawall's sensitive
discussion of the Fifth *Idyll* of Theocritus stops just short of saying flatly
what the wonderful animality of the poem figures forth, that the contest
between shepherd and goatherd is one between a sheep and a goat.[12] The
critical issue should not be who wins, but rather the ingenious inclusiveness of the perspectives. Theocritus, again with an art that can scarcely be
concealed by his pastoral disguise, in the First *Idyll* introduces us to the
pastoral world by a meticulous description of the wooden bowl set as a
prize for Thyrsis's rendition of a song about Daphnis: the scholarly
commentary on this bowl is exceedingly rich, virtually all of it recognizing that the carvings render a world antithetical to the pastoral ideal. But
even more significant is the way that world is reinvested with its authority in Thyrsis's song about the sorrows of Daphnis. Daphnis turns aside
from the claims of Priapus and of Pan, finally even those of Aphrodite,
refusing the life they offer, based as it is on the pains of love. This is no
mere lover's complaint; it is a suicide implicating all nature. (It is also
strikingly modern in its portrayal of psychological entropy.) And yet, of
course, it is also a prize song: the distaste for life it embodies is contained
by the splendor of the poetry and by the honor accorded Thyrsis as singer.
And though the bowl is carved with scenes of duplicity and failure—or of
the ages of man as they pass in the outside, mutable world—that record
too is assimilated to the pastoral decencies it denies. The double containment is itself a triumph of art and an embodiment of the distinguishing
pastoral mode of art.

Et in Arcadia ego—even I am in Arcadia: exile, forlorn love, the threat
of the savage, decay, death.[13] The Meliboeus of Virgil's *Eclogue I* is forced
from his homestead by the state and goes into uncertain exile. His
namesake, the sage Meliboee in the Sixth Book of *The Faerie Queene*,

is murdered by brigands who abduct his daughter, and the at last rea-
wakened Calidore must exert every energy to rescue Pastorella and subdue
the Blatant Beast, who as the book concludes is again loose and now
beyond vanquishment. The golden age is a cultural memory enshrined in
a pastoral longing that acknowledges the irrecoverability of the past, the
inevitability of its defeat, the inability to enclose the garden. At the same
time, the pastoral paradigm through its very vulnerability counters its
multitude of threats, minimizing their ultimate power, even subsuming
them within the unending principle of life.

> Die liebe Erde allüberall
>   Blüht auf im Lenz und grünt aufs neu!
>   Allüberall und ewig blauen licht die Fernen!
> Ewig . . . ewig . . . ewig . . . ewig . . . ewig . . . ewig . . . ewig.

Mahler's poignant suspension of an ever-recurring spring against the
necessity of human failure at the end of *Das Lied von der Erde* is a late
manifestation of the age-old pastoral balance that is discovered (and
rediscovered) in Theocritus, Virgil, Sannazaro, and Spenser.[14] It is just
present, perhaps by the accident of imitation rather than intention, in
Pope, but virtually disappears beneath the layers of enamel in which
French neoclassicism decorated the pastoral with a superficial gloss and
which, both in theory and practice, dominated British pastoral poetry of
the eighteenth century. It is tempting to deride this entire effort as
misguided—never did so many cultivated minds pursue the dead end of
vitiated taste with such single-minded lack of intensity—and yet, all
genres undergo necessary evolutions whose historical integrity is undeniable. From a modern perspective, however, it is obvious that the golden-
age pastoral, donnishly repeated without ever being truly recreated, had
neither past nor future to it. A stagnant genre of necessity creates a
countergenre, and it was thus that the pastoral recovered its traditional
dimensions in an unlikely guise.

II

While Strephon and Damon continued in their age-old stylized postures
to woo Phyllis and Amaryllis, uttering interchangeable arguments
against an unseducible coyness and bemoaning the sorrows of frustrated
adolescence, two pastoral traditions looked askance, as it were, from
opposite sides. One was serious, even devout, the other worldly-wise; but
the extremes met in their intolerance for mere attitude and masquerade.

    Renato Poggioli, one of the most influential of modern students of the
pastoral, insists that Christianity is incompatible with pastoral: "the
critical mind can only treat as failures all attempts to Christianize the
pastoral, or to translate pastoral into Christian terms. . . . the pastoral of
Christendom is as impossible as the tragedy of Christianity."[15] As a
misapprehension, Poggioli's must rank with Samuel Johnson's charac-

terization of pastoral in reference to *Lycidas* as "easy, vulgar, and therefore disgusting." The fact is that after Virgil, with a few exceptions
among later Roman and Hellenistic poets, there has been *only* a Christian pastoral. The true failures have been among the class of poets who
donned a spurious paganism and resolutely looked the other way. That is
not to say that a religious framework need be overt, only that the mythic
undertones lie deep within Western culture and of necessity implicate its
versions of pastoral.

For the early English Renaissance, Spenser most fully sets the paradigm in his *Shepheardes Calendar,* with its continual urge toward
allegory concerned with the state of country and church. By the early
seventeenth century the equation of shepherd and pastor was all but automatic, a dependable context for the subtle interweaving of typological
and scriptural threads that compose the underlying texture of Milton's
Lycidas.[16] For subsequent British culture, of course, the *locus classicus*
was *Paradise Lost,* with its representation of a golden age as true—no
mere mythic fiction—for its readers as it was tragically short-lived. As an
embodiment of mixed and often competing genres, *Paradise Lost* is
without peer in British literature; underpinning them all and presented
in its most radical form is the pastoral.[17] The lush effulgence of Eden, its
innocent sexuality, its nexus of human and divine are all the more prized
and poignant for our intruding upon it with a prior knowledge of the
fall. Not only do we catch our first glimpse of Paradise through the eyes
of Satan, sitting "like a Cormorant" (IV.196) on the Tree of Life, but
Milton frames the landscape between Satan's grandiose and despairing
soliloquies. The *hortus conclusus* is naturally vulnerable, easily violated.
In our sympathetic response to Satan's passion, we ourselves violate it.
Milton's subtlest casting of the pastoral balance includes lines commonly
celebrated by readers of the eighteenth and nineteenth centuries, though
without necessarily recognizing their generic implications:

> . . . The Birds thir choir apply; airs, vernal airs,
> Breathing the smell of field and grove, attune
> The trembling leaves, while universal *Pan*
> Knit with the *Graces* and the *Hours* in dance
> Led on th'Eternal Spring. Not that fair field
> Of *Enna,* where *Proserpin* gath'ring flow'rs
> Herself a fairer Flow'r by gloomy *Dis*
> Was gather'd, which cost *Ceres* all that pain
> To seek her through the world; nor that sweet Grove
> Of *Daphne* by *Orontes,* and th'inspir'd
> *Castalian* Spring might with this Paradise
> Of *Eden* strive . . . (IV.264–275)

On the one hand, a perpetual spring, a natural order supervised by the
pastoral deity Pan, and pure waters flowing from Parnassus; on the other
hand, mythic reminders of the passage of the seasons, the otherness of an
underworld, and with Daphne's transformation into a laurel tree the

dependence of poetry on suffering. The syntax embodying the endless present tense of Eden's dance is jarred by the mythic past (which is, on the time scale of the poem, yet the future): "Universal *Pan* . . . Led"— "*Proserpin* gath'ring . . . Was gather'd."

The knowing confusion of temporal values mirrors the way the Christian mythos transformed classical pastoral traditions. The paradise from which humanity is exiled is yet the far goal of time, as genesis presupposes apocalypse, and it wholly infuses the central event of Christian history, the birth of the Messiah, watched over by shepherds. The high noon of Theocritean pleasance in Christian pastoral becomes the deep midnight in the dark of the year, an incarnation into which all time collapses. So the pastoral elements of both "On the Morning of Christ's Nativity" and *Lycidas* insistently displace the temporal distinctions that intrude upon the poems. Jesus, the good shepherd, embodies the Eden from which humanity has fallen and the promised Arcadia to which he will lead his flock.

The continual pastoral strain in Milton's verse always reflects these associations and for subsequent poets becomes a conduit of Renaissance notions of Christian pastoral that serve as an alternative to the Virgilian conception. It is clearly discernible in Pope's further efforts in pastoral genres. *Windsor Forest* turns from its opening invocation to an explicitly Christian premise from which the rest of the poem derives motive force:

> The Groves of *Eden*, vanish'd now so long,
> Live in Description, and look green in Song. (7–8)

Although the aim of the poem is a panegyric on the reign of Queen Anne, this couplet establishes the eschatological context that comes to dominate the poem. Anne's peaceable kingdom is the type of paradise and her reign a foretaste of the millennium. When with the last line of the poem Pope subtly brings his entire fabric into line with Virgil's *Georgics* by quoting the opening of his own "Spring Pastoral," we are made to understand how fully within a pastoral framework the poem is conceived, how fully too that framework has been enlarged to allow for a reconciliation of classical and Christian paradigms as well as of the public world and the private retreat. A similar reconciliatory aim governs Pope's "Messiah: A Sacred Eclogue, in Imitation of Virgil's Pollio," where he transforms Virgil's Fourth *Eclogue* into the explicit celebration of Christ's birth it had traditionally been seen to prophesy.[18] The poem's comparative weakness may stem paradoxically from the extent to which Pope labors to touch every chord in the Christian pastoral harmony.

Virgil's messianic eclogue notwithstanding, the classical pastoral is fundamentally nostalgic, its claims for an undisturbed presence betraying a sense that it is already past. The Christian pastoral is conceived upon a more complicated paradigm. Eden exists, as Pope acknowledges, only in song, but the barred past prefigures the promised future. All of history may intervene, yet the momentary withdrawal from civilization seems a symbolic act of faith in the millennial redemption whereby civilization will be reabsorbed within the pastoral mode. The crucial question, however, is what to do in the meantime. If pastoral pleasance is understood as possible only in an irrecoverable past or an inscrutable future, the present it would celebrate cannot embody the pastoral. The double vision of classical pastoral thus threatens, within a Christian ethos, to become self-canceling.

Ironically, then, the inherent dynamic of Christian pastoral, with its acknowledgment of a fall from pastoral perfection, links it to the second strain of pastoral writing in the eighteenth century refusing the bondage of mere imitation, the antipastoral. As Pope seems the central figure both for simultaneously refining and exhausting the possibilities of classical imitation and for transforming the Renaissance Christian pastoral to the requirements of modern civilization, it is appropriate that the leading figure in tapping the rich potentiality of generic inversion should be his associate John Gay, who observes the connection between the two strains of pastoral, in the preface to *The Shepherd's Week*, by wittily portraying Milton's Satan stalking Eve—"As one who long in populous City pent, / . . . Forth issuing on a Summers Morn (9.445-447)—as the type of the pastoral poet. From *The Shepherd's Week* to *Rural Sports* to *The Beggar's Opera*—"What think you of a Newgate pastoral, among the thieves and whores there?" innocently asked Dean Swift—Gay, through his eye for realistic detail and his instinct for genial satire, pursued the antipastoral with such brilliance as to undermine the weakened integrity of the pastoral mode he parodied and virtually to substitute for it his own distinctive inversion. At least, it became a standard point of reference throughout the century whenever the inadequacy of contemporary pastoral was raised. That many readers took the parody seriously may be doubted, but the supposition furnished a standard literary anecdote later in the century. Johnson's balanced praise likewise was widely quoted, lending weight to the integrity of Gay's achievement: "the effect of reality and truth became conspicuous, even when the intention was to shew them groveling and degraded. These Pastorals became popular and were read with delight, as just representations of rural manners and occupations." Even more directly, Goldsmith credited Gay with recovering the authentic pastoral voice: "perhaps without designing it, he has hit the true spirit of pastoral poetry."[19]

Gay began from the most conservative of literary purposes, as the defender of Pope's mellifluous artifice against the "namby-pamby" simplicity of Ambrose Phillips. And yet *The Shepherd's Week*, in depicting the true simplicity of pastoral life in England, ultimately did greater honor to Phillips than to Pope. Most of all, it honored Theocritus, recapturing in parody the abundant good humor, the realistic vulgarity, and the unremitting vitality of the *Idylls*. Nature always wins out in the contest with art, as the pastoralists of the English Renaissance were fond of proving (with considerable art).[20] Pope's synoptic neoclassicism was, as his "Discourse" virtually acknowledged, a dead end. With Gay's reminder of Theocritus, it was as if the pastoral mode had been invented anew.

Johnson's and Goldsmith's reactions to *The Shepherd's Week* in the generation after Gay's death may reflect a large cultural shift involving a humanitarianism not commonly attributed to Dr. Johnson at least. Gay's intentions may be thought less kind than such testaments suggest. Indeed, his parody reflects the animus of an inveterate city-dweller against all that was associated with the bucolic in a self-consciously cultivated society. An uneducated, superstitious, bumbling peasantry, though portrayed with condescending good humor, represents neither the backbone of a nation nor an ideal of pastoral retreat. Still, Gay's hardminded realism, directly opposed to the literary nostalgia of neoclassical pastoral, at once established a new imperative for the mode.

The antipastoral of the eighteenth century had truth on its side; and with truth naturally followed the finest instincts of the century's satire. The inevitable result, we may suppose, is the fatalistic vision of George Crabbe's *The Village* of 1783, a poem that offers hope only through the offices of an enlightened landed gentry that will not allow the peasantry to sink wholly into the destitution that is their lot and seemingly their destiny. And yet, the stark view of Crabbe, increasingly applauded in modern criticism, pales before the wholesale inversion of his major predecessor, Charles Churchill. His mercurial, dissolute youth, short life, and enormous talent suggest a mind predisposed to self-destruction: in *The Prophecy of Famine: A Scots Pastoral* he displaced those instincts onto the pastoral genre with something of the precision of an ideologue. Written in 1763 when a renewal of the periodic Jacobite rebellions still seemed possible, topically consumed with vitriol for the Bute ministry and the sentimental nationalism of Allen Ramsay, *The Prophecy of Famine* possesses, now that its contemporary objects of satire have faded from consciousness, a Dantesque majesty. Churchill represents the counterweight to Macpherson in eighteenth-century characterizations of Scotland, dispelling the mists from a landscape of sublimely unrelieved barrenness.

> Far as the eye could reach, no tree was seen,
> Earth, clad in russet, scorn'd the lively green.
> The plague of Locusts they secure defy,
> For in three hours a grasshopper must die. (295–298)

Churchill's power comes not simply from his representation of a meager nature and destitute population but from his knowing deconstruction of pastoral paradigms. His ragged swains, Jockey and Sawney, finding "summer shrunk beneath a wintry blast" (336), are forced to take shelter within a cave. It is, with all its elements inverted, the cave of Virgil's Fifth *Eclogue*:

All creatures, which, on nature's earliest plan,
Were form'd to loath, and to be loath'd by man,
Which ow'd their birth to nastiness and spite,
Deadly to touch, and hateful to the sight,
Creatures, which, when admitted in the ark,
Their Saviour shunn'd, and rankled in the dark,
Found place *within*; marking her noisome road
With poison's trail, *here* crawl'd the bloated Toad;
There webs were spread of more than common size,
And half-starv'd spiders prey'd on half-starv'd flies;
In quest of food, Efts strove in vain to crawl;
Slugs, pinch'd with hunger, smear'd the slimy wall. (319–330)

In Virgil's cave Mopsus and Menalcus trade songs in tribute to the apotheosis of Daphnis, the singing shepherd transformed into fertility god, their cave representing the womb of nature and art allied. But the presiding deity in this cave is Famine, depicted with Spenserian exactitude, and the poem is taken over by her prophecy, which is in turn a careful inversion of the messianic Fourth *Eclogue* of Virgil. In her vision Scotland will triumph by preying on England, ravaging its bounty, pillaging its civilization. The final touch of this doubled irony is to make England almost by default into a vulnerable pastoral garden, innocent in its abundance, ripe to be ravaged. Scotland lives off death: rebellion is the civic complement to the anti-Nature manifested in Famine's secret cave.[21]

Churchill's literary method in *The Prophecy of Famine* is in remarkable concert with the tenor of his poem. His extreme satire preys on pastoral as Scotland would on England, gaining its own moral vision by sapping the life out of generic convention and the moral suppositions that attend it. The multiple inversions of the poem finally leave the reader with nothing but an almost paranoid guardedness. Churchill's is an irremediably fallen world, without hope for redemption. Such a vision is incompatible with the profession of his immediate follower, the Reverend George Crabbe, which perhaps suggests why *The Village* is such a perplexing poem, attempting at its end to find a saving grace where the poem gives no reason to expect one. Less extreme than *The Prophecy of Famine*, *The Village* is nonetheless similar in its aim to dispel the sentimentality and explode the pieties harbored by pastoral. But its differences in method are all-important. Crabbe's portrayal of rural life emphasizes members of a community, impoverished as it is. Though typed, the inhabitants are particularized, and their misery is shared. His subject is not pastoral ease but rural work: "What labour yields, and what, that labour past, / Age, in its hour of languor, finds at last" (3–4). The village is an economic entity, governed by rudimentary laws the science of which, with Adam Smith's pioneering treatise, had come into existence in the decade preceding Crabbe's poem. Its pessimism seems as much the result of Crabbe's contemplating mechanical laws of supply and demand as of his confronting the moral laxity of the poor. The viewpoint is hardly forgiving, but it is individualized and compassionate. So an aged shepherd sums his existence: "A lonely, wretched man, in pain I go, / None need my help, and none relieve my way" (ll. 222-223). Though the multiform destitution of this people is beyond easy solution, its relief is a solemn duty of the enlightened aristocracy celebrated at the end of the poem. Tory paternalism is, paradoxically, Crabbe's nostalgic refuge in the old pastoral.

Crabbe's realism is the underlying premise of all significant antipastoral in the eighteenth century. The generic inversion, however, in its systematic deflating of an artificial pastoral is constrained by the conventions, the venerable literary traditions, and the limits of apprehension that accompany the pastoral mode. If there is only hard labor to be faced, that does not alter the desire for ease; the inhospitable nature of a northern clime only aggravates fantasies of abundance. A portrayal of destitution and of unaccommodated man, as in Churchill and Crabbe, is thus susceptible to its own inversion, emphasizing simple comfort and fellowship. The harshness of eighteenth-century antipastoral, by the inherent logic of generic development, virtually necessitated its own countergenre, one no less committed to a realistic perspective but instilled as well with a sense of human dignity. Churchill's dark intensities are a throwback to Hobbes. The historical tides were with Shaftsbury and Rousseau, and they simply swept him away.

The eighteenth century itself testifies to its sense of a renewed pastoral instigated by the example of Collins's youthful *Oriental Eclogues*.[22] And yet they share something of the decadent assumptions of the mode they would replace: their self-conscious exoticism, duly complemented by learned annotations, is academic and bears the implication that pastoral can be revitalized only from a cultural distance. Collins's effort to transplant Arcadia to Arabia, with nomadic camel drivers supplanting classical shepherds, had little more than logic to support it. Few followers set off in search of blooms in Eastern deserts, but the colonial logic was itself congenial with the century's thinking and fired disparate imaginations. Perhaps the first fruit, certainly the most important, was *Five Pastoral Eclogues* anonymously published in 1745 and later attributed (it would appear erroneously) to Thomas Warton.[23] Here the pastoral was transposed only as far as Germany, but with the shepherds set in the midst of the current European war, the poems realistically depict the wasting of the countryside by contemporary struggles for political power. This pastoral retreat cannot survive, but not because it lacks self-sufficiency; it is simply in the way of brutal armies. The author was not a good enough poet to instill his situation with the requisite power and pathos; but if it were the young Warton, it is clear that Spenser's future apologist had already been to the master's school. In intention if not particularly in execution, the *Five Pastoral Eclogues* attributed to Warton recreate the realistic detail and the problematic vulnerability of pastoral before the unseeing eye of society which distinguish Spenserian pastoral. The effort is the more to be wondered at because it was so obvious and so very long in coming.

Another development in the transported pastoral is supplied a generation later by Thomas Chatterton, and, though scarcely to be credited with realism, it continues from the premises discernible in Collins and Warton. Chatterton's three *African Eclogues* of 1770 are deliberate in their obscurity, probably the extreme example, since unconstrained by any need for documentary history, of his penchant for inventing cultures.[24] These eclogues are exercises in brilliant coloration, surging with energy and primal emotions, interwoven with the grand designs of myth. But, of course, there is an intrinsic logic in connecting the primitive with the pastoral: in his way Churchill had done the same thing. There is a further element, also dictated by logic, but one with surprising ideological implications. In each of the *African Eclogues* European culture intrudes as an alien, hostile force. Especially is this the case with the first, "Heccar and Gaira," where Heccar recounts how his wife and children were captured by slave traders and vows an unslakeable vengeance against whites. However hyperbolic and sensational is Chatterton's version of pastoral, however removed from the pleasance of Theocritus and the melancholy calm of Virgil, he has given a poignant contemporary edge to the violated garden. His pastoral is not merely politicized, it reflects the preying of civilization upon the innocent denizens of paradise. A similar impulse underlies the antislavery pastoral of Edward Rushton, published anonymously as *West-Indian Eclogues* in 1787, which depict the mercilessly oppressed exploding in a murderous revenge.

Throughout the eighteenth century the pastoral had been more or less tinged with politics. Country-house poems relied on pastoral conventions to surround the aristocracy with an air of timeless stability. The self-consciously Augustan pastoralists, following the example of Pope, similarly used their simplified conception (or distortion) of Virgil to laud the expanding imperium of Britain. The town eclogue became a standard mode of satire, and, though often the designation meant only that it was a satiric poem in dialogue, the continuing pastoral overtones reminded readers that the town world was the opposite of the innocent freedom of the pastoral ideal. This is particularly the case with the *Political Eclogues*, on parliamentary machinations, that accompanied the *Probationary Odes* and *The Rolliad* in their numerous, expanding editions of the 1780s and 1790s. Churchill's *Prophecy of Famine* is in the end a fundamentally political poem. And yet, all such political offshoots of the pastoral, even in Churchill's stridency, shared a common ethos, a common faith in the stable structures of British culture. What Chatterton and Rushton suggest is the possibility within the mode for a radical critique of those structures.

Its lineaments are clear at least as early as 1788 with the publication of Hugh Mulligan's *Poems chiefly on Slavery and Oppression*, dedicated to William Wilberforce and introduced by four pastoral poems spanning the continents: "The Slave, An American Eclogue"; "The Virgins, An Asiatic Eclogue"; "The Herdsmen, An European Eclogue"; and "The Lovers, An African Eclogue."[25] The first and last of Mulligan's eclogues are virtually formulaic, though neatly mirroring each other. In the first Adala bemoans his slavery in Virginia and recalls the pastoral innocence of Africa; in the last Bura and Zilma escape their captors, watch the slave ship sink in a fearsome storm, and set off for the depths of the continent to find a pastoral happiness without threat from white civilization. The motifs are sharply united in the "Asiatic Eclogue," as two Indian temple virgins flee from the British despoiling their temple and comfort each other in their ruin. The "European Eclogue" is a dialogue set in Ireland, where father and son converse about the extensive wrongs of Europe, of America, and especially of Ireland. Their culminating vision of better times for the Irish, coming one decade before the Wolfe Tone rebellion, is ominous. So, perhaps, is Mulligan's connection between Irish oppression, British imperialism, and the enslavement of Africa. His four eclogues lack the incisive cultural penetration of Blake's sequence in the early 1790s of *America, Europe*, and *The Song of Los*, but a common ground is here being laid. The pastoral has thus become not merely political but revolutionary—a proletarian pastoral ready to do battle in the interests of the simple folk of the world against uniformly oppressive civilizations. By the curious logic of the protean form, we have returned to the implications of Virgil's First *Eclogue*.

And, as might be expected, there was a youthful scholar and budding poet who saw the point, the precociously learned and artistically ambitious Robert Southey of Balliol College, Oxford. In the fall of 1793, depressed by the French Terror, Southey first contemplated establishing a new Arcadia in the forests of America. Before this matured a year later into the scheme for a Pantisocracy in Pennsylvania, the nineteen-year-old Southey wrote his *Botany-Bay Eclogues*.[26] The *English Eclogues*, begun a couple of years later, are arguably the more important publications, certainly the more poetically sophisticated and, in their effect on Wordsworth and Coleridge, the more influential; but the *Botany-Bay Eclogues* have the virtue of their undiluted radicalism and of their shrewd transformation of generic traditions. Simply put, Southey follows Virgil's Meliboeus into exile on the morning after the melancholy shades of evening fall.

All the denizens of the new Arcadia are in exile, transported for life to the Australian penal colony of Botany Bay. Each of them reflects on the past, which means the inequities and injustices of English society. One has been transported for poaching, though it was to avoid starvation; others have been ruined in the army and navy; the sole woman, Elinor, was left in penury by the death of her father and sank into prostitution. In one way or another, all have been bought and sold by the system. Richard, the judge in the contest to decide whether John's army experiences or Samuel's naval service brought the greatest misery, in a nice turn upon the singing contests of the Sixth *Idyll* of Theocritus and the Third *Eclogue* of Virgil, "can give no judgment at all":

> My lads where the Deuce was the wit which God gave ye
> When you sold yourselves first to the army or navy?[27]

And yet all these victims have ironically been liberated from the market economy that ruined them, truly transported into a pastoral sufficiency. Thus Elinor speaks for them all:

> Welcome ye rude climes,
> The realm of Nature! for as yet unknown
> The crimes and comforts of luxurious life,
> Nature benignly gives to all enough,
> Denies to all a superfluity.

All the speakers in the *Botany-Bay Eclogues* express a sense of the strangeness of their surroundings. Like the studied transformations of genre practiced by Southey, the new pastoral takes getting used to, as again Elinor remarks:

> Welcome ye wild plains
> Unbroken by the plough, undelv'd by hand
> Of patient rustic; where for lowing herds,
> And for the music of the bleating flocks,
> Alone is heard the kangaroo's sad note
> Deepening in distance.

Pastoral, Southey suggests, is a state of mind, one foreign to the structures of modern civilization and not to be discovered in a nostalgic veneration for lost traditions. And yet, for all that pastoral as traditionally conceived may be irrecoverable, it is by no means inaccessible. The denizens of Botany Bay have found themselves just east of Eden in a realm both strange and somewhat savage, but with honest labor—georgic notes intrude throughout these poems—with self-respect, and with faith in providence a new paradise can be established. The religious note strongly sounded at the end of the first and last eclogues has a larger purpose than merely to clothe radical politics in respectable vestments. This is the religion of the poor, the outcast, the humble, all those promised first entry into the kingdom of God by Jesus. Whether or not the religious overtones convey a deeper substance, they establish a determined context for Southey in Christian pastoral.

Eighty years of generic experiment following Pope have issued in a pastoral turned inside out artistically and ideologically. The imperium centered in Windsor Forest is discovered, in retrospect, to be inimical to the pastoral. The impoverished proletariat so harshly depicted in realistic antipastoral is credited with the virtues of its dignified simplicity. An imperfect and at times inhospitable Nature is recognized to be sufficient. And the kingdom of God, if sought within, is acknowledged to be realizable on earth as well. Out of the wreckage of British civilization, the world will be turned upside down, almost literally, in Australia, as in Southey's adolescent experiment a Tory, reactionary, Anglican genre is transformed into one celebrating vernacular verse, uncouth folk, communal fellowship, democracy, and Methodist enthusiasm. Whatever the claims of the *Botany-Bay Eclogues* to high art (and they exist, deliberately it would appear, only in Southey's knowing play against conventional expectations), Southey's pastorals constitute a watershed in the history of the genre.[28]

And the flood that follows begins from the same generic and ideological premises, driving them to a serious, revolutionary conclusion:

> Paradise, and groves
> Elysian, Fortunate Fields—like those of old
> Sought in the Atlantic Main—why should they be
> A history only of departed things,
> Or a mere fiction of what never was?
> For the discerning intellect of Man,
> When wedded to this goodly universe
> In love and holy passion, shall find these
> A simple produce of the common day.[29]

III

In 1800, when William Wordsworth expanded to two volumes his experimental collection of two years earlier, he called it *Lyrical Ballads, with Other Poems*; he also extended the modest "Advertisement" of the one-volume edition to a lengthy and now celebrated "Preface." In 1802 that "Preface" was again enlarged to assume the final shape with which we are all familiar. Between 1800 and 1802, however, the poetic contents of the volumes remained the same, only being afforded a more complex and more fully descriptive title: *Lyrical Ballads, with Pastoral and Other Poems*. There is surprisingly little in the "Preface" pertaining to the nature and traditions of the ballad. On the other hand, there is virtually nothing that does not pertain to the pastoral. The "Preface" is, indeed, an extended defense of the new pastoral brought into being by Southey and here sophisticated by Wordsworth and Coleridge. Naturalizing and making contemporary in his poetry what had come to be understood as the most artificial and hidebound of traditional kinds, in his "Preface" Wordsworth audaciously claims that within this regenerated genre lies the basis for all poetry, its golden age, its lost Eden.[30]

Generic revision, because it so directly involves a new mode of apprehension, is the key to every element in the "Preface" tending to a poetic revolution. Underlying them all is the deliberate inversion of generic hierarchies. The last, whether as ballad or as pastoral, has suddenly become first. Rustic life is chosen as being most elemental. Colloquial language is used as being the discourse in which we are most natural and comfortable. The simple—"the meanest flower that blows"—contains an unstrained complexity. The poet, however cultivated and writing for the cultivated, is still "a man speaking to men." The well-known terms by which Wordsworth promulgated his new poetic are all appropriate not only to commentary on the pastoral but to the actual rubrics used for it during the eighteenth century. Were the paragraph where Wordsworth justifies his use of rustic life and language inserted with the necessary shifts of perspective into a contemporary introduction to Theocritus, for instance, it would seem perfectly in place. Hugh Blair's exasperation with the old and call for a new pastoral, quoted as epigraph to this chapter, finds its answer a generation later in Wordsworth's poetry. Yet, when the response came, it was not directly recognized, perhaps because it was so systematic and total as to seem something entirely new. The continual attacks on Wordsworth's "system" and on his studied simplicity by detractors like Jeffrey and Byron never explicitly relate Wordsworth's attempt to a generic reformation, and yet, once again, the terms of reproach and the standard critical vocabulary for treating pastoral—especially that of Theocritus—are the same.[31]

Nearly all the poems of *Lyrical Ballads* that record conversations, even in the 1798 edition, play against the traditions of the eclogue. If the Fifth *Idyll* of Theocritus, with its accretion of irreconcilable perspectives between shepherd and goatherd, establishes a suspended doubleness of viewpoint as an enduring aspect of the eclogue, that element notoriously governs poems that, read without reference to generic considerations, tend to perplex their critics. "Anecdote for Fathers" and "We are Seven" are obvious examples, but the characteristic is present in less dramatic form as well in the companion poems "Expostulation and Reply" and "The Tables Turned." These are all poems of relatively uncomplicated juxtaposition on a single plane of reference. Where Wordsworth's pastoral art begins to attain to something like a Virgilian complexity is in poems where the doubleness shadows forth an entire range of values and the reader is forced, or at least invited, to entertain the mutually exclusive as a whole.

Among the most powerful of these, in part because of their brevity, are the poems associated with the old schoolmaster Matthew: "The Two April Mornings" and "The Fountain, a Conversation." Here Wordsworth transposes the stock situation of old and young shepherd, preserving the helpful kindness of the one and youthful pleasantry of the other. Setting both poems in the retrospect of the narrative voice, Wordsworth places us in the middle of a conversation whose terms were not understood when it took place but which emerge with clarity, even as they preserve their indirection, in the retelling. And yet, there remains a baffling irresolvability in these comprehended perspectives, for innocence cannot be recaptured, as the mature poet is aware, and the lifetime of Matthew's memories, with the suffering that accompanied their indelible pastness, can never be fully communicated or comprehended even if they are now a portion of the poet's own memories. As his daughter Emma has died, so too has Matthew, who, like her, is both perfect and unrealizable in retrospect. The poems embody the doubleness of perspective that is their subject. And they suggest, in a wonderful recasting of generic convention, that the singing of prize songs is the natural effect of the vicissitudes of life and memory. The boy, sitting with his mentor by the fountain, thinks it an easy thing "to match / This water's pleasant tune" (9-10); but Matthew recognizes that the contest is unequal. The spring's flow is perpetual, and only a lack of consciousness permits Nature and innocent young poets to remain carefree: as the birds "Let loose their carols when they please" (39), so the boy claims, "I live and sing my idle songs / Upon these happy plains" (59-60). But for Matthew, to sum life's experiences is to realize a fundamental inadequacy; the numbers never add up: "many love me; but by none / Am I enough beloved" (55-56). And yet the singing contest must go on, even though one is doomed not to win it. So at the end of "The Fountain" Matthew accedes to the request of the youthful poet and turns the incongruous and the irreconcilable into song:

> And, ere we came to Leonard's Rock,
> He sang those witty rhymes
> About the crazy old church clock,
> And the bewildered chimes. (69–72)

One can be so struck by the ease and naturalness of Wordsworth's revitalization of pastoral convention in a poem like "The Fountain" as to ignore how deep it goes in its awareness of the nature of pastoral. Time intrudes upon the carefree; the edens of memory disturb the claims of the present moment to perfection; consciousness of mortality undermines the fecundity of the natural world. The learned schoolmaster imports his knowledge to a realm whose unity will necessarily be fragmented by it. And the cultivated poet studiously disguises convention in a complex act in which he both refreshes tradition and denies the spontaneity of pastoral song. This litany of the double perspective could be prolonged, but even a quick survey suggests how very much in the post-Virgilian line of pastoral Wordsworth is. It also suggests how very traditional (though traditional in the sense of great and intricate art) are some of the attributes of Wordsworth's genius, from multiperspectivism to an elaborate interplay of ironies, credited as original by phenomenological critics. We might instead, though to the same effect, honor him as the greatest of England's pastoral poets.

His simplicity of language, energy of expression, and ease with a colloquial vernacular link Wordsworth with Theocritus. It is a link that he seems at times self-consciously to foster. For instance, the Theocritean tone of voice uttered by "the homely Priest of Ennerdale" at the beginning of "The Brothers, a Pastoral Poem" (as it is called in the table of contents to the 1800 *Lyrical Ballads*) is unmistakeable:

These Tourists, Heaven preserve us! needs must live
A profitable life: some glance along,
Rapid and gay, as if the earth were air,
And they were butterflies to wheel about
Long as their summer lasted; some, as wise,
Upon the forehead of a jutting crag
Sit perched with book and pencil on their knee,
And look and scribble, scribble on and look,
Until a man might travel twelve stout miles,
Or reap an acre of his neighbour's corn. (1–10)[32]

The loquacious Priest, who views his graveyard as a repository of local history for the past 160 years, is in many respects a pastoral poet, his memory stored with tales of shepherds. The Theocritean ease of his celebration of the pastoral world, however, is soon subsumed by the Virgilian pathos of the returned Leonard, who seeks the stable paradise, itself a Theocritean vision, enshrined for many years in his own memory. The complexity of this collision, with Leonard confronting a mythic version of himself in the Priest's account as he had been obsessed with his own mythicized vision during his many years at sea, powerfully elaborates how pastoral ideals are created and why they persist, how imagination plays upon the memory until it renders a perfection into which life can no longer intrude, and thus why exile is so necessarily a theme of pastoral. As in the Matthew poems Wordsworth presents an outer frame that adumbrates the impulses it contains. For his pastoral poem, containing and forcing together the different mythic inventions of its characters, adds another score of years to the eight score in the Priest's memory, enlarging the myth and darkening its import. At the end, as we might expect of a poem so concerned with the nature and components of its own genre, Wordsworth insists on the pastness of his story and the presentness of his writing. Leonard, he notes, could not bear to reveal himself to the Priest, instead writing him a letter from the village to which he retreated: "This done, he went on shipboard, and is now / A Seaman, a grey headed Mariner" (434–435). The enjambment is deliberately wrenching. The garden enclosed from the vicissitudes of time is forced open.

Wordsworthian pastoral is self-conscious about its own making in a way that suggests a profound understanding of the nature and history of the form from Virgil on. Virgil's references to his pastoral art are a distinctive feature of the *Eclogues*, culminating in the Tenth, the poem written for Gallus to sing, where the poet calls attention to his distance and his craft, yet seems at the same time to identify the pastoral with the creation of an ideal art. Spenser, in revoking his identification with Colin Clout, as that figment breaks his pastoral pipes in despair, similarly reminds us that the enclosed garden of art is the true end of pastoral poetry. Likewise, *Lycidas* is structurally doubled, concerned that its art not be tainted by its grief or the insecurities it must confront: "th' uncouth swain" is distanced at the end and, matured by the experience of the poem, is sent forward "to fresh woods and pastures new," which is to say another and enlarged pastoral landscape. The multiple time frames of the Matthew poems and "The Brothers" have the same effect, complexly forcing temporal concerns upon the timeless realm of pastoral and making us aware that art can contain what it allows to threaten it from within.

This process is exemplified in "Michael," and made an explicit theme of "The Ruined Cottage," in both cases by means of a frame that calls attention to itself. In "Michael" Wordsworth achieves this end by virtually repeating as the last line of the poem its second line: this story is old, its principal characters are dead, and nearly everything associated with their suffering and hopes has been eradicated from the landscape. Only the heap of stones that would have been Michael's sheepfold, had it been completed, remain. And yet, if what is to be discovered in this sequestered vale is the unfinished pathos of life, the poem is conclusive, its closure emphasized, and it is made a whole to survive time—

> for the sake
> Of youthful Poets, who among these hills
> Will be my second self when I am gone. (37–39)

The implicit analogy with the sheepfold must be intentional. What is left unfinished and is never passed on in life can be held whole and transmitted in art. The sequestered vale was ironically open to intrusion: as Wordsworth leads us into it, like a local historian, at the beginning of the poem, he gently but firmly closes us in.

It appears as if *The Excursion* were intended in some sense to incorporate and enlarge upon the pastoral elements here discerned in "The Brothers" and "Michael." The churchyard becomes a locus for not one but a host of exemplary lives, forming a community in history. The family idyll of the pastor's household seems a deliberate attempt to recast ancient pastoral values in modern dress.[33] That the pastoral is a frame of mind is repeatedly, if negatively, illustrated by the Solitary's inability to draw sustenance from the literal enclosure of his isolated vale. And in the first book—first too in the chronology of his pastoral writings—Wordsworth both creates a self-reflexive pastoral mode and questions its value.

"The useless fragment of a wooden bowl" (*Ex* I.493) is all that remains to tell of Margaret's secluded existence. A worn-out life is represented by a stock property of a worn-out genre. And in the story that ensues, we are forced to confront literary convention with reality, to recognize that seclusion can bring insupportable isolation, that nature and humanity do not necessarily have the same goals, that dependence on pastoral enclosure makes the inevitable intrusion all the more destructive. Or is it that we are asked to look once again at pastoral not in its sentimentalized eighteenth-century forms but in its pristine state? Margaret's decline is a modern, demythologized version of the affliction of Daphnis recounted in Theocritus's First *Idyll*. An unfathomable, immedicable sorrow is translated into the wholeness of an art that recognizes that there must, indeed, be a harmonious interchange between humanity and nature if the pastoral ideal is even to be conceived as possible. It is in that transformation that the purpose of pastoral lies, and we know it because we recoil from our own fascination with a myth of entropy. So the Pedlar acknowledges:

> It were a wantonness, and would demand
> Severe reproof, if we were men whose hearts
> Could hold vain dalliance with the misery
> Even of the dead; contented thence to draw
> A momentary pleasure, never marked
> By reason, barren of all future good. (I.626–631)

The poet's struggle over nearly two decades to make this exemplary tale testify to a pastoral faith it denies, to convert the antipastoral into the true pastoral, called at last for its being remythologized, subsumed within a Christian consolation. The self-questioning is honest and radical, and that it should occur in Wordsworth's first attempt at a developed pastoral is remarkable. But, however uncomfortable he seems to have been with "The Ruined Cottage," as we judge from its continual revision, or however uncomfortable we may be with what appears to many to be a specious consolation in the final version, the connection of this poem with the great line of European pastoral is clear. It embodies and can never quite resolve the doubleness of vision characteristic of pastoral.[34]

If we think of the place "The Ruined Cottage" was meant to take in *The Recluse*, the three-part philosophical epic of which *The Excursion* was the second and only fully completed part, we suddenly see that this tragic pastoral is placed in exact juxtaposition with what is Wordsworth's most sustained celebration of pastoral pleasance, "Home at Grasmere." Much more than simply a celebration, it is, in a real sense, Wordsworth's version of the synoptic pastoral of Pope a century before, uniting pastoral and georgic elements, reincorporating the whole within a secularized version of the Christian pastoral mythos, and leading inevitably, as in Virgil, Spenser, and Milton, to an epic engagement that would remake the world. It is here that we recognize the full implications of Wordsworth's inversion of generic hierarchies: that it is, indeed, total.

"Home at Grasmere" begins characteristically in retrospect, yet the past thrusts forward, necessitating a shift in line 47 to a present tense that in its rhetoric continually enfolds both past and future. Time and space are coterminous: Grasmere vale enfolds past and future in its presence, just as it contains the wholeness of spatial dimension: "From high to low, from low to high, yet still / Within the bound of this huge concave" (43–44). The boy who at the beginning crosses "the verge of yon steep barrier" (1) inadvertently stumbles upon an Eden that has survived and subsumed the fall:

> What happy fortune were it here to live!
> And, if a thought of dying, if a thought
> Of mortal separation, could intrude
> With paradise before him, here to die! (11-14)

The pastoral ideal immediately calls up its opposition in mortality, but suspends the dialectic, in a rhetorical maneuver that will be repeated in many guises throughout the poem.[35] Wordsworth's evocation of the final lines of *Paradise Lost* is as deliberate here as it is in the first book of *The Prelude* (lines 14 and 640). The poet has returned with his sister Dorothy, "A younger Orphan of a home extinct" (78), their exile ended, to an Eden surpassing the original because of the knowledge that it had been lost and recovered (104-109). The "blended holiness of earth and sky" (144) is everywhere invested with the naturalized equivalents of sacred symbol. The flock of birds, wheeling above the vale in a "progress intricate / Yet unperplexed, as if one spirit swayed / Their indefatigible flight" (214-216) enacts "a perpetual harmony and dance / Magnificent" (202-203) that calls to mind angels and blessed spirits in heaven.[36]

A like remythologizing of the natural underlies the compounded harmonies of the following description, which qualifies as among Wordsworth's most dazzling demonstrations of verbal and rhetorical power:

> —How vast the compass of this theatre,
> Yet nothing to be seen but lovely pomp
> And silent majesty; the birch-tree woods
> Are hung with thousand thousand diamond drops
> Of melted hoar-frost, every tiny knot
> In the bare twigs, each little budding-place
> Cased with its several beads; what myriads these
> Upon one tree, while all the distant grove,
> That rises to the summit of the steep,
> Shows like a mountain built of silver light:
> See yonder the same pageant, and again
> Behold the universal imagery
> Inverted, all its sun-bright features touched
> As with the varnish and the gloss of dreams.
> Dreamlike the blending also of the whole
> Harmonious landscape: all along the shore
> The boundary lost—the line invisible
> That parts the image from reality;
> And the clear hills, as high as they ascend
> Heavenward, so deep piercing the lake below. (560-579)

Sphere upon sphere, every circle circumscribed by another, in the end even the mind's own containment is interpenetrated by what encloses it, and the boundary of separation between the mind and external reality is transcended. Moreover, these embedded spheres, like those which constituted the Ptolemaic universe, are in constant, naturalized motion within a perfect stillness.[37] Again, space and time are coterminous: the hoar-frost is melting in as yet bare "budding-place[s]"; winter is past and spring yet to come, the boundary being lost even here; and the landscape and the recorder of its image are both charged with an infinite potentiality. The ancient contention between art and nature is thus resolved within a new pastoral, as Wordsworth here conceives it; and the new pastoral itself, the "spousal verse / Of this great consummation" (810–811), which is the marriage of mind and nature, will translate that infinite potentiality from art to society, reforming both.

The inversion of generic hierarchies has its obvious ideological consequences for human society. No government intrudes on this paradise or on its denizens. All are free and equal, independent spheres within the large circumference, bound by natural exigencies, by tradition, by bonds of fellowship. The pastoral sufficiency allows no great inequalities of wealth or privilege: it is resolutely democratic. Nor does it foster the creation of a leisure class at the expense of the working poor, which is to say, a division between pastoral and georgic. Even the poet, relieved of obligations through the sufficiency provided by Raisley Calvert, has his duty, as he observes at considerable length (664–702), work demanded by the very environment and reflecting its perfect enclosure—*poesis*, making. A pastoral art will subsume epic pretensions: the boy "With paradise before him" has become a man with the same vision, but now he must realize it in art. The poet is the new *pastor*, who looks back to a lost Eden and leads his readers forward to another.

As with the sonnet and the ode, but more urgently, Wordsworth seems to have read the entire European pastoral tradition in a single glance and to have rendered from its fundamental elements a logic never before understood. This is so even to the suspension of contrary impulses discerned in the great line of pastoral. Wordsworth constantly obtrudes the problematic upon this paradise. The boy's first thought, as he looks upon the vale, is of death; the adult, returned to Grasmere with his sister, emblematizes them in two beautiful swans, whose death he immediately suggests. He acknowledges the harshness of the winter—"Bleak season was it, turbulent and bleak" (152)—immediately after a catalog of the perfections of the Vale. He praises exemplary figures among the inhabitants but allows that drunkenness is sometimes present too. What Kenneth Johnston has remarked as the characteristic rhetorical rhythm of the poem, an abrupt undercutting of what has just been celebrated, is, if construed within generic traditions, not a defect nor an indication of inner conflict but a concerted attempt to enlarge this enclosed garden so as to accommodate, but be ultimately invulnerable to, the world it contrasts with.[38] The author of "The Brothers," "Michael," and "The Ruined Cottage," pastorals of the harsh north, brooding on the tears of things, must find a means to enclose and justify his profound sense of human loss. In the prospectus that concludes the poem Wordsworth places himself in rivalry with Milton and on the same ground—"intent to weigh / The good and evil of our mortal state" (761–762). To create a theodicy within a pastoral mode requires a delicate complexity possessed by few poets. That Wordsworth never finished *The Recluse* perhaps speaks for itself. But the sense of joyful intensity that pervades "Home at Grasmere" is paradoxically dependent on the extent to which Wordsworth, artist as well as thinker, allows a Virgilian darkness, like Grasmere Lake, to mirror the sparkling brilliance of a Theocritean sky.

By 1806, with the final version of "Home at Grasmere" complete and *The Prelude* brought to a period, Wordsworth's decade of intensive preoccupation with the pastoral is finished. The genre had been utterly transformed. The nice irony is that pastoral had been modernized by being purified, returned to its classical roots. The Lake District is scarcely Sicily, but its principal occupation was the rearing of sheep. Its inhabitants were largely "Freemen," which is to say, owners of their own flocks and, where it was not common, land. By and large, women were economically equal. The life was simple, independent, and far removed from the center of political power. In that seclusion there was yet a heritage of at least moderate education for all and a deep sense of local tradition. The names attached through association to familiar features of the landscape are the rudiments of animistic myth, and the events of one generation, Wordsworth continually notes, become the legends of the next. The isolation and relative harshness of this world are a continual test of human endurance, and *otium* is the more prized because labor is so unending. The reality principle underlying eighteenth-century antipastoral is essential to this society, which will never create more than a pastoral sufficiency. And yet, Wordsworth fervently believes, that is exactly enough.[39] Here is the simple stuff of paradise, of human capacity fully realized, of virtue—honor, integrity, and mutual respect—nurtured by necessity, and mortality softened by closeness to the elemental rhythms of the earth. This is a pastoral whose accents are largely present in Theocritus and whose ethos is assuredly that of Virgil. So singular, however, was Wordsworth's transformation of it that it came to be identified as his personal vision. It is that, of course, but it has its roots as deeply in art as in life.

IV

As the expanded *Lyrical Ballads* in 1802 donned a new title, calling attention to the prominence of pastoral in its table of contents, it retained, besides "The Ancient Mariner," only two of the poems by Coleridge from the original edition. One was "The Foster-Mother's Tale," a poem in dialogue derived from *Osorio*, which tells of the rearing of a youth who is taught by nature and education alike to see beyond narrow religious superstitions, who is imprisoned by the Inquisition as a result, but who escapes to the New World and flees deep into the wilderness. If not quite an eclogue, "The Foster-Mother's Tale" is resolute in its claims for nature against society. The same claims are made on less political terms in the other reprinted poem, "The Nightingale, a Conversation Poem." Again, the poem lacks any relation to the ballad tradition so brilliantly recreated in "The Rime of the Ancient Mariner," but it is deeply imprinted with the concepts of pastoral. So, indeed, are all the lyrics now grouped together under the rubric of "conversation poems." They are, in their way, as subtle as the Matthew poems in their calling forth and recasting of the conventions of the genre.[40]

"The Nightingale" is a poem concerned with removing the encrustations of poetic tradition from natural features: the melancholy nightingale of poetic lore is a dead metaphor without relation to living reality. "In Nature there is nothing melancholy" (15), Coleridge asserts; on the contrary, the universal principle of the natural is joy. As a reiterated convention the literary nightingale typifies a stagnant poetic tradition, and particularly a tradition, like the enamelled pastoral of the eighteenth century, that has self-consciously "cultivated" nature:

> . . . youths and maidens most poetical,
> Who lose the deepening twilights of the spring
> In ball-rooms and hot theatres, they still
> Full of meek sympathy must heave their sighs
> O'er Philomela's pity-pleading strains. (35–39)

A true pastoral voice will find its impetus in reality, not convention.

But in defending a realistic base for pastoral, Coleridge links himself less with George Crabbe's satire of the traditional form than with Wordsworth's anathema against artificiality in the "Preface" at the beginning of the volume. Crabbe's antipastoral is simply an inversion of the literary commonplaces that Coleridge would wholly replace with a freshness of vision. And yet, the poem does nothing so superficially radical. Rather than step outside the boundaries of tradition, Coleridge reinvests it with symbolic meaning. As much as Wordsworth, but in his own distinctive way, Coleridge returns to the original focus of the pastoral eclogue, reforging its elementary ties with the *locus amoenus*. The singing contest of "The Nightingale" is between birds. The grounds of the abandoned castle, suggestive of courtly traditions that have died away, have reverted to a lush nature populated by nightingales:

> and far and near,
> In wood and thicket, over the wide grove,
> They answer and provoke each other's song,
> With skirmish and capricious passagings,
> And murmurs musical and swift jug jug,
> And one low piping sound more sweet than all—
> Stirring the air with such a harmony,
> That should you close your eyes, you might almost
> Forget it was not day! (56–64)

This is a revitalized Theocritean pastoral, even down to an unashamed indulgence in the pathetic fallacy, a high noon (though at night) of spontaneous song.

Coleridge calls his poem a conversation in verse, even though he makes us well aware that he does all the talking. Indeed, we are so aware of it that we necessarily shift the locus of the subtitle. "Conversation" is the very subject of the poem, which is an eclogue self-reflexively concerned with its own genre. The nightingales converse. The solitary nightingale whose song prompts Coleridge's poetic musings is, in fact, conversing with him. And that nexus in turn prompts, in line 40, a sudden introduction of fellow human speakers who, like the poet, disdain an artificialized nature: "My Friend, and thou, our Sister! we have learnt / A different lore." It is to them that Coleridge, in the fiction of the poem, tells of the castle grounds resounding with song. And he is not the sole auditor there. A young woman lives near the castle, visiting the grounds like a votary in the evening, accepted among the nightingales as they sing. Because in her presence the birds greet the sudden appearance of the moon "in choral minstrelsy, / As if some sudden gale had swept at once / A hundred airy harps" (80-82), Coleridge is reminded of his infant son, who when the moon appears "Suspends his sobs, and laughs most silently" (103). The infant is too young to talk yet and "Mars all things with his imitative lisp" (93), yet the principle of imitation suggests his maturing into joyful song in answer to the nightingales: "How he would place his hand beside his ear, / His little hand, the small forefinger up, / And bid us listen!" (94-96). At the end of the poem we seem to have wandered very far afield from its beginning, drawn on through the subtle intricacy of Coleridge's associative musings. But the distance only makes us realize the oneness of the discourse. Song draws forth song in conversation. The songs of nature prompt human art: conversation creates community, linking Coleridge with an unknown lady, linking her in turn with his inarticulate son, drawing both into a circle enlarged by the sympathetic receptivity of the Wordsworths. The central presence in the poem, Coleridge's poetic voice, draws nature and humanity into an indissoluble oneness, even as the poem itself comes to a conclusion: "Once more, farewell, / Sweet Nightingale! once more, my friends! farewell" (109-110). This is a benediction, not a parting, an assurance that both the natural and the human in their interchange will continue to "fare well."

Coleridge's version of a pastoral pleasance leaves little room for sorrow: melancholy is banished from nature and flourishes only where human society has artificially removed itself from natural impulses. Even infant nightmares, preverbal imaginings, are dissipated in the presence of nature. This world of joy may be tempered by the pathos of the Wordsworthian poems that accompany it in *Lyrical Ballads*, but it in turn accentuates the fellowship and resort to song in the Matthew poems, or the enduring hold of the pastoral on the imagination in "The Brothers" and "Michael." Darker timbres are deliberately introduced into other of the Coleridge conversation poems, and with them the balancing power of a Christian faith. But the underlying impulse, the exemplification of conversation, natural interchange, is always the same. "The one Life within us and abroad," as Coleridge phrases it in the first of the poems in this mode, "The Eolian Harp" (26), is the essential principle of pastoral, and its consequence is necessarily song.

That Coleridge's generic intentions are concealed in these poems is congruent with their overall design. Like the frost, pastoral operates by a "secret ministry" and is, by its intimate association with the vital imagination, discovered where least expected. Both in "This Lime-Tree Bower My Prison" and "Frost at Midnight" the true nature of pastoral is encountered by giving oneself over to doubts of its efficacy. In the first poem the bower is initially conceived as a prison, barring Coleridge from the affections of his friends and the large natural horizons of their walk. The enclosure evokes reflections whose underlying thread is the limitations of human nature, how doomed it is to decay.

> I have lost
> Beauties and feelings, such as would have been
> Most sweet to my remembrance even when age
> Had dimm'd mine eyes to blindness! They, meanwhile,
> Friends, whom I never more may meet again,
> On springy heath, along the hill-top edge,
> Wander in gladness. . . . (2–8)

The bower in which the poet sits in isolation, though a type of the cool pastoral retreat of tradition, is a precursor of the grave. Yet as the poet imagines his friends' walk through a landscape suggestive of endless possibility, he suddenly recognizes that the elements out of which he has composed this vision are all in his circumscribed vicinity. The bower is charged, a compressed chamber for imaginative play and, even in absence, for shared fellowship. The rook, who crosses the sky at the end of the poem, is a summarizing symbol. An ugly and raucous bird traditionally associated with death, the rook becomes virtually synonymous with the divine, forming the apex of a triangle linking the sequestered poet and his absent friends.

Even more directly does "Frost at Midnight" begin by opposing pastoral expectation with antipastoral reality. The isolated poet, in the deep of the night and the dark of the year, imagines a nature whose inner principles seem inverted. The "populous village" (11) is wholly silent; the only sound is an eerie "owlet's cry" (2); and the only sign of natural activity is the slow accrual of frost.[41] The activity of the frost is uncannily related to an opposite movement, the seemingly unmotivated "flaps and freaks" of a film, the stranger, above the all-but-extinguished fire. In both cases the operation seems to look like but actually be against nature, not dictated by a true vital principle but by a quirk of physical law. And yet, as the poem creates itself out of a complex of associated dialectical gatherings, it links the operations of these elements with those of the imagination and the memory and finally to the "gentle breathings" (45) of Coleridge's infant, whose sound, we realize, has underlaid and energized the entire poem: that systole and diastole is the "eternal language" (60) of God, who, Coleridge promises the sleeping infant, "shall mould / Thy spirit, and by giving make it ask" (63–64). The opposition between pastoral bower and grave has been enlarged to a universal natural rhythm, reuniting man and nature and both with God. The ensuing survey of the seasons again blends opposites with a swift, magical effect, returning us to the "secret ministry of frost" (72), which by the end of the poem seems the manifestation of divine grace, endowing life even from the materials of death.

The brilliance of Coleridge's re-Christianizing of pastoral should not blind us to its effect. Even where the sacred does not intrude, as with "The Nightingale," nature has become a symbol system of almost medieval intensity. As in the manger with its worshipful shepherds at Christ's birth, no element has integrity in itself, only through relation to the being who draws all of them into harmony. The pastoral bower in Coleridge's conversation poems becomes a place almost more of prayer than of song. And the effect is to intellectualize it into a state of mind rather than of nature. By no means is Coleridge alone in this tendency. All the major Romantic poets who approach pastoral either in terms of specific generic conventions or even as a mode tend to internalize it, making it a psychological perspective or conceptual arena. Only Wordsworth, for whom the reality of pastoral fellowship is assured by its social manifestations, also claims for pastoral a locus of natural values.[42]

Throughout this discussion it has perhaps been clear that one of the great pastoral artists of the time has been bypassed. William Blake's experiments with pastoral antedate those of the other Romantic poets, but they are anomalous in two diverse ways. First, *Songs of Innocence and of Experience* began to have a substantial impact on other poets only during the Regency, more than two decades after they were written; the *Book of Thel* and *Milton* were unknown beyond the small circle of Blake's friends and patrons. But also and paradoxically, Blake treats the mode wholly outside the main line of the tradition and in radical disagreement with it. He is perhaps unique in the entire history of European pastoral poetry for his elaborate use of pastoral convention and paradigm to support a determined and intellectually rigorous antipastoral. His is truly a countergenre, whose purpose is to prove the inadequacy of pastoral and to dispel the many cultural illusions reflected, supported, and thus strangely perpetrated by the continuance of pastoral traditions in literature. Blake's is assuredly a Christian pastoral, but it is written on a heretical, Gnostic plane.

And yet, no pastoral art is so meticulous in its representation of a double vision. This is clear enough in the many companion poems, some even bearing the same title, in the two sets of songs, but it is present even in the original separate *Songs of Innocence*, which contained three poems eventually to be shifted to the second set. Without question innocence is to be celebrated: it is, after all, the state of Eden. But its pretensions to sufficiency are specious and therefore dangerous, as any thinking reader discovers. Blake's method with these apparently simple poems has been justly honored, but it is in truth simply a deft employment of the traditional pastoral mode, playing our nostalgia for innocence and ease off against our civilized, mature awarenesses. We realize that the chimney sweeper is being exploited and recognize as well that the system of charity schools regiments children for the self-satisfactions of the rich. We know circular logic when we see it, as in "The Shepherd," and tend to wince at tautologies: "How sweet is the Shepherd's sweet lot." Catechisms are given to children, not to their elders: we may, content with our own self-satisfaction, so place ourselves as to answer questions definitively—"Little Lamb who made thee? . . . Little Lamb I'll tell thee"—but we are repeating by rote what we no longer believe in.

Having imported the city into this child's paradise, we discover that in a sense it was already there. The principal occupation of the children in *Songs of Innocence* is not playing, but—with heavy irony—weeping. There is scarcely a poem that does not literally introduce the tears of things into the garden, even when they seem to have been deliberately excluded: the child in the "Introduction" is so delighted by the poet's pastoral songs that "he wept with joy to hear" them (12). The oxymoron is pointedly exact. Desire is the essential antipastoral element in the world of innocence, portending the universal repetition of the fall. Blake centers attention on this nexus in *The Book of Thel* by naming the girl with the Greek root for desire, then focussing on its continual frustration. The *Songs of Innocence* are less taxonomic but implicitly reveal the same principle. The strongest indication comes in the "Nurse's Song," where the children plead to be allowed to continue playing even as twilight deepens.[43] Eventually, they will be, like the adults, out in the dark, which is the realm of the antipastoral.

> And their sun does never shine.
> And their fields are bleak & bare.
> And their ways are fill'd with thorns.
> It is eternal winter there. (9-12)

"Holy Thursday," as conceived in the *Songs of Experience*, is totally without sacramental meaning: holiness is ironic and alien here. The speaker, like an avatar of Charles Churchill, lives in a world that disallows firm values, necessitating a wholly antithetical reaction without creative perspective or even possibility. It is truly the pastoral turned inside out, emptied of a life principle. The very intensity of our desire for happiness leads us to tear down the walls enclosing the garden, then inexorably to a sense that beyond that putative enclosure no satisfaction will ever be complete or sufficient. The pastoral, on a psychological level, is indeed inseparable from the antipastoral it contains. But these contraries can never be suspended; rather they devour one another—and the being in whose mind they dwell. If, as Blake's subtitle to the *Songs of Innocence and of Experience* asserts, his poems show "the Two Contrary States of the Human Soul," they are the inheritance of original sin, manifestations of a fallen condition. The vision of Innocence is specious; the doubt of Experience is life-denying. The problem lies with pastoral itself, whose double perspective, if thought to compose a whole, is in truth a double bind.

It is probably fair to conclude that this is not the view Blake began with. The pastoral poems of *Poetical Sketches* (1783) and the intensity of joy depicted in "Laughing Song" or "Spring" suggest a mind predisposed to celebrate a world of ease and happiness. But his lengthy artistic tutelage in the mode appears to have taught Blake a much darker lesson, making him concentrate more and more on the inadequacies of the natural and thus convert his sets of *Songs* into a multifaceted rendering of human frustration with its condition.[44] The exploration led him eventually, after the Virgilian model, to his epic undertakings where he would see all of Western culture as deriving from our self-enslavement to the natural. Only after a decade of mythic endeavor was Blake able to integrate pastoral in a benign way into his vision. "There is a place where Contrarieties are equally True / This place is called Beulah," begins Book the Second of *Milton* (30:1–2), virtually defining pastoral in the terms Alpers develops from his exploration of Virgil's *Eclogues*. Beulah is a sleepy realm of pleasance, of happy dreams, of a Wordsworthian marriage of mind and nature. It is a state in which no one can remain forever, and it is dangerous for anyone who tries, as "The Crystal Cabinet" graphically demonstrates. But in its reminders of the original Eden, Beulah is a healthy locus of nostalgic retreat from which we return fresh for the labors of eternity. The true Eden, the state above Beulah, is forward- rather than backward-looking, burning with energy, with intellect, with imagination. It is a Higher Innocence, to use Northrop Frye's popular term, only in the sense that it is committed to creating paradise, but it is knowing rather than ignorant, self-projecting rather than self-enclosed, demanding freedom not protection. In *Milton*, for the one time in his later career, Blake writes poetry of natural description whose beauty is ravishing. But, as with Coleridge, the natural has been converted to transcendent symbol: skylarks become angels; the scent of thyme on the heath is an incense revealing the spiritual presence of the divine. As the pastoral is inadequate to human happiness but by its very insufficiency points to what alone can be adequate, Eden, so the natural becomes spiritualized—which is to say, humanized. The process is, as Blake emphatically understands, apocalyptic.

Yet Blake also recognizes that the conversion of natural detail into conglomerate symbol jeopardizes the integrity of the minute particulars that compose both reality and eternity. His struggle as an artist is to discover a wholly proleptic art, never static or finite, always in forward motion.[45] Like other pastoralists Blake understands the similarity of art to the enclosed garden, but in Blake's inverted view of the relationship, as the garden is a trap whose transcendence is imperative, so an art closed in on itself is self-devouring, mere decoration concealing an inner void. Even when art is reconceived as a city, Golgonooza, it is only a similitude of the ultimate city, Jerusalem, not a substitute for it.[46] All art is a fiction, and its importance lies precisely in that fact: the more we contemplate what does not exist, the more possible and even necessary it becomes to embody it in reality.

The accents are far different and the concepts less sophisticated in Keats's poetry, and yet, strange as it may initially seem, in his representation of art throughout his poetry Keats progressively works through the same problems to come to an understanding very much like Blake's. Art in the early verses is almost always connected with a lush pastoral bower, a cool retreat for imaginative reverie. Much of this is undoubtedly indebted to Leigh Hunt's program for the mythicized rustication of Hampstead Heath, and in the contemporary attacks on both poets there is an implicit assumption that the pastoral genre is no more than a fantasy spun by city dwellers—Cockney poets.[47]

Indeed, Keats's more ambitious early efforts, poems like "I stood tiptoe" or "Sleep and Poetry," are often mainly enumerations of the scenery visible from the bower or attempts to represent its qualities as materials for the artist: they are poems in search of a subject. Though Keats appears to treasure the intensity of such self-enclosure, he is also honestly aware of its inadequacy: revelling in the "realm . . . Of Flora, and old Pan" ("Sleep and Poetry," 101–102), he nonetheless recognizes that the poet's eventual subject must be "the agonies, the strife / Of human hearts" (124–125). He is, however, in no hurry to abandon the garden of his fiction, but rather in his poetry appears to buttress the walls enclosing it.

Much of the poetry that follows, written in 1817 and 1818, could be interpreted as Keats's attempt to summon the courage to forsake the garden of his fantasy.[48] He recognizes, almost from the beginning, that it is incapable of expansion: alone among the major Romantic poets, though in line with general eighteenth-century practice, Keats wishes to eroticize the pastoral. But the bridal bower and that of fantasy seem very much distinct. The despondent Endymion at the beginning of the poem, whose erotic dreams have made him unable to participate in the pleasance and communal celebrations of his pastoral society, is a portrait of a man split between conflicting desires. The pastoral kingdom is in its simplicity inadequate to his imaginative yearnings. And though four-thousand lines later the two are discovered at last to be congruent, the result fails the first test of all thought as Keats represented it, that its truth "be proved upon one's pulses" (*Letters*, I, 279). An art of true dimensions must by its nature escape the bower, however comfortable it appears. The

Apollo of the fragment that constitutes Book III of *Hyperion*, caught between his desire to remain the deity of his own isolated star and the "Knowledge enormous" (III.113) discerned in Mnemosyne's face, is in the process of becoming an epic poet and eschewing pastoral for good. In Keats's later poetry pastoral survives as a mental state, the garden of the mind in the "Ode to Psyche"—whose "branched thoughts new grown with pleasant pain" (52) are suggestive of the doubleness of sophisticated pastoral—or as irony, a trap as insidious as Blake's, in the death-urge of the "Ode to a Nightingale."

It is easier for us than for Keats's contemporaries to see this growing distrust in the lush pastoral of the mind. Byron, for one, reacted with aversion to what he saw as Keats's masquerading of adolescent wish fulfillment in the guise of mature poetry. His dismissal of Keats is in many respects a dismissal of pastoral. The psychological impulse to flee reality is certainly real, dangerously so, and Byron's willingness to honor that truth, in the episode of Juan and Haidee, creates one of the most memorable pastoral representations in Romanticism, whose achievement we will return to in the context of the complex generic design of *Don Juan*. Byron's one direct effort in the genre, however, though admittedly a slight poem, is also a remarkably deft critique of what he took to be a new artificiality pretending to naturalness: the alliance between art and nature is immediately suspect in Bryon's dim view. "The Blues: A Literary Eclogue," as the title suggests, is deliberate in its generic self-reflexiveness, a town eclogue that by implication upholds the values of the true pastoral against their perversion by decadent poets and their coteries.

The lecture room where Byron sets the first eclogue of "The Blues" is a hothouse of literary pretension—"the benches are crammed, like a garden in flower" (I.2)—or worse, a *hortus conclusus* of silk and dried blooms. Nothing in this artificial world is quite real: Inkel and Tracy, the men about town whose conversation dominates the two eclogues, are mainly concerned with eligible and moneyed young women; Scamp, the lecturer (customarily identified as Hazlitt), rides literary fashion as a self-promoter; the dull Botherby (Sotheby) rhapsodizes about imaginative flight in a string of clichés; and the poets who dominate the discussion earn their living through government sinecure. Chief among them and exemplary of this literary society is Wordswords, whose name implies a divorce between substance and rhetoric, between language and nature. He has clearly affected Lady Bluebottle: "the joy of my heart / Is to see Nature's triumph o'er all that is art. / Wild Nature!—Grand Shakespeare!" (II.113-115). Wordsworth's pastoral ideal, it is suggested, is a sham: the pedlars he celebrates are all versions of himself, currying favor among prospective buyers, turning a coat to secure a place. The clever turn to this antipastoral demystification lies in the fact that the sophisticated Inkel and Tracy, who represent Byron and a friend like Thomas Moore, embody the good fellowship, vernacular ease, and naturalness of the old pastoral. Every other element, whether in the lecture room, at Lady

Bluebottle's supper table, or emanating from the Lake District, is artificial, false. Enclosed bowers like these create a lifeless art infecting an entire society.

Byron's knowing play upon pastoral traditions and values alerts us to the extent to which Wordsworth's redefinition of the pastoral had become a standard, especially after his publication of the "Prospectus" to *The Recluse* as preface to *The Excursion* in 1814. Byron, who in the suppressed dedication to *Don Juan* had counselled the Lake Poets to "change your lakes for Ocean" (st. 5), in fact had only to invert Wordsworth's own inversion of hierarchies to set the stage for *The Blues*. But if we look beneath the easy targets of the poem, the underlying skepticism throws into doubt many of the assumptions linked with pastoral in the wake of Wordsworth's achievement. Byron's worldly perspective is as questioning of its sufficiency as is Blake's visionary transcendence. In Byron's view, the artful pretense to simplicity is by no means simple and may well distort reality. The pastoral bower of the mind substitutes fantasy for a true knowledge of the self or the world, then systematically mystifies the fantasy, drawing adherents into the enclosure, creating self-justified coteries. It links pastoral to the creation of a new order, but the marriage of the mind and nature grows stale, betraying the promise and falsifying the community. Whether or not Byron is fair in his antipastoral satire, he raises for the Romantic period the venerable question of how a pastoral vision, even when realistically construed, can accommodate rather than exclude reality. By so determinedly missing the point of Wordsworthian (or Coleridgean) pastoral, he raises the radical suggestion that there is none.

V

The subtlest and most extensive reinterpretation of pastoral in the generation after Wordsworth was undertaken by Shelley. His veneration for the early Wordsworth, and particular for his secular utopianism and simple humanity, is evident as early as the *Alastor* volume of 1815, where he also published his "Translation from the Greek of Moschus," indicative of the deep classical learning underlying all his revisions of pastoral. But even this early, and with increasing urgency later, a flickering presence of irony hovers over Shelleyan pastoral, forcing its engagement with the kinds of reality that in Byron's eyes it could not endure. The romance quest of "Alastor" is not intended to be realistic, but when near the end the Poet comes upon a pastoral paradise invested with symbiotic and mirroring relationships and can respond only by discovering his own mirrored ideal in the reflection of a well, the irony is pointed and complex. The inadequacy of the natural world to satisfy a spiritual hunger of such intensity is offset by our recognition that the narcissistic self-absorption of the Poet is by definition unnatural, portending his inevitable death. Yet, if these contraries are suspended in ambiguity, they are also of more than usual extremity, forcing us to question whether natural enclosure is compatible with that of the mind. Blake answered that question with an almost strident certainty, but Shelley's already mature skepticism leaves the tension unresolved.

What in the context of Romantic versions of pastoral makes Shelley's case of particular interest is that, unlike Wordsworth or Blake, he is not engaged by the presence of nature per se. To him in his philosophical idealism it is a neutral grounding for what does greatly concern him, the mind's internal adjustments, its translation of the objects of perception into mental points of reference. The pastoral enclosure near the end of "Alastor" is somewhat uncharacteristic of his earlier poetry, but a sign of things to come, particularly after his move to Italy, where like many British expatriates he felt the immediacy of its natural beauty and fertility. In "Julian and Maddalo" he celebrated Italy as the "Paradise of exiles" (57), neatly evoking the complex of opposites familiar from Virgil's First *Eclogue*. His fullest elaboration of that complex comes in the first large-scale effort of his own Italian exile, "Rosalind and Helen: A Modern Eclogue."[49] Generally relegated to minor status, "Rosalind and Helen" is perhaps most original for its realistic apprehension of generic possibility.

The poem is set on the shore of Lake Como, where the two friends after long separation are reunited and recount the events of the intervening years. They are necessarily long stories, accounts of utter ruination cataloguing every variation on tyranny and oppression Shelley can think of. The closest equivalent among other self-consciously modern eclogues is Southey's series of *Botany-Bay Eclogues*, but the differences are truly telling. Here the pressure of society is more extreme, the politics are more radical, and the human cost is virtually total. The tales are told within a forest clearing beside a fountain, a Theocritean setting against which the litany of sufferings reverberates ironically through an entire night:

> There is emotion
> In all that dwells at noontide here:
> Then, through the intricate wild wood,
> A maze of life and light and motion
> Is woven. But there is stillness now:
> Gloom, and the trance of Nature now. (126–132)

Pastoral harmony can serve only an ironic function where such human cruelties are ubiquitous. Like the natural impulses of Rosalind and Helen that contravened social statute, the pagan antiqueness of the clearing is remote from reality, not secluded so much as suppressed:

> A roofless temple, like the fane
> Where, ere new creeds could faith obtain,
> Man's early race once knelt beneath
> The overhanging deity. (108–111)

Creeds convert every natural element to their strictures, repressing its freedom. In this clearing, legend has it, a brother and sister had been discovered in incestuous union, and they and their child had been murdered. If so extreme a violation of the pastoral ideal exceeds the requirements of necessity or art, nonetheless it makes Shelley's point unmistakeable. There is no pastoral paradise possible outside the traditional distillations of collective memory, where, rather than compensating us for the corrupting influence of society, it lingers with merely ironic traces to intensify our embitterment.

> The accustomed nightingale still broods
> On her accustomed bough,
> But she is mute; for her false mate
> Has fled and left her desolate. (142-145)

So the pastoral ideal retains its purity, but with a purity so isolated from and indifferent to human concerns, irony intrudes on all its conventions. Both singers are in exile, and their songs are woeful laments for the loss of everything but existence. To the extent that pastoral is a state of mind, neither Rosalind nor Helen can recreate it, though they dwell in its midst. The epilogue does suggest a placid future in their seclusion, with the two women raising their children, a boy and girl, to a happiness they can never regain and a marriage of promise. But nothing intervenes to mitigate the threatening presence of the world beyond the garden. To it Eden is irrelevant.

"Rosalind and Helen" is actually the first of a trio of poems, written with increasing sophistication, in which Shelley tests the efficacy, especially in psychological terms, of pastoral. The second is "Lines Written Among the Euganean Hills," a loco-descriptive poem in which natural harmonies are tied to imaginative creativity and democratic liberty, and yet all of them made poignantly ephemeral, green isles "In the deep wide sea of Misery" (2). That sea is in one sense history, which continually breaks in upon the meditative mind harmonizing its surroundings. The climax of the poem (lines 285-319) is a dazzling representation of a Mediterranean high noon in autumn, suffused with "a soft and purple mist / Like a vaporous amethyst" (287-288), where synaesthesia complements the "Interpenetrated" elements (313) with such nuance as to reveal their internalized character: it is "the mind which feeds this verse / Peopling the lone universe" (319). The "lone universe" filtered through the creative imagination possesses a unified intensity, and yet the mental pastoral is even more vulnerable than that supposed to reside in nature, dependent both on vagaries of history that seem beyond individual control and (as Shelley subtly indicates through repeating the adjective) on "The frail bark of this lone being" (331) whose "antient pilot [is] Pain" (333). The poem ends with the imaginative projection of an island that would endure, where "a windless bower [might] be built" (344) so as to become a "healing Paradise" (355) encircled by love, and humanity would be drawn within the enclosure "And the earth grow young again" (374). It is, in the context of the poem, an impossible dream, yet one that will not fade from consciousness. Once again, Shelley reveals but does not resolve the tension that exists between a pastoral ideal so immediate in its psychological force and so distant in possible realization, between the green islands of the imagination and the process whose currents inexorably carry us past them.[50]

Such a primary tension is less certain to produce that suspension of contraries characteristic of pastoral than an antagonism between them. Recognizing the unlikelihood that the world can ever accommodate our pastoral yearnings increases the pressure on the mind to barricade itself from the hostile forces surrounding it. Yet even if that retreat were possible without destroying the equilibrium it was meant to protect, the problem lies deeper still, for the underlying assumption that rational will or imaginative vision can unify and control all mental activities is itself dubious. If in the internalized pastoral every element depends upon a perfect mental stability for unity, the psychological burden of holding it is almost sufficient in itself to guarantee failure. The concerted pastoral resonances in *Prometheus Unbound*, especially in Act II, focus pointedly but optimistically on these difficulties and will be reintroduced in the context of a later chapter. But they are also essential to a poem that, like "Lines Written Among the Euganean Hills," was written simultaneously with the lyrical drama and is oblique but nonetheless pointed in its incorporation of pastoral elements, even to its title: "Julian and Maddalo; A Conversation." Those elements are throughout the poem subjected to the forceful realism governing it, but not to the end of antipastoral satire so much as to an understanding of the extent that pastoral assumptions can withstand, or mitigate, the harsh realities of the world. The central context is immediately established in the epigraph, which is drawn from Virgil's Tenth *Eclogue*. "Julian and Maddalo" is an eclogue of serious and melancholy import, powerful in its representation of conflicting perspectives and deliberately inconclusive in their resolution, and focused directly on an implicit question raised by the Tenth *Eclogue*: What can a sympathetic poet offer to compensate for the grief of another's misfortune in love? The epigraph, a lapidary translation of lines 29–30 of Virgil's last eclogue, accentuates his intended irony:

> The meadows with fresh streams, the bees with thyme,
> The goats with the green leaves of budding spring,
> Are saturated not—nor Love with tears.

Love seems most truly natural when it is most unhappy.

The poem begins on another of Shelley's islands, but a realistically depicted one, the Lido of Venice: "a bare strand / Of hillocks, heaped from ever-shifting sand, / Matted with thistles and amphibious weeds" (3–5). There is nothing like this to be found in Virgil; it is an antipastoral setting more barren than Churchill's. But the setting actually enforces the crucial importance of psychological perspective in the poem. The fellow-ship of the protagonists harmonizes with the surroundings to create "aërial merriment" and "swift thought, / Winging itself with laughter" that "flew from brain to brain" (27–30). This is a realistic transposition of ancient pastoral song keyed to a mental perspective. As Julian remarks,

> I love all waste
> And solitary places; where we taste
> The pleasure of believing what we see
> Is boundless, as we wish our souls to be:
> And such was this wide ocean, and this shore
> More barren than its billows. (14–19)

Not only is the setting antipastoral, but the psychological impulses it fosters run directly counter to those traditionally associated with pastoral: we wish not to be enclosed but "boundless." Yet of course the garden is enclosed for a good reason, as Shelley had already acknowledged in "Rosalind and Helen." If the eschatological possibilities of Christian pastoral cannot now be fulfilled, making the world one garden (or one city, as in Blake), can a mental paradise be sustained without walls? The intrusions of society are pernicious enough, but even worse are the yearnings of the mind and spirit for love and community. They demand a satisfaction often beyond the means of the world to provide.

The center of this eclogue is a spontaneous song uttered, in indifference to his audience, by a maniac. He is enclosed in an asylum, "A windowless, deformed, and dreary pile" (101), an antipastoral setting if ever there were one, though isolated on its own island. He is even more profoundly enclosed within his own unsettled mind. His love complaint is longer and more clinically detailed than is customary in pastoral, but its sorrows are traditional in the literature. He is a test case for pastoral as for philosophy. Having heard the long lament, Julian reports of the friends, whose dispute over free will and determinism had prompted the visit to the asylum, "our argument was quite forgot" (520). But if philosophical questions are thus suspended before the prospect of such misery, what are the implications for literary ones, specifically for pastoral?

Partly at least, they are associated in this poem with the nature and necessity, and perhaps as well the inadequacy, of boundaries. Julian's creative idealism is fostered by the "boundless," but Maddalo recalls how, after their then sane subject had been abandoned by his lover, "he wandered then / About yon lonely isles of desart sand / Till he grew wild" (247–249). Once placed in the institution, "Some fancy took him and he would not bear / Removal" (251–252). The asylum at least has known limits to balance the uncertainties of human existence. Outside such artificially imposed limits all mental stability is precarious. The structures of art likewise translate process into codified, enclosed meaning: poets "learn in suffering what they teach in song" (546). The tranquil ease of pastoral is an imposed order, one that constantly reenacts, is

threatened by, and attempts to contain suffering, whether that of unsatis-
fied love expressed in the meditated vengeance of Simaetha in Theocritus's Second *Idyll* and in the despondency of Corydon over the fickle
Alexis in Virgil's Second *Eclogue*, or that caused by a solitary despair, as
in the First *Idyll* of Theocritus or in Wordsworth's story of Margaret. The
Maniac's tale combines both kinds of suffering, and, though Julian
contemplates the possibility of remaining in Venice and trying to cure his
madness, there is little that others can do for him. Daphnis dies despite
the best efforts of Priapus, Pan, and Aphrodite to turn him back to life.
Margaret's fate is the same, even though the Pedlar returns annually with
his sympathetic friendship. De Quincey's famous retort that he should
have done something other than talk misses the point. Pastoral exists on
its sympathy and its recognition that life comes out of death. The singing
contest of Thyrsis and the goatherd in the First *Idyll* subsumes the
affliction of Daphnis, transforming it into the finished perfection of art.
Wordsworth creates a like effect in the conversation of the Pedlar (or
Wanderer) and Poet in "The Ruined Cottage." Julian and Maddalo can
do nothing to cure the Maniac of his self-induced and obsessive affliction
(though Maddalo does provide for the necessities of life), but they can
respond with sympathy to his plight and to the inscrutable sorrows of the
human condition. The mind's hell is no foundation for paradise, but it
can be bounded by human fellowship and by the continuities of life.
Julian's remark that he did not remain in Venice to help the Maniac
because he was not "an unconnected man" (547) is by no means an
offhand defence. We love what is boundless but honor what binds us. The
pleasures of "sweet Venice" (549) are such as afford "little to recall /
Regrets for the green country" (557–558). Chief among them for an urban
pastoral is the fellowship of two friends—obviously in this poem two
disguised but great poets—whose singing contest is very real but whose
rivalry is contained by their capacity for sympathy.

Unlike Rosalind and Helen these friends do not occupy a paradisal
retreat. But unlike them too, they bear what there is of paradise—community, affection, art—within them. As "Julian and Maddalo" plays obliquely and realistically against the pastoral tradition, it also underscores
the delicate nature of a pastoral sufficiency. The Maniac wants paradise
on his own self-absorbed terms: Julian and Maddalo, inhabiting a poem
that is a deliberate fragment, know how to live within the range of the
possible and unpredictable. And that, to put it simply, is what Virgil
sings in the voice of his friend Gallus. Nothing can compensate for the
loss of Lycoris—love conquers all, even if we prove it ironically—but the
positive values of life continue, and we make as much from them as an
imperfect world allows. So, at the end of his despondent lament in the
Second *Eclogue*, Corydon wryly indicts himself for the uselessness of his
complaint and forces himself back to his pastoral labors. They are useful
and in their limited, bounded way pleasant, and they are sufficient to
satisfy the necessities, if not to provide for all the wish fulfillments, of

life: "invenies alium . . . Alexim." You will find another Alexis—though never the same.

To concentrate so on the limits of the pastoral world is not to deny that within those limits it is still capable of figuring forth the stuff of paradise, but it is to warn us that it may be, as it is for the Maniac, in Byron's fine phrase, "The unreach'd Paradise of our despair" (*Childe Harold's Pilgrimage*, IV.1096). Or, to place it within the Virgilian context, if the paradise represented in the messianic vision of *Eclogue IV*, the apotheosis of Daphnis in *Eclogue V*, and in Silenus' song of creation in *Eclogue VI* is the yearning desire to transform the earth at the center of pastoral, it is bounded by the reality of Meliboeus's exile in the First *Eclogue*, by Corydon's despondency in *Eclogue II* and Gallus's in *Eclogue X*. In the eschatological thrust of act II of *Prometheus Unbound*, Shelley deliberately plays against the aspirations of *Eclogues IV* and *VI*—the yearnings of pastoral are a key to human liberation—but even there he accentuates the mental conditions necessary for the creation of paradise. And to underscore the nature of pastoral perspective, in the 1820 collection of his poems he directly follows his optimistic lyrical drama with a pastoral fable in which the polarities of pastoral and antipastoral are superimposed upon the same garden—"The Sensitive Plant."[51] Nature is here the raw material for human fantasies of paradise or its inversion, both imagined as extremes, at whose center is a type of pure sensibility wholly dependent on the climate in which it exists. The Sensitive Plant is very much in the line of the Maniac, who describes himself "as a nerve o'er which do creep / The else unfelt oppressions of this earth" (449–450), flourishing in the Eden superintended by the beneficent Lady, destroyed by the storms and grotesque freaks of nature that arise when she disappears. The antipastoral eruption is Manichaean in its apocalyptic intensity:

> When winter had gone and spring came back
> The Sensitive-plant was a leafless wreck;
> But the mandrakes and toadstcols and docks and darnels
> Rose like the dead from their ruined charnels. (III.114–117)

The "Conclusion" of this poem has been variously seen as a model of Shelley's urbane style, an example of his Platonism, and, conversely, as indicative of an extreme skepticism; but from the standpoint of genre, it is most directly a self-reflexive commentary on how dependent are pastoral and antipastoral on our obsession with mutability. The ideal never changes, but it must be filtered through imperfect human perspectives, "our organs—which endure / No light—being themselves obscure" (23–24). Though "The Sensitive Plant" appears to reflect Shelley's own cravings for perfection and his mirror-like preoccupation with the nature of evil, it is also, in its collapsing of antipodes, a cautionary parable about the importance and yet problematic nature of pastoral self-knowledge. This garden is like the Maniac's too finely tuned mind: frustrated ideals can relapse into a psychological antipastoral. The significance of Shelley's urbanity in the "Conclusion" is that it implicitly recognizes both the dangers of an unreflective indulgence in the pathetic fallacy, of imputing to nature human desires and fears, and our responsibility for maintaining a skeptical equilibrium amid ultimate uncertainties. The result is at once to honor the eternity of our imaginative ideals and to temper our compulsion for their gratification.

To turn from the realistic pastoral explorations of Shelley's first year in Italy to the apocalyptic fable of "The Sensitive Plant" is necessarily to become aware of how broad and how learned was his engagement with the pastoral. To view him a year after the latter poem reverting to pastoral in *Adonais* may make one question how consistent he was. Here the learning is worthy of a scholar, and the synoptic recasting of the conventions of the traditional pastoral elegy is a feat of true artistry; but at the same time for Shelley to apotheosize Keats and then even himself is to force doubts as to how truly tempered are the poet's cravings for the ideal.[52] It could be argued that the particular traditions associated with the pastoral elegy wholly determine the thrust of the poem, but that would be to deny Shelley's creative independence and personal involvement in its issues. It would also unnecessarily beg the question of consistency. The synoptic learning underlying this poem is all charged with the same purpose, to secularize the traditional means of apotheosis, whether classical or Christian, to recognize in these impulses the highest ends of art, and to represent the entire experience as an internalized, psychological rendering of death into renewed life. If Shelley casts himself into the infinite at the end of the poem—"borne darkly, fearfully afar" (492)—he does so through the paradox of art, the enclosed garden of the human imagination, constantly vital in its creative possibilities though dependent on the always vulnerable mind of the individual artist. Though death and life meet and virtually exchange places in *Adonais*, achieving what would appear the ultimate suspension of contraries, the allusiveness of the poem testifies not to its uniqueness but rather to its indebtedness: the same process is at work in the apotheosis of Daphnis in the First *Idyll* of Theocritus and in Virgil's own recasting of it in the Fifth *Eclogue*.[53] At the center of the mind's enclosed garden, as at the core of the pastoral tradition, is the "burning fountain" (339) of life whose flow is never-ending. Its manifestations are continually obscured in our everyday existence but are ubiquitous in art. It is not coincidence that Shelley was speaking of the continuities of classical pastoral when in *A Defence of Poetry* he referred to them "as episodes to that great poem, which all poets, like the co-operating thoughts of one great mind, have built up since the beginning of the world" (p. 493). As with Byron and Shelley in "Julian and Maddalo," so with Keats and Shelley in *Adonais*, the singing contest is ultimately one act of humane fellowship in sympathy with and linking life and art, an act that claims victory over every aspect of the antipastoral as it is embodied in death. *Adonais* is Shelley's most detailed and profound reflection on the nature and ultimate values of the pastoral genre, a poem of almost abstracted generic purity.

It is scarcely necessary to lecture the author of "Lines Written Among the Euganean Hills" that we do not live in art, even if we refine our ideals within its enclosure. The elaborate formality of *Adonais* is perfectly congruous with the self-reflexive purity of its aims, but it is uncharacteristic of Shelley's usual pastoral mode, which is more oblique and delicate in expression. That timbre returns in his last months, in the poems to Jane Williams, lyrics in which the internalized pastoral—pastoral as a mental state—has become so natural a context that it is now implicit. But much appears to have been given up in the intervening years. The land has been sold off to pay a debt to experience, and the pastoral has been reduced to a spot of time; yet it is significantly not of this time, but distanced, celebrated in anticipation or retrospect.[54] Similarly, pastoral sufficiency has been translated into knowing that such moments, though necessarily isolated and unpredictable, are possible. The lyrics subtly interweave the melancholy of Virgilian pastoral with Faust's pact in Goethe (which Shelley was translating at the time) to give himself over to Mephistopheles if he should find such happiness as to say to the moment: "Verweile doch, du bist so schön"—"Yet remain, you are so beautiful." The poems are suffused with a tranquillity and ease, made all the more poignant because so removed from the normal state of life. The richest of them—"To Jane. The Recollection"—at its end returns us from the ephemeral garden to the antipastoral state of mind that governs reality.

> Though thou art ever fair and kind
> And forests ever green,
> Less oft is peace in S[helley's] mind
> Than calm in water seen. (85–88)

Though the green world remains, process inevitably intrudes upon the timeless bower of psychic peace.

The mental bower is all the more to be treasured for its being temporary. Shelley depicts it as containing and harmonizing contrary elements, folding in through repetition and echo upon itself. The techniques are similar to those employed in the pastoral retreat of "Alastor," though in this case, we realize, the poet looks for nothing beyond it. These are the central stanzas, replete with the conventions of pastoral but made fresh in their simple integrity.

> How calm it was! the silence there
> By such a chain was bound
> That even the busy woodpecker
> Made stiller with her sound
> The inviolable quietness;
> The breath of peace we drew
> With its soft motion made not less
> The calm that round us grew.—

There seemed from the remotest seat
    Of the white mountain-waste,
To the soft flower beneath our feet
    A magic circle traced,
A spirit interfused around
    A thrilling silent life,
To momentary peace it bound
    Our mortal nature's strife;—
And still I felt the centre of
    The magic circle there
Was one fair form that filled with love
    The lifeless atmosphere.

We paused beside the pools that lie
    Under the forest bough—
Each seemed as 'twere, a little sky
    Gulphed in a world below;
A firmament of purple light
    Which in the dark earth lay
More boundless than the depth of night
    And purer than the day,
In which the lovely forests grew
    As in the upper air,
More perfect, both in shape and hue,
    Than any spreading there;
There lay the glade, the neighboring lawn,
    And through the dark green wood
The white sun twinkling like the dawn
    Out of a speckled cloud. (33–68)

As masterful as Shelley is in accumulating natural detail here, it is all centered conceptually in the "magic circle" of time past, which endures only in the memory and in the pastoral art to which it has been translated: "The epitaph of glory fled," he calls it in the opening envoy (6).

Nature means nothing in itself in these poems. It assumes the character imprinted on it by the unifying imagination. And though each poem in its way asserts the echo of Faust in "To Jane. The Invitation"—"To-day is for itself enough" (40)—the magic circle is to be kept intact, reified, only through art. The circle is magical in its embodiment of opposite psychological states—a tenderness touched with ecstasy, a joy matched to a world-weariness very close to despair—and in their suspension within the texture of the poem. Yet, the triumph of art over nature is paradoxical, neither subsuming it within distanced artifice—Keats's "Cold Pastoral"—nor making unrealistic claims for the perfection of the mental bower. The simple capacity of art is to extend the pastoral moment seemingly to infinity, and through that process, though it cannot in any true sense alter "our mortal nature's strife," it mirrors an eternity that can be known no other way. The musical instrument celebrated in "With a Guitar. To Jane" is a personification of this pastoral art, and its capacities are precisely those of the circumscribed and internalized pastoral of the moment:

> For it had learnt all harmonies
> Of the plains and of the skies,
> Of the forests and the mountains,
> And the many-voiced fountains.
> The clearest echoes of the hills,
> The softest notes of falling rills,
> The melodies of birds and bees,
> The murmuring of summer seas,
> And pattering rain and breathing dew
> And airs of evening:—and it knew
> That seldom heard mysterious sound,
> Which, driven on its diurnal round
> As it floats through boundless day
> Our world enkindles on its way—
> All this it knows, but will not tell
> To those who cannot question well
> The spirit that inhabits it. (65–81)

The resonating music of the spheres in all its protective circularity is the true end of pastoral poetry.

Thus, paradoxically, a pastoral that retreats to the mind, dislocating itself from the garden as a place and even reducing the temporal process to an instant, invokes eternity, contains paradise in its essence. It might be argued that this is a moral retreat, accompanied by a quietism of dangerous implications, especially for a writer noted as a radical political visionary. Yet, on the other hand, Shelley's realistic reduction of pastoral to its psychic essence in these poems does not, like Byron's, issue in an antipastoral demystification, but instead confirms and extends the remarkably resilient hold of the pastoral ideal on the human imagination. The process of distillation begun in "Alastor" culminates in an *elixir vitae* that sustains life in the midst of its vicissitudes. It is a potent concentrate, as Virgil acknowledged by suddenly translating his pastoral pleasance into the messianic vision of the Fourth *Eclogue*. Shelley, having reduced the pastoral to a quintessence that honors the capacity of the human imagination to transfigure nature, discovers once more on earth the paradise never fulfilled but forever promised.

Yet to hardened and realistic thought that carefree pastoral, however to be desired, is not at all easy: the induction to Shelley's last poem, the fragment of "The Triumph of Life," allows us our alternative either to retreat to the intellectual passivity of a conventional pastoral harmony or to see through it to an inversion that is not so much an antipastoral as a mental liberation from all its sentimental associations. To the wakeful poet who projects himself among the stars, the green world may seem barely adequate. And yet, it contains the basic imagery and the enveloping ideology for a truly humane freedom. The pastoral of the mind at last enforces an inversion of conventional expectation that can be achieved only through assimilating the traditions and the ultimate anticipations of pastoral. It is perfectly what it is, but at the same time it is not sufficient, for it at once implies what it is not and promises what it could be. As always, the protean form demands its translation: "Sicelides Musae, paulo maiora canamus."

CHAPTER SIX

The Romance

The epithet *romantic* is always understood to deny sound reason to whatever it is fixed upon. . . . One of the most obvious distinctions of the works of romance is, an utter violation of all the relations between ends and means.

> John Foster, "On the Application of the Epithet Romantic,"
> *Essays in a Series of Letters to a Friend* (1805), I, 241, 273

Grecian is Mathematic Form   Gothic is Living Form   Mathematic Form is Eternal in the Reasoning Memory. Living Form is Eternal Existence.

> William Blake, "On Virgil"

> O golden-tongued Romance, with serene lute!
>   Fair plumed syren, queen of far-away!
>   Leave melodizing on this wintry day,
> Shut up thine olden pages, and be mute.
> Adieu! for, once again, the fierce dispute
>   Betwixt damnation and impassion'd clay
> Must I burn through.

> Keats, "On Sitting Down to Read *King Lear* Once Again"

I

THOSE WE CALL the British Romantics would be surprised by, and perhaps quite uncomfortable with, our common distortion of their contemporary sense of Romanticism. We can trace a British comprehension of the distinction between classical and romantic temperaments and cultures directly to August Wilhelm Schlegel's *Course of Lectures on Dramatic Art and Literature*, which after its translation into English in 1815 became at once influential and eventually a standard of definition for the age.[1] Yet, those who were subsequently most fixated on this distinction—especially in the early part of this century when the likes of Babbitt, Hulme, and T. S. Eliot used it to ground a conscious revolt against their own previous century—freely altered the historical demarcations of German thought, using Romanticism in the by then commonly accepted sense. Schlegel, however, was not lecturing on his own age, except insofar as it inherited the values of Western and Christian culture. For him the advent of Romanticism coincided with the spread of a Judeo-Christian culture, which for the seamless harmony of Greek and Roman ideals had rent a chasm separating the reality of this world from the imagined perfections of the next. To the extent that a universal irony attends his definition of the Romantic, it is an irony implicating all of modern

Western culture: its greatest literary exemplar is Shakespeare. As Keats bids farewell to the "syren" of Romance, he is, in Schlegel's terms, simply transferring his allegiance to the "fierce dispute" at the center of the Romantic. The two opposites, as we should expect with Keats, are intimately associated, and yet before we commit ourselves to the metonymy involved here, we should pause and consider how it was that this age— well before Schlegel's distinction gained currency—became so richly associated with a genre. The etymological root of Romanticism, it is easy to forget, is romance.

The seeds of this stock were sown for a full half-century before it issued in full bloom. As we conceive of the characteristic interests of Renaissance literature as stemming from the revival of Roman and especially Greek classics, so Romanticism was deeply influenced, and in a very real sense instigated, by one of the great scholarly achievements of the Enlightenment, the recovery of medieval literature as embodied in its romances. The ballad revival was actually a side event in the larger cultural resuscitation. Thomas Percy introduced the third volume of his *Reliques of Ancient English Poetry* (1765) with a seminal "Essay on the Ancient Metrical Romances" and in his researches collected, along with the ballads, twenty-six metrical romances that he hoped to publish separately.[2] The *Reliques*, coming on the heels of Thomas Warton's *Observations on the Fairy Queen* (1754; revised 1762) and Richard Hurd's *Letters on Chivalry and Romance* (1762), indelibly altered Britain's sense of its literary heritage. What modern criticism has dubbed "the Hurd instinct" was in its original dynamic a force of great power, and its resilience, which accounts for its sudden reappearance in unlikely manifestations well into the twentieth century, is underpinned by its deeply nationalistic character. The revival of romance led inevitably to its rewriting, in the subterfuges of Macpherson and Chatterton, and eventually to its recreation, in the decades upon which the century turned, as a central genre of British poetry. Indeed, it might be argued that the term by which we retrospectively define the period simply honors the primacy of romance in British poetry during this epoch.

It is perhaps difficult to transport ourselves into the thick of this excitement or to rekindle the heat that attended it. But the fact that Thomas Warton devotes two of the three volumes of his massive *History of English Poetry* to pre-Renaissance literature suggests the intensity of interest, as does the breathtaking acrimony of the prince of pedants, Joseph Ritson, in his attacks on Warton's scholarly sins.[3] The scholarship took place in something of a vacuum, since the independent verification that might be supplied with a text came relatively late. Disputes were rife from the mid-1760s on, but it was only in the first decade of the new century that the actual romances were republished—and then in a deluge. Ritson's *Ancient Engleish Metrical Romanceës* (3 volumes, 1802) were the culmination of his long battle for textual purity, printing twelve important romances in complete form. Walter Scott's *Minstrelsy of the*

Scottish Border (1801–1803) mainly concerned itself with ballads, but the planned fourth volume, his edition of the thirteenth-century romance *Sir Tristram*, was published separately in 1804. The attention it received convinced Scotland's finest antiquarian scholar to move into more creative paths, with major consequences for the history of European literature. In 1805 George Ellis, through a combination of extract and paraphrase, represented a further twenty romances in his *Specimens of Early English Metrical Romances* (again in three volumes), reinstating them within, and extending, the traditional Renaissance categories: Arthurian, Saxon, Anglo-Norman, on Charlemagne (the "Matter of France"), Oriental, and Miscellaneous. The decade ended with publication of the last of these three-volume sets, *Metrical Romances* edited by Scott's protégé Henry Weber (1810), in which ten poems were printed in complete texts. These eight years, it is safe to say, are without peer in the history of British literary scholarship; medieval romances may now figure in a relatively minor role, but especially for this time, their initial publication wholly altered the conception of British literature.[4]

But to concentrate on the recovery of Middle-English texts is to tell only half the tale. Each of these collections was prefaced by lengthy discourses on the nature of romance and of medieval culture—Ellis, for instance, printed some sixty pages of paraphrase of Geoffrey of Monmouth in his huge introduction—and the annotations were similarly prodigious. Moreover, the collections and translations were extensively reviewed by the critical journals in articles that are themselves often exercises in scholarly resuscitation.[5] General interest in romance was such that Henry John Todd could translate it into his variorum edition of Spenser (7 volumes, 1805), devoting most of volume II to the major commentaries on *The Faerie Queene* written by eighteenth-century critics; Warton's two-volume *Observations* was, significantly, republished in 1807. It is exactly at this point, half a century after the initial efforts of Warton and Hurd to resurrect Spenser, that classic status in British literature was finally accorded him. And the rest of Europe and even Asia was similarly enveloped. Both William Stewart Rose and Robert Southey published translations of *Amadis of Gaul* in 1803. Rose turned next to *Partenopex of Blois* (1807) and then to Italian romance: Casti's modern *Animal: Parlanti* appeared in 1819, then translations of both *Orlando Furioso* and *Orlando Innamorato* in 1823. It is important to recognize that Southey was almost as deeply implicated in romance antiquarianism as Scott. Partly because Bristol was his birthplace, Wales and the west of England figured large in his imagination: *Madoc* (whose hero was a twelfth-century Welsh prince), though not published until 1805, was Southey's first romance, basically finished in 1799. And in 1800, in collaboration with Joseph Cottle, he reedited the works of Chatterton to benefit the poet's surviving sister. The early years of the new century found Southey actively encouraging an edition of the Welsh national epic, the *Mabinogion,* and by 1807 he had laid the plans for an edition of the most long-lasting of Welsh-Cornish romances, Malory's *Morte Arthur*, which came into print a full decade later under the title *The Byrth, Lyf and Actes of Kyng Arthur*. Between the publication of *Madoc* in 1805 and *The Curse of Kehama* in 1810, this one-man literary industry, among numerous other projects, also printed an edition of *Palmerin of England* in 1807 and *The Chronicle of The Cid* in 1808. Still another vein of romance was opened in this decade—that of the *Eddas*—with William Herbert's two-volume translation of *Select Icelandic Poetry* in 1804. Ten years later Henry Weber was joined by his fellow Scottish antiquarian, Robert Jamieson, in the formidable endeavor to make available the major Teutonic romance sources, including the *Niebelungenlied* in *Illustrations of Northern Antiquities* (1814). Two years earlier Weber had edited another three-volume set, *Tales of the East: comprising the most popular Romances of Oriental Origin; and the Best Imitations by European Authors*, which brought the *Arabian Nights*, greatly expanded, back into the national consciousness.

One other set of three volumes suggests the tack that any such craze must take: *Tales of Yore* (1810), translated by the learned Germanophile and friend of Southey, William Taylor of Norwich, is an eclectic collection drawn from numerous European and Asiatic sources, ending with the first (and last) ancient Mexican romance, "Koxkox and Kikequetzel," a skillful parody of romance antiquarianism he ascribed to Wieland. The existence of such a parody suggests how very quickly the proliferation of romance resulted in the questioning of its excesses and its modern application. The tendency in the next few years would result in the translation of a number of burlesque romances, including Byron's rendering from the *Morgante Maggiore* of Pulci. That work was, however, merely an appendage to Byron's wholesale self-saturation in the style of burlesque romance, first in *Beppo* and subsequently in *Don Juan*, which he came to through reading the parody authored by John Hookham Frere, whose original title of 1817 in this context deserves full quotation: *Prospectus and Specimen of an intended National Work, by William and Robert Whistlecraft, of Stowmarket in Suffolk, harness and collar makers, intended to comprise the most interesting particulars relating to King Arthur and his Round Table*. That nothing in the title represented the true preoccupation of these ottava rima stanzas is beside the point. What matters most is Frere's credentials for writing them—extensive translations from *Le Cid* that so earned Southey's admiration that he printed them as an appendix to his edition.[6] Such burleques had an obvious literary progenitor in Cervantes: the initial burst of enthusiasm for romance explodes with innocent enthusiasm, but that spirit could not easily survive the world it was born to. Thus with Napoleon's invasion of Spain in 1807 and the introduction of British armies onto the Peninsula, the storied land of romance was enveloped in modern reality. So, it need hardly be added, were its readers.

If the signal difference between epic and romance is that the one embellishes upon historical truth and the other upon the improbable, the clear problem for the contemporary poet, coming to maturity in the midst of a craze at once scholarly and popular, was how to relate the improbable and probable.[7] More particularly, does the poet follow the antiquarian into the recesses of a past that comforts by its distance, its indifference, and its room for invention, thus evading modern history and a modern consciousness? Or does that past become a screen through which the poet frames and in a curious sense actually distances the modern so as to gain perspective on it? Unquestionably, to invoke Richard Hurd's memorable phrase, "a world of fine fabling" had been recovered, but what end it would serve became an essential issue. The number of extended metrical romances written in this relatively brief period of British literature runs well above a hundred, most of them intentionally escapist and exotic. And yet, it should be obvious that even fairy tales have literary integrity as well as cultural roots, and writings that intensely deny present reality are as much a commentary on it as those which allegorize or otherwise veil it. The Scottish fairy romances, like William Tennant's *Anster Fair* (1812) or the interpolated tales of James Hogg's *The Queen's Wake* (1813), tell us nothing about Luddite rebellions or the fanaticism of Scottish anti-Jacobinism, but they tap folk traditions going back centuries, translating them into ingenious plots and technically accomplished verse. The frank neo-Hellenism of Peacock's *Rhododaphne* (1818) seems wholly escapist until the reader contemplates the equal frankness of its sexuality. The same holds true for Hunt's tapestried *Story of Rimini* (1816).[8] There is likewise an astonishing wealth of talent (though perhaps of a largely superficial kind) to be discovered by modern antiquaries among the numerous neomedieval romances and, especially, epics prompted by the revival. Generally, customary piety and patriotism substitute for intellectual depth, but the energy, vitality, and descriptive overlay associated in the contemporary mind with the very nature of romance are abundantly present. Scott and Southey are the exemplary poets of a conventional romance in this period, and, though Francis Jeffrey might complain that the enduring feature of the latter was "childishness," he had to admit that the constant imaginative inventiveness of the child was among its attributes.[9] No one can read the depiction of the stag hunt that opens *The Lady of the Lake* (1810) without admiring Scott's instinct for exciting motion. Much greater poets in English, even among his contemporaries, have lacked what came naturally to him as a writer of verse.

Scott, however, is no mere nostalgic escapist; nor does Southey entirely mask his characteristic interests in trying mythologies on for size. They may not veil contemporary concerns in allegory, as did Shelley in *The Revolt of Islam*. Nor will they take generic self-reflexiveness to the extreme of Byron, whose "Romaunt" has more in common with the generic disquisitions of the antiquarians than with the metrical romances they prefaced. But their altogether profound learning as scholars of the field made them continually sensitive to its nature and scope, even where they seem most wholly to be captivated by the creatures of their imagination.

II

The first decade of the nineteenth century may appear in British literary history as something of a vacuum, a hiatus between two generations of Romanticism, each embodying independent and integral flowerings of genius. But, if we leave aside Wordsworth's *Poems, in Two Volumes* of 1807—a remarkable collection, though scarcely celebrated by its contemporaries—the truth is that if we discover a vacuum it is because we have been looking in the wrong places for fulfillment. The first decade of the nineteenth century found its actual center in the revival of romance, both as a scholarly and creative endeavor. Its towering figures, however neglected today, were Walter Scott and Robert Southey, who shared a scholar's devotion, immense learning, a wide readership—and virtually nothing else. Between them was divided, to adapt later terminology, the "matter of history" and the "matter of myth," the cultures of Britain and of the world Britain colonized, and, most significantly because most deeply imbued with their temperaments, a sense of beginnings and of endings. Scott, historically speaking and independent of his political interests, almost singlehandedly opposed the Napoleonic threat with a collective, historical sense of British intrepidness, while Southey rallied the faithful of many denominations for apocalyptic glory, a martyrdom that in the last days would finally ensure the reign of the saints.

That, at any rate, is the end attained in both *Thalaba* and *The Curse of Kehama*, which, transposed into exotic lands, enveloped by unfamiliar mythologies, and supported by thickets of learned annotations, are nonetheless marked with all the traditional features of medieval quest romances. *Madoc* sustains a more conventional geographic quest. Tracing the Welsh prince's tribulations among his barbarous people and his setting forth to found an empire in America wrested from the even more barbarous Aztecas, the poem, though with only the faintest of legendary authority behind it, pretends to epic verisimilitude, constantly reverting to the imperialist mission and the heroic ethos of *The Aeneid* and to its later reflection in Ercilla's colonial epic *The Araucana*. Southey, it would appear, took his cue directly from William Hayley's influential *Essay on Epic Poetry* (1782), which printed sixty pages of extracts and paraphrase from the Spanish epic in the notes to its third epistle and which likewise enjoined prospective bards to undertake even more extensive colonial enterprises:

> . . . if the Epic Muse still wish to tower
> Above plain Nature's firm and graceful power,
> Tho' Critics think her vital powers are lost

In cold Philosophy's petrific frost;
That Magic cannot her sunk charms restore,
That Heaven and Hell can yield her nothing more;
Yet may she dive to many a secret source
And copious spring of visionary force:
India yet holds a Mythologic mine,
Her strength may open, and her art refine:
Tho' Asian spoils the realms of Europe fill,
Those Eastern riches are unrifled still. (V.263–274)[10]

Southey's future program was fairly set out in this passage: so rifle the East he did. His characters and locations became standard frames of reference among contemporary writers, and his annotations became "a Mythologic mine" for many of them, whether for their representation of the complexities of Indian mythology or for drawing together in one convenient place the arcana—the several pages, for instance, on traditions of vampires in *Thalaba* had a particular effect—that so fascinated the poet.

Thalaba is an avatar of Galahad or Perceval—or, less far afield, of Spenser's Red-crosse Knight. Indeed, it could be claimed that Southey's first published romance is a barely concealed rewriting of Book I of *The Faerie Queene* with the same transformation of inexperienced knight into knowledgeable hero, the same kinds of temptations, the same intermittently present female counterpart. Thalaba's mission, though he does not understand its magnitude until the end, is to rid the world of evil through destroying the underworld realm of Domdaniel, a collective type of the Beast that Red-crosse must also at last confront. Types of Archimago constantly threaten to divert the hero from his task; at one point he succumbs to blissful embowerment; but he overcomes all his temptations and the immensity of the hostile forces arrayed against him through his talisman of Faith. At the end he willingly assumes his own destruction as the ultimate test of that faith and is translated into paradise as the world he leaves behind is purified of evil. The formulas had been tested by others beside Spenser and had proved their endurance as archetypes of inner growth and human commitment. Southey's achievement is to render them fresh and exciting by running them through a Muslim tributary. Yet in a sense he is betrayed by his own estimable learning. Though widely popular, the first quest romance of British Romanticism, not believing in the faith that empowers it and condescending to Muslim culture, is essentially uncommitted to its own mythos: unlike *The Faerie Queen*, *Thalaba* lacks the reverberations of an accepted allegorical matrix, and the quest, whether in terms of the hero's development or of the author's vision, is, to adapt Harold Bloom's important rubric, never internalized.[11] The same fault underlies the even more extravagant mythological fiction of *The Curse of Kehama*, where Southey elaborately turns his formulas inside out. For the hero of adventure we are given a heroine, Kailyal, practiced in patient suffering, and the attention is focused on the monstrous hubris of Kehama as he attempts to unseat the gods. The heroic quest is inverted with something like the scrupulous logic Milton gives to Satan, but Kehama is truly a paper tiger. His evil is total, but it is not very interesting. Though, once again, the poem fascinated some readers—the devil-ridden adolescent Shelley referred to it as "my most favorite poem" (*Letters*, I, 101 [11 June 1811])—its bombastic theatricality is innately ludicrous: "Epic and Pantomime for mast'ry strive / Till Momus cries, 'My sons, ye both may thrive.'"[12]

However self-evidently Southey delights in elaborating his machinery, there is more than mere showmanship involved. "Romantic mythmaking," as we now refer to it, owes its most immediate debt to Southey's quest romances, both for his enlargement of the horizons open to narrative poets and for his almost abstract focus on the individual's quest against and for evil powers. From the first Shelley owns his influence, but so, it might be argued does Blake, as he increasingly centers on climactic acts of self-annihilation in *Milton* and *Jerusalem*.[13] But the true mark of Southey's influence is not in particular characters or motifs but rather in the mythic invention that in its purity of excess encouraged among contemporary poets a liberation from narrowly rationalistic, didactic, and realistic constraints. Wherever the marvelous appears in the romances of this period (and, as we shall see, that is much less often than is customarily thought). Southey's influence is felt. And his impact might even be discernible from negative grounds, for whether among his associates and rivals in the first generation of Romantics or in his influence on the second, an objectification of a heroic quest like his, which separated it from psychological impetus or satisfaction, was recognized as a fatal mistake, paradoxically revealing the necessity for an inner grounding of the quest. That, at least, was what happened all around him, even with manifest borrowings from his poems.[14]

With Scott during this decade there is neither a quest nor an inner life of consequence (though *Marmion* hints at inner divisions that Byron almost immediately began to exploit). The imperative for Scott, it is clear, was historical. What may not be so clear is the particular reason behind his manifest urge to ground his fictions upon fact. And similarly, Scott's passion for history may, given his early passion for romance, appear somewhat anomalous. Not until *The Bridal of Triermain* (1813) did Scott indulge his interest in or exploit his great knowledge of medieval romance, and then he published the poem anonymously. The first three of his metrical romances—*The Lay of the Last Minstrel* (1805), *Marmion* (1808), and *The Lady of the Lake* (1810)—set the action in the first half of the sixteenth century, and *Rokeby* (1813) takes place a century later during the Civil War. As Scott's imagination during the Regency became captivated by prose, the historical setting became even more modern: *Waverley* is concerned with the final attempt, in the mid-eighteenth century, to restore a Catholic Stuart monarchy to Scotland. Only while his main concern was fictionalizing recent history could Scott as a poet revert to the medieval subjects that had compelled his youthful passion; but neither *The Lord of the Isles* (1815) nor *Harold the Daunt-less* (1817) greatly interested the public or, as Scott was candidly to admit in his introductions to the 1830 Abbotsford Edition, even their author. Such a record surely raises questions about why the early poems should be called romances, which simply become more insistent as we realize that there is only one truly improbable feature in any of the first four of them, the character of the goblin page in *The Lay of the Last Minstrel*, who, though fancied by Scott's public, is an incongruous and uninte-grated presence in the poem—as if Scott were so uncomfortable with the supernatural that he could not employ it without embarrassment.

To some extent Scott answered such questions, though behind a cloak of anonymity and uncharacteristic classicism, in his 1813 preface to *The Bridal of Triermain*, where he distinguished the romance from epic on the grounds that the former afforded its author carte blanche in directing his narrative: the romance "neither exacts nor refuses the use of supernat-ural machinery. . . . The date may be in a remote age, or in the present; the story may detail the adventures of a prince or of a peasant."[15] The romance, in other words, is simply fiction. That such a definition begs many questions is of less moment than the extent to which it still centers on a major one. However entertaining fiction may be, it is nonetheless not fact: "I cannot tell how the truth may be; / I say the tale as 't was said to me" (II.262-263), observes the Last Minstrel. Though Scott is the pro-genitor of historical fiction for modern Europe, he is almost obsessively aware that he is wedding contraries. That, indeed, is his most important legacy to his fellow poets, and the impact of his self-questioning and of the pressure for negotiation between contraries that underlies his poetical romances can be discerned everywhere in his wake.

The minstrel's stance as keeper of legend rather than of fact ironically reverses that of Walter Scott, who invents the legends (and, of course, the minstrel who tells them), then underpins the tale with footnotes laden with history and antiquarian lore. His Last Minstrel is a mediating figure and not just merely by connecting the past and present.[16] He once sang for nobility but is now reduced to earning his pittance by telling tales to peasants. His matter may center on the high-willed Lady Margaret, but the true concern is the test of manly wills that produces the continual Border warfare and that is resolved in a ceremonial tournament of cham-pions. Thus it is a man's world whose audience, in *The Lay of the Last Minstrel*, is pointedly feminine, residing with Anne, the widowed Duch-ess of Buccleuch, in the same castle where something like a century earlier the events of the poem occurred. This circle of fine ladies is entranced by what it is not, and at the end of the poem it confirms the wandering Minstrel's own distance from the legendary past he sings of by providing him permanent lodging on the estate and truly domesticating him. The last of his kind, he is the embodient of days that are gone, manners that are outmoded, a wildness now tamed. The world he sings of, though it can be historically validated, is improbable in the setting in which he sings. The world he sings to, another century later when Scott's poem is written as a tribute to the young and newly married inheritors of the Buccleuch title, is likewise an improbable situation in contemporary culture. For Scott, such a doubled act of mediating the improbable encloses yet keeps intact the essence of romance.

Early in 1806 Scott generously credited George Ellis with the exact achievement embodied in his own use of the minstrel as a framing device:

> Socrates is said to have brought philosophy from heaven to reside among men; and Addison claimed the merit of introducing her to the tea-tables of the ladies. Mr. Ellis, in his turn, had brought the minstrels of old into the *boudoirs* and drawing-rooms, which have replaced the founding halls and tapestried bowers in which they were once familiar; so that the age of chivalry, instead of being at an end for ever, may perhaps be on the point of revival.[17]

Romance is, as Scott conceives it, the enchantment of the present by the past. Even more artfully than in *The Lay of the Last Minstrel*, the nested frame he employs in *The Bridal of Triermain* recasts similar materials to draw together three totally separate periods of time. The earliest is the England of King Arthur, who, in the minstrel Lyulph's tale, after three months entranced by the Circean charms of Guendolen, returns from her castle to find his kingdom in disarray. Some fifteen years later the child of their union, Gwyneth, appearing suddenly at the Round Table to claim her birthright, repeats her mother's role as temptress by offering herself as bride to the greatest knight and produces carnage when they duel for her favor. This second threat to the kingdom is averted by the rising of Merlin's apparition, who dooms Gwyneth (the parallel with Brunnhilde is clear) to be imprisoned in an enchanted castle until a knight as intrepid as any of Arthur's finds the means to free her and claim her hand. Lyulph sings this tale five hundred years later in the castle of Sir Roland de Vaux (Scott borrowed the name from Coleridge's "Christabel," which was still unpublished), provoking the knight to set off in quest of the enchanted castle and princess, whom he wins only after undergoing a Spenserian moral test of considerable intricacy. Five hundred years have erased Druid powers, and Sir Roland and his bride lovingly unite. But this tale—and the core legend, too—are told by a modern Arthur courting the high-born Lucy, who is surrounded by the degenerate aristocracy of everyday England from whom he woos her by his minstrelsy—and the constancy of virtues it embodies. Thus Scott twice in *The Bridal of Triermain* shows the past being domesticated in the present, reaffirming in the contemporary, demystified, and emphatically democratic frame the chivalric virtues of both the legendary periods it subsumes. And thus, too, romance as a medieval genre is transformed into *romance* as amorous fantasy. Whether or not Lucy is as "Hoodwink'd" as Keats's Madeline in "The Eve of St. Agnes," both young women testify to the seductions of song and the centrality of the minstrel in the revived chivalric ethos.

In *Marmion* and *The Lady of the Lake* Scott drops the persona, explicitly placing himself in the minstrel's position. The shift is of particular importance to *Marmion*, which is by far the most complex and resonant of his metrical romances. Though the epistles to friends and fellow antiquaries that introduce each of the six cantos of *Marmion* were questioned as to length and propriety by contemporary readers, their insistent self-contemplation subtly recasts the fictional materials of the poem. Scott notes how time passes in its composition—halfway through, in the introduction to Canto IV, we encounter a second November—and suggests the durability of legend and tradition against the fleeting present. Two of his epistles are addressed to principal agents in the romance revival—William Stewart Rose and George Ellis—and reflect on the nature of romance and the pleasures of its composition. Others invoke the local scenery of the Borders, changed with the centuries from how it figures in the tale itself. Though it is true that the introductory epistles were advertised the year before *Marmion*'s publication as *Six Epistles from Ettrick Forest*, they possess little of an independent status. Their function in the poem is to remind us of our distance from its materials and yet of how the tissue of associations connected with landscape, culture, and scholarship inevitably draw us back to the distant past. Or, to invert the perspective, they continually intrude reality upon the created fiction, whether in the guise of the present-day shepherd, the contemporary hero (in the extended eulogies for William Pitt and Charles James Fox in the first epistle), or the modern bard.

The same tendency is strongly felt in the learned apparatus appended to the poem. *Marmion* is set in Catholic Scotland a generation before the Reformation; the annotations that deal with superstitions connected with this insular northern Catholicism, particularly those associated with the legendary St. Cuthbert, are both lengthy and sardonic. The legendary is thus artfully evoked in the poem and simultaneously exploded in the footnotes. And at times the demystification enters the texture of the romance itself. Sir David Lindsay appears as a diplomatic envoy in the poem and is noted as the man who later "broke the keys of Rome" (IV.133). Chrichtoun Castle, where Lindsay conducts Marmion, we are suddenly reminded, now "pens the lazy steer and sheep" in its "miry court" (IV.210, 209). Most serious because so heavily weighted is Scott's observation near the end of the romance that the ostentatious tomb of Marmion houses the remains of a peasant follower accidentally mistaken for him (VI.1107-18). This falsification of a fiction at the end of the poem is a double negative designed to reveal the author's manipulative hand. But we are constantly aware of his presence as Scott's instrusive "I" returns again and again throughout *Marmion*. By the end of the fourth canto, in which Scottish elements begin to predominate, Scott has styled himself "the Minstrel" (IV.687) of the romance he writes.

And yet what kind of minstrel holds his fiction up to so glaring a daylight? Chaucer, for one; Spenser for another. As much as pastoral, traditional romance carries its realistic antithesis within an almost marsupial envelopment. Comic deflation, like the Green Knight with his detachable head, is inherent in the kind. Southey did not recognize this element, nor, in all fairness, did Scott's many admirers who saw only the romance in his fictions. His few detractors noticed contradictions but were content to leave the charge without critical examination.[18] But the extent to which Scott deliberately accentuates and exploits the antiromantic is, in fact, the key to his crucial place in the development of the romance, whether in poetry or prose, and its impact on his contemporaries is palpable.

Marmion is poised on the meeting place between what is and is not. The modern minstrel in the first canto evokes a stirring pageantry that no longer exists, but balances it in the second with superstitious and barbaric religious practices that have also not survived the maturing of British culture. The "broken narrative" Jeffrey criticized forces the reader to alter judgment as the truth slowly impinges on appearances. The principal characters are not what they seem: the dashing hero is a ruthless villain; his faithful page is a disguised nun who has broken her vows and conspired to murder; the wizened palmer is a knight ruined by Marmion's treachery. In other words, what first appears romantic yields to a reality of lawlessness intolerable to modern civilized standards. As later in *The Bridal of Triermain* but with greater subtlety, Scott employs a nested time frame within the poem that enforces the realism accreting to his romantic narrative. In the third canto Marmion's squire Fitz-Eustace adopts the role of minstrel, singing "his favorite roundelay" (III.129), a traditional song about a wronged maiden that agitates the mind of the faithless Marmion. Fitz-Eustace is captivated by tales of knight-errantry, and when in the last canto he is charged with the safety of the heroine Clara de Clare, he adopts manners of archaic chivalry that reflect ironically both against the military folly of the Battle of Flodden Field and Marmion's villainy toward her. In his innocence he is a traditional squire, and yet his code is wholly out of place in the service of Marmion. His dream-world is perpetuated by the legendary tale told by the host of the inn where Marmion's entourage rests, of an encounter between King Alexander and the Elfin Knight three or four centuries earlier. Disturbed by Fitz-Eustace's song and the host's legend, in the middle of the night Marmion seeks out the spot of the encounter where he is surprised and almost killed by the man he ruined, De Wilton, his palmer's robe exchanged for armor. The legendary past intrudes upon the present to unhinge Marmion's pervasive skepticism, and yet that present is our legendary past another three centuries old as Scott writes it, and its romantic appearance disguises a *Realpolitik* that the modern minstrel, an inveterate skeptic himself, unveils. The nest of boxes implicitly questions the romance ethos each compartment encloses.

With this perspective we are able to realize why the events of the early sixteenth century should so impel Scott's romance endeavors. As *Waver-*

ley so graphically demonstrates—and the first six chapters of the novel, it is important to recognize, were written simultaneously with *The Lay of the Last Minstrel*—Scott is fascinated with the meeting grounds of cultures and epochs. His is truly a Border romance. The materials of his early metrical romances are all the same, unified by their concern for borders. Each centers historically on a dispute between political entities—the English and Scots in the first two, the Scottish throne and Highland tribes in the third—and between the cultures they embody. The cultures are as yet Catholic but are about to experience the Reformation. Knightly codes still command allegiance, but modern bureaucracies, typified by diplomatic envoys like Marmion, are supplanting the individual's claims to prowess. Early sixteenth-century Scotland is in every sense a liminal period, Janus-faced, and it was Scott's ingenuity, or genius, to recognize that the period offered an unlimited field not just for the creation of romance but for its simultaneous critique.[19] The simpleminded Scott of his own projection and of subsequent critical history was in fact an artist of subtle deconstructive manipulation. He gives nothing he does not at once take away, for he is obsessively aware that fiction is not fact, though fact is continually embroidered into fiction, and that the past is never the present, though its imprint is indelible upon it. He is at once a creator and an analytical scholar and as his genius was empowered by a scholarly revival, so was his legacy to his contemporaries. It is not medieval romance that they inherit, but a romance whose original elements have been transformed into a modern equivalence and whose tests, adventures, magical powers, and very improbability exist in a region defined by its borders with the antithetical.

III

That the subsequent course of romance during this period was determined by Walter Scott, who provided a full repertory of conventions and situations for either borrowing or inversion, should not surprise us. By the end of the opening decade of the nineteenth century he was the acknowledged master of British poetry. So Francis Jeffrey opens the August 1810 number of the *Edinburgh Review*: "Mr. Scott, though living in an age unusually prolific of original poetry, has manifestly outstripped all his competitors in the race of popularity; and stands already upon a height to which no other writer has attained in the memory of any one now alive."[20] What is surprising is that the first poet directly to set himself in competition with Scott was William Wordsworth. Although *The White Doe of Rylstone; or, the Fate of the Nortons* was not published until 1815, it was substantially completed in the month before *Marmion*'s publication. The reasons for Wordsworth's eight-year delay in publication are still obscure, but his sense of dissatisfaction with the manuscript he had transmitted to Longman's coincides with his anxious anticipation of reading Scott's second romance, and he may well have decided to suspend a competition rashly entered upon.[21] Whatever the case with Scott's second poem, there are obvious borrowings from the first. Using "The Rising in the North," a ballad printed in the first volume of Percy's *Reliques* as his source, Wordsworth looks directly to *The Lay of the Last Minstrel*, surrounding his tale with the apparatus of minstrelsy and superimposing multiple time frames upon its structure. The ruins of Bolton Priory suggest at once the continuity of the past and the mortal changes suffered by all things.

In 1843 Wordsworth added a short preface and replaced one of the two epigraphs to the poem. In both instances he stressed how antithetical to Scott's romances was his own. Any "comparison," he remarks, "is inconsiderate":

> Sir Walter pursued the customary and very natural course of conducting an action, presenting various turns of fortune, to some outstanding point on which the mind might rest as termination or catastrophe. The course I attempted to pursue is entirely different. Everything that is attempted by the principal personages in "The White Doe" fails, so far as its object is external and substantial. So far as it is moral and spiritual it succeeds.

Then, as if to ensure that we understand that the distinction is one about "conducting an action," Wordsworth prints as epigraph the powerful lines from *The Borderers*, finally published only the year before this late note:

> Action is transitory—a step, a blow
> The motion of a muscle—this way or that—
> 'Tis done; and in the after-vacancy
> We wonder at ourselves like men betrayed:
> Suffering is permanent, obscure and dark,
> And has the nature of infinity. . . .

The first canto of the poem purposely divests itself of any action except the appearance of a white doe outside the priory, which generates conjectures among the worshippers about it. The genesis of the poem is thus a multifaceted symbol demanding interpretation, an element of timeless lyricism that draws the poet into his element. The canto ends with Wordsworth reflecting on how he has strayed from the conventional focus assumed by his audience:

> Harp! we have been full long beguiled
> By vague thoughts, lured by fancies wild;
> To which, with no reluctant strings,
> Thou hast attuned thy murmurings. (I. 324–327)

Promising to proceed directly with his "tale of tears, a mortal story" (I.335), Wordsworth introduces us to his heroine, whose fate is not to act but simply and profoundly to suffer.

The quietism endorsed by Wordsworth's poem has troubled many readers and fostered critical commentary about the growing retreat of the poet from an active sense of engagement with the world. Yet, if there can be no question that his own suffering over the death of his brother John is reflected in the poem, the primary impulse behind it is generic, an extension of the mode of lyrical ballads into the world of romance. It is, indeed, a lyrical romance, whose central concern is not action but the functioning of symbols, both ironically as in the case of Emily's banner, which she embroiders with reluctance and which leads her entire family to destruction, and positively, in the force of the white doe, whose innocent affection serves to restore her from despair to a saving naturalness. Geoffrey Hartman has astutely observed how seemingly determined Wordsworth is to naturalize Catholic superstition into a "protestant romance," as he translates the sacramental associations and sense of mystery surrounding the doe into the normal but no less wonderful interanimation of nature and the imagination.[22] But the even more remarkable determination is to adopt the Border romance popularized by Scott and wholly to subvert its animating principle.

The general estimate of posterity has been that Wordsworth does not succeed in his experiment: the mode of the Scott Border romance is simply not congenial to so resolutely contemplative a poem. That may be the case, but still, Wordsworth implicitly recognizes that the aim of most quest romances is not a victory in battle or the stabilizing of a dynasty but rather inner fulfillment, and especially is this the case with those involving a religious quest. That for the Holy Grail is the most radical of all, since it pursues a visionary end, and the aim of seeing it is to be transported from this world. Thus, Galahad's quest must portend the ultimate destruction of the Round Table, for it is antithetical to any mundane solution, whether wrought in the name of communal progress or of individual virtue. Such mundane solutions in a Scott romance coalesce in a symbolic marriage, usually one uniting opposing factions or classes and promising to extend the reach of civilization. But the harmony that Wordsworth emphasizes is internal, reverting to the substructure of the many medieval romances where the convent and abbey contend with the court for superior claims. The genre associated with adventure, whose narrative mode tends to be episodic, will inevitably question the purpose of action and what continuities can be premised upon episode. In *The White Doe of Rylstone* action is not merely transitory, it is negative, a foolhardy embrace of self-destruction. Emily's sheer survival, Wordsworth intimates, though wholly lacking in adventure or any contention except with despair, is a true engagement with life.[23]

Wordsworth's subversion of the Border romance was finally published only after Scott had begun to transpose these materials into prose fiction. If in strict chronology it was the first poem to react against the model provided by Scott, its appearance in 1815 garnered little attention. The comparative value of *The White Doe of Rylstone* to the side, it came so late in the reaction to Scott that it appeared in the shadow of a series of poems, all of which show Scott's influence and the author's determination to plumb depths his fellow poet and countryman had covered over, Byron's Oriental Tales.[24] Scott himself ceded the field to Byron, gracefully exiting into prose as he observed Byron win the same sudden popularity that less than a decade earlier had catapulted him from obscure antiquary to honored bard. The exotic Mediterranean settings superficially conceal how very similar Byron's geography is to Scott's, with the same border between cultures, ideologies, religions, the same rough heroism asserting itself where law cannot reach, the same codes of vengeance, strong-willed women, and isolated men.

Yet the mere litany of these elements should immediately alert us to signal differences. None of the early Oriental Tales ends in marriage: in *The Giaour* the female is murdered, in *The Corsair* and *The Bride of Abydos* she dies of grief, and in *Lara* she is left to mourn. The role of women in this world is to be abused by masculine dominance. And there is no stabilization of civilized values: the Giaour ends his days an outcast in a monastery, and the tyrannical power opposed by the outcast heroes in the other three poems sustains its brutality, whoever dies in the attempt to overthrow it. Since the vengeful codes of honor are universal and thus interchangeable, oppressor and oppressed cannot be distinguished on moral grounds. Yesterday's brigand, if successful, would become today's despot. Adventure, then, exists for its own sake as an existential assertion of the self, and it culminates, whatever the complex of motives, in destruction. Jerome McGann's concentration on these tales as a critique of the masculine mystique is perceptive and enlightening; but the critique is even more far-reaching because it is accomplished within a mode whose inherent ideology is a reflection of male values.[25] The only positive, life-sustaining element in these poems is the feminine bower—Zuleika in the harem, Medora in her mountain retreat—traditionally associated, from Circe on to Vivien and to Acrasia, with ignoble ease and seduction from knightly duty.[26] But the bower is fragile, a sanctuary dependent on the masculine economy whether of sultan or pirate. And no children are ever born there.

The profound generic questioning of *Childe Harold's Pilgrimage* will be analyzed separately, but it is clear that the first two cantos, predating the Oriental Tales, establish a larger context for them, one in which the minstrel plays a central role. This context is a given for Byron's audience, who immediately insinuated him into the characters and events of the tales, thus personalizing his shrewd exploitation of contemporary fashion. Doubtless, had Byron not gone to the Levant, he would have found another subject—perhaps on the slopes of Loch na Garr. Yet, if the annotations to the Oriental Tales often read as if they were written by Southey, it is for the same reason that so many of the characters and incidents in the poems remind us of Scott. The audience was there for the asking. Still, Byron would never have had the instantaneous success he enjoyed had he merely dressed Scott's kilted warriors in Southey's kaftans. His power lies in exploiting the realism within romance, arousing fantasies that prove distasteful even as they entrance. Though these poems never stray beyond the realm of the probable, neither do they find refuge from the problematic. The broken narrative, borrowed from Scott and Samuel Rogers, conveys insecurity, inner threat, ultimate uncertainty. The duplicity of Marmion is intensified into the self-hatred of the Giaour and Conrad. The gallant masquerade of James V, in *The Lady of the Lake,* is inverted into the blindly cynical reconstruction of personality practiced by Selim in *The Bride of Abydos.* Behind the scenes stalks the specter of the modern warrior-chief, Napoleon Buonaparte, and a war to subdue his adventurism that had, when *The Giaour* was published, lasted twenty years. No less than Wordsworth, but more subtly and more powerfully because issuing from within the ethos of romance itself, Byron enforces a fatalistic quietism.

It was far from the genial temperament of Thomas Moore to disturb his audience (unless they were governesses or other protectors of the public morals). His major reach for permanent fame as something more than a pretty melodist came in the genre of romance, in his once celebrated and now wholly neglected *Lalla Rookh, An Oriental Romance* (1817), whose accomplishment is genuine if somewhat glossy. It was written for fame and fortune, a shrewd crowd pleaser best understood within the generic developments that had already produced crowds (and financial success) for Southey, Scott, and Byron. Yet, because of its careful bid for popularity, there is no more reliable index to the shifts that had taken place in public expectation and generic conception during the sixteen years after the publication of *Thalaba.* Byron had given Southey's orientalism a new lease on life, and Scott's techniques had survived as conventions even after his transmutation into "the Great Unknown." Moore had his own established credentials as the Irish minstrel (and as a corrupter of maiden propriety through lascivious verse). In *Lalla Rookh* he strung his harp so as to touch every one of these chords, even the last. Self-reflexiveness is no less complete for being done with wit.

Lalla Rookh is a collection of four oriental tales—two on Indian subjects, two on Muslim ones—interpolated within an elaborate frame in prose, in which the youngest daughter of Aurungzebe is being conducted with appropriately oriental pomp (much of whose choreography seems borrowed from Hunt's *Story of Rimini* of the year before) to the palace of the Arabian prince to whom her father had betrothed her. The tales are sung along the way by the emissary of the prince, the poet Feramorz, and he in turn is constantly belittled by his chamberlain Fadladeen. Despite the fact that Moore's Whig politics allied him with the *Edinburgh Review,* Fadladeen is transparently a caricature of Francis Jeffrey, admonishing Scott and belittling Southey in the name of common sense and Enlightenment canons of taste. Moore clearly intends his readers to identify Feramorz with himself as author of the Eastern romances, especially since the minstrel's lays inspire the young girl in his charge to fall in love with him. Propriety is, however, rescued at the very end, as

Feramorz turns out to be the very prince she is to wed—an outcome that every reader of *The Lady of the Lake* would have expected from the outset. Lalla Rookh is herself a representative of the public, particularly the female public, avid for romances despite the reductionist arbiters of literary taste. The frame—clever, light-hearted, and self-conscious—is as enthusiastic a defense of the value of romance as any of those by the antiquarians. The tales, however, are of a very different timbre, designed to outstrip Southey if at all possible in their diabolism and exoticism, their contrast between voluptuousness and terror, not to neglect the customary mythological and cultural learning of their notes.

Moore's poem in its debts to Southey, Scott, and Byron is a synoptic romance, revealing in clear detail what, after the explosion of original texts and modern recreations, had become conventional to the form. The romance of the Regency is seldom seen without a frame, and generally that frame is both more contemporary than the contents of the poem itself, enforcing multiple temporal vantages, and pointed in its self-reflexiveness. Scott's Minstrel not only was not the last but spawned innumerable variations, all of whom celebrate their own creativity, their distance from everyday business, and their centrality to a national cultural life. The isolated sensibility and self-regarding genius popularly associated with the Romantic poet is, indeed, an accurate representation of the romance poet conventional to this characterization.[27] Similarly, the demystification implicit in Southey's and particularly Scott's annotations—Southey's self-importance seldom allowing him to puncture his own fictions—is another constant, often carried forward from the back of the volume to impinge upon the narrative itself. The result, whether in Scott's borderlands, Byron's cultural and personal contradictions, Moore's playful contrast between wealthy domesticity and the demonic, or Wordsworth's deliberate subversion of action, is to cast the romance as a liminal genre; and this characteristic is only accentuated by the self-regarding frame. The creative invention of the poet and the action or pageantry of the poem are measured against the constraints of civilization. Fiction is placed in balance with fact. A world premised on exotic superstition, magical powers, supernatural intercession is embedded in Enlightenment learning and sardonic realism. The past is allowed to compel us nostalgically, but only within the insistent perspective of our modernity. Gothic horrors and primitive evil invade our consciousness, but again, only as distanced by time or geography or as explainable within a mythological construction foreign to modern European Christianity. Wherever the threshold is found, the door swings either way. The romance of British Romanticism tests limits, and it is no coincidence, but rather the inevitable carry-over from this defining genre of the period, that this is a fundamental aspect of all its poetry.

And simple logic would suggest that the result of such a testing would frequently be indeterminate, reinforcing the process itself without necessarily arriving at a conclusion. It is a nice irony that this is the exact paradigm from which we might date the beginning of the movement to recreate romance, in Coleridge's "Christabel," the first part composed in 1797, the second in 1800 (and its "Conclusion" in 1801), but the whole not published until 1816, when Coleridge prefaced the poem by remarking that if readers thought it derivative of Scott and Byron, they should realize that it predated their efforts. Indeed, Coleridge was well aware that both poets had known the poem in manuscript and that Scott had furthermore acknowledged its influence on *The Lay of the Last Minstrel* and had paid a second tribute to it by making Sir Leoline's estranged friend, Sir Roland de Vaux of Tryermaine, the hero of his own medieval romance. The narrative voice in the poem may not be as personalized as it generally became in the wake of Scott's poems, but its presence is sustained by a technique that calls attention to itself, the insistent asking of questions as a means of furthering the narrative. Some are answered, many are not, and even where answers are supplied they may be either tentative or inadequate to the reverberations of the interrogative mode. The most notable structural feature of the poem is that both parts end with announced "Conclusions," where, to adapt the fortuitous title Johnson supplied for the last chapter of his philosophical romance in prose, *Rasselas*, "nothing is concluded." The "Conclusions" are thus extensions of the interrogative mode, shifting us obliquely into unfamiliar territory, particularly in the case of the second, where the poetic fragment breaks off with narrative, moral purpose, and symbolic ramifications alike suspended. Interpretation of "Christabel" is among the most vexed in British poetry, and it is probably little help to its readers to suggest that the poem should be simply construed as an exercise in the mode of romance, its sheer inventiveness playing over traditional motifs without attempting to resolve them in a unified whole. Well before the actual revival of romance at the end of the eighteenth century, in Warton's and Hurd's defenses of Spenser, romance had been identified with, in Warton's words, "the careless exuberance of a warm imagination and a strong sensibility" rather than neoclassical rule.[28] Coleridge intimated how he expected to resolve the poem, but the fact that he never did so—and that three years separated the composition of the two completed parts—suggests that critics who follow what they conceive were his intentions in seeking an arching unity for the poem are likely to be misled. The two parts are themselves disunified by a "broken narrative": what Coleridge left behind are episodes, tantalizingly mysterious, of the essence of romance—innocent and temptress, distant lover and misunderstanding parent, minstrel and estranged friend, enveloped by portentous symbols and intimations of the supernatural and situated in the far north where spring is late and enlightenment never comes.

Such a view of "Christabel" is lent weight by the existence of at least one other poem in the period that is a romance in this abstracted, self-regarding way. Shelley's "The Witch of Atlas" is more finished but no less enigmatic for its interpreters, most of whom attempt to fashion a sustained allegory out of its mysteries. Yet, if they can unite in the view that Shelley's Witch is an avatar of imaginative ideals, they disagree profoundly on her function in the world, the meaning and purpose of her adventures, and her relevance to morality and culture. The most provocative account of the poem, by Jerrold Hogle, insists, however, that such critical questions are misplaced: the subject of the poem is its own activity, which is purely imaginative play.[29] The poem, then, is in the present context a romance about romancing, an invention concerned with its own inventiveness: "What, though no mice are caught by a young kitten, / May it not leap and play as grown cats do . . .?" (5-6) In the abstract, romance is merely a making of fiction, a fiction that needs no rules, pursues no ulterior moral end, and requires no justification, except perhaps that it engage other imaginations and liberate their flight. "The Witch of Atlas" attains its integrity by insisting on the absolute value of the improbable.

Such a poem, self-content in its own propensity for play, can be written only by a mature poet who is assured of his powers. Shelley's earlier ventures into romance are far less limited in their generic endeavors, also less assured. *The Revolt of Islam* is unquestionably the most ambitious neo-Spenserian romance in the period, perhaps in all of English literature, both for its major length, its adeptness with the technical difficulties of the stanza, and its goals, which, as intimated earlier, are more to be associated with epic than romance. Its attempt to convert Southey's means to realize Milton's ends is perhaps inherently incongruous; but a poem whose barely disguised aim is propaganda for political reform at least remains as a monument to the intensity of the contemporary fascination with romance. And it suggests as well that political undercurrents well beneath the surface of a school of poetry that in the hands of Southey, Byron, and Moore has escaped war-weary Europe only to collide with the despotism and fanaticism inseparable from Britain's view of the Muslim East.

Far more interesting for later interpreters, and for its crucial representation of the inner stresses of the romance mode, is Shelley's first sustained effort within it, "Alastor." The dawn that broke with Earl Wasserman's influential exploration of multiple viewpoints in the poem might have come much earlier had the poem been placed within its proper generic context, which is provided generally by Scott and most specifically by its recodification by Byron in the first two cantos of *Childe Harold's Pilgrimage*.[30] Shelley places himself in the familiar role of minstrel to his tale, which is, with his hero's death, irrevocably past. His own attempt to find a stable satisfaction in the everyday contrasts with, and is questioned by, the intensity of his protagonist's quest. The poem is thus balanced on the liminal, which it explores with perceptive nuance and compassionate evenhandedness. The psychological projection that many readers sense behind the poem is probably true, but paradoxically it reinforces its objectivity and compassion. It is small wonder, however, that the ends are indeterminate: the genre promises us as much, even if the normal complexity of human desire should not.

But whether or not the poem is a therapeutic self-analysis for its author, its importance for the genre lies in its recognition that the quest is innately psychological. "Alastor" is the crucial poem in British Romanticism for enacting the internalized dynamics of the quest romance. The continual play of reflective imagery in the poem suggests the extent to which the quest is always for a completed self, and the hard irony against which Shelley forces his protagonist and his poem is that the only completion is that of death. The various tellers of the Perceval-Galahad legend had enveloped the same truth in the transcendental promises of Christianity, but in his customary way Shelley resolutely secularizes the dynamic. The improbable ethos of romance is rooted in our desire for total liberation, an impossible psychological state. Insofar as what we know constitutes the limits of the probable, the only way beyond it is to embrace our own death. A lifelong quest for an ideal may be the inner striving of the spirit against the constraints of the probable, but it is also a striving against life and in the pursuit of death. The transcendental and the entropic are one and the same. Distilled to such an essence, the romance is an oxymoronic mode—which is exactly why Schlegel adopted the term to distinguish a sensibility that can never be satisfied with the mundane. Wherever one casts the threshold, it must be between two antithetical realms. Shelley as narrating minstrel may at the end bemoan the failure of his visionary protagonist, for it does prove the intractable nature of the human condition, but he also recognizes the inner contradictions of the quest. His protagonist spurns love; his only sexuality is involuntary and unproductive; and though he is called the Poet, he never puts pen to paper. He also covers most of the known earth in his compulsive travels and discovers nothing new. In fact, as Shelley knowingly inverts the conventional dynamics of the genre, throughout his career the visionary poet literally does nothing.

That both protagonist and narrator are poets, however, raises to the surface what had been implicit in the recreated genre since *The Lay of the Last Minstrel.* Far more than the ballad—though Wordsworth in a poem like "Simon Lee" may call attention to himself as author—the romance continually invokes the conditions of its creation. With a frame so self-regarding and even self-congratulatory enclosing a distanced poem whose imaginative inventiveness is accentuated as a generic hallmark, it is inevitable that romancing becomes an issue, even a problem.[31] That the narrator of "Alastor" writes a romance and the visionary poet, who never writes, lives one sharply focuses the problem. Those who write presume a readership, establish communion, speak for and to humanity. But one who lives in and for his imagination has no mediating function and is necessarily possessed by his own solipsistic vision. It is precisely the writer's awareness of the liminal that separates him from the visionary. "Alastor" acknowledges the paradox implicit in romance: that imaginative escape, which compels the genre, must be temporary, that the imagination empowered and celebrated by it is, as Johnson's Imlac so perceptively remarked, a "hunger . . . which preys incessantly upon life." The visionary's *alastor* is by definition a *kakodaimon*, an evil daemon who must be controlled—or, in the structural matrix of contemporary romance, framed.

Keats's *Endymion: A Poetic Romance* has generally been considered a response to Shelley's "Alastor," but since most of the direct comparisons confuse Shelley with the visionary poet, their conclusions are suspect. Yet, if the comparison is just, then it seems fair to remark that Keats posits a hero who, without regard for Shelley's pointed ironies, seemingly gets to have his cake and eat it too—which, if this were the actual case, would relegate his romance to adolescent fantasy rather than mature art, with its claims to our attention vastly overrated. In earlier criticism the question was whether the poem were a contrived allegory of a Spenserian cast or simply an extended test of inventive powers, both of which would be justified by the genre. The latter view, however, sounds suspiciously like another version of the impossible cake, one that celebrates unthinking genius and casts Keats in the line of Southey, rifling the mythologic mine provided by Lempriere's *Dictionary*. Whether or not the allegory is wholly integrated and congruous, *Endymion* possesses a manifest seriousness of concern, of which we are most immediately aware through Keats's frame. And whether or not it was Keats's intention to set his poem against the context of "Alastor," the generic self-regard is similar and works toward a similar end.

Each of the four books of the poem is prefaced by an authorial intrusion that by 1818 was simply customary to the romance. The first, borrowing from the seasonal focus of Scott's epistles in *Marmion*, celebrates the pastoral bower as the animating principle of poetry, a notion that, as we observed in the previous chapter, the events of the ensuing book question, if not wholly contradict. The second proem shifts to question the customary materials of romance, tales of adventure, which pale before the quiet intensities of love: these darken into fatality as the hero encounters first Venus and Adonis and then Alpheus and Arethusa. A stark note of modernity is touched at the beginning of the third book, as Keats exclaims against the "baaing vanities" (III.3) of kings and public officials, whose pomp and majesty are tinsel compared with the universal presence of the moon—this to preface a book in which Endymion's responsibilities to his fellow humanity are, in the usual reading, Keats's focus. The last proem celebrates the integrity and independence of a British muse and the poet's sense of his cultural responsibility to prepare for Endymion's sense of split allegiances, his despondency, and last-minute rescue. It is surely possible to overread Keats's intentions as romance narrator to his first extended work, but what appears to distinguish these four proems is their sense of poetic, even generic, growth and their independent, if not antithetical, posture in respect to the verses that immediately follow, which in every case are intimately associated with the prefatory matter.[32] The intimacy of the association, however, is the very point of the allegory discerned through the baroque apparatus of the romance, which, to borrow one of Blake's diabolic proverbs, suggests that "Eternity is in love with the productions of time" (*Marriage of Heaven and Hell*, 8.10).

Endymion is no more to be identified with Keats than is Shelley's visionary with himself, though both are necessarily projections of the poet's voice, inspiration, sense of purpose, and even ambivalence. Indeed, much more directly than Shelley (though still short of Byron's monumental achievement), Keats transforms the self-reflexive romance into a vehicle of self-creation and thus into a liminality that is utterly pure. The emphasis in its preface is not merely self-deprecatory, as it might appear, but rather generically defining:

> The imagination of a boy is healthy, and the mature imagination of a man is healthy; but there is a space of life between, in which the soul is in ferment, the character undecided, the way of life uncertain, the ambition thick-sighted. . . .

Endymion has its necessary failings, but its most remarkable achievement is to spin an allegory of the "space of life between," reverting continually to the maturing powers and apprehension of its speaker and enacting at every stage the marriage between his mortal limitations and the ideal of art that is recast in the intrusion of his narrative self upon the myth he would recreate, by which he would be recreated. The quest romance figures forth the quest for poetic identity of its singer.

The irony that flickers between narrative intrusions and the recast myth in *Endymion* is an agent of maturation, forcing Keats to distance himself from the myth's potentiality for extension into mere fantasy. But it is also, like other elements in the poem, indicative of his future development. Irony was to become Keats's characteristic rhetorical mode. In returning to the romance, he has his usual advantage of coming late in the generic development and of building on the logical possibilities inherent in it. It is an interesting fact that the only titles Keats used in presenting his three poetic volumes to the public are romances: *Endymion* is followed in 1820 by *Lamia, Isabella, The Eve of St. Agnes, and other Poems*, whose identified titles are romances in the mode of the Greek (in couplets), Italian (in ottava rima), and British (in Spenserian stanzas). The narrative voice is subtler than in earlier examples in the period, is less formal in its framing, and dispenses with annotations as a distancing technique. But its ironic presence is ubiquitous, felt in the vernacular diction that distinguishes a modern sensibility from its legendary matter, or in the sudden imposition of a second temporal frame, as in the apostrophe to Boccaccio in stanza 19 of "Isabella" or the celebrated shift of tense by which we enter the final stanza of "The Eve of St. Agnes." Jack Stillinger, particularly in the title essay of his book, *The*

Hoodwinking of Madeline, shrewdly argued that these poems, so long read as straightforward romances, were in truth antiromances, indulging in romance conventions and thus lulling us into an escapist world that exploded before our eyes. More recently in a long, cogent exposition, Tilottama Rajan has characterized these poems as inherently deconstructive, affirming and rejecting the values of romance at one and the same time.[33] Rajan's *via media* is deftly responsive to the curious experience of reading Keats's late romances, but, in truth, her characterization, allowing for distinctions among poets and the evolution of the genre, applies to the entire corpus of Romantic romance.

Keats's poems are distillations of its very essence and bring us at last to verify the intuitive perception that made August Wilhelm Schlegel adopt the term "romantic" as comprehending an ironic sensibility.[34] Keats in his romances writes wholly within the liminal. The art is polished to a high sheen, but it is without question the art of Scott and of Shelley, and even, with its touches of wit, the art of Moore. Most particularly, it is the art of Byron, who in *Childe Harold's Pilgrimage*—with its sinuous, associative structure, its doubled sensibility, its innumerable thresholds between antitheses, its endless demystification, and equally inexhaustible quest—wrote the quintessential romance of the period.

IV

Childe Harold's Pilgrimage, a Romaunt, unlike the works we have been considering, begins from the perspective of antiromance or from that of the author of *English Bards and Scotch Reviewers,* who there satirized the new romance of Southey and Scott and who now plots its deliberate inversion. Its protagonist is contemporary, an antihero incongruously clothed at first in an archaic Spenserian diction.[35] His quest is away from, not for, a stable center. He is existentially disengaged in a world whose superstitions he sees through and whose magic is chimerical. He is fictional, as Byron was at pains to remark in the original preface and in his later addition to it, but there is no fiction for him to enter upon. He is less a presence than is his minstrel, who never leaves the center of the stage to which he introduces us in the first stanza. It is the minstrel, whom we might expect to be disengaged or at least distant, who is passionate in his commitments, and yet he is committed—far more universally than Scott's singer—to what no longer exists and, indeed, seems mainly concerned to determine whether it ever did. Byron's is a romance *manqué* shadowed by the spiritual entropy of Harold, a pilgrimage in search of a shrine, a quest for an object worthy of empowering a quest. Yet out of nothing, or worse, a "Vitality of poison" (III.299), and out of the ruins of empires and aspirations declining toward the void, there arises an opposing force, a creative inventiveness that is the inner soul of romance. From so unrelenting a vision of the antiromantic, an irony so pure that it inverts even itself, Byron proves the enduring power of the genre.

Byron's is the most extreme example of "broken narrative" in the Romantic period, functioning not like Scott's, to suspend reality in appearances that slowly dissipate, but rather, through a continual test of values for their flaws and a restless search for a whole that can reconcile the parts, to displace any resolution of the quest. Yet "broken" is not a truly apt term for the structural dynamic of *Childe Harold's Pilgrimage*. Though the antiquarian revival was not so critically sophisticated that it could categorize defining structures of medieval romance with precision, Byron appears to have intuited the principle of "interlaced structure" that Eugene Vinaver has seen as central to romance narrative.[36] Before Byron, Spenser is the last great practitioner of this structural mode, in which characters and themes disappear from view or are left in suspension, only to reappear with added resonance from intervening episodes: the whole finally achieving—in Vinaver's brilliant analogy—the intricate delicacy of the interwoven vegetation, lacking any point of origin or end, in the illuminated capitals of medieval books.

Another medieval analogy of startling congruence is offered by Donald Howard's application of the interlace to labyrinths figured in the pavement or walls of cathedrals and other shrines of Christendom and their relation to the experience of pilgrimage and the structure of Chaucer's *Canterbury Tales*.[37] Harold's completion of "Sin's long labyrinth" (I.37) is Byron's starting point, and he elaborates his own labyrinth as a righting of the negation of spiritual values that has led his protagonist to a void. That such refinements of modern literary scholarship were not available to Byron is true enough, but we should not underestimate the extent to which his culture conceived of romance as offering alternate models of structure. Warton's defense of Spenser and Ariosto against neoclassical rules has already been alluded to. Bishop Hurd continually distinguishes the Gothic from Aristotelian models in his *Letters on Chivalry and Romance*. It is not yet Ruskin's Gothic, but there is a common awareness among the defenders of romance that an organically unfolding idea is fundamental to its structure. Byron reverts to such a notion repeatedly, from the epigraph to the first two cantos in which Louis de Monbron compares the universe to a book whose pages are all alike to the assertion in the last canto that "History, with all her volumes vast, / Hath but *one* page" (IV.968–969). *Childe Harold's Pilgrimage* unfolds elaborately, but its informing ideas turn and return through its progress. It is their pilgrimage that grasps our fixed attention, not Harold's. That the protagonist is only fitfully the central focus and then disappears without explanation in the third canto may continue to trouble readers, but it is true to the structural norms of the "romaunt" of Ariosto and Spenser and, indeed, serves to direct our attention to the substructure of ideas that truly impels the poem.

The associative and episodic dynamic of the poem is one element that identifies it with contemporary romance.[38] Its doubled narrative perspective is another. The alternation of animated energy and descriptive calm is a third element that is manifest with increasing sophistication and accretion of import as the cantos develop. Even more pointedly than Scott, Byron anchors the emotional force that gathers around his vision of fragmentation and failure to dryly factual annotations. The last canto, surging with enormous rhetorical power between wonder and despair, actually enlists two powerful agents of scholarly ballast, John Cam Hobhouse and Ugo Foscolo, to ground it with a separate volume running hundreds of pages—*Historical Illustrations of the Fourth Canto of Childe Harold: containing Dissertations on the Ruins of Rome; and An Essay on Italian Literature*. History intervenes with increasing urgency as the cantos develop, and with its force come the myths and legends by which it is memorialized. Figures from older romances continually cast their shadows on the landscape, whether Roland in Spain (I, sts. 34-37), Odysseus on Calypso's island (II, sts. 29-30), German knights on the castled Rhine (III, st. 49), or the chivalric world created by Ariosto (IV, sts. 40-41). The spatial and temporal frame shifts continually, most dramatically in the deliberate wrench that leaps from Spain to Parnassus in Canto I, stanza 59. Wherever the pilgrimage leads, there is the clash of armies, either contemporary as with Byron's tour behind the Spanish battle lines in Canto I, or in recent history (the Battle of Waterloo memorialized in Canto III), or in classical antiquity—Agamemnon's tomb (II, sts. 5-6), Actium (II, st. 45), Marathon (II, sts. 89-90), Thrasimene (IV, sts. 62-65). The scenes of high adventure—and carnage— alternate dialectically with nodes of religious worship.

The pilgrimage is a religious quest, and it visits literally dozens of shrines, a fact curiously absent from the voluminous critical literature on *Childe Harold's Pilgrimage*. Byron emphasizes the primacy of the religious quest as a structuring principle in the poem by making the terminus of the first pilgrimage, Cantos I and II, the seat of the Byzantine church, Haija Sophia in Constantinople (II, st. 79), and of the last canto, the seat of Western Christianity, St. Peter's in Rome.[39] And yet, except for the final, epitomizing structure, most of the shrines are in ruins or have been perverted from their original function. The first such building, ironically, is Newstead Abbey, or at least the fictive version of it in which Harold resides:

> Monastic dome! condemn'd to uses vile!
> Where superstition once had made her den
> Now Paphian girls were known to sing and smile. (I.59-61)

Human fallibility likewise inverts the purity of religious impulses, forcing the gods to descend not to inspire but to be chained to the earth. Harold's first resting point on the pilgrimage, amid the empty palaces of Cintra, is at "our 'Lady's house of woe'" (I.255) and nearby is its fitting complement: "Deep in yon cave Honorius long did dwell, / In hope to merit Heaven by making earth a Hell" (I.259-260).[40] Byron himself writes from Parnassus as a votary of its "holy haunt" (I.644) but then enlarges his vision to encompass all of Greece: "Where'er we tread 'tis haunted, holy ground" (II.828). And yet its relics of worship are unregarded by its inhabitants and, worse, plundered by others: "The last, the worst, dull spoiler" (II.94) is Lord Elgin, who, with his countrymen, "could violate each saddening shrine, / And bear these altars o'er the long-reluctant brine" (II.98–99). The world has been demythologized, its romantic impulses and objects of veneration brought to earth—or to museums.

And yet Byron inherits this fall, embodying it in the harshly realistic vision of his poem. Both the first and second cantos begin with an appeal to a muse who will not answer:

> Oh, thou! in Hellas deem'd of heav'nly birth,
> Muse! form'd or fabled at the minstrel's will! (I.1–2)

> Come, blue-eyed maid of heaven!—but, thou, alas!
> Didst never yet one mortal song inspire— (II.1–2)

Religion is the ultimate romantic fiction, the minstrel's fable of the improbable; and, as "Even gods must yield—religions take their turn" (II.23) in any survey of history, so before the demystifying gaze of an Enlightenment minstrel there is nothing to inspire but "shrines [that] no longer burn" (II.22), the ruins of romance. The questing poet is truly "By pensive Sadness, not by Fiction, led" (II.319) through these ruins that, however splendid in their variety, are unified in their decay. They can be surveyed but cannot be revived.

The monuments to unavailing fictions are the spatial determinants of Byron's poem, all of them marking "the unreach'd Paradise of our despair" (IV.1096). The temporal is similarly abstracted, not simply in the reduction of history to one page, reiterated again and again, but in its very essence, the action that impels all romances. Harold is its immediate embodiment: "To horse! to horse! he quits, for ever quits / A scene of peace. . . . Onward he flies, nor fix'd as yet the goal / Where he shall rest him on his pilgrimage" (I.324–329). On his reappearance in the third canto, Byron observes that Harold, "once more within the vortex, roll'd / On with the giddy circle, chasing Time" (III.97–98). Action is indiscriminate impulse, undertaken for its own sake. Traveling is one of its lighter manifestations, a solitary and unsocial action. When societies act, they produce the carnage of Talavera, represented in the first canto (sts. 38–44), or its repetition at Waterloo (III. sts. 25–28), or its prefiguration at Thrasimene (IV, sts. 62–65). Glory, fame, courage—the very stuff of romance—reduce to an abstract violence. The bullfighting arena of modern Spain (I. sts. 68–80) simply ritualizes the passion for destruction, as did the Roman Coliseum (IV. sts. 139–142). As we build monuments so as to have ruins, we do to undo.

Byron's systematic demystification of the spatial and temporal elements of romance extends to its protagonists, heroes of action and vision—Napoleon and Rousseau, respectively—the towering poles from which he suspends the structure of the third canto. They are both described as living oxymorons, whose "spirit[s]" are "antithetically mixt" (III.317). "Conqueror and captive of the earth" (III.325), Napoleon is both "more or less than man" (III.334). He is possessed of "a fire / And motion of the soul" that "once kindled, quenchless evermore, / Preys upon high adventure" (III.371–376) with universally fatal results. He is, in other words, the incarnation of the abstracted destructive action surveyed throughout *Childe Harold's Pilgrimage*. And yet his philosophical counterpart cannot escape the same inner division, whose friction inevitably drives to the same end. Rousseau retreats from action, but remains a "self-torturing sophist" (III.725), "Kindled . . . and blasted" (III.736) by the perfect ideal he could conceive but never discover on earth. There is fire here as well, but it represents (as Byron originally wrote, III.749) the "spirit's self-consuming heat." And yet that fire in the hands of others "set the world in flame, / Nor ceased to burn till kingdoms were no more" (III.763–764), and the result was that "good with ill they also overthrew, / Leaving but ruins" (III.774–775). These ruins, like all the others in the poem, testify to dead fictions, the human hunger for the improbable. If we could purify ourselves to the condition of the Zoroastrian priests, worshipping from mountain peaks the fires of the distant universe, as Byron represents them in a pointed metaphorical enclosure of the third canto (sts. 14 and 91), we might escape the destruction wrought by the friction of a universal contrariety; "but this clay will sink / Its spark immortal" (III.123–124). No one knows this better than the poet, who weaves his metaphor so sinuously through the entire canto, centering it first in himself as "A whirling gulf of phantasy and flame" (III.58). It is because of this that he writes, creating the "Soul of my thought! with whom I traverse earth, / Invisible but gazing" (III.51–52).

Increasingly in *Childe Harold's Pilgrimage*, as Byron demystifies the materials of romance and therefore his capacity to write a modern romance, he posits a *tertium quid* against ruined shrines and ruinous action: art for the sake of art. It too is a self-propelling activity. If it has a moral, it rests with the reader to create it, as the last line of the poem affirms. If the poem is to be a living monument, that too is left to others to sustain. Art does not necessarily redeem the artist, as Rousseau's life indicates, nor does it alter the conditions of society, as Italy's history abundantly demonstrates. Byron, in other words, does not abandon his universal demystification in order to place his art on a pedestal of self-congratulation. But his pilgrimage in quest of an ideal order becomes more and more a quest for art and a quest through art. Romancing is the universal thirst of humanity for its ideals. Even out of the universal decay of fictions, the poet, who knows himself to be "A ruin amidst ruins" (IV.219), recognizes that "still teems / My mind with many a form which aptly seems / Such as I sought for" (IV.58–60). He will embody those forms, evanescent though they may be, because, like the victims of violence—the bull "disdaining to decline" (I.785) or the dying gladiator who

"Consents to death, but conquers agony" (IV.1254)—any assertion of integrity is a shrine to the ideal. The ruins of history are like those of the Coliseum, once an arena for sanctioned destructiveness: "A ruin—yet what ruin! from its mass / Walls, places, half-cities, have been reared" (IV.1279-80). And so his monumental poem acquires its form and inner life, paradoxically "Prey[ing] on high adventure" and on the "spirit's self-consuming heat" in order to validate romance out of its very ruins.

With the "magic circle" (IV.1295) of the Coliseum (Shelley appears, with his borrowing of this phrase and so many others, to have used Byron as Rome did the Coliseum), Byron begins to develop an intricate architectural metaphor that will ultimately emblematize his own poem. The "Arches on arches" (IV.1144) of the Coliseum ascend toward heaven and return to earth, building layer after layer upon the impulse of Byron's pilgrimage. The Mole of Hadrian is another enclosing circle. To the circle the Pantheon, a shrine to all gods, adds an enclosing dome, and the principle is enlarged to breathtaking proportions in the largest architectural structure in the world, St. Peter's Basilica. "But lo! the dome—the vast and wondrous dome" (IV.1369), a monument to the fiction that has endured the centuries and organized much of the world within its mythic confines, itself as perfect a rendering of the improbable as art has ever created. Stone upon stone, through perfect balance, employ the stress, the mutual friction, of contraries, to defy the force of gravity that draws all things, including gods, to the earth. It is a metaphor for all art, but most particularly for Byron's poem, a grand assemblage of jarring oppositions, the stanzas each being building blocks of a structure that here at last can contemplate itself as a whole: "Vastness which grows—but grows to harmonize— / All musical in its immensities" (IV.1399-1400). Byron's poem, too, can only be observed "piecemeal" (IV.1405); it transcends its mere materials, because it is always a process, is always, like the stresses in the building-blocks of the dome, in arrested motion. As the poet well recognizes, he has another analogy present in his poem from its early stanzas, originally a metaphor for instability and transience, now redeemed as an image of the transcendent ideal that his romance has served through all its denials. St. Peter's Basilica is like the ocean (IV.1407), its grandeur poised between the ebb and flow of contrary stresses: both are "The image of Eternity—the throne / Of the Invisible" (IV.1644-45), as Byron describes the ocean. His "pilgrim's shrine is won" (IV.1567) in St. Peter's not through conversion but through finding a fit metaphor for the improbable. But the grail cannot be fixed and stabilized. In the same stanza where Byron proclaims his victory, he relinquishes himself and the fiction of himself to the ocean, that universal ebb and flow that mirrors the vicissitudes of human life as well as eternity, and mirrors too the poem in which Byron triumphantly mediates between them.[41] The poem may end, but the pilgrimage casts itself upon the ocean where the quest continues, doomed but universal and therefore unending: "there are wanderers o'er Eternity / Whose bark drives on and on, and anchored ne'er shall be" (III.669–670).

By the time the last canto of *Childe Harold's Pilgrimage* was published in 1818, its author had become the foremost poet of European Romanticism. It is not too simple to say that it happened precisely because he wrote *the* romance for an age that had lost all its fictions. His was a revival beyond the reach of scholarship, and its success came not from his contemplating himself in the poem, but from his contemplating a genre in himself. *Childe Harold's Pilgrimage* is truly an internalized quest romance, whose ringing notes of triumph at the end signal the improbable recovery of a genre, a mode of apprehension, from its ruins.

CHAPTER SEVEN

The Epic

READER, if instant thy soul-lighted eyes
Perceive the claims of GENIUS as they rise,
Welcome this noblest effort of the NINE,
To deck with Epic wreath their English shrine;
Since there they rose, to emulate, at length,
The Mantuan sweetness, the Meonian strength,
And our green vales and silver streams along
Pour'd Eden's grand, imperishable song. . . .
Thus, for the glory of the nineteenth age,
The EPIC MUSE awakes her sacred rage.

Anna Seward, "Verses written in the
Blank Leaves of Southey's *Madoc*" (1805)

A correspondent wrote us lately an account of a tea-drinking in the west of
England, at which there assisted no fewer than six epic poets—a host of
Parnassian strength, certainly equal to six-and-thirty bands. . . . How un-
reasonable then is it to complain, that poetry is on the decline among us!

Edinburgh Review, 11 (1808), 362

. . . such [is] the overflow of genius and talent among us, that we have to
boast of more than one poet, who can send forth yearly, or even monthly,
compositions of this kind, of a length which would formerly have employed a whole life of ordinary duration.

R. Payne Knight, Preface to *Alfred* (1823)

I

THE ROMANCE REVIVAL, by its intensity and by the popularity of the new
poetry that accompanied it, has marked the period from 1790 to 1825
indelibly with its name. Yet, the truly amazing phenomenon during this
time is the proliferation of epics in England, which is unique in the
history of Western literature. If we are inclined to smile at the pretensions
of a culture that anticipated several epics every year, we perhaps testify
less to our taste than to our own shift in values and lowered expectations.
Every major poet planned an epic (though not all were executed) and
minor bards issued them in profusion. For many, it must be remembered,
the distinction between romance and epic enforced in this discussion was
at best blurred. Throughout the opening decade of the nineteenth century
the annual *Poetical Register and Repository of Fugitive Poetry* separated
for prior reviews a category first termed "Epic and Heroic Poems," then
in 1812 "Epic Poems and Romances": the rest of the year's publications

were merely "Miscellaneous." George Ellis, who knew a romance when he saw one, discussed the first cantos of *Childe Harold's Pilgrimage* from the perspective of epic; Scott's *Marmion* was talked of in similar terms; and though we might draw so fine a distinction as to conceive of *Joan of Arc* as Southey's only true venture in the form, we are left with Byron's memorable expectation of "an epic from Bob Southey every spring" (*Don Juan* III, 97.4), or, if we wish to adopt a more generous contemporary attitude, with the *Annual Review*'s description of *Madoc* as "the best epic poem, which, since the Paradise Lost, has quitted the British Press."[1]

There are a number of impulses, some of them wholly antithetical, converging upon this phenomenon, one of which was clearly the romance revival itself. Another was the popularity of Cowper's *The Task* (1785). Though its colloquial tone and desultory method had an extraordinary impact on contemporary poetry, particularly with Wordsworth and Byron, it was less the substance of Cowper's poem than the readership it attracted—middle-class, devout Dissenters, and serious readers of long poems—that influenced the course of epic poetry. The sense of historical urgency, even destiny, that accompanied the fall of the Bourbon monarchy in France and which then was brought to a head with the British declaration of war is everywhere evident. Its presence is felt in the sudden outpouring of nationalistic epics, particularly in the years at the turn of the century when invasion threatened; in attempts to adapt the typology of Biblical subjects to the historical crisis; in radically subversive and visionary works that would liberate all nations; and naturally in those poems which endeavored to translate national missions into epic dimensions. Epic poetry, it had been said, is "doctrinal and exemplary to a Nation." Milton's observation stands behind the entire epic outpouring. More important still, so does the poet.[2]

The 1790s were a period of intense interest in Milton, with several important editions coming into print, remarkable sets of illustrations to his works epitomized by Fuseli's "Milton Gallery" and by Blake's first group of designs, a variorum edition of *Paradise Regained* edited by Charles Dunster (1795), and the three-volume folio, *Poetical Works of John Milton. With a Life of the Author*, by William Hayley (1794–1796). Hayley also commissioned Cowper, who lived under his protection at Felpham in his last years (his successor was, of course, Blake), to translate the Latin and Greek poems of Milton into English. Henry John Todd's seven-volume variorum edition of the poetry in 1801 and Charles Symmons' seven volumes of prose in 1806 culminated this burst of energy. It is undoubtedly an aspect of the entire pattern of literary revival we have observed in previous chapters, and it is linked as well with the surge of interest in Shakespeare centered around the great Boydell edition. But the differences are telling. Locked in a desperate and intractable conflict with the French, and with pressures at home more explosive than had been experienced since the constitutional settlement of 1688, the British naturally drew their national treasures into the array of battle. Shakespeare was perhaps the chief of these. But Milton was part of the battle itself, an apologist for the people against monarchy, defiant before invested authority whether in church or crown, a peerless intellectual, and the author of not one but, emphatically in this period, two epic poems stressing human responsibility within the providence of God. And yet, his unswerving faith and his sense of British destiny made him a man for all seasons, embraced by a conservative Anglican prelate like Todd, by a radical enthusiast like Blake, and by the Jacobins of the 1790s. In a sense they all strove to place him in the vanguard of a cause. Historically speaking, the liberal Whigs had the advantage. In terms of literary posterity, however, it was decidedly in favor of those who saw to the roots of their culture and diagnosed its manifold diseases. "[T]he sacred Milton was, let it ever be remembered, a Republican, and a bold enquirer into morals and religion," exclaimed Shelley in the preface to *Prometheus Unbound* (p. 134). The boldest enquirers among the British Romantics were those most deeply imbued with Shelley's sense of Milton's example, but his specter shadows every attempt to write a poem of epic scope. Frequently, as might be expected, the contrast overwhelms the poet who vies with him; but, unlike the eighteenth century, which had generally dodged possible comparison, no anxiety of influence bars the dozens who, starting in the 1790s, set their eyes on the high slopes of Parnassus and with a deep breath began the ascent. The faith is at once comic and moving.

The bards carried their Virgil from school; a few packed Homer, or at least Pope's version of Homer.[3] A thumbworn Milton accompanied them all. And William Hayley provided the guidebook. Southey's encomium to his *Essay on Epic Poetry* (1782) was noted in the previous chapter, but his estimate of the critical importance of this work merits elucidation. Had Hayley written a decade later, doubtless he would have experienced some problems in holding to the high Enlightenment strain he adopted. But the very distance from the confusion of values that soon followed allowed his learning, his program, and his ideological focus to serve as clear beacons to his readers. One of his major endeavors is to expand the canon of approved models: Lucan is raised from his disregard; the medieval Latin epics principally by Italians are surveyed with taste and discrimination; the *Divine Comedy* is celebrated and its first three cantos translated in terza rima in the notes; Ercilla is granted major attention and Camoens highly praised. Only the French are without true contenders for the laurels, Voltaire's *Henriade* being considered stillborn. Instead, as Hayley views their fortunes, they turned aside to write the rules for epic poetry, rules that no true bard could abide and that resulted in feeble academic exercises when followed.[4]

In the history of literature, as Hayley perceives it, there will always be "slaves of System" (III.173), but no great poet is one. Ariosto, for instance, was "Born every law of System to disown, / And rule by Fancy's boundless power alone" (III.155–156). From the first line ("Perish that critic pride") to the last, Hayley argues that "Freedom is the soul of Art" (I.298) and vows to "Free the young Bard from that oppressive awe, / Which feels Opinion's rule as Reason's law" (I.31–32). And his means and ends are exactly congruent: the new national epic, he enjoins the poets of Britain, should have as its highest aim to celebrate "The splendid fane of British Freedom" (V.300). Milton, who did not live to see it, is its inspiriting force, and thus Hayley explicitly directs the ambitious bard:

> If from his commerce with the'inspiring Muse
> He seeks to gain, by no mean aims confin'd,
> Freedom of thought and energy of mind;
> To raise his spirit, with aetherial fire,
> Above each little want and low desire;
> O turn where Milton flames with Epic rage. . . . (IV.320–325)

It is hard to imagine such thumping couplets inflaming anyone's imagination, and yet Hayley's enthusiasm, his learning, and his humane principles were taken to heart by his culture. The first note in harmony was struck in 1790 with *The Revolution,* an epic poem in twelve cantos anonymously written by the Manchester reed maker, James Ogden, and published by Joseph Johnson, whose circle in the 1790s included every prominent liberal intellectual in London. It was followed in 1791 with an exploratory first canto of another anonymous epic, *The Revolution; or Britain Delivered* (Edinburgh: William Creech, and London: Thomas Cadell), dedicated to Lord Thurlow, the Lord High Chancellor (whose nephew would inherit the title in 1806 and make a nod or two toward the epic muse himself). Though the expanded version of this second epic celebrating the Bloodless Revolution of 1688 was not published until 1800, the preface of 1791, "asserting the laws of justice, and rights of mankind, in opposition to the dictates of slavery and despotism" (p. 5), and the invocation—"Descend, fair Freedom, from that awful height . . ." (1. 7)—testify to the clear influence of Hayley.[5]

By the turn into the new century the British reader had a number of candidates for the great national poem the country lacked. As the political repression deepened, however, it became more difficult to celebrate a constitutional accord whose true existence was in doubt, and difficult even to praise anything resembling a revolution without threat of penalty. The result was an inevitable turning to the legendary past. Joseph Cottle's *Alfred* (1800) was succeeded by another *Alfred* by the poet laureate, Henry James Pye, in 1801. In 1801, also, John Ogilvie's *Brittania: A National Epic Poem in Twenty Books* on the founding of Britain and *Richard the First* by Sir James Bland Burges issued from the press. John Thelwall, surveying the contemporary scene as he published specimens of his own medieval epic, *The Hope of Albion; or, Edwin of Northumbria* in 1801, was led to observe that "he finds . . . the press teeming, and, perhaps the public already satiated with National Heroics, which, when his principal work was first projected, was a *desideratum* in English Poesy.''[6] It may well have been the case that the public taste was satiated with these poems. At least, two decades were to pass before the subjects were again essayed in Eleonor Ann Porden's *Coeur de Lion; or the Third Crusade* (1822) and Richard Payne Knight's last bow in print, *Alfred; a Romance in Rhyme* (1823).[7] Of all of these poems Cottle's is surely the best, and his minor success (there were new editions in 1804 and 1816 and an American imprint in 1814) is directly attributable to the company he kept. The prefaces to the first and second editions affirm the suitability of the plain style of the Lake poets for epic endeavors and emphasize the values of uninflated realism and charged dramatic encounters. The epics on Richard the First, on the other hand, resort to what had become traditional machinery, openly borrowing from Milton and Southey, with Burges having the government of France virtually run by Satan and Belial and Porden resorting to the whole tribe of evil genii that *Thalaba* had wiped from the earth to justify Saladin's feats in battle. Richard Payne Knight, inveighing in his preface against the superstition and bloodletting sanctioned by early Christianity, retains a supernatural machinery by employing "of the different modifications of Christianity . . . the only one entirely compatible with the now generally received system of the universe," which is to say "the system of emanations" (p. vii) projected by Emanuel Swedenborg and—significant in such a context—already in use by William Blake.[8]

The high acclaim accorded Southey's *Madoc* in its time seems singly responsible for a second line of national medieval epics involving Wales. Joseph Cottle's second poem in the genre, *The Fall of Cambria* (1809, 2nd ed. 1811), devoted twenty-four books to the campaign of Edward I to join the separate kingdoms into a united Britain; and his success was followed by M[ary] Linwood's brief epic on the same subject, *The Anglo-Cambrian*, in 1818. Underlying these poems is the assumption that Scott and his successors had already cornered the northern market; but Cottle's poem at least shows the same Bristol prejudices of Southey being incorporated into a celebration of national unity. Perhaps there is also a sardonic nod in the direction of Gray as Cottle dons the bardic cloak to celebrate the English victory that precipitated Gray's bard from the cliff. The kinds of researches Gray promulgated during his lifetime actually enter the epic lists very late in the period. William Herbert, the translator of the Eddas, produced his *Helga* in 1815, reducing, to cite the stricture of the *Edinburgh Review*, "the gigantic forms of Scandinavia" to "a pretty, modern, melting love-story . . . fit and pleasing ornaments for the boudoirs."[9] Far better—and, indeed, not a poem to have been so wholly lost from modern consciousness—is Henry Hart Milman's *Samor, Lord of the Bright City* (1818), whose hero is Eldulph de Samor, Earl of Gloucester (etymologically, according to Milman's preface, the Bright City) in the time of the late Roman domination, who defends Christianity against the pagan Hengist and after a dazzling battle scene in Book XI (which runs over a thousand lines) defeats the Scandinavian forces. Conventional in

its patriotism, with encomiums to Britain sung at the beginnings of
Books I, V, and XI, and conventional, too, in a religious fervor befitting
the future Dean of St. Paul's, it is nonetheless the most polished and
gifted of these attempts to create a national epic from medieval sources. It
was succeeded by another Saxon epic, *Rogvald*, by John Fitzgerald Pennie (1823), whose greatest significance is that its second book begins with
a paean to the poet of *Beowulf*. It would appear to be the original
introduction of the Anglo-Saxon epic into modern literary influence.
With appropriate irony, at the end of this period of intense effort to cull a
national epic from medieval sources there emerges at last the true one.[10]

The other major line of epics during this age is religious in character,
the legacy of a different but certainly no less formidable eighteenth-
century revival, the Evangelical Movement. Methodism found its bard in
William Cowper (though he staunchly defended his Anglican faith), and
his high moral earnestness invests all of the more traditional epics on
religious subjects that followed him. Historically distant, Milton is nonetheless the figure to whom they all revert. The significant problem they
face, however, is a definition of the subject matter. Milton clearly confronted the same difficulty and resolved it with customary brilliance by
elaborating in both epics what were relatively sketchy biblical texts. Only
one religious epic during the Romantic period attempts to find room for
invention in Holy Writ, James Montgomery's *The World Before the
Flood* (1812); yet, if its claims to literary significance probably excel any
of the others, it cannot escape the solemn piety that universally afflicts
these poems. But the others founder as well on the rock of ages so to
speak, for being wholly unwilling to put out to sea.

Yet, they are not barren of instruction for literary history. Far from it,
they allow us to see Milton's direct influence from an obvious, though
previously unexamined, perspective. By the late eighteenth century the
process by which Milton had been assimilated to Scripture was complete.
George Gregory, the translator of Bishop Lowth's *Lectures on the Sacred
Poetry of the Hebrews*, acknowledges this fact with bemusement:

> I cannot help observing, that the whole fabric of Paradise Lost, except the
> mere naked narrative of the Fall, is founded upon the most slender authority
> imaginable, two or three short, obscure, and ill-understood passages, chiefly
> in the Epistle of St. Jude; and yet it forms at present a part of our popular
> theology. Our grandsires, and even perhaps many grave Doctors of Divinity,
> would exclaim against the impiety of that man who would dare to question
> a syllable of the authenticity of all that he has related, of the war in heaven,
> of the rebellious spirits, &c. &c. This is a new proof of the preponderancy of
> Milton's genius, as well as of his popularity.[11]

This is the implicit assumption of what, historically speaking, is the first
complete epic of the period, *Calvary; or the Death of Christ* (1792) by
Richard Cumberland. Cumberland, whose modest dramatic gifts are
occasionally remembered with a nod to *The West Indian*, left the stage

after his Methodist conversion and devoted himself to unexceptional literary endeavors. (His novel *Henry* [1795] is *Joseph Andrews* as Wesley might have written it.) *Calvary* enjoyed a high regard among the pious and was handsomely reprinted in two volumes in 1800. It is written in the plain Miltonic style, that is to say, the style of *Paradise Regained*, and it begins exactly where Milton's brief epic ends, with Satan recalling the events leading to his defeat in the wilderness and summoning a council of devils who resolve to tempt Judas to betray Jesus. Scripture is filled in by this infernal machinery and, at the end, by the resurrected Moses conversing with Gabriel about paradise; otherwise the Bible is, in truth, followed assiduously, sententiously. From the first, of course, it was the particular character of the epic to spawn successors, with Virgil carefully picking his way around *The Iliad* and *The Odyssey* and assimilating Homer into his own distinctive structure. But Cumberland conceives himself as Milton's exact follower, and in turn after his death he was to provoke a sequel from a Mrs. [Charlotte Eliza] Dixon, *The Mount of Olives, or the Resurrection and Ascension; a Poem. In Continuation of Calvary* (1814), which apostrophizes Cumberland in heaven and leads Christ (whom Cumberland had left after his harrowing hell) into his place among the saints. And as Cumberland had begun where Milton ended, so the ill-fated Henry Kirke White appears to have planned some manner of revision of Cumberland's epic as well. At least, the three hundred lines of his fragment, *The Christiad* (published by Southey among the *Remains* in 1807), begin precisely at the same point, with Satan's report to his legions on the failure of his temptation and his anticipation of revenge through the crucifixion.[12] There is one further variation on this theme worth noting, another epic by James Ogden, whose *The Revolution* of 1790 had signalled the beginning of the collective national effort. Again anonymously, in 1797 he published *Emanuel; or, Paradise Regained: An Epic Poem in Nine Books*. It is clear that he had read Cumberland's *Calvary*, for he also introduces Moses (and, for good measure, Elias) into the structure of his poem. But unlike Cumberland, who treats *Paradise Regained* as an extension of scripture, Ogden actually has the temerity to challenge the master and rewrite his poem. The result is, however, truly dismal: everything radical in Milton's brief epic becomes conventional; its restraint is discarded; its profound interiority is opened out and trivialized.[13] And, on top of his literary sins, the Whig apologist has in these short years turned reactionary, associating democratic politics with Satan. Yet, Ogden is one of only two epic poets of the period willing to confront Milton rather than simply assimilate him to Scripture. The other, of course, is Blake, to whom we will return.

A second wave of post-Miltonic epics begins in the new century, and all of their authors, including even Cumberland, revert to the Old Testament for subjects. In 1807 his collaboration with Sir James Bland Burges, the first four cantos of a projected ten, was published as *The Exodiad, A*

Poem. By the Authors of Calvary and Richard the First. It is, they acknowledge in the Advertisement, the first such partnership "in the epic line," but one that never extended to a completion of the poem. The same year, however, offered a second epic on the subject, *Exodus*, by Charles Hoyle, Domestic Chaplain to the Duke of Marlborough, which was published by J. Hatchard, "Bookseller to her Majesty." The connection with the aristocracy and crown is probably indicative of the strains of the Napoleonic wars (and perhaps, too, the loose living of the Prince of Wales). But such encouragement—more than a century had passed since Richard Blackmore was knighted for the bloodless thunders of *Prince Arthur* (1695)—also reflects the public standing of epic poetry, particularly the pious variety, in this age. Hoyle's *Exodus* is the most thoroughly Miltonic of the Romantic epics, attempting to capture the organ tones of the grand style and continually reverting to *Paradise Lost* for characters and situations as well as style. What is most characteristic about the Hoyle and Cumberland–Burges epics drawn from Exodus, however, is that they are, once again, clearly conceived as sequels to Milton, picking up the second book of the Old Testament as he had the first.[14]

Another way of conceiving such a sequel is to concentrate on the exact point where Michael suspends his historical narrative in Book XII of *Paradise Lost*, with the crowning of David as typological precursor of Christ. This is the climactic moment of both William Sotheby's *Saul* (1807), which at its best achieves a stark spareness of effect, and J. F. Pennie's *The Royal Minstrel; or, The Witcheries of Endor* (1817). Joseph Cottle's *Messiah* of 1815 also devotes its last third to David and in the final canto translates him into heaven, where Raphael assumes Michael's role and shows the future intervening until the Messiah's descent. The concentration on the struggle between Saul and David allows all three poets to introduce the battle scenes absent from the various derivatives of *Paradise Regained*. But except for the last canto of Cottle's *Messiah* these Old Testament epics lack the cosmic dimensions of *Paradise Lost*.

An attempt to restore them is made in 1815 by the Rev. George Townsend with the first eight of twelve projected books of an epic entitled *Armageddon*. Like Hoyle he is identified as a graduate of Trinity College, Cambridge, and like him too his publisher is Hatchard and the epic is patronized by nobility, here the Duke of Devonshire. Townsend's preface also expresses gratitude for the solicitude of Richard Cumberland, who had recently died, in his effort. This is a world, it would seem, that has become increasingly constricted. Unfinished as it is, *Armageddon* at least branches out from biblical texts to attempt an apocalyptic grandeur of its own. It also draws on the popularity of *The Curse of Kehama*, enlisting various Indian gods (who are all in the service of Satan and have a special dislike for Britain) in the destruction of the earth. The result is little more than a curiosity, but the extent to which the materials of romance are assimilated to what had become conventional to religious epic indicates an urge to break free of the twin scriptures of the Bible and Milton.[15]

As suggested earlier, the one religious epic of the period that succeeds in this endeavor is Montgomery's *World Before the Flood*, published in 1812. And it does so by virtually transforming its materials into those of a romance. Its hero is a minstrel whose life in exile among the descendents of Cain has grown intolerable and who escapes to return to his threatened people, led by Enoch, the first of the post-Adamic types of Christ in *Paradise Lost*, Book XI. Through the central importance of this fictional hero, Javan, the power of song and its reflection of heavenly harmony become as much concerns of this epic as they are of the contemporary romance. And until the last canto, when the venerable Enoch is translated into heaven, there are neither miraculous events (except those memorialized from the past or the revelations of dreams) nor supernatural machinery. The love of the minstrel Javan for Zillah effectively humanizes the poem. Yet, on the other hand, a sentimental epic that trades on Scott lacks the dimensions customary to the genre; and the exemplification of patient endurance of one's martyrdom, while good Methodist teaching, leaves a vacuum where heroics are anticipated. The incongruities of mode are as blatant and unresolved in Montgomery's poem as they are in Shelley's *Revolt of Islam* (which may, indeed, have been influenced in this regard by Montgomery's popularity). Montgomery does in fact break free from the grip of biblical and Miltonic scriptures, but his poem cannot truly sustain either epic purpose or pressure. His later attempt to wed epic achievement and religious piety through the experience of eighteenth-century Moravian missionaries, a five-canto fragment of *Greenland* (1819), is perhaps doomed by its unpromising subject but reveals his active search for a means of escaping the impasse into which religious epics had, on principle, strayed. The actual escape for Montgomery was into fantastic allegory, in a poem that defies generic categorization and perhaps even meaning, *The Pelican Island* (1827).

So extensive a survey of comparatively minor poems with major pretensions is unlikely to rescue any from neglect. But it does accentuate the difficulties of writing an epic poem, even in an age that thrived upon them. The requirement of genius to the side, if no successful epic is written by following the rules, neither is there an example of one made by copying models. James Ogden's urge to rewrite Milton is actually the inherent thrust of the epic mode, even if he went about it in exactly the wrong way, replacing the conventions that Milton had subverted in the first place. Hayley's injunction to his countrymen to stand up for freedom both ideologically and generically proved hard to put into practice, particularly in the midst of a war to restore ancient privilege. But there were those with the vision to see what he meant, though not always to practice successfully what he preached. The libertarian epic that flourished in the shade of sanctioned piety and patriotism also was capable of foundering in its turn, but truly for want of genius rather than conception. Subversion is, after all, the life blood of the epic genre.[16]

II

Joan of Arc was published by Joseph Cottle early in 1796, several months before Robert Southey attained his majority. It was at its time a stunning achievement of precocity and is only less so in retrospect because of the early successes of Shelley and Keats. Everything about the poem projects an image of the *enfant terrible*, and, indeed, Southey went out of his way to ensure it (as Shelley also did in *Queen Mab*). The Homeric epigraph in Greek is balanced by a knowledgeable critique of classical epics in the preface and a defense of Homer against his translators: "Pope has disguised him in foppery, and Cowper has stripped him naked."[17] Indeed, the critique expands to cover ten epic poems that Southey handles with little deference to authority. "There are few readers who do not prefer Turnus to Aeneas" (xxiii); "I do not scruple to prefer Statius to Virgil" (xxiv); "I have endeavoured to avoid what appears to me the common fault of epic poems, and to render the Maid of Orleans interesting" (xxv); "It has been established as a necessary rule for the epic, that the subject should be national. To this rule I have acted in direct opposition" (xxvii): direct opposition—subversion.

Southey's literary and political aims are wholly and very cleverly integrated in the poem. In a climate of growing repression of Jacobin sympathizers, accompanied by a concerted attempt to muzzle the press, he audaciously celebrates a French campaign for liberation from British rule. His central figure, true to the poet who would head his 1797 *Poems* with verses addressed "To Mary Wollstonecraft" and a lengthy account of "The Triumph of Women," is not a man but a woman of courage, fortitude, and vision—also, as one might expect in the 1790s, of sensibility. Though there are stirring accounts of battle that suggest a close study of classical epics, Joan and her cohorts denounce the ravages of warfare as they engage their brutish and unchivalrous adversaries. His purpose, Southey suggests in the opening lines, is to sing "War's varied horrors, and the train of ills / That follow on Ambition's blood-stain'd path / And fill the world with woe" (1797: I.1-3). With Church and King mobs being openly encouraged by the government of Pitt, Southey represents the clerisy as both crafty and vicious and the court as degenerate, composed of fops and factions. That, of course, is what the British generally thought of the French, but the portrait of the Dauphin Charles, on a second glance, is a telling likeness of the Prince of Wales. As John Aikin remarked in reviewing the poem, "a strong allusion to later characters and events is manifest, and we know not where the ingenuity of a crown lawyer would stop, were he employed to make out a list of innuendos."[18] Moreover, in crowning the Dauphin King of France at the very

end of the poem, Joan does not mince her words but concludes her lecture
by pointing to the consequences of his swerving from his duty:

>   "Believe me, King! that hireling guards,
> Tho' flesh'd in slaughter, would be weak to save
> A tyrant on the blood-cemented Throne
> That totters underneath him." Thus the Maid
> Redeem'd her country. Ever may the ALL-JUST
> Give to the arms of FREEDOM such success. (1797:X.743–748)

True to the argument of Hayley, Southey celebrates freedom, but it is
French liberty, equality, and fraternity (and sorority) that he holds up
to the British public as an example to contemplate. Southey's protest
against rules in his preface is somewhat disingenuous: never did moral
purpose and the need to educate princes so dictate the course of an epic
poem.

   Southey's antiwar and anti-imperialist ethos is shared by his Oxford
classmate Landor, and, though his *Gebir* (1798) has more of romance
than epic in its makeup, in the context of Southey's epic and of the
contemporary war Landor's political sentiments are one of the few clear
elements in his poem.[19] No reader of 1798 could miss the implications of
a colonial power in Egypt, where Napoleon had just landed his armies
and usurped the Marmaluke government. But the anticolonial ethos of
the poem implicates the British as well as the French.[20] The only nationalist faith endorsed by *Gebir* is the right of a people to be left to their
own devices. The natural end of colonial governors, even well-inten-
tioned ones like Gebir, is assassination. Though the poem has a number of
generic signals suggesting its epic claims—conventional invocations, a
visit to the underworld—Landor wholly subverts the notion of epic
heroism, of Virgilian duty. (This would have been even clearer had he
fulfilled his initial eccentric notion of writing the entire poem in Latin.)
Public responsibilities forestall personal satisfactions and are wholly
antithetical to the supreme value of love that Landor honors in Book IV.
The poem is alternately wonderful and baffling, as much as *Joan of Arc*
the product of adolescent ambition, and it is thus risky to presume
Landor's overall intentions. And yet he appears purposefully, and with a
sophisticated literary understanding, to have pitted the genres of romance
and epic against each other, valuing the pastoral romance to which
Gebir's brother Tamar gives his allegiance over the public, imperialist
duties of his epic hero. Reveling in his luxuriance of style, Landor knows
the difference between writing and doing.

   In both *Joan of Arc* and *Gebir* Virgil is the model who is dethroned,
and with him the value of an imperial mission and the warfare that
sustains it. That this is not simply the bravado of two disgruntled Oxoni-
ans who never finished their undergraduate degrees can be easily seen in
the shared views of Joseph Cottle. *Alfred* is, in a sense, Cottle's response
to the epic he printed for Southey, recast so as to celebrate a national hero

of Britain. Its main action is the defeat of the imperialist Danes by Alfred's Saxons, and the single battle is cast three-fourths of the way through the epic, in Book XVIII, the book ending with the outcome still in doubt. The Danes, we subsequently learn, have been defeated, and the remainder of the epic is spent on Alfred's politic means of effecting the peaceful surrender of the Danish chieftain, Guthrum, and his conversion to Christianity. Cottle's is virtually a pacifist epic, and he makes his point very clear in his preface, where he discusses battle as not only disgusting in itself but also a cliché of epics:

> . . . it is not an unfair supposition that, if Alexander had not heard of Achilles, Charles the XII. would not have emulated Alexander, in which case, the world might have been benefitted by the talents of two extraordinary men, the evil of whose characters seems principally to have arisen from an early and indiscriminate passion for arms.[21]

This is a delicate way of putting Blake's passionate conclusion to "On Homer's Poetry": "The Classics, it is the classics! & not Goths nor Monks, that Desolate Europe with Wars" (p. 267). If we place *Joan of Arc, Gebir,* and *Alfred* in the context of the various derivatives of *Paradise Regained* in the 1790s and the two epic defenses of a revolution that was, in the popular memory, bloodless, there emerges a clear pattern of epic subversion, fostered alike by critical public events and Milton's two attempts to find a subject "Above Heroic."[22]

There was another obvious epic subject of the Southeyan kind that would touch much closer to home than fifteenth-century France, the American Revolution. Thomas Northmore's *Washington, or Liberty Restored* appears from internal evidence to have been written in the 1790s but held back until a more favorable climate for printing such a poem might occur. Thus it was finally published in 1809, bearing the imprimatur of the respected and wholly unradical firm of Longman, Hurst, Rees, and Orme. Its political motivation is clear from the preface, where Northmore defends his enthusiasm as "aggravated by the proclaimed increase of the influence of the crown, and the gigantick strides of modern corruption" (p. iv). The epic ends with yet another passionate apostrophe to Liberty as the "Spirit divine" to whom "the Muse / Owes her best fires" (X.262-264). For all its good intentions, however, *Washington* is made ludicrous by Northmore's borrowing the conventional machinery already hackneyed by his contemporaries and employing it full force in a modern environment. To have the Spirit of Liberty remove the film of mortality from Washington's eyes so that he can see the future might seem a valuable asset to any future head of state, but when what he sees is the entire infernal host floating above the Appalachian Mountains, the effect is almost as deflating as the later representation of Satan at the ear of Cornwallis. Northmore's unintentionally self-subverting epic, however, allows us a useful perspective to bring to the work that almost certainly impelled its publication, an epic poem that not only has been unjustly ridiculed but is the most radical of all the epics that have so far entered the discussion in its revision of the material, conventions, and purposes of the genre.

> Almighty Freedom! give my venturous song
> The force, the charm that to thy voice belong;
> Tis thine to shape my course, to light my way,
> To nerve my country with the patriot lay,
> To teach all men where all their interest lies,
> How rulers may be just and nations wise:
> Strong in thy strength I bend no suppliant knee,
> Invoke no miracle, no Muse but thee.

This is the epic invocation of Joel Barlow's *The Columbiad* (I.23–30).[23] Even more explicitly than Cottle and Southey, Barlow turns away from the classical epics, devoting a considerable portion of his preface to a demonstration of their corrupting influence on all subsequent culture. Distinguishing between the fictional and real (that is, ideological) design of *The Iliad*, he praises the first and decries the second:

> Its obvious tendency was to inflame the minds of young readers with an enthusiastic ardor for military fame; to inculcate the pernicious doctrine of the divine right of kings; to teach both prince and people that military plunder was the most honorable mode of acquiring property; and that conquest, violence and war were the best employment of nations, the most glorious prerogative of bodily strength and cultivated mind. (pp. vii–viii)

Barlow concludes that Homer's "existence has really proved one of the signal misfortunes of mankind" (p. viii). The ideological thrust of *The Aeneid* is virtually the same: "Virgil wrote and felt like a subject, not like a citizen. The real design of his poem was to increase the veneration of the people for a master, whoever he might be, and to encourage like Homer the great system of military depredation" (p. ix). The political ends of *The Columbiad* are exactly the opposite, as Barlow makes certain his readers understand:

> ... the real object of the poem ... is to inculcate the love of national liberty, and to discountenance the deleterious passion for violence and war; to show that on the basis of the republican principle all good morals, as well as good government and hopes of permanent peace, must be founded; and to convince the student in political science that the theoretical question of the future advancement of society, till states as well as individuals arrive at universal civilization, is held in dispute and still unsettled only because we have had too little experience of organized liberty in the government of nations to have well considered its effects. (p. x)

The Columbiad is truly the epic written to Hayley's prescription, though its sense of the inherent logic of its subject, honed by over two decades of reflection, goes far beyond what Hayley invited or initially might have countenanced.[24] Barlow's ideological thoroughness forces him to cast his epic outside the boundaries established by classical tradition. He clearly has Milton's sanction in turning away from heroic action; he also has Milton's example of how to achieve it.

The vision of subsequent history that Michael offers Adam from the height of Pisgah was Milton's reversal and extension of the underworld prophecies of *The Odyssey* and *The Aeneid* in order to remark the consequences of the fall in history and to place his own culture subtly within that perspective. The device in later hands lends itself both to didactic and proleptic purposes, and, as Gray's "Bard" reminds us, need not be confined to epic poetry. Milton's achievement in this culminating section of his poem provided the model for a set piece borrowed by his emulators and usable in a variety of situations. It was so much a set piece for Southey that he removed "The Vision of the Maid of Orleans" from *Joan of Arc* and printed it separately. There is a fictive prophetic vision in *Gebir*, and, as a concluding book, in Cottle's *Messiah* and Richard Payne Knight's *Alfred*.[25] But to make such a vision the substance of the poem itself is to alter the very nature of epic.

The fiction of *The Columbiad* is that Columbus, returned to Spain, is cast into prison to languish in despair while the new world falls prey to Spanish arms. Hesper, the Guardian Angel of America, appears to him there and unfolds the future course of the hemisphere, including its ultimate leadership in ridding the old world of its encrusted political, social, and religious institutions. The fiction is simply a frame for the historical vision, and in turn it is continually buttressed, on the one hand, by the leveling equality of science and, on the other, by Barlow's representation of America as a source of mythic potentiality. His projection of the federated nations gathering to discard their outworn superstitions is truly the stuff of myth, one that immediately attained an independent status that retains its vital impulse still. But the immediate effect, which appears never to have been noted, was on the early apologists for the French Revolution, specifically on the Count de Volney, whose widely known *Ruins of Empire*, published in 1789, two years after *The Vision of Columbus*, expands on Barlow's example, making explicit its disestablishment of all religions through a congress of nations. Barlow, however, is important not just as an index to his culture or as an influence in its impact on French thinking, but also in the way he promotes a generic shift in the Romantic epic. His visionary epic replaces martial valor with peaceful nation building and finally with the creation of a world federation that transcends all nationalisms. The philosophical cast of the poem is deeply embued with Enlightenment values, yet at the same time its literary progenitor is *Paradise Regained*, both in titular subject and intellectual mode. The ethos of the classical epic has been reversed. Where *The Columbiad* looks back, it sees the failed mission of Columbus, so it casts its eyes to the future, to the creation of a new myth rather than the representation of an old one. Without question it is a national and public poem—two of its ten books relate the events of the

American Revolution—but the pressure is on what is yet to come. Mythic beginnings frame the poem, but the thrust is toward the mythicized congress of nations where all people and nations are equal and the heroism is of the mind. A rigorously secular and public epic, still it serves the interiorized ends of *Paradise Lost*, where the creation of a "Paradise within" replaces the field of battle, and a determined responsibility for the future is all that survives the irrevocable pastness of the mythic center.[26]

Barlow's visionary, supranational, and libertarian epic is not the last poem of the Enlightenment; there is one more, published four years later—Shelley's *Queen Mab* (1813), whose similarities to Barlow's poem, starting with its original conception in ten books, are as striking as they have been unremarked. The assumption among its scholars has been that Shelley borrowed heavily from Volney's *Ruins*, but since Volney himself appears to have been indebted to Barlow, the line of transmission may be simpler than thought.[27] What Shelley would have found in Barlow was a visionary survey of past, present, and future, combined with a reduction of all mythologies and religions to a naturalistic base and a concomitant introduction of scientific principle into his materials. But Barlow is explicitly a propagandist for American republicanism, distanced from the social structure of Britain. Shelley's emphasis on the evils of that system, attentuated through all European culture, and his brilliant translation of Dalton's new atomic theory into social metaphor, gives his poem an urgency, an intensity, and a wholeness of conception not to be found in Barlow. And the fictive framework of the poem carefully relates its public exposition to a psychological base, so that the interiorization of the vision is itself symbolic of the educative process Shelley is engaged in. The customary encyclopedic knowledge of the epic is represented by the astonishing learning and coherent social critique of the notes. Those notes have understandably received the widest attention from scholars because they had considerable influence on social thinking in nineteenth-century England. The array of Shelley's sources and the remarkable cohesiveness he draws them into are, however, mirrored in the poetic structure. Although, as we have seen, conventional epic endeavors continued through the Regency, two decades of experiment come to a true point in *Queen Mab*. It follows Southey in being centered around a heroine who is virtuous and independent, but her heroism is of the mind, she is a contemporary figure, and her vision elaborates the process by which she comes to see past, present, and future free of cultural prejudices. As the vision is liberating for her, so its recital educates the reader. The evils of war, empire, and entrenched power contrast with her imaginative flight, but if that is the only action countenanced by the poem, it is not a flight away from the realities of the world but rather into seeing them directly and whole. The mind that contains those realities can also transform them, enacting a peaceful revolution in the public realm congruent with the paradise found within. *Queen Mab* is the logical end of the epic of visionary and libertarian subversion, and paradoxically it is, without question, the one Romantic epic that sustained an independent life as a national poem in the nineteenth century.

Against such a context the fragment of *Hyperion* assumes a cast strikingly different from the customary one. It should be emphasized that Keats is the only British poet of this period to revert to the classical pantheon for epic subject matter. It is actually a daring gambit, as is his clear borrowing of situation from *Paradise Lost*; for in both cases he effects a new construction on traditional materials, playing against the expectations of the reader and forcing a novel perspective from them. His approach is more nearly that of Milton than any of the other Romantic writers of epic, with the exception of Blake, as he borrows to subvert and engages the reader in the process. His epic too records a fall, but it is a necessary and desired one. It also records a revolution.[28] Neither in *Hyperion* nor in its recasting as *The Fall of Hyperion* does Keats specify the political nature of that revolution, for his interests seem more psychological than ideological. And yet, the carefree life and genial self-satisfaction of the Titans in their golden age are unmistakeably those of the *ancien regime*, whether of French aristocrats or English country gentlemen. And the troubled ambivalence that Apollo grows into is the mature mental state of those who survived the debacle of the French Revolution, recognize that the clock cannot be turned back, and with some reluctance assume responsibility for establishing a new order from the ruins. The vision of *Queen Mab* is radical and apocalyptic, a product of aristocratic enlightenment; that of *Hyperion* is liberal, in the nineteenth-century sense, imbued with the hard-won values of a stable owner's son. But it too—and even more is this the case with *The Fall of Hyperion*—recognizes that what the mind imagines, the world becomes, and that therefore the process of psychological liberation is the true epic subject of the modern world.

III

When Virgil combined the main actions and themes of the two Homeric epics, he made it possible to define a genre whose great examples before him had been marked more by a disparity in means and ends than by similitude. His hero is not merely a representative man but a national leader who is as courageous and valorous as Achilles, as selfless in purpose as Hector, and as politic as Odysseus. He epitomizes his culture as warrior, as imperialist, and as explorer of the unknown; and where heaven makes demands, he seeks an earthly accord. Supporting his heroic exploits are a panoply of truly arbitrary conventions: councils of men and of gods, the descent of those gods, a human descent into the underworld, celebratory games, various catalogs suggestive of what we know about nations and nature, tests of human endurance and purpose. That many of these conventions reflect an oral formulaic tradition and serve as a means to record history, culture, and physical knowledge where there is little writing is an understanding conditioned by twentieth-century scholarship, but that the effect of these was to engage a breadth of knowledge that is virtually encyclopedic was acknowledged by Virgil and became traditional among his followers.

What makes the epic so fascinating a genre is precisely that there are so few examples, that the rules are so arbitrary and so arbitrarily insisted on by readers long after they have shed their cultural relevance, and that, against that critical expectation, the only great successes come from bending or openly breaking those rules so as to reform the cultural link. The idea that Homer should provide models for the France of Louis XIV is inherently ludicrous, though Le Bossu endeavored to twist him into shape by an incongruous Aristotelian logic. By the late eighteenth century in England, at least, the incongruity was too obvious to stand unchallenged. Hugh Blair, remarking that Le Bossu had reduced Homer to the level of Aesop, scorned his theory as "one of the most frigid, and absurd ideas, that ever entered into the mind of a Critic," and he offered his own simple definition in its stead: "The plain account of the nature of an Epic Poem is, the recital of some illustrious enterprise in a Poetical Form."[29]

The Scottish urge for common sense is, as always, understandable and, as usual, too facile. Not only is the defining phrase wonderfully ambiguous, but Blair has excluded any traditionary authority from a genre that has no existence except as defined, even through counterstatement, by tradition. That is the unstated assumption underlying the whole of Hayley's *Essay on Epic Poetry*. Yet, as Hayley also understood, the reservoir of that tradition has always been channeled through its last commonly accepted example. The epic poets who set themselves to emulate Milton generally did not follow Hayley's injunction against servitude: hence the spectacle of a demythologized age fearlessly threatening itself with satanic legions made of cardboard. The true exemplum offered by Milton, and understood by the sophisticated artists among his emulators, was an epic of mental exploit, whether in Abdiel alone among the rebellious angels, or Jesus alone in the wilderness, or Adam and Eve as they first create a solitude amidst plenty and then must rediscover their sole place in a universal scheme they have redefined. For Romanticism the last epic hero in the British tradition was the Jesus of *Paradise Regained*, whose "illustrious enterprise" is simply to define the god within: warfare, past and future history, the high achievements of human culture, all must give way to that exploit of the mind. The compression is ingenious and brilliant, but it leaves his followers with so refined an epic inversion, so pure a non-act, that it is hard to conceive of following it. And most did not even try but were rather content to adopt the superficial attributes of Milton's epics or endeavored, like Southey in *Joan of Arc*, to have it both ways, inveighing against war and writing rousing battle scenes. But those with a clearer sense of Milton's example only increased the odds against imitating it successfully. Keats's problem in both *Hyperion* poems is to elaborate the dynamics of a moment of conversion, and he is unable to find an enveloping narrative frame that allows for narrative progress. At the opposite extreme, the problem faced by Barlow and Shelley is also how to invest their encyclopedic analyses with a carrying fiction so that the result is art rather than philosophy. Milton moved the epic into the mind, but he did not tell future generations how to act convincingly in such an arena.

The different methods by which *The Prelude, Don Juan,* and *Prometheus Unbound* seek to accommodate this recreated epic mode are the subject of the next chapter. Yet, there is a direct and profound response to Milton's epic example in the two completed epics of William Blake, *Milton* and *Jerusalem,* both of which pursue the logical possibilities of the Miltonic mode and invest it with the distinctive cultural concerns of the Romantic epic. Blake went to unusual lengths to appear neither a slave of tradition nor a representative of his culture, but in fact his epics are epitomes in both senses. We may suppose that before Blake felt his genius under threat from the values of an eighteenth-century gentleman, William Hayley had something to do with how Blake conceived his epic vision.[30] The successor to William Cowper immediately set upon his own "task" under Hayley's patronage, and it was one informed by the epic traditions and contemporary endeavors in the genre it would seek to turn on end.

Both *Milton* and *Jerusalem* reflect the religious and nationalistic impulses of the Romantic epic, though the former is more deeply concerned with revealing the dynamics of a conversion process and the latter with the attempt to relate them to the character of the nation. But the prefatory plate to *Milton* summarizes the ends pursued by them equally:

> I will not cease from Mental Fight,
> Nor shall my Sword sleep in my hand:
> Till we have built Jerusalem,
> In Englands green & pleasant Land. (1.13–16)

The logical end of generic self-reflexiveness is to convert epic purpose into epic writing, "Mental Fight," to translate Milton's concentration on the process of self-knowledge, psychological enterprise, into the creation of the artist as epic hero. The entirety of *Milton* is concerned with this process, which is in the fiction of the poem an envelopment of Milton so as to reincarnate him within a changed culture, to alter him so as to alter oneself. Milton must be subverted in order to be reclaimed, brought down from the pinnacle and, like his tested Jesus, forced to enter on his human ministry:[31]

> I come in Self-annihilation & the grandeur of Inspiration
> To cast off Rational Demonstration by Faith in the Saviour
> To cast off the rotten rags of Memory by Inspiration
> To cast off Bacon, Locke & Newton from Albions covering

To take off his filthy garments, & clothe him with Imagination
To cast aside from poetry, all that is not Inspiration (41.2-7)

Blake's mythicized self-creation is of such intensity and daring that it is easy to take its rhetorical grandeur at face value, as representing an actual self-portrait. Yet, that object of anathema called Memory is never simply cast off in this poem (or in *Jerusalem*); it is, rather, recharged and reborn. Blake is conscious that Milton's life is lodged in Hayley's *Life*, that his poetry is encapsulated with its accrued commentary in Todd's edition. Milton's journey out of Eternity to meet his match in Blake's pastoral garden is the process by which his spirit is freed from the letter. And with it the epic spirit from epic tradition. Yet, Memory cannot be denied; it can only be redeemed. "Say first! what mov'd Milton" (2.16): the very epic formula suggests epic formula as the answer. The journey is conventional, so much so that the term for it is an odyssey. Milton returns home, or like Aeneas voyages to a new home, into the allegory of his garden where William Blake writes, a garden that is not a memory irrecoverably past but a reservoir of infinite potentiality. He is impelled to this mental act by a bard's song, reciting mythic memories of yet another dispute among the gods that will descend to trouble humankind, an epic episode that must be internalized, rewritten in the psyche. The bard surrounds his song (usually several plates after the information is needed) with genealogical catalogs of the divinities; other catalogs intrude again and again to disrupt or frame the episodes of Milton's and Ololon's descent. An encyclopedia of myth must be drawn in by poet, by reader, so as to expand the possibilities of interpretation, so as to subsume history within its types. The very nature of the discourse is symbolic of the transmutation of memory into renewed art, of epic tradition into epic poetry. Blake has read his Hayley; he has also read his classics. The result in *Milton* is a radically different "Essay on Epic Poetry," but, along with the many other attributes of the poem working to the same ends, the recasting of convention is so constant that the poem mirrors its own creation as well as the attendant recreation of its author that is its culminating event. It would appear from Hayley's attempts to woo Blake to more mundane and popular projects that he never recognized the extent to which the subject of *Milton* was the very inspiration he had called upon the epic poet to give his age.

Milton embodies a prelude to vision, in Thomas Vogler's fine phrase.[32] *Jerusalem* is conceived as vision itself, with Blake representing himself at the beginning as called to his task in sleep in order to awaken his country. Blake's knowing play against epic traditions continues in *Jerusalem*, though it is complicated by a richness of biblical referentiality that seeks to accommodate the scriptural mythos to epic traditions, by an extensive historical allusiveness, and by the development of Blake's own myth in lengthy episodes. But even these last implicate traditional epic themes:

the character of Jerusalem is intended to remind readers of *The Iliad* of Helen of Troy, who has dishonored her people by whoredom. Epic councils to indict her lead to epic battles among the sons and daughters of Albion, but there is no honor on any battlefield. The Daughters rightly fear for their existence and, assuming the historic role of Dido, seduce the warriors from their exploits. Since that cannot long succeed, they castrate them, and then in turn are pursued with murderous vengeance. Los watches all of this with the eye of a scholiast, seeking some way to emend the text and convert these endless heroics, the law of the sword, into the inner peace promised by God. Among his many similitudes, he is a scholar of epic poetry, tracing the six thousand years of history through its cultural embodiments, rereading the same pages time and time again, converting the variations into the underlying conventions that organize human culture and trammel human thought. The consequences of his failure, he is aware, will be dire indeed: *Jerusalem* is the most outspokenly antiheroic poem in the epic tradition, as it envisages the heroic ethos to eventuate in the obliteration of humanity itself.

Similarly, irony accompanies the nationalistic overtones that are heard throughout. The superimposition of Druid motifs on the epic structure should be read not simply thematically, as part of Blake's continuing critique of natural religion, but also and more importantly as a generic subversion. Blake follows his countrymen in incorporating primitive British history into his national epic. But he discovers nothing to emulate there, only a bloody tribal warfare sanctioned by religious code. The new sacrificial victim of Chapter 3 is Shiloh, which is to say France, whose destruction is but the latest in the long series of vengeful acts that constitute British history. And yet, even where the irony is pointed, no epic is more deliberately framed by its nationalism. Albion is an embodiment of ancient Britain, collective in his humanity. And Blake elaborates that humanity through a striking transformation of convention, cataloguing and peopling the British landscape. The cathedral cities, who in their civilized values constitute the Friends of Albion, attempt to revive him. Erin, with long experience at the couch of death, solemnly keens over the body of Albion at the close of Chapters 1 and 2. Most remarkable of all are the several recitals of the counties of Great Britain, both as organized by the self-righteous and self-destructive Sons and Daughters of Albion and in their potential manifestation as homes of the lost tribes of Israel. Cataloguing in *Jerusalem* serves the organic purpose of rendering the fragmented body of Albion whole and reborn and irreducibly human. And repetition is similarly linked to a functional purpose, both the codification of error that is Los's duty and the invocation of Jesus, who represents the solution to a world doomed to traditional epic repetition. At the precise moment in which the impasse is broken, Blake reverts to formula, employing an epic repetition separated by only two lines, suggesting that from this point on the moment he records will recur without interruption: "As the Sun & Moon lead forward the visions of Heaven and Earth / England who is Brittania enterd Albions bosom rejoicing" (95.21-22; 96.1-2).³³

This is the moment when an entire culture is redeemed, a nation is discovered from within. *Jerusalem* is a fearsomely difficult poem, and yet, however strange and formidable to the uninitiated, it is truly *the* British national epic—of this period, perhaps of all periods—a poem that mythologizes Britain's past, but so as to demand renewal and transformation, to create its future. Its hero Los is a type of its poet Blake, struggling in uncertainty and obscurity to write the epic that will subvert the host of *Alfreds* that compete for prominence and establish a new national identity in their place. Aware that a war-weary England has no myth to fall back on which is not merely nostalgic and sentimental, devoted enough as a Protestant Christian to demand that a religious epic reenact rather than reiterate exemplary truth, Blake invests his epic with a daunting fiction of his own creation, one that enforces enormous demands on his creative power as mythmaker and on his audience, so accustomed to the classical pantheon and Christian pieties. And yet his machinery bears a striking resemblance to what is conventional in his time. Into his poem, like those of most of his contemporaries, there enters the figure of Satan, but he is protean, demanding continual redefinition. He is Urizen in one manifestation, Luvah in another; "I in my Selfhood am that Satan," cries Milton to the benumbed Eternals (14.30), and so acknowledges Blake in the touching simplicity of his ballad introduction to Chapter II of *Jerusalem*:

> Spectre of Albion! warlike Fiend!
> In clouds of blood and ruin roll'd:
> I here reclaim thee as my own
> My Selfhood! Satan! armed in gold. (27.73-76)

The easy sanctimoniousness of the traditional machinery that survives in contemporary epics lacks mythic resonance and disowns the self-testing verities of true religion. Blake's Satan is not simply the empty counter who wanders about contemporary epics with the key to the machinery; he is mythically vital, a mirror held before poets and readers who pride themselves on their purity and at the same time cheapen epic magnitude by succumbing to unexamined convention.

The process of testing and subverting traditional epic conventions is an aspect of Blake's "Mental Fight." As with Milton before him, by subverting epic expectation, Blake forces reflection upon narrative events, drawing external action into mental space. The complex equation he forces between the cultural myth and the mind framed by and contributing to it is deeply embedded in the process of the poem. Jerusalem is both holy city and an emanation of the psyche, a way of life dependent upon an attitude of mind. An embodiment of its own process, *Jerusalem* is an extension of its title character, an epic *in potentia*, even as Britain is as yet unawake and still fragmented, and the labors of the creator of its national epic are lifelong. Hayley's injunction to sing "the splendid fane of British Freedom" is, Blake knows full well, the true challenge for an epic poet, because it does not exist except in vision. The end of *Jerusalem* is to create a national identity by recreating a national mentality. The interiorization of the epic forged by Milton and his successors among the British Romantics is, as Blake conceives his purpose, not an abandonment of its public and historical functions but the only way that they truly can be represented. Almost forty years after Hayley set the subject of the Romantic epic, Blake's rich and complex response was at last finished. At its core lies the simplest of propositions: "JERUSALEM IS NAMED LIBERTY AMONG THE SONS OF ALBION" (pl. 26).

CHAPTER EIGHT

Composite Orders

. . . it is one world which includes in its bosom so many diversities; *one* is its form and essence; *one* the mode by which all its parts are with discordant concord connected and conjoined, without any thing wanting, yet with nothing superfluous or unnecessary: Thus, I judge, that, by an excellent poet, (who for no other reason is called divine, but because he seems to partake of divinity, by the similarity of his operations to those of the Sovereign Artificer,) by an excellent poet, may be formed a work in which, as in a little world, we may read of armies in array, of land and naval fights, of sieges, skirmishes, jousts, and duels; in one place, descriptions of thirst and famine, in another of tempests, prodigies, and conflagrations. Here, we may find celestial and infernal councils; there, seditions, discords, wanderings, adventures, and enchantments; with deeds of cruelty, audacity, or generous courtesy; with happy or hapless, joyful or joyless incidents of love. Yet, still the poem, which contains such variety of matter, may have unity; *one* may be its form and fable, and all this diversity may be so disposed, that the latter parts may correspond with the former; each may regard the others, and every event have such a necessary, or probable dependence on a preceding one, that the alteration or removal of a single member would bring ruin on the whole. This simple variety will be laudable too from its difficulty; for it is an easy matter, and a thing of no industry, to introduce a great diversity of accidents in a multitude of separate actions; but that in a single action the same variety should be found, *Hoc opus, hoc labor est.*

> Torquato Tasso, *Discourses on the Heroic Poem,* tr.
> John Black, *Life of Torquato Tasso; with an Historical and
> Critical Account of his Writings* (1810), II, 133–134

I

IN RENAISSANCE generic formulations the epic is first in the hierarchy of genres because it is the most inclusive of forms. The Homeric epics were conceived as a repository of cultural knowledge—from the organization of the Olympic pantheon to the history of the eastern Mediterranean kingdoms assembled on the plain of Troy to the geography charted by Odysseus' wanderings, even to the proper construction of ships so as to weather storms at sea. A minor sidelight of a poem that contained all the known arts and sciences and set the rules for governance of homes and empires alike is that it also subsumed the lesser genres, providing in Scaliger's formulation "the universal controlling rules for the composition of each other kind."[1] That Scaliger's conception is impossibly anachronistic is immaterial, for whatever his claims to an absolute truth, he voices for the Renaissance its inherent expectation of the epic. The most inclusive of narrative forms will by its very nature subsume multiple modes of apprehending the world.

That by the later eighteenth century such a grandiose vision was no longer automatically associated with the epic can simply be deduced from the kinds of epics that proliferated from the 1790s on. But that the association survived, at least in some minds, is unquestionable. In 1797 Coleridge counselled Joseph Cottle that it would require twenty years of labor, half of the time spent in acquiring "universal science," to produce a true epic poem.[2] Wordsworth saw *The Recluse* as the beacon star and justification of his life's work, but also, in the famous analogy to a cathedral, as its enveloping form. And if we are as yet uncertain about the precise dates of composition of Blake's last epic prophecy, it is nonetheless clear that *Milton* and *Jerusalem* aspire directly to the encyclopedic grandeur of Renaissance conceptions of the epic. Scaliger was no longer the arbiter, but the masterpiece he used for epic reference, *The Aeneid*, was still a staple of British education. Less culturally distant was *Paradise Lost*, whose generic capaciousness was recognized as one justification of its claims to preeminence among modern epics.

By no means is the epic alone in its capacity to subsume or otherwise absorb other poetic genres. We have already observed the protean nature of the pastoral and the extent to which romance situates itself upon borders with pastoral, with epic, with satire. In the preface to his first collected edition of 1815 Wordsworth adopted the term "composite order" to cover poems that seemed to escape normal generic classification, specifically Young's *Night Thoughts* and Cowper's *The Task*. Poems of this sort combine modes of didacticism, philosophical satire, and the Idyllium, a term Wordsworth uses as a catchall for poetry descriptive of either external or internal processes (*Prose*, III, 27–28). *Genera mixta* were much debated during the Renaissance, and again the terms of that debate were largely submerged by the late eighteenth century. But that the four major poems in English during the eighteenth century— *The Dunciad, The Seasons, Night Thoughts*, and *The Task*—were of this sort reminds us both that the stringencies of neoclassical rule demanded exception and that mixed forms retained their inherent value long after the local arguments for or against them were forgotten.

And yet to call a form mixed can mean many things. Composite orders are inherently risky, for where there are no recipes or assured conventions the experiment can be unintentionally grotesque or incongruous, which is generally the historical verdict on a poem like *The Revolt of Islam*. A mixed form does not abandon conventional expectation: on the contrary, the precision of generic signals is all the more an imperative if the poet seeks to combine disparate forms for a larger end than can be achieved from a narrower generic construction. Beyond making separate modes, with their attendant ideological and cultural expectations, compatible, the poet who aspires to a formal assimilation is contracting with the reader for a new mode of apprehension created through that assimilation. The mixture of genres naturally calls attention to its larger purposes, the world view it serves, the contexts from the past it invokes as guidelines, the vision of the future that will result. No less than a traditional genre do *genera mixta* embody ideological means and ends.

Though the ensuing discussion focuses on works that are epic in theme or dimension, a brief recovery of known territory, largely excluded from earlier discussion because of its very familiarity, will quickly illustrate the point. When Wordsworth and Coleridge designated their original collection *Lyrical Ballads*, it was with an assured sense that throughout the volume they had endeavored to reconcile opposing literary, and even philosophical, modes. Deliberately playing against the general interest in ballads precipitated by Percy's *Reliques*, they drew on both Gothic and folk materials for their collection. But whether invoking the wonders of the supernatural, as in "The Rime of the Ancyent Marinere," or tales of mundane human effort, as in "Simon Lee," they stall the reader exactly on the issue of action. The mere shot of a crossbow or, more radically, Simon Lee's inability to uproot a tree stump transforms the traditional objectivity of the ballad into a lyrical—which is to say, psychological— confrontation. Not the action itself, but its psychic motivation or conse- quence, becomes the dynamic force of poem after poem. Two decades later, surely influenced by these efforts, but even more so by the quicken- ing romance revival, Keats knowingly creates the impasse recorded in "La Belle Dame sans Merci" by juxtaposing a knight's duty to act against the uncertainties of his fantasy life. At its base the impasse is actually generic, between the ballad's recital of unelaborated event and the roman- ce's emphasis on imaginative projection. These examples could be com- pounded, but they illustrate on a relatively simple, if brilliant, level how dependent is the artistry of a composite form on the poet's first being aware of the network of associations isolated within the genres involved, and then being alert to ways to draw from the reader that implicitness of meaning already foregrounded in literary tradition. As the form becomes more complex, so are the requirements on author and reader alike. The poems to which we now turn—*The Prelude, Don Juan*, and *Prometheus Unbound*—are perhaps the most enduring monuments of literary aspira- tion in British Romanticism. Only *Don Juan* was called an epic by its author—and then to a general disbelief among its readers—but each of these poems attains to a plateau of greatness that is inseparable from the richness and profundity of its generic conception. Such amplitude is the characteristic mark of the true epic.

II

Was it truly, as Wordsworth wondered about *The Prelude*, "a thing unprecedented in Literary history that a man should talk so much about himself" (*WLEY*, 586)? Certainly, he could have claimed two precursors among the poets of composite order in the eighteenth century, Pope and Cowper. Pope more than any other major writer in the century after Milton made his own genius the explicit standard for universal judgment, particularly in the *Epistles* and *The Dunciad*. By nature far more retiring, Cowper nonetheless channeled the local prospects of Olney through his refined sensibility and in a sheer paradox transformed the intensely private man into a universal arbiter. Yet, if these examples gave Wordsworth a progressive generic foundation for the extended monologue of *The Prelude*, it is truly to Milton that he was indebted for his tone and tenor, elaborating from the authorial intrusions into *Paradise Lost* an entire mode of epic poetry. As Milton had consciously centered the myth of human fall and redemption on himself as blind bardic visionary, so Wordsworth conceives of the interior process by which a sensitive child grows into mature artist as the essential, though truly self-reflexive, epic argument.[3]

The epic signals of *The Prelude* are so extensive that debate over the poem's subsuming genre should be, at this point in critical history, a moot issue.[4] The poem begins *in medias res*, with the poet about to undertake a new phase in his life, and proceeds by flashbacks to fill in earlier history. That there is only flashback and that the poem ends, as it began, *in medias res* suggests once again Wordsworth's characteristic way of thinking through arbitrary conventions to their inherent values, which is true of how he employs other epic signals as well. There is a descent into the underworld, but it is redefined as London. There is epic warfare—a conflict between France and Britain that might alter the destiny of the world—but the hero is initially on the wrong side, subsequently finds neither side worthy of allegiance, and translates the contest into a psychomachia demanding a truly diplomatic resolution. All Wordsworth's trials are thus ultimately of the spirit, especially as he records his journeys into the unknown—which is to say, to Cambridge, and then twice to France. Wordsworth's muse is likewise transformed from convention, as Coleridge is cast in the role; but then, this poet depicts himself at the beginning as self-motivated and directs his hope to inspire the same capacity in his muse, reintegrating his isolated brother poet so that together they may establish a new dispensation among their countrymen. The poem, beginning in the southwest of England, then enveloping the northwestern Lake District, the east in Cambridge, and the south in London, quietly effects a breadth of geography, climates, and inhabitants, which is extended by the European tours. And similarly there are catalogs, though the reader must keep eyes alert to recognize their gesture toward tradition, since lists of possible epic subjects in Book I, of types of pastoral in Book VIII and of romance in Book IX, not to say of Wordsworth's childhood reading in Book V, may seem to convert epic inclusiveness into a library's card catalog. Yet, surveying the inhabitants of London, Wordsworth does recapture the traditional sense of wonder inherent in the epic catalog, and he subtly distends it so as to include the monstrous, even the demonic, in the ironic amplitude of his catalog of Bartholomew Fair:

> All moveables of wonder, from all parts,
> Are here. . . .
> All out-o'-the-way, far-fetched, perverted things,
> All freaks of nature, all Promethean thoughts
> Of man, his dullness, madness, and their feats
> All jumbled up together, to compose
> A Parliament of Monsters. (1850: VII.706–707; 714–718)

It may well be the case that the numerous traditional conventions of epic that inform *The Prelude* are so transmuted by Wordsworth's deliberate grounding of them in a modern sensibility that they are less immediately apparent than the genres and modes he incorporates within it. Some of these are minor, if very obvious, intrusions, like the mock heroic card game of Book I, or the eulogy to Ann Tyson that opens Book IV, or the dream vision of the Arab with stone and shell in Book V. Others are more extensive, requiring a noticeable shift in tone and decorum: Book VII ("Residence in London") constitutes Wordsworth's most successful venture into satire, while Books X and XI are largely versified history. The most important secondary form empowering *The Prelude* is the verse epistle, and Wordsworth wields it with shrewd dexterity, at once justifying a vernacular freedom of style and language that can rise to emotional intensity, specifying the nature of the audience he writes for, and giving implicit force to the correspondences that are both vehicle and purpose, the inseparable form and content, of his poem. Throughout *The Prelude* the epistle functions with an independent integrity, above the mixtures, the conflicts, the revaluations that attend other generic elements, its intrinsic principle of harmony continually bringing pressure to bear on the disruptive in experience or in the literary modes that shape it. Most potent in this regard are the claims for primacy of two other genres whose relationship with epic is in a constant process of renegotiation throughout the poem: the pastoral and romance.

The Prelude begins with a return from the city to a pastoral solitude, but the questions broached by the change of situation immediately imply an epic transformation:

> What dwelling shall receive me? in what vale
> Shall be my harbour? underneath what grove
> Shall I take up my home? and what clear stream
> Shall with its murmur lull me into rest?
> The earth is all before me. (1850:I.10–14)

The tag from *Paradise Lost* is clearly intentional; and yet it is more complicated than it initially appears. Wordsworth has inverted the Miltonic situation, reentering the Eden from which Adam and Eve had been exiled but with the felt necessity to instill it with the true dimensions, the epic inclusiveness, that Milton had shown humanity relinquishing. The freedom is itself intimidating, even if the epic subjects Wordsworth proposes to himself (I.166–225) are all histories of liberation.[5] It is small wonder that, enveloped in multiplying ironies, the poet finds himself frustrated, unsure how to proceed, turning back to his earliest memories for guidance: "Was it for this . . . ?" (I.269). This open-ended question, which is in fact the originating phrase of the two-book *Prelude* of 1799, focuses the inception of Wordsworth's poem on a problem of genre, the relationship between the lowest and highest in the hierarchy, between "The simple ways in which my childhood walked" (1850: II.3) and "some philosophic song / Of Truth that cherishes our daily life" (1850:I.229–230). To revert to the terms of our earlier discussion of pastoral, what Wordsworth records at the beginning of *The Prelude* is how arduous and uncertain a task it is to put into practice his program for a systematic inversion of generic hierarchies without sacrificing epic inclusiveness. It requires the expansion of the pastoral enclosure until it can envelop and harmonize not only the peaceful and innocent but all those diverse elements which threaten its fragile order.

The premise that opens the very next verse paragraph after Wordsworth asks that loaded question supplies its essential answer:

> Fair seed-time had my soul, and I grew up
> Fostered alike by beauty and by fear. (1850: I.301–302)

The artlessness of this beginning, appropriate as it is to the pastoral mode, should not blind us to its resonance, for it permeates every aspect of the poem that follows. In this formulation the familiar suspension of contraries that distinguishes pastoral is allied with the process of, rather than a retreat from, experience, creating a mythos of continuing maturation of the self and simultaneous enlargement of the field of perception. The dialectical rhythm between opposing impulses is the motive force driving *The Prelude*, characterizing both its renowned spots of time and its cultural and historical encounters, responsible for the mode of development that Geoffrey Hartman has analyzed as spiritual purification through the *via naturaliter negativa*, and at last even converted into epic theodicy.[6] For in the end Wordsworth explicitly celebrates his attainment of creative power as a transformation of the fundamental terms he embeds in the opening formulation:

> To fear and love,
> To love as prime and chief, for there fear ends,
> Be this ascribed; to early intercourse,
> In presence of sublime or beautiful forms,
> With the adverse principles of pain and joy—
> Evil as one is rashly named by men
> Who know not what they speak. (1850: XIV.162–168)

The conversion of the aesthetic contraries, the sublime and the beautiful, involved in childhood perception into the ethical categories of mature

awareness does not alter the underlying balance they share. Yet, so pronounced a shift of dialectical significance indirectly accentuates the
means by which Wordsworth is able to enlarge his conception to an epic
wholeness. The seeming vulnerability of the pastoral suspension, tested
by experience and even hardship, retains such resilience that all epic
endeavors, a true comprehensiveness, are implicit within it.

The crucial section of *The Prelude* for understanding Wordsworth's
generic aims is Book VIII—"The Retrospect"—in which the poet summarizes and recasts the first half of his work. It contains the most extensive defense of a realistic pastoral in all his writing, emphasizing—in
climate, in human character, and in experience—how much more varied
and inclusive than the traditional literary pastoral it is, and carefully
establishing a bridge from it to the larger social realms it might appear to
exclude. The true shepherd, known to Wordsworth from earliest memory
as the embodiment of the pastoral balance, becomes the very type of
humanity:[7]

> Thus was Man
> Ennobled outwardly before mine eyes,
> And thus my heart at first was introduc'd
> To an unconscious love and reverence
> Of human Nature; hence the human form
> To me was like an index of delight,
> Of grace and honour, power and worthiness.
> Meanwhile, this Creature, spiritual almost
> As those of Books; but more exalted far,
> Far more of an imaginative form,
> Was not a Corin of the groves, who lives
> For his own fancies, or to dance by the hour
> In coronal, with Phillis in the midst,
> But, for the purposes of kind, a Man
> With the most common. (1805: VIII.410–424)

Wordsworth's sudden pun—"the purposes of kind"—suggests how
closely linked are his social and literary conceptions, yet at the same time
it helps to accentuate the ambiguity felt here between "a Man / With the
most common" and the "imaginative form" the shepherd takes within
the mind. In the end Wordsworth wishes to claim, wishes his pastoral
epic to claim, that they are one and the same. The agent in this coales-
cence of image and reality, as the poet implicitly acknowledges by shifting the generic focus halfway through Book VIII, is romance. Romance
itself has an ambiguous function in *The Prelude*. Its archetypes provide
models of commitment to a high vocation, like that sudden sense of
irradiation that inspires the poet in Book IV, or of transcending and thus
ennobling mere mortality, as in the examples Wordsworth cites in
Book V. His dream of the Arab, "With the fleet waters of a drowning
world / In chase of him" (1850: V.137–138), racing to save science and art
from the deluge, is prompted by his reading *Don Quixote*—which sug-

gests that romance, however fantastic or distorted its vision may be, serves the largest ends of human aspiration. But its vision does uniformly distort, as Wordsworth, with good humor at his own expense, testifies in shifting perspective in Book VIII:

> Where the harm
> If, when the woodman languished with disease
> Induced by sleeping nightly on the ground
> Within his sod-built cabin, Indian-wise,
> I called the pangs of disappointed love,
> And all the sad etcetera of the wrong,
> To help him to his grave. (1850: VIII.437-443)

As is the case with *Endymion*, romance is the natural outgrowth of the imagination's desire for something beyond mere sufficiency—"something evermore about to be," as Wordworth puts it in the Simplon Pass description (1850: VI.608)—and is thus inherently in conflict with pastoral fixities. And yet, as interpretation of the poem has generally agreed, in *The Prelude* nature itself fosters the imagination's urge to break its confines; in generic terms, pastoral opens naturally into romance. The result, however, is not to effect a break with pastoral, but to force its enlargement so as to encompass the imaginative pressure exerted upon it. This dialectical exchange between romance and pastoral occurs again and again in the poem and indeed constitutes its underlying dynamic principle. The "Retrospect" of Book VIII is, if viewed abstractly, devoted to its operation. It is even more clearly delineated in an extensive passage originally intended for this retrospect but left in rough draft in the manuscript known as MS Y, where Wordsworth traces the natural development of a child's mind:

> . . . when in fine
> That great Magician, the unresting year,
> Hath play'd his changes off, till less and less
> They excite in us a passionate regard;
> Then attestations new of growing life,
> Distinct impressions and unbounded thought,
> To appease the absolute necessities
> That struggle in us, opportunely come
> From the universe of fable and [romance?]—
> Trees that bear gems for fruit, rocks spouting milk,
> And diamond palaces. . . . (MS Y. 76-86, p. 573)

Some never outgrow these indulgences of childish fantasy—"Untutor'd minds stop here, and after life / Leads them no farther" (MS Y. 120-121, p. 574)—but the child of nature enters a "season of his second birth" (MS Y. 168, p. 575) in which nature is discovered to be wholly adequate to his awakened desire.

> He feels that, be his mind however great
> In aspiration, the universe in which

> He lives is equal to his mind, that each
> Is worthy of the other; if the one
> Be insatiate, the other is inexhaustible. (MS Y. 171–175, p. 576)

Thus the mode of romance enlarges the pastoral enclosure to universal proportions. The result is epic.

Yet, the same revisionary rhythm that obtains between romance and pastoral also operates between romance and epic. The very failure of romance to sustain its promises is an agent of imaginative and moral growth. The failure is inevitable, and, in truth, wherever Wordsworth invokes romance, we can be sure that a crisis is impending. It is the underground motive of the unsettling encounters with mutability in Book V, and it surfaces with powerful effect in Wordsworth's confrontation with London:

> There was a time when whatsoe'er is feigned
> Of airy palaces, and gardens built
> By Genii of romance; or hath in grave
> Authentic history been set forth of Rome,
> Alcairo, Babylon, or Persepolis;
> Or given upon report by pilgrim friars,
> Of golden cities ten months' journey deep
> Among Tartarian wilds—fell short, far short,
> Of what my fond simplicity believed
> And thought of London. (1850: VII.77–86)

The disenchantment that ensues disturbs the young poet to the quick, impelling him to an extremity of aversion that disturbs psychic equilibrium and generic balance. Wordsworth slips naturally (though with shrewd artistic foresight) into an uncongenial mode, satire, that enacts the very psychological distancing that for him is London's most hateful characteristic. The balance is restored as he returns to the Lake District and the contrast of Helvellen Fair with Bartholomew Fair, out of which the retrospect of Book VIII develops. At its very end is a tribute to a London wonderfully transformed—as unified polis, a center of "majesty and power . . . thronged with impregnations like the Wilds / In which my early feelings had been nursed" (1850: VIII.631, 633–634) rather than the "monstrous ant-hill on the plain / Of a too busy world" (1850: VII.149–150) he had conceived it earlier. The demystification of romance, which imperils imaginative vision, is itself dissipated by being unable to survive within the restorative pastoral garden.

In the generic revision of Books VII and VIII Wordsworth establishes a dynamic model for the much more severe deflation of the romance ideal that follows as he again attempts, in revolutionary France, to find in the world of epic action a complement to his interior balance. His friend Michel Beaupuy is portrayed as a modern chivalric exemplar, a knight bound by oath to rectify injustice among his people: "unto the poor / Among mankind he was in service bound" (1850: IX.303–304):

> He through the events
> Of that great change wandered in perfect faith,
> As through a book, an old romance, or tale
> Of Fairy, or some dream of actions wrought
> Behind the summer clouds. (1850: IX.298-302)

There is no ironic note on Wordsworth's part here, although his readers cannot help but carry forward a sense from their earlier encounter with romance that the trial of the champion will take place in the tournament of reality. That is kept before our eyes as Wordsworth charts the downfall of Beaupuy's ideals in the Terror and the apparent revival of French imperialism. It is not until the failure is manifest and Wordsworth has returned to the torments of alienation in England that he allows his own retrospective commitment to the cultural romance to well over.

> Bliss was it in that dawn to be alive,
> But to be young was very Heaven! O times,
> In which the meagre, stale, forbidding ways
> Of custom, law, and statute, took at once
> The attraction of a country in romance!
> When Reason seemed the most to assert her rights
> When most intent on making of herself
> A prime enchantress—to assist the work,
> Which then was going forward in her name!
> Not favoured spots alone, but the whole Earth,
> The beauty wore of promise—that which sets
> (As at some moments might not be unfelt
> Among the bowers of Paradise itself)
> The budding rose above the rose full blown. (1850: XI.108-121)

The rhetorical energy of this great passage and the extent to which it sounds a veritable proclamation of Romanticism again does not allow us to take it ironically; and yet the deflating pressure of reality is implicit in the past tense in which it is cast. And the remembrance of this social romance is so placed as to be immediately cast into question, as the poet discovers himself overwhelmed by the "meagre, stale, forbidding ways" he had misconstrued and within two hundred lines plunges to his "soul's last and lowest ebb" (1850: XI.307). Once again, however, resort to the pastoral allows the defeat to be transformed into victory. The ancient, peaceful interchange of man and nature cannot be disrupted by momentary social failures but reasserts itself and its inherent rhythm to envelop the disaffected and to offer promise of an ultimate, natural community. The imaginative vision that invests society with the aura of romance may falsify on a superficial level of reality. But it also testifies to its own power, its own faith in a reality that must eventually exist: "the bowers of Paradise" remain even as humanity reaffirms its exile from them. The poet who suffers over such human willfulness only confirms that those bowers are implanted in the mind and flower in his verse.

In the retrospect of Book VIII, having charted the course of his education through layers of pastoral and romance, Wordsworth arrives upon a
visionary plateau, which he introduces with an epic signal:

> Enough of humble arguments; recal,
> My Song! those high emotions which thy voice
> Has heretofore made known; that bursting forth
> Of sympathy, inspiring and inspired,
> When everywhere a vital pulse was felt,
> And all the several frames of things, like stars,
> Through every magnitude distinguishable,
> Shone mutually indebted, or half lost
> Each in the other's blaze, a galaxy
> Of life and glory. In the midst stood Man,
> Outwardly, inwardly contemplated. (1850: VIII.476–486)

Among these mutually indebted frames of things—indeed, operating much
like the geometrical forms Wordsworth celebrates early in Book VI—are
the mixed literary genres of *The Prelude*. Constituting modes of apprehension, of mental organization, of experiential diversity, they retain
their integrity even as they blend in harmony to a single end. In *The
Prelude* Wordsworth combines genres as ways of seeing and of growing.
Although they are hierarchically arranged, the hierarchy is associated
with stages of maturation. But, as we everywhere observe, the inherent
pressure within the poet is to convert loss into gain, or to rediscover what
has been assumed to be lost in a new form, or to have the present
energized by being reintegrated with the past. His mixture of genres is
thus a dialectical progression toward a oneness of personality. The intricate balance of *The Prelude* among pastoral, romance, and epic genres,
reflecting the process leading to psychic equilibrium, embodies an inevitable and inclusive vision.

III

In his preface to *The Excursion* in 1814 Wordsworth propounded the
famous analogy of his poems to a cathedral, *The Prelude* having a
relationship to *The Excursion* that "the antechapel has to the body of a
Gothic church." Throughout *Don Juan* Byron ridicules that "drowsy,
frowsy poem, called the 'Excursion,' / Writ in a manner which is my
aversion" (III.94, 7–8). Presumably he had read the preface as well as the
poem, for he appears in *Don Juan* deliberately to have recast its architectural analogy to accord with his secular predispositions, as well as his
memories of Newstead Abbey, describing the country seat of the Amunde-
villes, Norman Abbey, as a similitude of his poem:

> Huge halls, long galleries, spacious chambers, joined
> By no quite lawful marriage of the arts,

Might shock a connoisseur; but when combined,
   Formed a whole which, irregular in parts,
Yet left a grand impression on the mind,
   At least of those whose eyes are in their hearts:
We gaze upon a giant for his stature,
Nor judge at first if all be true to nature. (XIII.67)

The spaciousness of *Don Juan* has asssuredly left "a grand impression" on literary posterity, and Byron's witty claims for its epic stature are now, in general, seriously weighed.[8] But what this stanza emphasizes is Byron's equal awareness of generic mixture: if his epic is unique, he suggests, it is largely because of its spurning of the normal conventions of literary wedlock. Love and matrimony, as Byron never ceases to say, are incompatible, and his poem, to preserve its liberty—to see with its heart—will witness "no quite lawful marriage of the arts."

Wordsworth's dialectical order, by which pastoral and romance through their limitations impel an epic vision that subsumes and redeems them, is far from Byron's subversion of systematic design. And yet, Byron's mixture of genres is as complex and far-sighted—and as formally congruent with the ideology of his epic—as Wordsworth's. His method is not so much one of negation, as Brian Wilkie terms it, as it is of ironic inversion, of double ironies leading to impasses that, by the very nature of life, cannot be sustained. Wilkie observes from Byron's deliberate avoidance of cumulative plan that in *Don Juan* he creates a poem that is "less than the sum of its parts."[9] But, viewed from the perspective of genre, it is much more. "One system eats another up," Byron remarks at the opening of the Fourteenth Canto. As with religions or ideologies, so with genres: if no system is sufficient to accommodate the variety of life, we are left paradoxically, like Wordsworth, with "something evermore about to be," a poem whose open-ended inclusiveness is proved by the inadequacies of generic category.

Byron's customary strategy can be most easily viewed in his last full canto. "Knights and Dames I sing, / Such as the times may furnish" (XV.25, 1-2). Having brought together his assembly of the modern peerage and their retinue, Byron subtly insinuates an antiromance into the texture of the poem. Juan's first encounter with the ghostly Black Friar prompts Lady Adeline to tell the legend in an interpolated ballad that could come straight out of a Scott romance. But the idea of this paragon of polished civility placing herself in the guise of the Last Minstrel—or, more aptly, in that of the romantic Flora MacIvor of *Waverley*—wholly undercuts the authority of her supernatural tale. She plays the harp as perfectly as she writes ballads, not because she is possessed by passion or thrilled by superstition but because they are accomplishments of a cultivated lady. The discontinuity between appearance and reality deepens as Lord Henry and Lady Adeline turn to the business of the day, Lord Henry's "public day," where instead of accepting feudal loyalty, the two must entertain the boring local gentry and Lord Henry must pass judgment on such responsibilities of his liege as a poacher and a pregnant servant. The incongruities are brilliantly consolidated in the resolution of the mystery, as the terrifying Black Friar is reduced to "The phantom of her frolic Grace—Fitz-Fulke" (XVI.123, 8), who shines in intrigue but is scarcely a damsel in distress, nor a lady to be placed on a pedestal. And yet, in the midst of this satire on the modern world's toying with romance, Byron wholly reverses the ground. Reality is, as it were, remystified as Juan, awakening to the attractions of Aurora Raby, discovers renewed those "feelings which, perhaps ideal, / Are so divine, that I must deem them real" (XVI.107, 7–8):

> The love of higher things and better days;
>   The unbounded hope, and heavenly ignorance
> Of what is called the World, and the World's ways;
>   The moments when we gather from a glance
> More joy than from all future pride or praise,
>   Which kindle manhood, but can ne'er entrance
> The Heart in an existence of its own,
> Of which another's bosom is the zone. (XVI.108)

All the superannuated relics of feudalism, the indulgence of romantic posturings, the mannered chivalric elegance by which Don Juan finds himself surrounded only foster by their contrast the ethos of romance he is beginning to cultivate as the poem breaks off. To claim one attitude as more "real" than the other would be equivalent to ignoring the truth that Aurora Raby and the Duchess of Fitz-Fulke, however opposite in disposition, share the same gender.

Canto XVI deliberately enacts a generic standoff, as romance is at once demystified and reified. In this process the canto typifies the entire poem, which realigns itself according to the conventions of one genre after another, analytically deconstructing each as to sufficiency or even adequacy, yet always, if obliquely, reinforcing them. The romance of Canto XVI is simple in its patterning compared with the pastoral, as exemplified in the episode of Juan and Haidee. This is the one sustained episode of the poem that vies in popularity with Byron's earlier tales, but its mode is inherently that of pastoral rather than romance. And yet, the mode is subverted from the very beginning. Haidee is assuredly beautiful and innocent, but the first detail the barely conscious Juan registers as a fire is kindled to warm him is that "Her brow was overhung with coins of gold" (II.116, 1). True as it may be that "A day of gold from out of age of iron / Is all that Life allows the luckiest sinner" (III.36, 3–4), we are well aware that someone must pay for it. "The greatest heiress of the Eastern Isles" (II.128, 2), who provides the convalescent Juan with "a bed of furs, and a pelisse" (II.133, 1) to soften the rocky realities of his cave, has more than a touch of Marie Antoinette about her. Her pastoral fantasies are purchased by piracy, slave trading, and murder. Nonetheless, they are pure and spontaneous. The pastoral enclosure created by Juan and Haidee is as innocently physical as that of Adam and Eve, to whom they are pointedly compared (II. 189, 193). Its impossibility is balanced by its humanity, its innocence by our knowledge of inevitable consequence. Byron renders the chiasmus in a couplet whose delicately suspended poise, even to its gentle wit, possesses the soul of pastoral: "And thus they form a group that's quite antique, / Half naked, loving, natural, and Greek" (II.194, 7-8). The last line gives back far more than its predecessor can take away.

The balance is sustained, as Lambro leaves the lovers to their own devices—"for them to be / Thus was another Eden" (IV.10, 1–2)—and the Petit Trianon is, as it were, moved into the Palace of Versailles. "[T]heir bower . . . Amidst the barren sand and rocks so rude" (II.198, 4–5) is essentially unaltered by the translation into these new circumstances, whatever the rich cushions and tapestries that surround them, the jewelry they lavish on themselves, the crystal and gold with which they dine, or the bountiful feast they share with one and all. We are like them, drawn to fantasies of the golden age, even as we know better. The central emblem for this pastoral feast is fittingly paradoxical:

> A band of children, round a snow-white ram,
> There wreathe his venerable horns with flowers;
> While peaceful as if still an unweaned lamb,
> The patriarch of the flock all gently cowers
> His sober head, majestically tame,
> Or eats from out the palm, or playful lowers
> His brow, as if in act to butt, and then
> Yielding to their small hands, draws back again. (III.32)

The indulgence of the ram in pretending to lambhood is akin to that of Byron, or of his readers, and is no less sincerely felt for being impossibly retrogressive. An explosion of this fantasy is certain, but Byron's touch is unexpected, for it arrives as yet another version of pastoral, one incompatible with that of Juan and Haidee. Her cutthroat father sees in Haidee's innocence "His only shrine of feelings undefiled" (III.52, 8), "The only thing which kept his heart unclosed / Amidst the savage deeds he had done and seen" (III.57, 3–4). Juan has unwittingly violated one bower to establish another. Both will be destroyed in the collision.

There is still a further perspective to bring to bear on these irreconcilable pastoral fantasies, and once again it comes in an unexpected way. The laureate of this island kingdom, "a sad trimmer" (III.82, 1) obviously related to Southey, indicts the entire community in his song "The Isles of Greece." This bower, whoever commands it, is specious: citing the "Pyrrhic dance so martial" (III.29, 7) that has first alerted the returning Lambro of something amiss on his island, the unheeded singer extracts the hidden irony:

> You have the Pyrrhic dance as yet,
> Where is the Pyrrhic phalanx gone?

> Of two such lessons, why forget
>   The nobler and manlier one?
> You have the letters Cadmus gave—
>   Think ye he meant them for a slave? (st. 10)

This island paradise is not merely purchased by illgot gain; it is also a land of slaves whose presumed liberty is the product of intoxication. Juan, who barred the stores of rum from the mariners during the shipwreck of Canto II, is in this setting as ignoble as he was noble before. So, with a leap from fiction to contemporary fact, is Robert Southey. What at first appears in the midst of this scene as the usual Byronic drollery at the expense of the Lake Poets is, as we observe it to be in "The Blues," directly linked to their notion of pastoral, and in *Don Juan* the point is as sharp as a stiletto: "Such names at present cut a convict figure, / The very Botany Bay in moral geography" (III.94, 1–2). True pastoral demands freedom. The mature laureate has not simply turned his politics or coat but has retreated in vision, transported himself so to speak, from the realities he exposed in his *Botany-Bay Eclogues*. Suddenly we realize that the attack on pastoral in "The Isles of Greece" itself implicates two further versions of pastoral, alike incompatible. The pastoral of the Lake Poets is politically irresponsible, purchased by government sinecure and thus as illgot as Lambro's island. But the alternative posed by "The Isles of Greece" is to overthrow oppression, and that requires the intervention of war and the dependence of pastoral on heroic effort. Curiously enough, this reflection of Southey, his mirror inversion, in the context of pastoral tradition looks very much like Edmund Spenser.

Between the pastoral of Juan and Haidee with its innocent gratification—"they were children still, / And children still they should have ever been" (IV.15, 1–2)—and the deferral of pastoral possibility enjoined by the sad trimmer lies a gulf of experience. Yet the inevitable failure of Juan and Haidee to restore the paradise of Adam and Eve does not make their desire less intense nor their instinct less natural. And is the jeremiad of "The Isles of Greece," resolving into a plunge from slavery into the sea of death, any less involved in failure? Thus we reach the end of this episode, even with Byron's powerful shift of tense and mood—"That isle is now all desolate and bare" (IV.72, 1)—honoring Haidee's assertion of pastoral purity in the face of all that threatens it. If anything, in retrospect that isolated bravery is all the more attractive after Byron's exposure of the realities of heroism in Cantos VII and VIII. For there Christianity is at least going through the pretense of liberating the West from Turkish imperialism, which is what the trimmer would hope for Greece. But to lay waste a city is scarcely to establish a pastoral garden in its place. The only end of such savagery is ruin. In the midst of the bloodbath of Ismail's siege Byron intrudes a natural contrast, but one wholly unanticipated after the multiple failures of pastoral observed earlier: a seven-stanza encomium to Daniel Boone and the backwoodsmen of Kentucky (VIII.61–67):

Motion was in their days, Rest in their slumbers,
  And Cheerfulness the handmaid of their toil;
Nor yet too many nor too few their numbers;
  Corruption could not make their hearts her soil;
The lust which stings, the splendour which encumbers,
  With the free foresters divide no spoil;
Serene, not sullen, were the solitudes
Of this unsighing people of the woods. (VIII.67)

This stanza—and the entire passage it climaxes—touches every virtue associated with the pastoral and explicitly frames it politically, with a free land and free people. It is the mature alternative to the childish indulgences of Juan and Haidee, nurturing and not sacrificing life, embracing the pastoral enclosure and not simply retreating into it. Boone is "An active hermit, even in age the child / Of Nature" (VIII.63, 7-8). The suspension of contraries here is pointed; it is also perfect in its encompassment.

Has Byron then arrived at a point of unconditional affirmation, one that contravenes the false pastoral models earlier exhibited? It is not his way. For one thing, Boone's Kentucky is a man's world: there are no Haidees here. It is also dependent on a political dispensation it did not effect, one produced by George Washington, who is the only genuine modern hero admitted into *Don Juan*, standing in solitary contrast (VIII.5; IX.8) to the inhumanity that universally masquerades under the nomenclature of heroism. And of course, Boone's pastoral world stands isolated in geography from the European arena encircled by Juan's travels: though a forceful alternative, it is literally outside the possibilities of the poem itself. Assuredly, it deflates any claim to adequacy of Haidee's paradise, but then in its isolated circumstances it escapes the harsh realities of the ancient Mediterranean world where pastoral began.

This is a generic impasse of remarkable complexity, shifting with possibility even as it actually hardens over a number of cantos. Though reverting with a subtle knowledge to pastoral paradigms in the first half of *Don Juan*, Byron enforces an insistent relativism that questions the sufficiency, even the efficacy, of any of them. Yet if they constitute valid modes of perception or of ideological compression, then so radical a standoff raises serious questions about the reliability of archetypal pattern and the futility of the human instincts that demand it. More significantly still, it questions the very nature of truth, which is "the grand desideratum" (VII.31, 2) of Byron's poem, invoked again and again as its novel characteristic, essential to both sides of the major generic equation by which, late in the poem, he defines *Don Juan*, "this Epic Satire" (XIV.99, 6). It would seem unthinkable that an epic vision, whether in its most limited definition as a rendering of the probable or in its largest claims as a cultural epitome that is "doctrinal and exemplary to a Nation," could be conceived apart from general truths that link culture or nation. Even more stringent are the demands of satire, which simply cannot exist apart from accepted moral standards.

And in *Don Juan* it does not: instead, the accepted moral standards become the subject of Byron's incessant attack, for they themselves do not accord with the truth of the world or of human life. But a true satire cannot be simply negative, and Byron's brilliant ploy—by this point in his life it is probably as much mature instinct as literary strategy—is to deconstruct satire by turning its tools on itself. "[T]his poem's merely quizzical" (IX.41, 3), he insists, not relying (like Southey, for a prime example) on any absolute standard of measurement. The greatest of satires is *Don Quixote*, but Cervantes' "noblest views" are "for mere Fancy's sport a theme creative, / A jest, a riddle" (XIII.10, 5-7). Byron, confessing himself "but a mere spectator" (XIII.7, 6), points the lesson Cervantes teaches:

> I should be very willing to redress
>   Men's wrongs, and rather check than punish crimes,
> Had not Cervantes, in that too true tale
> Of Quixote, shown how all such efforts fail. (XIII.8, 5-8)

Moreover, the increasing emphasis on philosophical skepticism in the late cantos questions the possibility of truth and even the authority of fact. The interchangeability of hero's names by which Byron debunks bulletins from the battlefront in Canto VII implicitly acknowledges how dependent fact is on subjective observation, and that in turn universally involves national or political prejudices as well as the inherent distance of spectators from the events they report. After the Siege of Ismail Byron expects no demurral from his readers when he defines "History" as "the grand liar" (IX.81, 4), even though it contradicts his own putative reliance on fact. Having insisted earlier on his unique veneration for fact, Byron slowly and deliberately undermines himself after the war cantos. He asks his reader to "recollect the work is only fiction" (XI.88, 4), observes that "Don Juan . . . was real, or ideal,— / For both are much the same" (X.20, 1-2), and celebrates lies as "but / The truth in masquerade":

> I defy
> Historians—heroes—lawyers—priests, to put
>   A fact without some leaven of a lie.
> The very shadow of true Truth would shut
>   Up annals—revelations—poesy. . . . (XI.37, 1-6)

The serious and self-reflexive undercurrent here cannot be glossed over as merely Byron's ubiquitous sense of play. He is deeply aware of the consequences of seeing so clearly into the uncertainty of all things:

> There's no such thing as certainty, that's plain
>   As any of Mortality's conditions;

So little do we know what we're about in
This world, I doubt if doubt itself be doubting.

It is a pleasant voyage perhaps to float,
    Like Pyrrho, on a sea of speculation;
But what if carrying sail capsize the boat? (IX.17, 5-8; 18, 1-3)

To insist that all facts are subjective approximations and that no truth is pure is the truth asserted throughout *Don Juan*. The inconclusive and the inclusive are one and the same. Epic can accommodate such a radical skepticism, but satire cannot.[10] "He who doubts all things nothing can deny" (XV.88, 5) is Byron's refined distillation of his vision in the poem. There is an ethics and a general humanity implicit in it suggestive of satire turned inside out. Byron does not forego incisive judgment—innumerable stanzas end with the resounding clang of a cell door—but he affects no pretensions of reform nor even a finality of judgment, leaving such satirical ends to those who write against him. Turning satire on itself, he achieves its effects while denying its ends:

My natural temper's really aught but stern,
    And even my Muse's worst reproof's a smile;
And then she drops a brief and modern curtsy,
And glides away, assured she never hurts ye. (XI.63, 5-8)

The insufficiency of pastoral, romance, and satire almost by default lend force to Byron's epic claims in *Don Juan*. But he does not shift his strategy in turning to the most encompassing generic conception. Rather, as Wilkie has perceptively shown, he deconstructs the genre mercilessly, intermixing mock-epic and epic themes, casting contemporary meanness against older models of heroism, but then suggesting how equally unattractive are the classical models and how much more extensive are the possibilities for heroism in the modern world.[11] He openly admits to inserting epic conventions, like the shipwreck or the Siege of Ismail, as set pieces to prove his mettle. Although with the siege Byron certainly appropriates heroic conventions with an eye to subverting them, creating from the extremity of his representation the most repugnant vision of epic warfare in the Romantic period, that aim seems almost secondary to their mere employment: "The Muse will take a little touch at warfare" (VI.120, 8), he remarks offhandedly at the close of Canto VI. At times, *Don Juan* seems to be more a recipe for concocting an epic than the thing itself.

But the self-consciousness of the generic anatomy is, in effect, what is so truly subversive about *Don Juan*: "Heroes are but made for bards to sing" (VIII.14, 5). As Milton centers the myth of the fall and divine grace in his blindness and inspiration, as Wordsworth finds epic breadth in the enlargement of his creative powers, Byron creates his epic vision from a totally demythologized presentation of what he sees, thinks, creates.

Juan, in his haphazard way, tags along as Byron encircles Europe, drawing in modern headlines and ancient history, contemporary writers and classical authorities, and the general subjects of all literature:

> Love's the first net which spreads its deadly mesh;
>   Ambition, Avarice, Vengeance, Glory, glue
> The glittering lime-twigs of our latter days,
> Where still we flutter on for pence or praise. (V.22, 5–8)

What accrues in this desultory fashion is truly encyclopedic (though badly in want of an index for critical purposes), enveloping Western culture even as it refuses to systematize it. Wilkie suggests that Byron "play[s] against one another different attitudes toward epic" as part of the process of "emptying *Don Juan* of meaning."[12] But is it not exactly to forestall a nihilistic end that Byron engages in the strategy? It is of a piece with his approach to the lesser genres subsumed by the epic. He empties a form by subjecting it to his skeptical awareness of the insufficiency of any single system, but in doing so he only reinforces its hold on the human imagination—his own imagination, self-conscious in its independent creativity: "I have more than one Muse at a push" (X.5, 4). Byron recognizes that what unites all epics is not a universal truth but simply and profoundly a generic conception, what Tasso represents in his notion of the poem as heterocosm.[13] As the world we live in depends on opposites for its ongoing life, so must its microcosm *Don Juan* and so, too, its author who glories in his inconsistency (XVII.11). Byron as epic poet is as much a tour de force of generic capaciousness as the artifact he creates. Both are unexclusive in what they will contemplate, inconclusive in what they can know, bounded only by human inventiveness and the limits of mortality. "If you have nought else, here's at least satiety" (XIV.14, 5).

IV

Prometheus Unbound, a Lyrical Drama in Four Acts, begun in 1818 while Shelley was living in Byron's rented estate at Este, contains so many studied allusions to Byron's poems as to constitute a deliberate counterstatement.[14] At the same time, and as an equal manifestation of their remarkable artistic interchange, Byron started work on *Don Juan*. These two poems, intimately associated in so many respects, are also the major experiments in extended mixed genres published during the Romantic period. As one might expect, Shelley's approach, though conceived in terms of *Childe Harold's Pilgrimage* and *Manfred*, is wholly opposite to Byron's. The difference is fundamentally ideological, permeating every aspect of form in his lyrical drama.

Shelley's generic designation is uncommon, though not unique; in the Romantic period lyrical drama is a term applicable to any serious dramatic effort containing music, from opera to choral drama.[15] Though no music was intended to accompany the drama, musical imagery is a significant element throughout, and the generic subtitle likewise accentuates and justifies the large number and variety of lyrical intrusions in the work. The designation also has a second effect, however, for it prompts a comparison with the Wordsworth-Coleridge experiment of two decades earlier. From the very first Shelley alerts us to a mixture of modes even more purely antithetical than those of the *Lyrical Ballads*: the distanced presentational objectivity of drama, allowing for no authorial voice, its familiar Horatian unities requiring strict chronological development, being linked with an effusion of emotional intensity divorced from time or circumstance or even personality. With such a generic designation we are prepared for a work centering on the balance between subject and object, whose mixture of modes will continually enlarge the frames of reference so as to mediate between an internal psychological state and its enveloping political organization, between one mind and the whole of human culture, between time and eternity, spatial fixity and the infinite. Where Byron attains his epic vision by representing irreducible discords, the polarities of Shelley's generic subtitle impel *Prometheus Unbound* to intricately modulating harmonies that in its last act aspire to the music of the spheres.

Not that discords are absent from a work that begins on the stage of high tragedy. "Ah me, alas, pain, pain ever, forever!" is Prometheus' despairing refrain in the first act (I.23, 31, 635), an encapsulating formula for the tragic mode of apprehension that engulfs all characters in the act. Shelley borrows from Aeschylus a limbo of agony, its inception and its promised cessation alike so far removed that time seems stopped amid "wingless, crawling Hours" (I.48). The tragic mode wraps others in its blanket of irony: the mountain waste where Prometheus is chained is "Black, wintry, dead, unmeasured; without herb, / Insect, or beast, or shape or sound of life" (I.21-22)—an antipastoral enclosure of death. Similarly inverted are the traditional messenger speech, with the Phantasm of Jupiter called upon to repeat Prometheus' original curse rather than to relate some new and crucial event, the dream visions offered by the Furies that, in the crucifixion of Christ and the debacle of the French Revolution, represent promise not fulfilled but forestalled, even the alternative visions of the Spirits of Love, who sing of ruin, desolation, and pain along with selfless courage and honor. Generic conventions are thus introduced with their associations deliberately reversed to accord with the tragic premise of the act. Prometheus' summation—"There is no agony and no solace left; / Earth can console, Heaven can torment no more" (I.819-820)—characterizes a limbo in which no movement is possible, no mode of seeing is free from the universal denial of possibility. After this, Prometheus speaks only one further line in Act I, in response to Panthea's reminder of the Oceanides' enduring vigilance; yet by implication it wholly reverses the multiple ironies of his tragic apprehension: "I said all hope was vain but love—thou lovest. . ." (I.824). The manifestation of fellow-feeling, begun with Prometheus' acknowledgement that he pities Jupiter for presiding over a system of slavery (I.53), here quietly comes full circle, enclosing and separating the tragic perspective whose elements have been anatomized throughout Act I.

Prometheus is unaware that he has liberated himself by altering his perspective. The reader discovers the fact as Act II unfolds, and, though there are many indications of it, Shelley carefully marks the change by a telling generic restitution. That is, to place this act in condensed perspective, it opens with a messenger speech of true communication, with Panthea herself being the agent of dream visions of promise, not futility. It is followed by the descent of Asia and Panthea through an effulgent Virgilian pastoral into a quest romance of initiation that results in Asia's transfiguration. And in the end we experience another antiphonal chorale matching the Furies and Spirits of the first act, a love duet or epithalamion between Asia and the disembodied voice of Prometheus. Love empowers all things, especially generic conventions as avenues of perception. Genres bloom in this universal spring, reversing the tragic winter of Prometheus' imprisonment.

Music is heard everywhere, doubled in the echoes that lead Asia and Panthea to Demogorgon's cave, threading through each change of landscape or alteration of mode, drawing together all conditions of life. The rich pastoral realm of the second scene, like Coleridge's untended castle garden, is flooded with the songs of nightingales, but there are also, as the fauns describe their surroundings, unseen spirits of the woods who sing continually. The fauns break off their contemplation of this interwoven choral texture to tend to Silenus' goats, moving us suddenly into Virgil's Sixth *Eclogue* and the satyr's cosmic mythography, songs "which charm / To silence the unenvying nightingales" (II.ii.96–97). The self-contemplating, constantly reechoing pastoral world is represented, as these images accumulate, not as repressed and closed off, but as charged with potentiality. It returns in the process of being fulfilled with Asia's final song, itself a musical self-contemplation, prefiguring "A Paradise of vaulted bowers / Lit by downward-gazing flowers" whose inhabitants (in the last words of Act II) "walk upon the sea, and chaunt melodiously" (II.v.104–105, 111). The richness of effect here is uncanny: so minor a detail as the internal rhyme of the last line itself exemplifies the notion of echo that touches every detail of the act, from Panthea's echo of Asia and Asia's of Prometheus, to the fauns' conversation and the natural sounds that suffuse their world, to Demogorgon's echoes of Asia's very words in their crucial exchange. And the paradise where people "walk upon the sea" on a grand scale echoes the vision of Christ in Act I, suggesting that his pastoral promise has been at last realized, though in a secular way. The entire act is epitomized by Asia's song about singing, a lyrical contemplation of the nature of lyricism, endlessly creative, spontaneous, timeless, the type of paradise.

Such uninterrupted self-reflexiveness is at no point redolent of narcissism. Instead, it focuses our continuing attention on interior processes, whether of thought, feeling, resolve, or responsibility. The entirety of Act II is a reflection of Asia's mental world as its potentiality is liberated: the interconnecting generic modes suggest the range of that interior possibility, from the communion of the pastoral enclosure to the romance encounter with the giant form of self-transformation embodied in Demogorgon. Even the variety of lyric measures Shelley creates in the act serve to expand the range. They cover what appears an entire spectrum, from the mercurial reflections of impulse and inspiration heard in the echoes and the songs of spirits to the sonorous and impassioned high style of Asia's final verses.

The process continues, simplified so that its implications are more boldly apparent, in Act III. The first scene, in which Jupiter's fall is enacted, is the stuff of grand heroic drama, full of pomp and posture, whose false style betrays the true nature of the despot. As the trappings of his grandiose stage-set collapse about him, Jupiter plunges to his doom with a reminiscence of Prometheus' refrain: "I sink . . . / Dizzily down—ever, forever, down" (III.i.80–81). It is the fall of tragedy itself. The ensuing scene renders the first of three messenger speeches in the act, each reflecting a different aspect of the fall and its effects, all together emphasizing the signal importance of perspective and the enriching amplitude of their variety. The first of these is in the exchange of Ocean and Apollo, ancient Titan and young god, not in this resolutely humanist work to be construed as deities but rather as primal elements, water and fire, no longer in contention. The other messenger speeches will conclude the act, as the childlike Spirit of the Earth rhapsodizes over its wonders and the mature Spirit of the Hour anatomizes the psychic alterations that coincide with the dethroning of Jupiter. The perspectives are complementary, not exclusive, suggestive of fields of human endeavor, partial in isolation but here implicitly harmonized. The discourses of science, of imaginative wonder, and of social and psychological anatomy constitute, as it were, a university.

All such elements in Act III center on the cave to which Prometheus and Asia will retire, not to retreat from human obligation but to serve as its dynamic core. Here the pastoral motifs of the second act recur and coalesce:

> There is a Cave
> All overgrown with trailing odorous plants
> Which curtain out the day with leaves and flowers
> And paved with veined emerald, and a fountain
> Leaps in the midst with an awakening sound;
> From its curved roof the mountain's frozen tears
> Like snow or silver or long diamond spires
> Hang downward, raining forth a doubtful light;
> And there is heard the ever-moving air

> Whispering without from tree to tree, and birds,
> And bees; and all around are mossy seats
> And the rough walls are clothed with long soft grass;
> A simple dwelling. . . . (III.iii.10–22)

This is the pastoral of a restored golden age, simple, bountiful, harmonious. But as Prometheus' description unfolds, the contents of the cave are transposed from such natural details to mental processes. The cave is so richly detailed not by way of wish fulfillment but because it is a symbol of the regenerate human mind, a fertile plenum in which contraries are balanced and charged with purpose: the "unexhausted spirits" of Prometheus and Asia will "Weave harmonies divine, yet ever new, / From difference sweet where discord cannot be" (III.iii.36, 38–39). The tragedy of isolation and frustration has been transformed by thought, the impulse of fellow feeling, into a domesticated pastoral comedy. But the transformation is even more radical than that, for, as we have slowly gathered that Prometheus and Asia themselves represent the two major faculties of the mind, intellect and emotion, their reunion constitutes a generic internalization and reformation. In this description Shelley elaborates the essential core of his mental pastoral.[16]

Act III of *Prometheus Unbound* is the only act without lyric effusions. Their quiet absence prepares for the astonishing proliferation of lyric forms in the fourth act. It is designed as a celebratory marriage masque, a universal epithalamion even to the point of introducing earth and moon in magnetic embrace.[17] The explosion of lyric forms reflects not only the vital energy of the regenerated world but also its inexhaustible variety. No element, no perspective, escapes the universal harmony. The virtuoso flair by its very nature conveys inclusiveness, as in this juxtaposition of rapid and prolonged phonetic units in the Chorus of Hours:

> Ceaseless and rapid and fierce and free
> With the spirits which build a new earth and sea
> And a Heaven where yet Heaven could never be—
>
> Solemn and slow and serene and bright
> Leading the Day and outspeeding the Night
> With the Powers of a world of perfect light— (IV.163–168)

As with these complementary voices on a small scale, so with the multitude of lyric forms that compose Act IV of *Prometheus Unbound*: each is an integral prism of perspective coexisting, much like musical cadences, in democratic equality. When, in Demogorgon's concluding enjoinder to all elements in the universe, he calls upon the stars and they respond in a single voice as "Our great Republic" (IV.533), Shelley suggests by inference why he has created such a galaxy of lyric differentiation in Act IV.

The regenerate universe of *Prometheus Unbound* is a psychic creation. To adapt Blake's aphorism from *Auguries of Innocence*, "The eye altering alters all." The only generic perspective at last excluded from the universe is tragedy (though its inclusion in the first act of the drama actually allows Shelley to project a wholeness that is absolute and reminds us that a tragic inversion of this regenerate universe is again possible). Appropriate to its internalized nature, in no other work of literature do genres serve so fully and self-consciously as modes of apprehension. Nor, we might add, is there a major experiment equal to *Prometheus Unbound* in the formal ramifications of its democratic ethos. No sense of generic hierarchy is allowed to intrude upon Shelley's drama: whatever form they assume, hierarchies are still the creations of Jupiter. Rather, the mixture of genres implies an uncompromising multiperspectivism, a constant process whereby the mind reorders the elements that constitute its universe. In so wholly honoring received generic traditions, Shelley paradoxically creates a monument of revolutionary art whose concern is the nature of the ultimate human revolution. Its insistently humanist vision must almost by necessity be richly imbued with humane traditions. Yet, the triumph of his conception lies in the seemingly inexhaustible stores of those traditions as they spill into *Prometheus Unbound*. Genre so self-reflexively considered becomes virtually a metaphor for the poem itself, the purpose of whose mixture of forms is to celebrate human inclusiveness.

Prometheus Unbound is the most compressed of major endeavors in mixed kinds among the British Romantics. Its union of form and content is brilliant, representing the truth enunciated by Shelley in his preface, that poets "are in one sense the creators and in another the creations of their age" (p. 135). Simply put, a work of such intricate generic complexity could not have been conceived without the universal sense of formal possibilities that marks the age of British Romanticism. Nor, of course, could that sense have existed without its concentrated and ranging literary revival. Shelley's ringing statement of a poet's creed in the same preface—"one great poet is a masterpiece of nature, which another not only ought to study but must study" (p. 134)—is very much of its time, both in its faith in ongoing creativity and in its veneration for the models of the past.

CHAPTER NINE

Form and Freedom in European Romantic Poetry

Natur und Kunst, sie scheinen sich zu fliehen
Und haben sich, eh man es denkt, gefunden;
Der Widerwille ist auch mir verschwunden,
Und beide scheinen gleich mich anzuziehen.
Es gilt wohl nur ein redliches Bemühen!
Und wenn wir erst in abgemessnen Stunden
Mit Geist und Fleiss uns an die Kunst gebunden,
Mag frei Natur im Herzen wieder glühen.

So ists mit aller Bildung auch beschaffen.
Vergebens werden ungebundne Geister
Nach der Vollendung reiner Höhe streben.
Wer Grosses will, muss sich zusammenraffen.
In der Beschränkung zeigt sich erst der Meister,
Und das Gesetz nur kann uns Freiheit geben.

Johann Wolfgang von Goethe,
"Natur und Kunst"[1]

I

THE COMPOSITE ORDERS of Wordsworth, Byron, and Shelley are the most daring and sophisticated formal experiments in British Romantic poetry. The poets' knowledge of their literary heritage is brilliantly tempered to a determined conceptual purpose, and yet their individual ideologies, if clearly associated in a shared concern with the values of process and progress that dominate their culture, are as distinctive in constitution as they are in purpose. The generic inclusiveness of *The Prelude, Don Juan,* and *Prometheus Unbound* is of such complexity that each poem becomes the locus for an encompassing world view, and thus it is natural for us as readers, generally speaking, to refer the entire canon of the authors to these supreme embodiments of their genius. So enveloping a synoptic form, we are wont to say, must constitute the poet's largest and ultimate vision of life. The critical instincts by which we enforce an ideological centering of such intensity are not only natural, but they also accord with our own experience, moral no less than aesthetic.

Nevertheless, they are implicitly reductive. We have only to look at the wanderers elsewhere in Wordsworth who cannot discover meaning or solace—his Female Vagrant, his burned-out old soldiers, the intellectually dessicated Solitary of *The Excursion*—to temper any simple sense of Wordsworth's faith in his progressive imaginative liberation. Providing the obverse of or necessary balance to Byron's fluid comic vision are the four historical tragedies he wrote contemporaneously with *Don Juan*, all centering on heroes ground down by cultural fixities each vainly tries to escape. And there can be observed in Shelley's writing another way of construing a universal democratic paradigm that inhibits any urge to read the final act of his lyrical drama sentimentally, the republic of despair enacted in *The Triumph of Life*. What is most to be celebrated in these poets, and their fellow artists of the Romantic movement as well, is not an encompassing ideological vision, but that they never remained still, even when formulating structures encompassing ceaseless mental movement. And the preceding chapters as a whole suggest an even more cautionary injunction against too facile an equation of art and life among these poets. If poetic forms embody a logic that constrains the intellect to its dictates and if genres necessarily presuppose that certain values will be honored over others, even with composite orders—perhaps most especially with composite orders—such interwoven generic constraints, though they may well enable creativity, exert a continual ideological pressure on imaginative vision. That is not to say that a genre constitutes an ideological absolute. The history of literary genres within the Romantic period suggests that, whatever the metal from which an artistic superstructure is formed, even an alloy of intricate molecular complexity, it is always malleable. Bend it as the poet wills, however, the metal does not change.

And yet, the continuing implication of this discussion, whether involving sonnets or epics, is that the ideological pressure of a genre can, at least in the hands of a major artist, be liberating. Classical pastoral offered Wordsworth a model for a democratic sufficiency of such balanced clarity that it took him a decade to plumb its implications. An entire generation in Blake's life as a poet issued from his endeavor to grapple with the logical possibilities inherent in the epic as it was left by Milton to his successors. The shift in cultural values that transpired during the Enlightenment allowed the entire period to reconceive, from a necessary distance, the ethos of the English Renaissance. In these instances, and many more suggested by the foregoing pages, recovery stimulated a process of reformation, of reimagining the past; and that in turn, at least from the midpoint of the eighteenth century to the political realignment that took place between 1827 and 1832, equally prompted the reimagining of the present, which, by the perverse logic of history, had in the Enlightenment lost much of its past and all of its mythology. The received traditions of literature, particularly as channeled through the centuries by their generic momentum, could compensate where other cultural embodiments had been emptied of palpable meaning. Against the failure of myth, the factionalism and proliferation of religious sects, the dissolution of iconographical knowledge, their resilient conceptual syntax kept its integrity and was thus able to counter and assimilate the demythologizing rationalism whose stream forged a new and dangerously rapid tributary in the eighteenth century.

The result was not so much a universally understood program—though there are assuredly contentious manifestoes among Romantic poets—as the necessary adjustment of European culture to fundamentally altered circumstances. The peculiar isolation of Britain from the continent coincided, fortuitously it would appear in retrospect, with the pressure of Enlightenment rationalism to create the charged arena of Romanticism in which a skeptical epistemology closed with, and transformed, its literary heritage within a single generation. The Renaissance hierarchy of genres was tested, inverted, then reconstituted through those inverted values. To place that transformation within a sharper ideological and cultural framework, where the literary inheritance had been conceived upon an aristocratic model, resolutely tempered to sacramental purposes, and generally secured against openended philosophical speculations, the shift of underlying cultural values necessarily subjected it to a democratic ethos, a progressive secularization, and the skeptical assumptions of Berkeley and Hume. Byron may disagree profoundly with Wordsworth's sense of the decorum appropriate to such an inversion, asserting the worldly voice of Pope and Gay against a reincarnation of "namby-pampy" Phillips, but he participates in the same process; and, indeed, his entire poetic career, viewed in a glance, is one extended inversion of the traditional genres in order to reconstitute them according to an aristocratic notion of the democratic, secular, and skeptical. As Byron's example suggests, the inherent logic of such a thorough transformation tends to force a genre to pivot on its axis. In such a process of turning inside out, it is no wonder that paradox invests the entire process. Not the least of its results is that the more resistant to altered circumstances are the conventions of a genre, the more likely they are not to be discarded but rather forced into new alliances flaunting their shifted values. Of all the major Romantic poets Byron might be counted the least likely to write a religious quest romance, which, without our overstraining the logic, is probably why he did so. Yet also, as even such a reverse of expectations as this attests, the transformation of generic convention resolves itself in a continual process of testing. The consequences are major and, as the previous pages continually exemplify, they are twofold. Because the constituents of a genre cannot be simply appropriated without question, they become self-conscious in their application, which is to say self-reflexive in their very conception. Moreover, this process of testing also necessarily forces them into organic relationship with the overall artistic purpose, as Coleridge so perceptively argued from his own experience.

We have ourselves inherited a common metaphor for representing at least one element of this studied inversion, which is the mode by which light, enlightenment, is seen to be transmitted by the means of art. There are, on the one hand, mirrors and, on the other hand, lamps; and these two means of representation, which are not in fact means at all but simply metaphorical tropes, imply a rude dichotomy between simple mimesis and a self-conscious creativity. In the rough, this metaphorical extrapolation from the tangled maze of the history of consciousness helps to separate its strands. The accepted function of literature did perceptively shift ground in the eighteenth century, partly because the potential readership and the number of publications both vastly expanded, contributing to and being reinforced by the attendant alteration in cultural values we have been remarking. But to conceive that shift as also involving the spurning of tradition or a disregard for the generic underpinnings of that tradition is to be seduced by the apparent logic implicit in simplistic metaphor. In our own time that logic has become something of a historical assumption, and, unquestionably, there were some few souls in the nineteenth century who also pursued it. It is, however, significant that at least in England those who grasped for such an understanding did so while standing in the perplexing trough of genius that separated a definable Romantic period from what would come to be discerned as the early manifestations of Victorian art. John Stuart Mill's "What is Poetry?" of 1833 and John Keble's lectures from the Oxford Chair of Poetry from 1832 to 1841, published in 1844 as *De poeticae vi medica*, redefine poetry as the mere expression of lyrical emotion, an art of spontaneous overflow empowered by an aesthetic clearly derived from what were mistakenly conceived by the writers to be Wordsworth's notions of his art. That the chief beneficiary of this aesthetic in Great Britain, the short-lived Spasmodic School, bowed in and then out with less effect than the inhabitant of the previous generational trough sixty years earlier, the Della-Cruscan school (of which, it might be said, its lamp was the Spasmodics' mirror), should give us both pause and historical perspective. But, at least with Mill, the cultural ramification has been wrongly construed from the first, for the driving question of his essay is actually the nature of fiction, and it had far more importance for conceiving the ground rules of the Victorian novel as a repository of cultural stresses than for influencing in any lasting way its poetry. As an assessment of Romanticism, it participates in the fantasy by which Browning was to clear ground for his genius, defining the previous two generations as centers of lyric verse and ignoring their notable achievements in narrative poetry. The arguments by which Mill and Keble safely encompassed, and distorted, the poetry of the previous half-century are as transparently indicative of the insecurity of their decade as Shelley's celebration of his culture in the *Defence of Poetry*, separated by a mere dozen years from Mill's essay, is also inimitably of its time. Since, however, Mill and Keble provide the most substantial evidence adduced to promulgate the myth of a generic breakdown in British poetry, they have assumed an importance beyond their intellectual means and a centrality that masks their fearful belatedness.[2]

Yet, to give due credit to the sources of a distorting misapprehension, it

is surely possible that the generation that followed the Younger Romantics mistook the remarkable freedom with which they learned to manipu-
late traditional genres, not the least from the example of Wordsworth and
Coleridge themselves, for a total liberation from them. Though attempts
to distinguish the two generations of British Romanticism generally
founder because of the signal contributions of the older poets to the
poetic ferment of the Regency, the patterns discernible from the evidence
of the preceding chapters suggest that what may have been tentative
generic experiments in the first generation quickly established firm principles for the artistry of the second. Yet against what in retrospective logic
might be anticipated—and, perhaps because the logic seems so obvious, it
has now been fairly embalmed in customary literary history—the enlarging skepticism of the Younger Romantics paradoxically coincides with
an increasing preoccupation with generic possibility. A moment's contemplation should explode the seeming paradox and comprehend why
inherited traditions would prove so imperative to a school of poetry that
is self-professedly engaged in social and psychological liberation.

Where the Younger Romantics inherit the democratic, secular, and
skeptical ethos of their predecessors, an ethos invested in a revitalization
of generic traditions, they implicitly assume a notion of genre as both a
mode of apprehension and a repository of conflicting values, exemplified
in Wordsworth's resurrecting the paradigms of classical pastoral against
Renaissance Christian allegory or eighteenth-century aristocratic man-
nerism. Through all these cultural manifestations, they recognize, the
conventions remain and the metal bends to necessity. So from Ephesus to
Haija Sophia to St. Peter's, Byron pursues his religious quest. So Keats,
in *Hyperion*, juxtaposes the Miltonic fall into knowledge with its equivalent in classical myth. So Shelley, in *Prometheus Unbound*, intrudes a
vision of the crucified Christ before the eyes of his hero martyred by
Jupiter. As certainly as a conceptual syntax embodies an ideological
syntax, it resists any single system of belief; and especially where such
systems are brought into confrontation, the syntax allows the contemplation of essential mysteries of human experience through multivalent
contexts and a liberating artistic perspective. What we learn from the
ubiquity of deconstructive strategies in British Romantic poetry is that
the generic perspective, if the poet is clever enough, can be profoundly
exploratory. The art that results is therefore likely to have no purpose
beyond that of exploration.

Needless to say, it is a defensible political posture. In an age of reaction,
and with a European conflict that seemingly disallowed every alternative
to a British compromise that had in those stresses barely held together—
that had indeed through those stresses proved that the compromise was
more a matter of conventional rhetoric than of law—not to serve, but to
stand and wait openly, is perhaps the only comprehensible stance for
those who can neither revert to the past nor do more than hope for the
future. From our comfortable distance it is easy either to accord faith in a

remythologized prospect as though it were a program uniting the culture, or to puncture those seemingly inflated hopes as if unaware that they were, as Shelley said of *Prometheus Unbound*, only saving "idealisms of moral excellence." One extreme of critical perspective inevitably produces its alternative, yet neither ultimately is true to the conditions of the culture.[3] What is profoundly true is that literary traditions, particularly those associated with generic tradition, allowed a neutral, yet critical and self-integrating, stance for poets who stood ineffectually outside it.

What we learn from the concentrated generic transformations of British Romanticism is a simple truth that can be expressed without resort to theoretical jargon or reductive abstractions, which is that art continually recreates life as well as further extensions of art. In one sense or another every poem of substance in the Romantic period reveals the pattern. Form is a refuge from the systems of belief forced, and understandably so, by a culture in siege and at war. It is a link with the past as a conceptual repository, its contents not construed as involving (though it was, of course, the case) even more constricting belief systems, but rather liberating imaginative structures that reaffirm the commitments all of us have to what transcends the necessary limitations of any cultural epoch. Shelley's remark in *A Defence of Poetry* that the poetry of Dante and Milton is essentially distinct from their religious beliefs is characteristic of how we may imagine they were read as well by a great many less candid admirers: "The distorted notions of invisible things which Dante and his rival Milton have idealized, are merely the mask and mantle in which these great poets walk through eternity enveloped and disguised. . . . The Divina Commedia and Paradise Lost have conferred upon modern mythology a systematic form" (pp. 498–499). A different time—indeed, a later time trying to contain the fearful energy released by Humean skepticism—might revert to the repository of traditional Christian paradigms for moral comfort or philosophical distance, as Arnold does in his claims for literary touchstones. But the British Romantics look to genre for a much more radical purpose, to supply a geometry for art that is, or can be made to be, itself both morally neutral and a driving force.

II

But does that then mean that an isolated Britain, however distinguished the literary productions of its Romanticism, is to occupy a no-man's-land, sharing an identifying term with continental literatures from which it would be better to differentiate it? By no means. And yet the very question suggests that the relationship between British and continental Romanticisms is complex and requires a continual adjustment of cultural perspective if it is to be viewed without distortion. First of all, we have to recognize that Romanticism, conceived as a European phenomenon, lasted well over a century, yet at the same time occurred in national phases. Thus Goethe was already being enthusiastically celebrated as a genius before any of the Italian or French Romantics were born and stood as sage and septuagenarian when the great commotion of French Romanticism began with the *Méditations Poétiques* of Lamartine in 1820. Just four years after that milestone, with the death of Byron, the flowering of British Romanticism had abruptly ceased; but the central figure of the French movement, Victor Hugo, did not die until 1885, leaving, true to his nature as a cultural monument, two epic poems to be published after his death. The anomalies interwoven within such dates could be multiplied considerably but would only underscore the extent to which, even when we identify Romanticism as pan-European, it is keyed to the discrete exigencies of national cultures.[4] And yet the effort to discuss it in a transnational setting inevitably encourages a discourse about what is shared in, rather than what separates, these national Romanticisms, with the result that vital distinctions easily become blurred.

If we attempt to define the movement by contrast, we are bound to renew the polemical debate over classicism and Romanticism, but even that debate is culturally determined, surfacing in Germany in the 1790s, where it occupied something less than a decade of spirited polemics, reerupting in Italy in the 1810s, slightly tinging the British cultural scene at the same time, and then being suddenly resuscitated in France during the 1820s and 30s. The latter, almost comic, gesture of belatedness should alert us to the fact that the dispute between classic and romantic, so vague though noisy in its polemics and so incongruously reconceived within every stirring of national literatures, is a component of Romanticism itself, the surest mark of the self-consciousness by which the movement, in country after country, came to understand its power and to galvanize its momentum. Moreover, on close inspection it is almost impossible to mark a dividing line and identify anticlassical Romantics, at least among the intellectual and artistic giants of the period. In Italy one must rule out Foscolo, who so celebrated his birth on a Greek island that, even without his translation of *The Iliad*, claim might be made for him as Greece's Romantic poet, as well as Leopardi, who prided himself on his ability to read classical Greek poetry with the stylistic discernment of a native-speaker. In Germany we must exclude Hölderlin, who not only reinvented the Greek pantheon but earnestly tried to believe in it, and the arch neo-Hellenists Goethe and Schiller, who defended classicism in the preliminary debate; but also, if we regard Friedrich Schlegel as their chief antagonist, we are faced with the irreducible fact that he was a learned antiquarian, wrote a history of classical poetry, and was by appointment a professor of Sanskrit. The Younger British Romantics all resuscitate classical myth, and it might even be said that Byron gave his life for the sake of a myth he had assiduously deconstructed. It is true that the study of Greek rather gave way to Roman martial arts under Napoleon's empire, but if the posthumous publication of Chenier's bucolics in 1819 offered the French Romantics their point of departure, Hugo's odes a central voice, and Sainte-Beuve's celebration of classical models in the

1840s and 50s a new impetus, the French debate appears to have continued at least into the 1870s when Rimbaud introduced modernism at the age of seventeen. And yet it is entirely symptomatic of this century of debate that the first indication of Rimbaud's prodigious genius was a Latin prize poem written at the age of fourteen.

Even when we locate the classic-romantic debate within Romanticism itself, however, it does not escape the inevitable cultural determinism. Broadly speaking, we might wish to see it in T. S. Eliot's terms, as a confrontation of a tradition and the individual talent, and often that was how the argument ran. But whose tradition and in relation to what talent? Foscolo's conception of himself as neo-Hellenist empowers his writing and, indeed, even mythologizes it in a poetry of endless exile: his Greece is irrecoverable, but incarnate in him. In a sense, that frees Foscolo from other components of literary tradition that any Italian poet must inherit, the quattrocento, and behind it, the heritage of Latin literature. And yet, for Foscolo's countrymen it would appear a specious freedom for a dispirited, partitioned, and repeatedly occupied country—if that term is even applicable—to throw off what gave it identity, continuity, and dignity.

If we cross the Alps, the entire argument shifts. Classical order becomes profoundly antinationalistic, at least as the Schlegels or Madame de Staël represent it. The romantic signifies the northern, the rugged poetry of the heroic past: the pine tree, not the palm, as Heine would succinctly mark the distinction. In generic terms Romanticism is the romance, Germany's indigenous mode, competing with the Homeric and Virgilian epic for literary primacy. Toward the west the issues are more academic and perhaps subtler. The neo-Hellenism of the British Romantics is, as we have continually remarked, an easy inheritance, one already assimilated in the Renaissance, but revived, along with the formidable classical scholarship spearheaded by Richard Porson, as a respectable cloak for skeptical, non-Christian thought. The very late classical revival of France had first to contend with the legacy of the Empire's Roman trappings and then with the academic canon of French literature. Sainte-Beuve's new classicism coincided exactly with the recovery of the French Renaissance, particularly Ronsard.[5] Yet, as the debate raged, it is apparent that both elements became crucial to the liberation the Romantic faction wanted. If classicism is seen as a lapidary, unchanging, and aristocratic order, then it is an aspect of rationalism, or benevolent despotism, or Aquinean Catholicism. But if it resides in the mythmaking of Hesiod, the dynamic energy of Homer, or the erotic spontaneity of Theocritus on the one hand, and on the other the plain honesty of Horace, the brooding double vision of Virgil, or the lyric virtuosity of Catullus, it represents an ancient freedom from the constraints of modern culture. The other side of the European defense of classicism, in other words, is Romanticism.

As British Romanticism constitutes a renaissance of the Renaissance, both a recovery of its earlier literature and of that earlier literary recovery itself, we can reliably transfer the applicability of this entire complex, with due allowance for what the past meant in each national literature and the extent to which it had been obscured, to the whole of western European Romanticism. And if we add to that recognition a balanced awareness that what writers do and what they propound are often distinct, we are also able to extend the significance of traditional forms that we have observed in British Romanticism to the poetic ferment on the continent. There is clearly a link binding British experimentation with genre to Hölderlin's attempts to forge a new free verse form in German from Greek iambs and hexameters and Schiller's recovery of the grand style, to Foscolo's *Odes and Sonnets* of 1803 and his driving Pindaric ode, *Dei Sepolchri*, of 1806, and to the splendid incongruity by which French Romanticism trumpeted its originality in Lamartine's elegies, Hugo's odes, and Musset's epyllions.[6] Yet if we concentrate attention just on the reappropriation and central positioning of the ode in all three cultures, we must acknowledge that what binds these revivals are radically different notions of the form. It is not the same kind in any of them, and even where there are certain correspondences, they are apt to strike us as anomalous rather than as generically constitutive. For instance, the early odes of Coleridge—"Ode to the Departing Year," "France: An Ode"—do share the public themes and hortatory inflations of Hugo's odes of a generation later. Yet, their poetical models are as different as their politics. Coleridge's poems derive their impetus from the political odes— particularly the Whig progress piece—of the British eighteenth century, whereas Hugo's are conditioned by the alexandrine encomium and by seventeenth-century French stage conventions. A new form of the ode will arise among the second group of French Romantics to compete with the grand rhetoric and dramatic postures of Hugo, but it will derive from reclaiming Ronsard, whose odes have nothing in common with Pindar's, to the French literary canon. The Pindaric odes of Hölderlin, Schiller, and Foscolo do stem from a single source but are similarly filtered through very different national understandings of classical form, the former two reconceiving Winkelmann's marble, the latter a Mediterranean passion. The characteristic odes of the later British Romantics, on the other hand, derive their power, as we have noted, from the choral odes of Greek tragedy, converting the oppositional structure of strophe and antistrophe into dialectical rhythms demanding a synthesis that usually the poet is unable or unwilling to effect. In each case Romanticism is dependent not simply on classicism but on versions of classicism that themselves betray the biases of the nation's scholarship and probably its program of education. Even more is this the case with the hymn. We can compare, but it is probably more fruitful to contrast, Novalis's *Hymnen an die Nacht*, Manzoni's *Inni Sacri*, Shelley's "Hymn to Intellectual Beauty," and the hymnic meditations of Lamartine. The religious climate of each culture is so distinct, so enveloped by centuries of national development, and so infused with contemporary European politics that only the fact of the kind itself allows common ground.

The complexity of these formal problems seems far removed from what might appear normative a century before, and therein lies an expansion of the singular paradox observed earlier in the relationship of British Romanticism and the Enlightenment. To survey European literature around 1750 is to discover common ground, something approaching an observed and universal canon over which reigns the flexible Voltaire. It was that because—at least in Britain, France, and Germany—it was so small a cultivated tract. Though neither Italy nor Spain ever lost its principal heritage, in the other three countries Romanticism coincides as a movement with reclaiming the wilderness beyond—which is to say, particularly medieval literature, and in England and France the sixteenth century as centered in Spenser and the Pléiade. The explosion of lyrical forms in Romanticism is exactly the reverse of poetic anarchy; rather, it testifies to the revelation of literary possibility from the past against which the dull sameness of heroic couplets and of bifurcated alexandrines suggested undeserved, long-endured, and wholly unnecessary poverty. Yet at least in the initial stages of this recovery, it is for obvious reasons intensely nationalistic, though connected to a further common ground in the resurgence of classical scholarship. Everywhere in European literature the observed canons were revealed as inadequate to encompass the burden not just, as a strictly historical overview might have it, of startling new material and creative conditions, but of a revived heritage. And after the first wave, national recovery, came its sharing through translation.

Another feature of that early Enlightenment landscape was the codification of generic rules by French arbiters of taste: Boileau, Rapin, Le Bossu, et al. But again, the British experience is written large when one crosses to the recovery of continental literatures. There were no rules to encompass the verse of the Troubadors and Minnesingern, or the *Niebelungenlied*, or the succession of Italian Orlando poems, or the ballad. Not only had neoclassical categories constricted literature to a small number of approved texts and an implicit hierarchy of genres, but it had through its exclusivity reduced generic possibility itself. The gradual critical enlargement of the number of stipulated genres we observe in England during the eighteenth century occurs throughout Europe as the history of literature was at last understood and for the very first time written. The hegemony of rules could not survive such a test. For a history of national literature is perforce diachronic and evolutionary, even when, as was the case with Bishop Percy and Thomas Warton, it is obsessed with prehistoric sources. To such a history critical arbiters of another culture and an opposite ideology—representing, as it were, a synchronic poetics—were irrelevant. It is not, then, to choose a single case, that the numerous attempts to write a new epic in England and France threw the prescriptions of Le Bossu to the wind. History had done so in the revival of romance throughout Europe. The dialectical relationship between the two perspectives on narrative offered intellectual and artistic challenge, and it was accepted on all sides, first in England and then, with a life force that is truly astonishing, throughout nineteenth-century France, culminating in the posthumous publication of Victor Hugo's unfinished theosophical epics, *La Fin de Satan* and *Dieu*.[7]

To underscore the extent to which European Romanticism grounded itself in an Enlightenment program whose dynamics reached far into the nineteenth century, however, is not to deny major shifts in sensibility and concomitant generic developments in literature. The pastoral, for instance, does not disappear but becomes so transfigured and, so to speak, naturalized that it takes a second glance to recognize how deeply it embues the exotic landscapes of Hugo's *Orientales*. On the continent, indeed, Wordsworthian naturalism is less discernible than Churchill's or Crabbe's austere antipastoral, which only accords with a generation of warfare on Europe's pastoral plains. French Romanticism truly finds its first voice, echoing across the gulf of history, in Chenier's *Bucoliques*, written in prison before his execution under the Terror and first published in 1819. His representation of the lambs of eighteenth-century aristocracy being led to their slaughter is, arguably, the farthest-reaching of modern antipastorals, inasmuch as its inversions mark the doom of an entire culture as well as its unfortunate author. Yet something of its like also emerges in the terrifying calm of Leopardi's "Canto notturno di un pastore errante dell'Asia"—"Night Song of a Wandering Shepherd of Asia." Leopardi's youth was spent in studying the classics, and his career began with translation of the bucolic poetry of Moschus. In the "Canto notturno" he systematically inverts the pastoral conventions he knew by heart: alienation intrudes where we expect fellowship; the nomad's illimitable desert blurs into an infinite sky instead of the *hortus conclusus* of the pastoral bower; the menace of midnight replaces the otium of noon; and even Virgil's melancholy shadows—his reiterated "umbrae"— are exaggerated into an "Abisso orrido, immenso"—the horrid, immense abyss into which all of value disappears. This haunting song of despair, however, issues in a compassion that is exactly commensurate with the assurance of its metrics and the refinement of its style, reproducing the balance between the beauty that sustains and the entropy that threatens in the First *Idyll* of Theocritus and the First *Eclogue* of Virgil. As great pastoral subsumes the antipastoral, insisting on the vulnerability of its enclosed circle, in the "Canto notturno" the circle is expanded to cosmic dimensions and the vulnerability is proportionately infinite.

One notable feature of the European Romantic landscape, self-evident in even the most cursory of surveys, is its remarkable exfoliation of verse forms, both in new patterns of rhyme and meter and revivals of older models. Despite the occasional experiments in prose poetry (such as Aloysius Bertrand's exercises in hortatory medieval exoticism, *Gaspard de la Nuit*) or gestures toward *vers libres* (Hölderlin's neo-Hellenist odes), it is almost impossible to think of unrhymed French and German verse during this period. Indeed, rather than concentrate on Bertrand's self-conscious experimentation, we should recognize its actual context, which is the tyranny—and astonishing resilience—of the alexandrine couplet or quatrain in nineteenth-century French verse. As late as the dazzling surrealism of Rimbaud's "Bateau Ivre" of 1873, its preeminence is taken for granted, so much so that Hugo created an uproar, and eventually his reputation as the national arbiter of poetic taste, by daring to shift the position of its caesura. Rhyme is scarcely the only constituent of poetic form, but especially in reference to German poetry, the mere examples of Eichendorff and Heine, who polished an already glistening marble, should keep the theoretical pronouncements of the Jena school about liberating poetry from its constraints in necessary perspective.[8] So, in fact, might the actual achievements of Friedrich Novalis, all too briefly its major poetic genius. For, though his *Hymns to the Night*, with their combination of breathless, rhapsodic prose and chiselled hymnody, vaunt their freedom from classical restraint, they do so from within the framework of Gothic lyricism provided Novalis by medieval German mystical poetry and the Christian meditative tradition. In Italy, significantly, the formal terms are wholly different. To unrhyme Italian verse seems to have been a cultural effort going back at least to Dante; so the relative delicacy of a Leopardi in this respect, and his concern for refined syllabic symmetries, have their indigenous cultural underpinnings that mirror these other constants.

It is true that rhyme and meter can be freely reconstituted for the circumstances of the moment and therefore have no necessary connection with the long tradition of European poetry, with generic expectation, or with the example of precursors. Yet, if we look specifically at the kinds of continuities in form examined in the early chapters, we discover not only their presence but even more importantly their revival and dissemination across national boundaries. The sonnet in England, as we have traced its path, has a truly resilient formal continuity. It had a potent prehistory for Italian poets as well, much less so for the French (who recovered the form before resuscitating its French history), and virtually none for the Germans. Yet, given that disparity, what we can immediately observe as a constant of comparative Romanticism, without quibble or cultural adjustment, is the ubiquity of sonnets on the sonnet, a self-reflexive subgenre containing multitudes. The epigraph to this chapter, Goethe's sonnet "Natur und Kunst," is a studied import, proclaiming Goethe's adherence to a pan-European literary tradition and, in effect, Germany's union with it: "Und das Gesetz nur kann uns Freiheit geben": only that law will give German poetry its freedom. Wordsworth's independent view in "Nuns fret not at their Convent's narrow room," the prefatory sonnet to his 1807 collection, is exactly congruent, even to the adoption of the same imagery of confinement: "In truth, the prison, unto which we doom / Ourselves, no prison is." In the perspective of Goethe's sonnet, Wordsworth's resolute return to the nature of the Petrarchan and Miltonic sonnet forms in his 1807 volumes, to ground their dynamics in the psychology of perception, takes on added resonance. Wordsworth's use of the form as a metaphor for the self's reaching out to center space and time, to effect a unity between the mundane and supernal, is not only uncannily what it enacts, but, as with Goethe's sonnet, a statement about the nature of art itself. His comparison of the sonnet to an orbicular construction, the cosmos of a drop of dew, nicely invokes the geometric shape that, in Marshall Brown's view, haunts German Romanticism, particularly among the Jena school.[9] Though not so systematically self-reflexive as Wordsworth, Foscolo appears to have something of the same ends in mind in the sonnets he published in 1803, where the form becomes a bridge that reunites the isolated voice with human and mythic continuities from which it has been exiled. In England during the Regency, as we have seen, Leigh Hunt took up the quiet intensities with which Wordsworth had invested the form and domesticated it to his suburban circle, and Keats and Shelley in turn stretched its newly discovered elasticity to see just how much of the sublime could be held and intensified within its constraints. But Wordsworth's most striking influence is unexpected, for Sainte-Beuve also seems to have drawn from his sonnets possibilities for the domestication of the poetic voice. His introduction of the sonnet into French Romanticism had far-reaching consequences.[10] Nerval converted its polarities into an enclosed tabernacle enshrining symbolic mystery. Baudelaire similarly found in the sonnet what he called a "Pythagorean beauty" and through his long career continually elaborated its "constraining form" to reach a "more intense idea" of inherent correspondences.[11] And, deliberately following in their wake, finally Mallarmé compacted the sonnet into the oxymoronic *tombeau* of an art sustaining its vitality within an impenetrable labyrinth. Indeed, with French symbolism the sonnet is converted from the Miltonic reaching out toward cultural ideals into the embodiment of an art without relationship to anything else but its own dynamics. In an art that exists for its own sake, form is essential.

Yet that very fact should underscore why form was so inescapable a necessity for Romantic subjectivity, a ground for either commitment or disengagement, but always a ground for self-mirroring and self-creation. And simple logic would suggest the necessity within such a dialectical field of a complementary mirroring and recreation of the predicated other as well. Hence the crucial importance of Coleridge's definition of "organic form" as art's "self-witnessing and self-effected sphere of agency." What Coleridge's term presents, and what Romanticism as a whole wanted to embrace, was the challenge of definition from the inside out, in life as in art. Sonnets are not written according to Petrarchan rules but according to the inherent dynamics and geometry of the form (to which Petrarch's own understanding is of course a guide), and that in essence is the most universal urge of generic development throughout Western literature. The sonnet's prominence throughout Romanticism and its remarkable candor in artistic self-reflexiveness make it a simple index to the nature of poetic form in culture after culture. Its history in the nineteenth century, with the necessary adjustments made for formal continuities and experiments, is replicated in the ode, the elegy, the ballad, the romance, the epic, and in every shade between.

Yet, its history also traces a growing disengagement, an involution into formal self-witnessing as a refuge from bourgeois culture, that could not have been intended by the Enlightenment renaissance, even if it was, by the strange quirks of history, its principal inheritance for modernism. The customary division of nineteenth-century French poetry between Romanticism and Symbolism, though notoriously hard to place, testifies to a general awareness that Romanticism, though forced to wait out the Napoleonic Wars, did not embrace its disengagement with pleasure or with pride. Indeed, generally speaking, it turned to art as a resource of forms of intellectual power, as a means to reconceive and expand a European conceptual syntax too restrictive to accommodate the new historical forces represented by the French Revolution. For Romanticism form became a guarantor of intellectual freedom, at once a framework for psychological exploration and a means, through reimagining the past, to enlarge future possibilities. Although the past chapters have indicated numerous ways in which this was accomplished, here at the end we might contemplate two opposite strategies—the one deconstructive and the other modelled on the total organization of scientific system—which, in their sum, demonstrate how imperative formal means were to the Romantic enterprise and how intellectually liberating was the result.

The Fall of Hyperion, composed at the end of Keats's tragically foreshortened career and resonant with the knowledge of what impends, bears witness through its strategies of ideological displacement to an intellectual bravery that will neither succumb to convention nor pretend to its irrelevance. The poem represents Keats's reassimilation and testing of the values tentatively asserted in the fragmentary trial of *Hyperion* a year and a half before. Yet this second fragment, even if it is far more intense in its multiple confrontations, never even approaches the point of forcing the cosmological impasse upon which the original poem faltered. The shift of generic models is the key. For the supposedly objective truths of epic tradition Keats substitutes the mode insinuated upon the genre by Dante, the dream vision, which forestalls distance and accentuates the ways in which truths are perceived and ordered within the mind.

But the genre is adopted only to be insistently questioned even as it organizes the poem. The first episode within its fiction is the poet's dream of a deserted Eden, our most primordial of cultural myths and memories, which, simply because it is so unavailing of satisfaction, gives way to a second and antithetical dream. There the poet comes upon dispossessed collosi, who, with their strange mythic distance, embody our exclusion from the paradise at the infancy of our cultural and psychological development—or our primal alienation. After a struggle to attain an equilibrium, figured as a matter of life or death (and perhaps, after all, that is exactly what it is), the poet looks deeply within the inarticulate eyes of Moneta and is afforded his third vision, which appears to be the culminating one. For a month, immobile, he contemplates the similarly immobile and inarticulate Titans, lost like them in an extended day-dream in the twilight of the gods. Yet, whatever internal recognitions might have been elicited by that reverie are never articulated: they consti-tute a marked resemblance to the deep eyes of Moneta into which the poet stares and upon which he is reflected. As an oracle Moneta has nothing whatsoever to tell; she only parts the curtains on a scene, where, though we assume it to be a *tableau vivante,* nothing occurs through the month-long vigilance. Yet she does speak before unveiling this enigmatic vision, and then it is to question the understanding and pronouncements of "dreamers weak," which, if we have managed to keep our bearings in this conceptual labyrinth, is to question the very dream in which she appears. As it starts to assimilate the cosmic myth of the earlier poem, *The Fall of Hyperion* breaks off, having intimated a majesty and a portent of mean-ing that it will not allow us to delimit. Relatively short as it is, it offers an accumulation of visions, not just those described but also those far interwoven in the vortex of their succession, all displacing meaning into a further interior, transferring symbolic import to that distance which is never reached. The effect is exactly, yet symmetrically, opposite to the breaking-point of the original experiment, *Hyperion,* where Apollo is left forever in the process of coming convulsively to a knowledge neither he nor we will ever comprehend.

The state in which *The Fall of Hyperion* suspends its discourse, if such a term applies where there is no reality principle in evidence, is either a plenum of too many visions compacted or a vacuum in which all are mutually canceling, a visionary intensity or a visionless emptiness. In either case it is a state that questions the value of its own enterprise as sharply as Moneta—or as formatively as does its own preliminary prem-ise: "Fanatics have dreams." The proem frames the dream vision by questioning its value, and the dreams accumulate without answer. They all begin from the inception of Cartesian mental process: "Methought I stood where trees of every clime. . . ." The enclosed and self-referential mind contemplates the paradise of its own elaboration—its desperate, never-satisfied need—and can assert but one sole assurance, that it thinks, or that in doing so, it once forced a poem to be conceived: "Methought." The term, removed from the present moment by its tense no less than its archaism, by its nature implies self-questioning, and in its purity intro-duces us to visions that elaborate that self-questioning beyond the point where any answer is ascertainable. Is there then no truth in these em-bedded enigmas, no assurance that impels us forward? The very recogni-tion of the reader's momentum ironically enforces what is the one solemn certainty that we can ever know from *The Fall of Hyperion,* which is at least a more comforting truth than is to be gleaned from the similarly involuted fragment of a dream vision with which Shelley ended his career. In "The Triumph of Life" Shelley looks metaphor directly in its face and recognizes that there may be nothing else. Keats's vision pursues the larger conflation of values, the conceptual syntax that is genre, affirming that there is in human history a legacy of dream visions, all of which testify to a genuine desire for universal truth, and which are, by the nature of art, composed of and recognized by conventions that are utterly arbitrary. That they have no intrinsic meaning Keats is at pains to demonstrate, but that they allow him to structure a poem that represents the deeper and deeper search for ultimate certainties is a value to be exemplified, even self-reflexively celebrated. "There is a budding morrow in midnight" he claimed on behalf of the blind bardic visionary who impelled Western literature on its course through endless traces of imaginative conception. Having characteristically represented an oxymoron at the very inception of generic traditions, Keats pursues his fascination with the Phoenix that forever survives its own consuming in this complicated visionary experience in which he juxtaposes multiple planes of reality, all of which are traditionally sanctioned and all of which, even as they deny what they affirm, leave untouched the shrine of affirmation they can never reach. That shrine is the embodiment of human desire that systems of belief may ultimately codify but that visions empower and genres organize. The seemingly arbitrary structures that compose the genres of literature are the means by which a poet realizes what in another context Keats called the negative capability of art. Genres allow an imaginative creation to be compounded of "uncertainties, Mysteries, doubts" (*Letters*, I, 193) and even, in the extreme case of *The Fall of Hyperion*, to embody a charged fullness empty of defined meaning, only and profoundly capable.

At the opposite pole from this fragment of dissipating visions lies the most extensive composite order of European Romanticism, Goethe's *Faust*, almost a lifelong undertaking, only finished within the year of the poet's death. Whether or not its multitude of scenes, composed over so many years, all quite fit together, it is the supreme example of *genera mixta* in all of literature, the consummate *Gesammtkunstwerk*. As the defense of the mixed genre invariably rested, Tasso states it clearly, on the poet's duty to create a heterocosm of God's universe in all its varied majesty and contradiction, so Goethe, though he hedged somewhat on the vexed question of God, pursues a like aim. He does so, first, through deliberately embodying and reconciling the debate between Romantic and classical ideals in the elaborate parallels he draws between Christian and Hellenistic structures of thought and art in the two parts of *Faust* and, second, through the most ambitious reclamation of genres that exists in literature. It is sufficiently ambitious that *Faust* should attempt to revitalize every mode of drama practiced on Western stages, from its double prologue to the opera libretto conceived for one scene of Part II. (Goethe went so far as to inquire of Meyerbeer whether he had time to volunteer his services and furnish the required music.) Even more striking, however, is the panoply of verse forms and of their attendant decorums with which he invests the work: though, as it were, the figured bass of *Faust* is provided by the heroic couplet conventional to the German stage, one scene is written in the stately alexandrine of French neoclassical tragedy, and an entire act re-creates Greek tragic decorum. These form a backdrop to interpolated verse forms of almost every variety imaginable: from the antique balladry of "The King of Thule" to the homely *Knittelvers* of folk tradition to the breathless lyrical effusion in dimeter of "Gretchen am Spinnenrade"—and even, with startling appropriateness, to one scene being composed in prose to render the moment of Faust's total demoralization in Part I. It is not simply a multitude of genres and forms that are thus assimilated, but with them the concerns of every major religion of the West from primitive cult worship to ethical culture, the range of human sciences, and the vision of Europe's greatest poets as well: Euripides in Act Three of Part II, Dante in the final scene, even in the Euphorion episode the touching tribute to Byron.

The result goes beyond anything contemplated in Wordsworth's term composite order. Rather, Goethe aspires, in Angus Fletcher's phrase, to a "transcendental form," reaching for the infinity of human potentiality that was the subject of his art for sixty years. For Goethe the human lot is a continual striving to become—"immer streben"—against all odds and through every conceivable form. Goethe's attempt to rear a Gothic cathedral from the page, *Faust* in the multiple perfections of its parts incarnates the "Alles Vergängliche" of its final chorus, that "something ever more about to be" that Wordsworth characterized as human destiny and that a later time would come to see as a credo of Romanticism. Goethe poured his life, his art, and an encyclopedic learning into that capacious mold in the faith that it might contain even what he might only imagine and everything he could hope to know. And every block in its construction is a form retrieved, rethought, transformed. In this, as it is the grandest, it is also the exemplary conception of European Romanticism.

Notes

Chapter 1. Of Form and Genre

1. Among numerous discussions of iconographical traditions, the writings of Erwin Panofsky and E. H. Gombrich have been most influential; on typology, see the collection, *Literary Uses of Typology from the Late Middle Ages to the Present*, ed. Earl Miner (Princeton: Princeton University Press, 1977), and the more intensely localized consideration by Paul Korshin, *Typologies in England: 1650–1820* (Princeton: Princeton University Press, 1982); on scientific and cosmological structures in the Renaissance, see S. K. Heninger, *Touches of Sweet Harmony: Pythagorean Cosmology and Renaissance Poetics* and *The Cosmographical Glass: Renaissance Diagrams of the Universe* (San Marino: Huntington Library Press, 1974; 1977); and for the most authoritative treatment of numerology, see Alastair Fowler, especially *Spenser and the Numbers of Time* (London: Routledge & Kegan Paul, 1964). On Homeric structure consult Cedric Whitman, *Homer and the Heroic Tradition* (Cambridge: Harvard University Press, 1958). John Hollander's monograph, *Rhyme's Reason* (New Haven: Yale University Press, 1981), though brief, is weighted with a craftsman's knowledge; see also Paul Fussell's now classic study on the uses of prosody, *Poetic Meter and Poetic Form* (New York: Random House, 1965; rev. 1979). I borrow the term "conceptual syntax" from my perspicuous colleague Barbara Herrnstein Smith.

2. The first quotation is from *Les genres du discours* (Paris: Seuil, 1978), p. 46; the second from *The Poetics of Prose*, tr. Richard Howard (Ithaca: Cornell University Press, 1977), p. 42. In very recent years, as Todorov's injunction might suggest, French post-structuralist theory has begun to turn to the dynamics of conceptual transmission in literature. Gérard Genette has formulated the term "architext" to indicate how generic pressures impinge on literature in a *"transcendance textuelle"*: see *Introduction à l'architexte* (Paris: Seuil, 1979), esp. pp. 87–90. The comparative weakness of this history of generic thinking in the West is that it is keyed to the Aristotelian triad. Genette's further elaboration breaks free of that constriction to explore what occurs when authors transform earlier literary models through parody, travesty, pastiche, antiforms, sequels, etc. This mode Genette terms hypertextuality: see his stimulating *Palimpsestes: la littérature au second degré* (Paris: Seuil, 1982).

3. Paul Hernadi focuses *Beyond Genre: New Directions in Literary Classification* (Ithaca: Cornell University Press, 1972) on how academic and unpragmatic is the traditional tripartite division. Todorov, perhaps more sharply than any other generic critic, has recognized how ironically reinforcing are all deliberate subversions of rules: see his critique of Maurice Blanchot in *Les genres du discours*, pp. 44–47. On a less theoretical plane is the elegant testimonial of a practicing poet, John Wain, "On the Breaking of Forms," in *Professing Poetry* (New York: Viking and Penguin, 1978).

4. The essay by Hans Robert Jauss, translated into English as "Theory of Genres and Medieval Literature," is, because of (not despite) its careful historical orientation, probably the single most stimulating, capacious, and dependable examination of generic theory in modern criticism. The complexity of medieval genres, the levels of culture and problems of transmission they reflect, and the dearth of previous commentary demand of Jauss an encompassing perspective and a delicacy in the relation of particularities which constitute a model for criticism. Jauss's essay was originally published in *Grundriss der Romantischen Litteraturen des Mittelalters*, 6 (1972), and is translated by Timothy Bahti as Chap. 3 of Jauss's *Toward an Aesthetic of Reception* (Minneapolis: University of Minnesota Press, 1982).

5. Although he is reflecting on the dynamics of narrative plot, Mikhail Bakhtin's gnomic injunction is particularly appropriate to the history of poetic genres: "A literary genre, by its very nature, reflects the most stable, 'eternal' tendencies in literature's development. Always preserved in a genre are undying elements of the *archaic*. True, these archaic elements are preserved in it only thanks to their constant *renewal*, which is to say, their contemporization. A genre is always the same and yet not the same, always old and new simultaneously. Genre is reborn and renewed at every new stage in the development of literature and in every individual work of a given genre. This constitutes the life of the genre. Therefore even the archaic elements preserved in a genre are not dead but eternally alive. . . . A genre lives in the present, but always *remembers* its past, its beginning" ("Characteristics of Genre," in *Problems of Dostoevsky's Poetics*, tr. Caryl Emerson [Minneapolis: University of Minnesota Press, 1984], p. 106).

6. *Literature as System: Essays Toward the Theory of Literary History* (Princeton: Princeton University Press, 1971), Chap. 5. The preceding chapter, "On the Uses of Literary Genre," is equally important for its understanding of how imperative for criticism is an accurate assessment of the historical emplacement of genre. On the relations between parody and anti-genres, and on the hermeneutic problems of boundary genres, where contradictory generic expectations coexist in a single work, see Gary Saul Morson, *The Boundaries of Genre: Dostoevsky's Diary of a Writer and the Traditions of Literary Utopia* (Austin: University of Texas Press, 1981).

7. See Joan Malory Webber, *Milton and His Epic Tradition* (Seattle: University of Washington Press, 1979).

8. This appears to have been the orientation of the International Colloquium on Genre held at the University of Strasbourg in the summer of 1979, at least as one can judge from the papers from it assembled in *Glyph*, Vol. 7 (1980). It may be that the Olympian distance and inconclusiveness of Jacques Derrida's "The Law of Genre" (pp. 176-229) relate to this assumed problematic; but then again, it may simply be elevated caprice: see the note by his translator, Avital Ronell (pp. 229-232), on the ineffable difficulty of rendering into English the wholly negating pun on *naitre—n'être*, indistinguishable in a delivered paper.

9. In all fairness, Marxist critical methodology leads it to emphasize formal elements as cultural indices, but its origins in German Romantic thought often lead to a subordination of received traditions that influence and are countered by writers to a Hegelian (and Coleridgean) organicism hardly dissimilar from Crocean expressionism. Even where due credit is given the dimensions of a literary heritage, a rough sociology is likely to intervene before the more delicate questions of generic subversion; and there is a curious way in which the realistic novel is always given priority, even in a culture in which it does not exist. The ideological issues are comprehended, if not resolved, in comparing *Marxism and Literary Form*, ed. Frederick Jameson (Princeton: Princeton University Press, 1971) with Terry Eagleton's handbook, *Marxism and Literary Criticism* (Berkeley: University of California Press, 1976). The latest sophistication of the relationship of Marxism and form, in Chap. 2 of Jameson's *The Political Unconscious: Narrative as a Socially Symbolic Act* (Ithaca: Cornell University Press, 1981), is so conceived against the sociology and ideology of the late nineteenth-century novel that I, at least, find it difficult to extrapolate from it an interpretive model that can encompass earlier poetic forms.

10. See "The Dialectics of Poetic Tradition," Chap. 2 of *A Map of Misreading* (New

York: Oxford University Press, 1975), for an eloquent consolidation of Bloom's argument for "the presentness of the past" in the atmosphere of belatedness that clings to all post-Miltonic literature. It is interesting to note that, before Milton, that mighty systematizer of the Renaissance, Julius Caesar Scaliger, suggested that the whole of the Western literary tradition lay embryonically within *The Iliad* and *The Odyssey*, an argument that extends the anxiety of influence—conceived in the form of generic transmission—to the dawn of Western literature: see *Select Translations from Scaliger's Poetics*, ed. E. M. Padelford (New York: H. Holt, 1905), p. 54.

11. Rosalie Colie, *The Resources of Kind: Genre-Theory in the Renaissance* (Berkeley: University of California Press, 1973); Alastair Fowler, *Kinds of Literature: An Introduction to the Theory of Genres and Modes* (Cambridge: Harvard University Press, 1982); Barbara Kiefer Lewalski, Paradise Lost *and the Rhetoric of Literary Forms*, (Princeton: Princeton University Press, 1985). In particular, I should note that the care and complexity with which Fowler pursues this subject have allowed me a comparative brevity here, though, since he also subscribes to the myth of a breakdown of genres in Romanticism, he is of less help in respect to the continuities traced in later chapters. Paradoxically, however, one of the book's implicit values is its recognition of generic regulation in the poetry of the last hundred years.

12. The classic histories of generic theory of poetry in the period are by H. T. Swedenberg, Jr., *The Theory of the Epic in England: 1660–1800* (Berkeley: University of California Press, 1944), and J. E. Congleton, *Theories of Pastoral Poetry in England: 1684–1798* (Gainesville: University of Florida Press, 1952).

13. See Chap. 2, "*Mel* and *Sal*: Some Problems in Sonnet-Theory," of *Shakespeare's Living Art* (Princeton: Princeton University Press, 1974).

14. Lest my tone suggest I am pursuing a clandestine cavil, I should hasten to note that I am all the more sensitive to this procedure from having overargued the case for Shelley's tragic sense of things in *Shelley's Cenci: Scorpions Ringed with Fire* (Princeton: Princeton University Press, 1970), which occasioned the attempt to see Shelley working within the patterns established by Dante and Milton in *Shelley's Annus Mirabilis: The Maturing of an Epic Vision* (San Marino: Huntington Library Press, 1975) and which, I fear, through the inevitability of a logic that never seems to end conclusively, has prompted as well this attempt to lay the ghost at last to rest.

15. Especially in this context, we should remember and give due weight to Wordsworth's elongated and emphatic dependent clause: "but though this be true, Poems to which any value can be attached, were never produced on any variety of subjects but by a man who being possessed of more than usual organic sensibility had also thought long and deeply" (Preface to *Lyrical Ballads* [1800], *Prose*, I, 126).

Chapter 2. The Second Renaissance

1. The most valuable modern studies of how the historical milieu affected the literary scene are Carl Woodring's *Politics in English Romantic Poetry* (Cambridge: Harvard University Press, 1970) and Marilyn Butler's *Romantics, Rebels, and Reactionaries: English Literature and its Background, 1760–1830* (London: Oxford University Press, 1981; New York, 1982).

2. That audience was built and nurtured in the first two decades of the century by annuals and periodicals that attempted to catch even the smallest fry among the various schools, casting their nets over the waves of verse, either to remark the numerous volumes of poetry, to collect poems from newspapers and magazines, or to patronize promising talent: e.g., *Flowers of Literature*, edited by Francis William Blagdon; *The Poetical Register and Repository of Fugitive Poetry*, edited by R. A. Davenport; *The Annual Review*, edited by Arthur Aikin; and the two years' worth of monthly installments of a periodical whose title characterizes the age, Richard Ackermann's *Poetical Magazine; Dedicated to the Lovers of the Muse, By the Agent of the Goddess*.

3. *Childe Harold's Monitor; or Lines Occasioned by the Last Canto of Childe Harold,*

including Hints to other Contemporaries (London: J. Porter, 1818), p. 38. This poem is erroneously attributed to Thomas James Mathias in the Bodleian Library copy—along with *Saeculomastix* (1819)—as well as in a review by the *Gentleman's Magazine*, 88.ii (1818), 137.

4. C. Colton, *Hypocrisy. A Satire, in Three Books* (Tiverton: T. Smith; London: W. Button, 1812), p. 47.

5. "First and Last Romantics," *Studies in Romanticism*, 9 (1970), 226. The essay is reprinted in *The Ringers in the Tower* (Chicago: University of Chicago Press, 1971).

6. *Quarterly Review*, 4 (1810), 167: the critic is Barron Field. In other words, just fourteen years earlier Herrick had been virtually unknown, to be fitfully resurrected by literary antiquarians like George Ellis and Nathan Drake and finally, in the face of a still active prejudice against earlier literature, accorded an edition of 250 pages. The process is exemplary, as the opening of this review suggests: "These new books are all old, and are intended to flatter that appetite for reprints, which is one of the symptoms of the bibliomania now so prevalent. . . . [S]elections or reprints . . . are daily issuing from the press" (p. 165).

7. The best modern exposition of Warton's achievement is provided by Lawrence Lipking in Chap. 12 of *The Ordering of the Arts in Eighteenth-Century England* (Princeton: Princeton University Press, 1970).

8. The annotations are skillfully separated and represented by George Whalley in the first volume of *Marginalia, The Collected Works of Samuel Taylor Coleridge*, 12 (Princeton: Princeton University Press, 1980), 37-87. John Bell's *The Poets of Great Britain Complete from Chaucer to Churchill* (1777-1787) in 109 volumes represents only Chaucer, Spenser, Donne, and Waller before Milton. Even as late as Chalmers's 1810 edition, only seven of the twenty-one volumes covered pre-Restoration poetry.

9. "On the Revival of a Taste for our Ancient Literature," *Blackwood's*, 4 (1818), 264. The history of this revival was an aspect of Earl R. Wasserman's learned and ranging doctoral dissertation, later published as *Elizabethan Poetry in the Eighteenth Century* (Urbana: University of Illinois Press, 1947); see Chap. 5 especially. Wasserman ignores formal matters but fluently demonstrates the impact of the revival on poetic style. It is worth noting that the parallel emphasis on recovering seventeenth-century poetry comes a full generation after the Elizabethan revival, not reaching its full dimensions until after Chalmers's edition.

10. *From Classic to Romantic: Premises of Taste in Eighteenth-Century England* (New York: Harper, 1946), pp. 169-170.

11. *Lectures on the British Poets*, in *The Works of William Hazlitt*, ed. P. P. Howe (London: Dent, 1930-1934), V, 161-162; hereafter cited in text.

12. "On Poesy or Art," collected with the *Biographia Literaria*, ed. J. Shawcross (London: Oxford University Press, 1905), II, 262.

13. *Coleridge on Shakespeare: The Text of the Lectures of 1811-12*, ed. R. A. Foakes (Charlottesville: The University Press of Virginia, 1971), p. 107.

14. As late as 1807, *The New Encyclopedia* will simply plagiarize its "Poetry" entry from Newbery, adding nothing to his generic categories.

15. On how Blake and Scottish songs reflect decided shifts in the nature and respectability of song in the later eighteenth century, see Leopold Damrosch, Jr., "Blake, Burns, and the Recovery of Lyric," *Studies in Romanticism*, 21 (1982), 637-660.

16. *Retrospective Review*, 8 (1823), 49; 2 (1820), 167. When "others" are introduced in connection with Leigh Hunt, the designation usually refers to Keats and, perhaps, Shelley.

Chapter 3. The Sonnet

1. Johnson, "Sonnet," *A Dictionary of the English Language* (London, 1755). This pronouncement is repeated by almost every writer on (or, for that matter, of) sonnets later in the century.

2. The veneration of Wordsworth, Coleridge, and Keats for these sonnets reveals an independent literary taste that runs against the weight of contemporary opinion. See Wordsworth's "Essay, Supplementary" of 1815 (*Prose*, III, 69); Coleridge's *Marginalia*, ed.

George Whalley (*The Collected Works of Samuel Taylor Coleridge*, 12 [Princeton: Princeton University Press, 1980]), I, 41-43, 81-87; Keats's *Letters*, I, 188-189. The *Retrospective Review*, writing late in the Renaissance revival, carefully limits its praise for Shakespeare's sonnets in comparison with Milton's, a conventionality of viewpoint that does not prepare one for the surprising conclusion of its brief survey of sonnets, the quotation of Keats's "On First Looking into Chapman's Homer" (*Retrospective Review*, 7 [1823], 392-403).

3. *Petrarca: A Selection of Sonnets from Various Authors* (London: C. and R. Baldwin, 1803), pp. xxi, xxxiii. As late as 1833, Wordsworth was urging Alexander Dyce to overcome his distaste for a poetry of conceits and include Donne's "Death be not proud" in his forthcoming collection of sonnets (*WLLY*, II, 604).

4. *Edinburgh Review*, 6 (July 1805), 297: attributed to William Herbert.

5. Note to "Stanzas suggested in a Steamboat off St. Bees' Heads" (1833), in *WPW*, IV, 403.

6. "Preface to the First Edition," 4th ed. (London: Dodsley, Gardner, and Bew, 1786), p. iii. The successive editions were considerably enlarged and always richly annotated to suggest, especially in respect to Petrarch and Milton, both Smith's links to tradition and her claims to poetic stature.

7. Seward's antipathy is expressed throughout her letters: see Hesketh Pearson's prefatory essay in *The Swan of Litchfield* (London: Hamish Hamilton, 1936), p. 27. Many of the hundred sonnets she published in *Original Sonnets on Various Subjects; and Odes paraphrased from Horace* (2nd ed., London: G. Sael, 1799) are conspicuously dated over a span of thirty years, quietly claiming at least a decade of priority over Smith in concentrating on this form; there are as well three sonnets "written in the character of Werter" (nos. 88-90). Whatever Seward's independence, Charlotte Smith's sonnets were directly influential on many other contemporaries. At least two other collections bear the title *Elegiac Sonnets*: by William Ashburnham (London: Cadell and Davies, 1795) and Melmoth Roblewood in the second volume of his *Poetry Original and Selected* (Glasgow: Brash and Reid, 1796-1799). The *Gentleman's Magazine* printed two sonnets written to Smith (59 [1789], 839; 64 [1794], 1035) and another also composed for her novel *Celestina* (61 [1791], 760: signed "H. H."). In her *Sonnets, and Other Poems* [Mrs.] B. F.[inch] portrays herself as "following, at humble distance" in Smith's footsteps "with a design of gathering a few of those straggling wildflowers she may have passed by unregarded" (London: Black and Parry, 1805), p. vi. The fifty-first of the seventy-five *Sonnets of the Eighteenth Century*, published anonymously by Thomas Davison in 1809—entitled "Wonders"—pays tribute to Smith: "she, whom fix'd in fast despair / Sooth'd the sad sonnet, as to Cynthia pale / Mourn'd her lorn harp's inimitable gale." An interleaved copy of the fourth edition of *Elegiac Sonnets* in the Folger Library contains sonnets, in a woman's hand, in response to particular sonnets of Smith's, mainly suggesting consolations for her sorrow. In one case the writer has rewritten Smith's sonnet to alter its despairing conclusions (Folger cat. no. MS. M.b.4).

8. Bannerman's "Werter" sonnets first appeared in her 1800 poems; those from Petrarch and others were added to the 1807 edition—see *Poems* (Edinburgh: Mundell, Doig, and Stevenson, 1807), sonnets no. 45-54, 69-74. Earlier, Alexander Thomson also published a series of sonnets based on Goethe's novel in *Essay on Novels: a poetical epistle . . . with six sonnets from Werter*, remarking in his prefatory note that he "had once some intention of throwing into sonnets all the most brilliant passages of the work" in a hundred or so poems (Edinburgh: P. Hill and J. Watson, 1793), [p. 16]. Armstrong published his *Sonnets from Shakespeare* under the pseudonymn "Albert" (London: J. Debrett, 1791). The quotation from Mrs. Robinson, testifying to the rapid proliferation of sonnets and to a vigorous debate over their formal decorum, occurs in the preface to *Sappho and Phaon. in a Series of Legitimate Sonnets, With thoughts on poetical subjects, and anecdotes of the Grecian poetess* (London: for the author, 1796), pp. 9-10. The series was reprinted in her three-volume *Poetical Works* of 1806 (London: R. Phillips). William Beckford, under the pseudonym J. A. M. Jenks, wittily satirizes the entire literature of sensibility, with travesties of the sonnets of Mary Robinson, Charlotte Dacre, and other women poets in *Azemia, A Novel Containing Imitations of the Manner, both in prose and verse, of many of the authors of the*

present day, 2 vols. (London: Sampson Low, 1798). Among these are an "Elegiac Sonnet to a Mopstick" and a Della-Cruscan extravagance beginning, "Oh! Darkness! hide me with thine ebon ray." That Beckford, who set many of the conventions of the Gothic novel, also lengthily parodies Anne Radcliffe's recent successes is an incidental interest of this work for literary historians, as is the appendix in which he reviews his novel according to the style of the principal periodicals of the 1790s.

9. *Poetical Works*, 2 vols., ed. George Gilfillan (Edinburgh: James Nichol; London: James Nisbet, 1855), I, 1. The fulsome praise for Smith in Bowles's advertisement to the second edition is tempered by veiled criticism: *"It having been said that these Pieces were written in Imitation of the little Poems of Mrs. SMYTH, the Author hopes he may be excused adding, that many of them were written prior to Mrs. SMYTH'S Publication.* He is *conscious of their great Inferiority to those beautiful and elegant Compositions; but, such as they are, they were certainly written from his own Feelings"* (*Sonnets* [Bath: R. Cruttwell, 1789], p. 7). (Bowles's claims for precedence over Smith are highly unlikely.) This second edition will be used for poetic reference in the discussion, since it was clearly here that Coleridge came upon Bowles's sonnets. Its organized unity is somewhat altered in ensuing editions, as Bowles revises, adds, and deletes sonnets.

10. *Poetical Works*, (1855), II, xiii. It is of incidental interest to this discussion to observe that Gilfillan, in his interesting commentary on distinctions between the eighteenth and nineteenth centuries, calls Bowles "the father of modern poetry" (II, v, xii).

11. Bowles appears to have recognized the logical incongruities of this sonnet, since he rewrote the sestet to remove them, replacing it with a sentimental commonplace.

12. Three copies of this pamphlet survive: in the Cornell University Library, the Huntington Library, and the Victoria and Albert Museum. The Huntington copy is bound with the second edition of Bowles; Paul M. Zall has analyzed its contents in "Coleridge and 'Sonnets from Various Authors,' " *Cornell Library Journal*, (1967), 48–62, and has reprinted both this essay and the pamphlet in *Coleridge's "Sonnets from Various Authors"* (Glendale, California: La Siesta Press, 1968). The Victoria and Albert copy, in the Dyce collection, is bound with Bowles's fourth edition and has been described in detail in *Marginalia, The Collected Works of Samuel Taylor Coleridge, 12*, ed. George Whalley (Princeton: Princeton University Press, 1980), I, 716–717. The preface, slightly revised and entitled "Introduction to the Sonnets," is to be found on pp. 71–74 of Coleridge's *Poems, 2nd ed., to which are now added Poems by Charles Lamb and Charles Lloyd* (Bristol: J. Cottle; London: Robinsons, 1797). Quotations from the preface refer to this edition as being the most practically available.

13. *Poems on Various Subjects* (London: G. G. and J. Robinson; and Bristol: J. Cottle, 1796), p. x.

14. Reprinting the sonnet in his 1796 *Poems*, Coleridge eliminated direct reference to Pitt by retitling the poem "To Mercy." Whether caution or his own apostasy intervened, he withdrew it from all subsequent editions (except for that of 1803 when Addington had succeeded as Prime Minister); it was restored to the canon only in 1852. Coleridge's political sonnets are not unique in this period. In 1795 the bulk of John Thelwall's *Poems Written in Close Confinement in the Tower and Newgate, Under a Charge of High Treason* consisted of a sonnet sequence of twelve poems.

15. This inclination can be seen earlier. The sonnet "On Bala Hill" (1794) is virtually a transcription of Southey's sonnet on gaining the summit of Lansdown, the second of the anthologized sonnets. Similarly, the sonnet to Sarah Siddons is credited to Charles Lamb in both the 1796 and 1797 editions: it was probably "loaned" to Coleridge for the *Morning Chronicle* series. To be fair, the sonnet rage among this circle frequently resulted in a totally collaborative effort. Thus Coleridge notes in his personal copy of the second edition, "There were 3 or 4 Sonnets of which so many lines were written by Southey & so many by me, that we agreed to divide them in order to avoid the ridiculous anxiety of attributing lines in the same short poem to two different authors" (*Poems*, 2nd ed., Harvard University Library, cat. no. *EC8.C6795.796pb(C), p. 82: reprinted by permission of the Houghton Library).

16. See Zall, "Coleridge and 'Sonnets from Various Authors'," *Cornell Library Journal*, 2 (1967), 50-51.

17. Coleridge later regretted this statement: "A piece of petulant presumption, of which I should be more ashamed, if I did not flatter myself that it stands alone in my writing. The best of the joke is that at the time I wrote it, I did not understand a word of Italian, and could therefore judge of this Divine Poet only by bald translations of some half dozen of his Sonnets" (MS note, *Poems*, 2nd ed., Harvard University Library, cat. no. *EC8.C6795.796pb(C), p. 71: reprinted by permission of the Houghton Library). The poet was not the only one who took exception to his high-handed dismissal of the past. Capel Lofft's "Sonnet. On Sentiments Expressed by Mr. Coleridge, in the Preface to his 'Sonnets,' adverse to the Petrarcan Model" (dated 6 February 1804) found its way into the *Poetical Register and Repository of Fugitive Poetry for 1805* (London: F. and C. Rivington, 1807), p. 407.

> THOU, who hast amply quaff'd the Muses' rill,
>   And bath'd thy locks in pure poetic dews;
>   Canst thou disparage the PETRARCAN MUSE:—
> To her sweet voice deaf, cold, fastidious still?
> Examine if unprejudic'd the Will[,]
>   COLERIDGE, which can to *her* high praise refuse;
>   And of perverseness her fair laws accuse,
> Which through the enchanted ear the bosom fill.
> Her various, cadenc'd, regularity
>   HE, who o'er Epic heights hath soar'd sublime,
>   And magic SPENSER, lov'd—The mighty Dead
> Have Followers, haply to Posterity
>   Not unendear'd.—O! scorn not these, who led,
> In many a graceful maze, the full harmonious rhime.

18. "Introduction to the Sonnets," *Poems*, 2nd ed., pp. 72, 73. Despite Coleridge's views about a rhymeless sonnet, the only one of note in Romantic poetry—so formally inconspicuous that its audacious experimentation has never been credited—is Blake's "To the Evening Star," published the year before Charlotte Smith's first appearance in print, in the *Poetical Sketches* of 1783.

19. *Laura*, 5 vols. (London: B. and R. Crosby, 1814). Lofft reflects contemporary taste in all but passing over Sidney, Spenser, and Shakespeare in his over two-hundred page history of the form (mainly Italian), but he celebrates Milton in fifteen enthusiastic pages that begin with the marginal identification "John Milton—Giovanni Miltono" (I, cxli).

20. *Edinburgh Review*, 6 (July 1805), 297.

21. Robert Fletcher Housman, *A Collection of English Sonnets* (London: Simpkin, Marshall, and Co., 1841), quotes Herbert twice in his introductory remarks (pp. ix, xvii). The quoted comments are on pp. xxiv, xxx-xxxi: they sharply illustrate a shift from the taste of fifty years before.

22. The other Shakespearean sonnets are mere exercises: "To the Evening Star" (1790?), "On Seeing a Youth Affectionately Welcomed by a Sister (1791), and "With Fielding's 'Amelia'" (1792). The two Italian sonnets are "Pantisocracy" (1794)—which he may not have authored—and "To Robert Southey."

23. "Introduction to the Sonnets," *Poems*, 2nd ed., p. 73. It is interesting to observe as well that none of the anthologized sonnets has strict regularity.

24. *Quarterly Review*, 2 (November 1809), 281—a review by John Hoppner of William Lisle Bowles's *Poems, Never Before Published*. Hoppner appears to echo the complaint of Mary Robinson quoted above, but she directs her criticism at a misuse of the form by novice poets, not to its contents.

25. This notebook, now known as DC MS.44, survives in an incomplete state, but its contents and order have been shrewdly resuscitated in the prefatory matter and Appendix I

of Jared Curtis's edition of *Poems, in Two Volumes, and Other Poems, 1800–1807* (Ithaca: Cornell University Press, 1981), cited for reference throughout this discussion.

26. The opening line of the "Prefatory Sonnet," which was written about the same time as the first passage quoted, clearly reflects the same notion. Compare "Nuns fret not at their Convent's narrow room" to the "narrow room" in which the poet crowds his effects.

27. "Note to 'Miscellaneous Sonnets'," 1843, in *WPW*, III, 417. Dorothy's journal entry for 21 May 1802 is more laconic and presumably more accurate: "Wm wrote two sonnets on Buonaparte after I had read Milton's sonnets to him" (*Journals*, ed. Mary Moorman [London: Oxford University Press, 1971], p. 127). There are actually four sonnets among Wordsworth's juvenilia: his very first publication was an unabashed indulgence in sensibility, "Sonnet on Seeing Miss Helen Maria Williams Weep at a Tale of Distress," printed in *The European Magazine*, 40 (1787), 202.

28. Wordsworth rendered the translations at the request of Richard Duppa for his *Life and Works of Michel Angelo Buonarroti* (London, 1806)—see Curtis, *Poems, in Two Volumes*, pp. 143–145, 410. George Henderson's *Petrarca* (1803) is, despite its title, mainly concerned with modern examples; it was not until 1814, when Capel Lofft published his five-volume history (and diatribe) in *Laura*, that an extensive selection of sonnets from the Italian Renaissance became available in England.

29. That this was Wordsworth's intention in the "Miscellaneous Sonnets" is clear from his comments on the sequence in his letter to Lady Beaumont of 21 May 1807 (*WLMY*, I, 145–151).

30. Lee M. Johnson, *Wordsworth and the Sonnet*, Anglistica 19 (Copenhagen: Rosenkilde and Bagger, 1973), p. 49.

31. In DC MS.44, the Coleridge notebook, the fourth line significantly read "Young Vane, and Cyriac Skinner, Milton's Friend." This may simply be a tribute to Milton's sonnet to Skinner, listed first by Wordsworth among those he most admired in the November 1802 letter quoted from earlier (*WLEY*, 379); but it suggests as well how deeply within the spirit of Milton's sonnets Wordsworth has entered at this point in the sequence. Also, it should be noted, this litany of Whig heroes has decided political overtones for Wordsworth's contemporaries.

32. For instances, see Lord Byron in *Monthly Literary Recreations*, 3 (July 1807), 65–66; Francis Jeffrey in the *Edinburgh Review*, 11 (October 1807), pp. 230–231; and Lucy Aikin in the *Annual Review*, 6 (1808), 527: reprinted, respectively, in Donald H. Reiman, *The Romantics Reviewed* (New York: Garland Press, 1972), Part A, II, 661–662; II, 437–438; I, 19.

33. Mary Wordsworth noted that the *River Duddon* sonnets "all [to]gether comprise one Poem"; and the poet himself observed that the sonnets of the second sequence had the effect of stanzas in a single poem: see *WPW*, III, 357.

34. Yet even this last sequence has had its defenders, the most recent of whom is Seraphia Leyda, "Wordsworth's *Sonnets Upon the Punishment of Death*," *Wordsworth Circle*, 14 (1983), 48–53.

35. One composer of sonnets who should never have disappeared into this oblivion is Thomas Doubleday, who anonymously published his *Sixty-five Sonnets; with Prefatory Remarks on the Accordance of the Sonnet with the Powers of the English Language: also, a few miscellaneous Poems* (London: Baldwin, Cradock, and Joy, 1818). (Both the Bodleian and British Libraries make this attribution.) The preface is shrewdly and wittily argued; and the sonnets, though tending to moralize, are technically accomplished. Housman knew the volume well enough to quote from its preface in his *Collection of English Sonnets* in 1841. In 1822 *Blackwood's*, printing thirteen of the poems, had "no hesitation in saying, that, next to Wordsworth and Bowles, this anonymous poet, for he *is* a poet, is the best writer of Sonnets in our day" (*Blackwood's*, 12 [1822], 228). There being neither money nor fame to be secured in such a small arena, Doubleday went on to write noble Roman costume dramas. As an example of his prowess, his no. 28 transforms the conventions of the prospect sonnet in ways that suggest the later pre-Raphaelites:

Far off the rook, tired by the mid-day beam,
    Caws lazily this summer afternoon;
    The butterflies, with wand'ring up and down
O'er flower-bright marsh and meadow, wearied seem;
With vacant gaze, lost in a waking dream,
    We, listless, on the busy insects pore,
    In rapid dance uncertain, darting o'er
The smooth-spread surface of the tepid stream;
The air is slothful, and will scarce convey
    Soft sounds of idle waters to the ear;
    In brightly-dim obscurity appear
The distant hills which skirt the landscape gay;
While restless fancy owns th'unnerving sway
    In visions often changed, but nothing clear.

36. In his *Journal* entry for 17–18 December 1813, Byron writes: "Redde some Italian, and wrote two sonnets on [Genevra]. I never wrote but one sonnet before, and that was not in earnest, and many years ago, as an exercise—and I will never write another. They are the most puling, petrifying, stupidly platonic compositions. I detest the Petrarch so much, that I would not be the man even to have obtained his Laura, which the metaphysical, whining dotard never could" (*L&J*, 3, 240). (Compare *Don Juan*, 3.8: "Think you, if Laura had been Petrarch's wife, / He would have written sonnets all his life?") Byron also wrote a "Sonnet on Lake Leman" in the Miltonic mode during the summer of 1816.

37. This remark is recorded by Thomas Medwin: see *Medwin's Conversations of Lord Byron*, ed. Ernest J. Lovell (Princeton: Princeton University Press, 1966), p. 194.

38. *Toward* Samson Agonistes: *The Growth of Milton's Mind* (Princeton: Princeton University Press, 1978), p. 134. The entire section, "The Sonnets: The Exemplary Poet and His Evolving Politics" (pp. 128-144), is valuable for Milton's legacy in this form. So, too, is the more expansive treatment of Anne K. Nardo, *Milton's Sonnets and the Ideal Community* (Lincoln: University of Nebraska Press, 1979).

39. The Nile contest occurred on 4 February 1818; it is possible that Shelley's "Ozymandias" came from such a contest with Horace Smith several weeks earlier, though possible too that Smith simply wrote "On a Stupendous Leg of Granite" in response. For text and commentary, see M. K. Bequette's note in the *Keats-Shelley Journal*, 26 (1977), 29-31.

40. Among earlier sonnets structured around catalogs, see "After dark vapours have oppressed our plains" and the tour de force on the notion of "blue" ("Blue!—'Tis the life of heaven—the domain"). On metrical and other formal, as distinct from generic, concerns, the reader should consult Lawrence John Zillman, *John Keats and the Sonnet Tradition* (Los Angeles: Lymanhouse, 1939) and relevant chapters in Walter Jackson Bate's *Stylistic Development of John Keats* (New York: Modern Language Association, 1945).

41. François Yost, "Anatomy of an Ode: Shelley and the Sonnet Tradition," *Comparative Literature*, 34 (1982), 232.

42. To these sonnets should perhaps be added Coleridge's late bloom, "Work without Hope" of 1825, which inverts octave and sestet, separates all nature from its author, and in its final, tellingly Shakespearean couplet, seals the poet into his static polarity, Death in Life.

Chapter 4. The Hymn and Ode

1. Paul Fry, in *The Poet's Calling in the English Ode* (New Haven: Yale University Press, 1980), pp. 5-10, following Kurt Schlüter (*Die Englische Ode; Studien zu ihrer Entwicklung unter dem Einfluss der Antiken Hymne* [Bonn: Bouvier, 1964]), derives the ode from the hymn, emphasizing the criterion of congregationalism as a distinction. But his primary example (p. 280), Addison's "The Spacious Firmament on high" (which the poet

entitled "Ode"), gives pause inasmuch as it represents so distinctively an Anglican hymnody.

2. The most valuable elucidation of the development of the hymn in the eighteenth century is by David B. Morris in *The Religious Sublime: Christian Poetry and Critical Tradition in 18th-Century England* (Lexington: The University Press of Kentucky, 1972).

3. Chalmers, *Works of the English Poets from Chaucer to Cowper*, 18 (London: C. Whittingham, 1810), 473–491.

4. On Wordsworth's remark, consult Walter Jackson Bate, *John Keats* (Cambridge: Harvard University Press, 1963), pp. 265–267; also Robert Gittings, *John Keats* (London: Heineman, 1968), pp. 166–168.

5. *Notebooks*, ed. Kathleen Coburn (New York: Pantheon, 1957), I, No. 1646 (November 1803).

6. Hunt's hymns were included in *Juvenilia; or a Collection of Poems Written between the Ages of Twelve and Sixteen* (London: J. Whiting, 1800), whose three editions gave him early fame; Browne's poems (London: Cadell and Davies, 1808) were advertised as written between ages eight and thirteen.

7. *LSTC* (November 1819?), IV, 974–975.

8. *Poems*, p. 377. The note prefaced the poem in its first printing in the *Morning Post* in 1802 and in its reprint in the *Poetical Register for 1802*. Shelley would appear to have read the "Hymn" in the version published in *The Friend*: see Charles E. Robinson, *Shelley and Byron: The Snake and Eagle Wreathed in Fight* (Baltimore: Johns Hopkins University Press, 1976), p. 36.

9. *Blackwood's*, noticing "Mont Blanc" in its review of Mary Shelley's *History of a Six Weeks Tour*, thought the poem "often very beautiful," but "at times too close an imitation of Coleridge's sublime ode on the vale of Chamouni": 3 (July 1818), 416.

10. Paul Fry comes to the same conclusion simply on the grounds of the private, noncongregational emphasis of the poem: *The Poet's Calling in the English Ode*, p. 8. For a different and illuminating perspective, see David Robertson, "'Psalm 90' and 'Hymn to Intellectual Beauty'," Chap. 4 of *The Old Testament and the Literary Critic* (Philadelphia: Fortress Press, 1977).

11. Schlüter, *Die Englische Ode*, p. 29.

12. As noted, Schlüter organizes his study around the ode's relationship with hymns; Paul Fry attempts to link odes and their authors in phenomenological terms, but this approach elides differences in history and culture and tends to make odes urgent struggles for apotheosis. More straightforward historical accounts include Carol Maddison's comparatist treatment, *Apollo and the Nine* (Baltimore: Johns Hopkins University Press, 1960); Robert Shafer, *The English Ode to 1660: An Essay in Literary History* (Princeton: Princeton University Press, 1918); and George N. Schuster, *The English Ode from Milton to Keats* (New York: Columbia University Press, 1940). For its detailed knowledge of both poetry and critical attitudes Norman Maclean's monograph, "From Action to Image: Theories of the Lyric in the Eighteenth Century," in *Critics and Criticism Ancient and Modern*, ed. R. S. Crane (Chicago: University of Chicago Press, 1952), is in a class by itself.

13. Cowley published his *Pindarick Odes*, accompanied by a modestly self-extolling preface (and an epigraph from Horace), in 1656; his reputation was such that when Congreve published his "Discourse on the Pindarique Ode" in 1706, forty years after Cowley's death, he couched his criticism in fawningly deferential terms. To place this in historical perspective, it is interesting to observe the footnote appended in 1823 to this statement in the *Quarterly Review*: "Congreve, we are told by the great critic of our country, was the first to teach us that Pindar was not irregular in the structure of his odes.— Dr. Johnson was no great reader of our old poets, or he might have known that some of them, and particularly Ben Jonson, had taught us this more than a century before Congreve was born" (*Quarterly Review*, 28 [1823], 412; review of Abraham Moore's translation of the complete *Odes of Pindar* [1822]). The chronology is askew, but the recognition is otherwise sound.

14. On the surprisingly sparse knowledge of Pindar in England before the eighteenth century, see Shafer, *The English Ode to 1660*, pp. 69-78.

15. There were actually three separate translations of Pindar into English in this one year: a wholly new version by the Rev. J. L. Girdlestone (Norwich: R. M. Bacon); Francis Lee's completion of the West translation (London: W. Miller); and a composite translation by Gilbert West, Henry James Pye, and Robert Berkeley Greene (Oxford: J. Munday). Comparing the first two for the *Quarterly Review*, Reginald Heber advances the improbable notion that Walter Scott gives a better sense of Pindaric style than either (*Quarterly Review*, 5 [1811], 448-449).

16. Maclean, "From Action to Image," p. 435. Maclean's offhand conclusion is, I hope to demonstrate, radically understated: "This principle controls the progression of many other neoclassical odes."

17. John Hollander ends *The Untuning of the Sky: Ideas of Music in English Poetry, 1500-1700* (Princeton: Princeton University Press, 1961) with a consideration of Dryden's ode, which, in his last sentence, he terms "a brilliant performance whose only lesson is its own worth" (p. 422).

18. Maclean's monograph, for all its immense learning, is simply wrong in its thesis, which transposes into a historical progression—"From Action to Image"—the ode's inherent dialectic between public celebration and private mental or emotional states.

19. This reduction may have not been the intention of the opening pages of Harold Bloom's *The Visionary Company* (rev. ed., Ithaca: Cornell University Press, 1971) and his continual references to "the Bards of Sensibility," or of such essays of Geoffrey Hartman's as "Blake and the Progress of Poesy" and "Romantic Poetry and the Genius Loci" in *Beyond Formalism* (New Haven: Yale University Press, 1970), but the effect can be sharply discerned in a critical study that, however perceptive its readings, has taken the next step and personified its age in its subject, Paul Sherwin's *Precious Bane: Collins and the Miltonic Legacy* (Austin: University of Texas Press, 1977).

20. *Restoration and Eighteenth-Century Poetry: 1660-1780 (The Routledge History of English Poetry*, Vol. 3) (London and Boston: Routledge & Kegan Paul, 1981), pp. 154-157.

21. John C. Sitter, in Chap. 4 of *Literary Loneliness in Eighteenth-Century Literature* (Ithaca: Cornell University Press, 1982), offers an insightful comparison of the odes published by Akenside, Collins, and Joseph Warton in 1745-1746.

22. "In the [sublime] class Pindar stood without a rival till Gray appeared." "Gray is the first and greatest of modern lyric writers; nay I will venture to say of all lyric writers" (Robert Heron [John Pinkerton], *Letters of Literature* [London: G. G. J. and J. Robinson, 1785], pp. 33, 131).

23. William Preston, for instance, strongly defends the irregular ode in his "Thoughts on Lyric Poetry" (in *Poetical Works* [Dublin: J. Archer, 1793], II, 3-14): "The introduction of strophe, antistrophe and epode into English poetry is not only unnecessary, but unaccountable" (II, 6).

24. In Chalmers, *Works of the English Poets*, 10, 301; a similar account can be found in the preface to Gilbert West's *Odes of Pindar*: Chalmers, 13, 142.

25. *The History of the Rise and Progress of Poetry, Through it's Several Species* (Newcastle: L. Davis and C. Roymers, 1764), p. 125.

26. Pye, *A Commentary on the Poetics of Aristotle* (London: John Stockdale, 1792), p. 231; Hunt, note to his "Imitation of the First Pythian of Pindar," *The Poetical Register and Repository of Fugitive Poetry for 1806-1807* (London: F. C. & J. Rivington, 1811), pp. 92-93.

27. *Quarterly Review*, 5 (1811), 444-445.

28. "The heroic ode is evidently of a dramatic character, and was the primitive source from whence the regular drama was produced"—*A Dictionary of Arts and Sciences*, compiled by G.[eorge] Gregory (London: Richard Phillips, 1807), II, 464.

29. See, for instance, the "Observations on His Genius and Writings" by J. Langhorne, attached to Collins's *Poetical Works* in 1765 and in subsequent editions; or R.[obert] Potter,

An Inquiry into some Passages in Dr. Johnson's Lives of the Poets (London: Dodsley, 1783), pp. 15, 21.

30. Tr. G.[eorge] Gregory, 3rd ed. (London: Thomas Tegg, 1835), Chaps. 25-28.

31. *The Art of Poetry*, II, 40; it has been claimed that this work was at least revised by Oliver Goldsmith (Prior, *Life of Goldsmith*, I, 389). Its wide influence made it a standard authority: the *Encyclopaedia Perthensis* of 1807, for instance, plagiarizes this passage (18, 54-55).

32. Batteux, tr. John Miller (London: B. Law, 1761), III, 20-21; Blair (London: Strahan, Cadell, & Creech, 1783), II, 355.

33. *Classical Arrangement of Fugitive Poetry*, 16 vols. (London: John Bell, 1789-1794), Vols. 12-16; Drake, *Literary Hours, or Sketches Critical and Narrative* (London: Cadell & Davies, 1798), p. 378.

34. Though less conducive than the sonnet to supplying filler, odes also furnished a poetic staple for the periodical press. The late eighteenth century saw a large increase in parodies of the ode, the most pointed being that by Soame Jenyns, whose last stanza forms the epigraph to this chapter. The tradition of laureate odes has been ignored here, but whenever the position fell open in this period, it called forth a supposed contest among British bards for the honor. The first of these, widely influential for parody surveys, are the *Probationary Odes* of 1785, which included Thomas Warton's actual poem on the king's birthday among the twenty-two parodies as well as a "Table of Instructions" from the king and supposed "Thoughts on Ode Writing" by Warton. (Warton was also parodied by Peter Pindar [John Wolcot] in his *Ode upon Ode; or A Peep at St. James's; or New-Year's Day; or What You Will* [London: Kearsley, 1787].) The *Probationary Odes* was a collective venture by young wits, including George Ellis, Richard Fitzpatrick, Lawrence Joseph Richardson, and Richard Tickell, who subsequently produced a mock-epic on a parliamentary place-man, *The Rolliad*. The success of the latter served to keep the *Probationary Odes* in circulation into the early years of the nineteenth century. When the laureateship fell open upon Pye's death, the notion was revived (prompted by the recent success of Horace and James Smith's *Rejected Addresses*) in John Agg's pseudonymous *Rejected Odes; or Poetical Hops, Steps, and Jumps of a Dozen Popular Bards for the Obtainment of the Situation of Poet Laureat*, ed. Humphrey Hedgehog (London: J. Johnston, 1813). Following the example of the *Probationary Odes*, Agg included an actual poem by Southey among his twelve parodies. Far more than the earlier parodies, however, Agg's carry political overtones, since virtually all celebrate, sometimes graphically, the Prince Regent's devotion to wine and women.

35. *Blackwood's* maliciously reported overhearing the great classicist Porson offering to produce 134 examples of faulty Greek from it: 2 (1817), 12.

36. The only reading that professes to consider the poem formally as an ode does so through a neo-Hegelian perspective that many would find distorting; it does, however, offer continually perceptive readings: see Cyrus Hamlin, "The Hermeneutics of Form: Reading the Romantic Ode," *Boundary 2*, 7.iii, 1-30.

37. The long first version to Sara Hutchinson was written on 4 April 1802; lengthy passages (addressed to Wordsworth) were included in a letter to Sotheby of 19 July; others were sent to Southey on 29 July and Wedgwood on 20 October (*LSTC*, II, 790-798; 813-819; 831-832; 875).

38. See A. Harris Fairbanks, "The Form of Coleridge's Dejection Ode," *PMLA*, 90 (1975), 874-884.

39. That same species has been, in a famous modern definition, renamed "The Greater Romantic Lyric": see M. H. Abrams's essay in *From Sensibility to Romanticism*, ed. Frederick W. Hilles and Harold Bloom (New York: Oxford University Press, 1965). pp. 527-560. For Wordsworth's conception of the properties of an ode, see Joseph Sitterson, "The Genre and Place of the Intimations Ode." *PMLA*, 101 (1986), 24-35.

40. *The Poet's Calling in the English Ode*, p. 76.

41. It is only fair to note that the new text of the "Ode to Napoleon Buonaparte"

established by Jerome McGann deletes, according to what seem to be Byron's second thoughts, the final stanzas in which the displacement onto Washington occurs.

42. *Medwin's Conversations of Lord Byron*, ed. Ernest J. Lovell (Princeton: Princeton University Press, 1966), p. 114.

43. I have pursued the linkages among these poems in Chap. 5, "Purgatorial and Prophetic Odes," of *Shelley's Annus Mirabilis* (San Marino: Huntington Library Press, 1975).

Chapter 5. The Pastoral

1. What appears to be the oldest commentary on pastoral poetry in existence—the Codex Ambrosianus 222 (c. 1250)—observes that "the bucolic is a mixture composed, as it were, of every form": see J. E. Congleton, *Theories of Pastoral Poetry in England: 1684-1798* (Gainesville: University of Florida Press, 1952), p. 15.

2. Paul Alpers sees this sort of suspension as the distinguishing characteristic of Virgilian, and by implication all, pastoral: *The Singer of the* Eclogues: *A Study of Virgilian Pastoral* (Berkeley: University of California Press, 1979). Likewise, Harold Tolliver calls attention to "the dialectical, tensive structure characteristic of all worthwhile pastoral" in *Pastoral Forms and Attitudes* (Berkeley: University of California Press, 1971), p. 5. Tolliver is a very helpful guide to Renaissance pastoral, but his treatment of Wordsworth and Keats is, at least for me, often beside what I see to be the real point.

3. Thomas G. Rosenmeyer emphasizes the significance of the noon hour in *The Green Cabinet: Theocritus and the European Pastoral Lyric* (Berkeley: University of California Press, 1969), pp. 76-77, 88-91. This much-praised and valuable book is at the same time narrowly fundamentalistic, establishing paradigms for pastoral from the example of Theocritus, then denying later developments in the genre efficacy because they naturally break the mold. As the present argument suggests, a migratory form cannot be so constricted.

4. Colie, *Shakespeare's Living Art* (Princeton: Princeton University Press, 1974), Chap. 6. It is clear that the acceptance of tragicomedy as a mixed form with its own decorum arose from the debates surrounding Guarini's attempt to expand the range of pastoral into drama. For the extensive influence of pastoral drama on English opera, see Ellen T. Harris's *Handel and the Pastoral Tradition* (London: Oxford University Press, 1980), especially Chap. 4. Thomas Warton's view—argued in the Latin preface to his edition of Theocritus, *Theocriti Syracusii quae supersunt* (Oxford, 1770), pp. xxi-xxvi— that Greek pastoral grew out of early comic drama, though generally disputed, was widely known in the late eighteenth century.

5. Peter V. Marinelli argues that "pastoral and epic imply each other continually": *Pastoral* (London: Methuen, 1971), p. 19.

6. René Rapin, *A Treatise de Carmine Pastorali* (1659), tr. Thomas Creech (London, 1684)—in Augustan Reprint Society, Series 2, No. 3 (1947)—p. 13. Pope repeats this formulation almost verbatim in the "Discourse on Pastoral Poetry" prefacing his *Pastorals*.

7. Hugh Blair explicitly notes the significance of this in his *Lectures on Rhetoric and Belles Lettres*, III, 114-115.

8. *The Singer of the* Eclogues, p. 1.

9. The insignia on Madame Eglentyne's brooch, *Amor vincit omnia*, though generally proverbial, derives from the admission of erotic necessities in *Eclogue* 10.69. The title of Alpers's study is taken from Dante's designation of Virgil, in colloquy with Statius, in *Purgatorio* 22.

10. Alpers's commentary follows two others of high merit: Michael Putnam's *Virgil's Pastoral Art: Studies in the Eclogues* (Princeton: Princeton University Press, 1970) and

Eleanor Winsor Leach's *Virgil's* Eclogues: *Landscapes of Experience* (Ithaca: Cornell University Press, 1974).

11. *A Treatise de Carmine Pastorali*, p. 6; for Rapin as source of this dictum, see Congleton, *Theories of Pastoral Poetry*, pp. 64-65. Though not focussing on this issue per se, Raymond Williams decries the extent to which Virgil's "living tensions are excised" by Renaissance and later pastoral writers in his influential study, *The Country and the City* (London: Chatto and Windus, 1973), p. 18. The most extensive account of the misappropriation of Virgil in this period, concentrating on its political ramifications, is provided by Annabel Patterson in "Neoclassicism and the Fête Champêtre," *Huntington Library Quarterly*, 48 (1985), 321-344.

12. *Theocritus' Coan Pastorals: A Poetry Book* (Cambridge: Harvard University Press, 1967), Chap. 5.

13. Panofsky's classic essay of 1937 on the iconography of this trope has been widely reprinted; it is easily accessible in Eleanor Terry Lincoln, ed., *Pastoral and Romance: Modern Essays in Criticism* (Englewood Cliffs, N.J.: Prentice Hall, 1969); for the extent to which all Virgil's *Eclogues* contain dark and threatening elements, see the succinct summary in Leach, pp. 48-50.

14. Sannazaro's claims to this company can be measured by a simple perusal of the first of his *Piscatory Eclogues*, which is haunted by death. The *Piscatory Eclogues* and *Arcadia* are available in a modern translation by Ralph Nash (Detroit: Wayne State University Press, 1966).

15. Poggioli, *The Oaten Flute: Essays on Pastoral Poetry and the Pastoral Ideal* (Cambridge: Harvard University Press, 1975), pp. 19, 106. Poggioli's argument appears to be twofold: that pastoral invariably enacts a retreat from the serious responsibilities of the world, which Christianity disallows its adherents, and that pastoral looks backward to a golden age in contrast to the eschatological thrust of Christianity.

16. The fullest exposition of these will be found in Joseph Wittreich's *Visionary Poetics: Milton's Tradition and His Legacy* (San Marino: Huntington Library Press, 1979). For the extent to which the seventeenth century Christianized traditional pastoral themes, one should consult William Browne's *Brittania's Pastorals* or, especially, the *Piscatory Eclogues* of Phineas Fletcher, which represent Christ as the Fisherman.

17. The most direct discussion of this subject is undertaken by John R. Knott, *Milton's Pastoral Vision: An Approach to "Paradise Lost"* (Chicago: University of Chicago Press, 1971). For reconsiderations, see Barbara K. Lewalski, "The Genres of *Paradise Lost*: Literary Genre as a Means of Accommodation," and Balachandra Rajan, "*Paradise Lost*: The Uncertain Epic," in *Milton Studies*, 17 (1983)—*Composite Orders: The Genres of Milton's Last Poems*, ed. Richard S. Ide and Joseph Wittreich—75-103, 105-119.

18. That J. E. Congleton should remark that "Pope's 'Messiah,' which is called 'An Eclogue,' is hardly a pastoral" (*Theories of Pastoral Poetry in England*, p. 8) suggests how little credit has been given to the survival of the Christian pastoral tradition in the eighteenth century. The result is an inevitable distortion both of literary history and of specific poems imbued with the tradition.

19. *Lives of the English Poets*, ed. George Birkbeck Hill (Oxford: Clarendon Press, 1905), II, 269; Goldsmith's assessment is quoted on II, 269n. Wordsworth records Johnson's sentiments with approval in the 1815 "Essay Supplementary" (*Prose*, III, 72). Praise for Gay's achievement is a commonplace in Romantic assessments of eighteenth-century pastoral—from the prefatory note to Southey's "English Eclogues" (*Poems*, II [1799], p. 183) to John Thelwall's *Poetical Recreations of THE CHAMPION* (1822), pp. 60-61.

20. On the dynamics of this contention see Edward Tayler, *Nature and Art in Renaissance Literature* (New York: Columbia University Press, 1964).

21. The structure of Churchill's poem, with the eclogue preceded by the epistle to John Wilkes, publisher of *The North Briton*, tends to invert even the implied tribute to England as pastoral paradise. Ignorance is by no means bliss, nor is innocence to be trusted:

> [From Scotland] simple bards, by simple prudence taught,
> To this *wise* town by simple patrons brought,

In simple manner utter simple lays,
And take, with simple pensions, simple praise. (135-138)

22. Collins's commentator Langhorne allows "that in simplicity of description and expression, in delicacy and softness of numbers, and in natural and unaffected tenderness, they are not be equalled by any thing of the pastoral kind in the English language" (Chalmers, *Works of the English Poets*, 13, 210). Nathan Drake indulges in comparable hyperbole: "no eclogues of ancient or modern times, in pathetic beauty, in richness and wildness of description, in simplicity of sentiment and manners can justly be esteemed superior"—*Literary Hours or Sketches Critical and Narrative* (London: Cadell and Davies, 1799), p. 234.

23. The question of authorship is ambiguous. Although Warton's sister assured his first editor, Richard Mant, that Warton disclaimed authorship, they were commonly reprinted under his name both during and after his life: see Clarisa Rinaker, *Thomas Warton: A Biographical and Critical Study* (Urbana: University of Illinois Press, 1916), p. 25n. One certain follower in Collins's path was John Scott of Amwell, who wrote three oriental eclogues, setting the first in Arabia, the second in the East Indies, and the third in China. His *Moral Eclogues* of 1778 earned him a contemporary recognition that has not lasted.

24. Chatterton also wrote four "medieval" eclogues. Tyrwhitt, his first editor in 1777, noted the incongruous title Chatterton had supplied for one notebook: *Eclogues and Other Poems by Thomas Rowley.*

25. London: W. Lowndes, 1788. Mulligan's introductory note observes that "*The* First *and* Fourth *of these Eclogues were published some years ago in a respectable periodical publication, and evidently furnished the hint to some publications which have since appeared.*" More likely than not, the reference is not so much to pastorals as to the considerable amount of antislavery poetry that began to appear in the periodical press in the 1780s. Cowper's "The Negro's Complaint," for instance, had wide circulation. Mulligan's sense of his own influence contrasts strongly with the comparative rarity of his volume, and that in turn (though full-scale censorship was yet a half-dozen years off) may stem from how far beyond the accepted political boundaries his pastorals diverge. The other (and realistic) possibility is that poems of such questionable artistic merit suggest publication in relatively few copies. Mulligan was from Liverpool and was clearly influenced by Edward Rushton's *West-Indian Eclogues*. Rushton celebrated their long friendship in "On the Death of Hugh Mulligan," *Poems* (London: J. Osted, 1806), pp. 27-30.

26. The publication of one of these in the *Morning Chronicle* in autumn, 1794, accomplished through Coleridge's connections, was Southey's first appearance in the London press. His first volume of poetry, in combination with Robert Lovell, was published by Richard Cruttwell of Bath, Bowles's publisher, about the same time. The *Botany-Bay Eclogues* did not appear there but were reserved for the first (1797) of the two volumes of his *Poems* (1797-99). Since, like most of Southey's verse, these poems were much revised later, all quotations are from the 1797 volume, where the *Botany-Bay Eclogues* occupy pages 77-104.

27. Southey's rough anapestic vernacular in this eclogue perhaps sounds silly to modern ears, but it should be respected as the first successful attempt in English after Spenser to capture the jocular tone and country dialect of Theocritean pastoral. The experiment paves the way for its further elaboration in *Lyrical Ballads*, published the following year.

28. In his prefatory note to "English Eclogues" Southey scoffs at neoclassical pastoral: "No kind of poetry can boast of more illustrious names or is more distinguished by the servile dulness of imitated nonsense. Pastoral writers 'more silly than their sheep' have like their sheep gone on in the same track one after another." Well aware of the risks he had taken, Southey defends himself: "How far poems requiring almost a colloquial plainness of language may accord with the public taste I am doubtful. They have been subjected to able criticism and revised with care. I have endeavoured to make them true to nature." (*Poems*, II, [1799], p. 183.)

29. "Home at Grasmere," lines 800-808. To paraphrase this passage from Wordsworth's prospectus for his life work, accentuating its pastoral context, neither an irrecoverable Eden

nor an inimitable Theocritus bars us from the pastoral paradise; it is merely contingent on the proper state of mind, one that will unite the simple and the common in humanity and in nature.

30. Stephen Parrish is precisely on the point in observing, "It seems hardly too much to say that the *Lyrical Ballads* with their critical prefaces were simply Wordsworth's version of pastoral, his contribution to the sustained eighteenth-century debate over the nature and value of pastoral poetry" (*The Art of the* Lyrical Ballads [Cambridge: Harvard University Press, 1973], p. 162). As this discussion suggests, I would question Parrish's narrowing the context so that Wordsworth follows in the line of Burns and the Scottish pastoralists. Nor would I want to exclude the impact of late eighteenth-century ballad literature on Wordsworth. Its weight has been very well demonstrated by a number of scholars, foremost among them Karl Kroeber in Part I of *Romantic Narrative Art* (Madison: University of Wisconsin Press, 1960); Albert Friedman in the exemplary scholarship of *The Ballad Revival: Studies in the Influence of Popular on Sophisticated Poetry* (Chicago: University of Chicago Press, 1961), Chap. 9; and Mary Jacobus in several detailed chapters of *Tradition and Experiment in Wordsworth's* Lyrical Ballads *(1798)* (Oxford: Clarendon Press, 1976). Earlier attempts to integrate these genres probably had no actual influence on Wordsworth, but Shenstone's four "pastoral ballads" were well known and much admired well into the nineteenth century. They have an agreeable prettiness but are still fancy-dress affairs, not rustic in any realistic fashion.

31. For Wordsworth's acquaintance with and references to Theocritus, as well as an extensive argument on their similarities, see Leslie Broughton's doctoral dissertation, *The Theocritean Element in the Works of William Wordsworth* (Halle: Max Niemeyer, 1920). Surprisingly little has been said on Wordsworth as pastoral, as distinguished from nature, poet. Harold Tolliver devotes a chapter of *Pastoral Forms and Attitudes* to what he sees as "Wordsworth's Two Natures," the one sensuously observed, the other transcendentally immanent. Lore Metzger notes Wordsworth transferring authority from classical sources to local oral traditions in "Wordsworth's Pastoral Covenant," *Modern Language Quarterly*, 37 (1976), 307–323.

32. In the 1800 edition Wordsworth appends a footnote to "The Brothers" to "apologise for the abruptness with which this poem begins," observing that it was originally "intended to be the concluding poem of a series of pastorals, the scene of which was laid among the mountains of Cumberland and Westmoreland." In the *Biographia Literaria* Coleridge praises this poem as "that model of English pastoral, which I never yet read with unclouded eye" (*BL*, II, 62n).

33. In this case the word "idyll" is used in the generic sense meant by Virgil Nemoianu in *Micro-Harmony: The Growth and Uses of the Idyllic Model in Literature* (Bern: Peter Lang, 1977), as the portrayal of a small and secluded domestic circle. As Nemoianu surveys the type in late eighteenth-century European literature, it is best exemplified in French and especially German literature. The concluding books of *The Excursion*, which Nemoianu does not treat, actually constitute its fullest manifestation in English Romantic poetry.

34. True to the protean character of pastoral, "The Ruined Cottage" is generically recast as tragedy by Jonathan Wordsworth, *The Music of Humanity: A Critical Study of Wordsworth's "Ruined Cottage"* (London: Nelson, 1969).

35. Kenneth Johnston, " 'Home at Grasmere': Reclusive Song," *Studies in Romanticism*, 14 (1975), 1–28. The argument is incorporated within Johnston's *Wordsworth and* The Recluse (New Haven: Yale University Press, 1984).

36. M. H. Abrams uses "Home at Grasmere" as the introductory and exemplary text for his analysis of the secularization of sacred theme and symbol in *Natural Supernaturalism: Tradition and Revolution in Romantic Literature* (New York: Norton, 1971).

37. That the circling birds are meant to be seen within the same framework is particularly evident from Wordsworth's initial draft, called MS. B:

> Behold them, how they shape,
> Orb after orb, their course, still round and round,

Above the area of the Lake, their own
Adopted region, girding it about
In wanton repetition, yet therewith—
With that large circle evermore renewed—
Hundreds of curves and circlets, high and low,
Backwards and forwards, progress intricate. . . . (MS. B, 292-299)

38. Johnston, "'Home at Grasmere': Reclusive Song," *Studies in Romanticism*, 14 (1975), 1-28.

39. On the practical base for this conception, see Chap. 7, "Wordsworth's Labor Theory: An Economics of Compensation," in Kurt Heinzelman's *The Economics of the Imagination* (Amherst: University of Massachusetts Press, 1980). In a paper delivered at the Philadelphia meeting of the Northeast Modern Language Association (March, 1983) Heinzelman stressed the equality of women in this economy. Both in a note to *The Excursion* and a letter to Lady Beaumont (*WLMY*, I, 521) Wordsworth praises the intention, though questions the achievement, of John Dyer, author of *The Fleece*, a pastoral georgic. These passages suggest his own sense of continuity with Dyer's enterprise.

40. Coleridge also plays against generic expectation and convention in his "Fire, Famine, and Slaughter: A War Eclogue," written, it would appear, in 1796 and first published in the *Morning Post* on 8 January 1798. The three personifications celebrate the devastation of pastoral possibility.

41. Coleridge, with his uncommonly catholic taste, could well have found in Donne's "Nocturnall upon St. Lucies Day," where the poet spins an involved conceit around the notion of a vital death principle, a model for the inversion he creates at the beginning of this poem.

42. For reasons of space and because their works in the mode, though highly popular and conspicuous in their day, show little attempt truly to rethink the genre (except to give it a contemporary note of realism), I omit from this discussion a number of works from which we could define a "Romantic georgic poetry." These include gestures toward science in William Mason's *The English Garden* (1772-82) and, in particular, Erasmus Darwin's *The Botanic Garden* (1789-91) and *The Temple of Nature* (1803); the writings of Robert Bloomfield, particularly *The Farmer's Boy* (1800), James Grahame's *British Georgics* (1809), and John Clare's *Shepherd's Calendar* (1827); also the more realistic compositions of the Ettrick Shepherd, James Hogg, who was indeed a shepherd and therefore, in his own mind at least, a truer pastoralist than the mere plowboy, Robert Burns.

43. See also the dalliance of boy and girl picking grapes to the left of the second plate of "The Ecchoing Green."

44. Edward Wagenknecht concentrates on "pastoral ignorance" as the object of Blake's analysis, though my own reading would suggest that the critique is both far more extensive and more deeply rooted in the traditions of pastoral: see *Blake's Night: William Blake and the Idea of Pastoral* (Cambridge: Harvard University Press, 1973).

45. The most complicated view of the problems this caused Blake, partly because they are seen to include a temperamental resistance to his own ideological position, is provided by Leopold Damrosch in *Symbol and Truth in Blake's Myth* (Princeton: Princeton University Press, 1980).

46. This distinction has been raised by a number of readers of Blake; a particularly subtle elaboration is provided by Thomas R. Frosch in *The Awakening of Albion: The Renovation of the Body in the Poetry of William Blake* (Ithaca: Cornell University Press, 1974), pp. 152-159.

47. There can be no question that Leigh Hunt conceived of his first mature collection of poems, *Foliage* (1818), as centered in pastoral values. He divides the volume between "Greenwoods," his original poems, and "Evergreens," those he has translated, among which are seven *Idylls* of Theocritus, and poems by Bion and Moschus, including the latter's "Elegy on the Death of Bion." The "Preface, Including Cursory Observations on Poetry and Cheerfulness" recommends a Theocritean simplicity and *otium* as essential

poetic elements. In 1820 Hunt published a translation of Tasso's pastoral drama, *Amyntas*, which prompted Horace Smith to write his talented (if strange) *Amarynthus, The Nympholept: A Pastoral Drama*, with a brief preface extolling the virtues of pastoral drama, in 1821. The argument could be advanced that Hunt was more interested in the genre than Keats and the better poet in using it.

48. This is in essence the thesis pursued by Morris Dickstein in *Keats and His Poetry: A Study in Development* (Chicago: University of Chicago Press, 1971). Stuart Peterfreund sees the struggle in terms of Virgilian georgic in "Keats and the Fate of the Genres: the Troublesome Middle Term," *Genre*, 16 (1983), 249-277.

49. The poem was actually begun in England in 1817 and then was revised to reflect its Italian scenery in August 1818, with the result being an uncomfortable split between the political involvements of the one year and the strange dislocation from such concerns Shelley felt during his first months in Italy.

50. Shelley returns to this complex in the culminating vision of *Epipsychidion*, where the accretion of imagined perfections in his island paradise finally collapses from its own weight, throwing us back upon the fictive nature of the vision.

51. Though Neil Fraistat is primarily interested in complex thematic interplay rather than generic resonances, I am indebted here to the critical possibilities opened up by Fraistat's discussion of Shelley's 1820 volume in *The Poem and the Book: Reading Romantic Volumes* (Chapel Hill: University of North Carolina Press, 1985).

52. There is no room here to demonstrate either the subtle recastings of convention or the extent of the poem's paradoxical commitment to the ongoing business of life. I have attempted to do both, as well as to suggest the extent to which Shelley incorporates Keats's own poetic vision, in *"Adonais* in Context," published in *Shelley Revalued: Essays from the Gregynog Conference*, ed. Kelvin Everest (Leicester: Leicester University Press, 1983), pp. 165-182.

53. Further embodiments and extensions of this tradition are to be found in Bion's "Lament for Adonis," in Moschus's "Lament for Bion" (quoted in the epigraph to *Adonais*), in Spenser's *Astrophel*, and in Milton's *Lycidas*.

54. A similar emphasis impels the sustained excellence of William Keach's treatment of these poems, but where I read pastoral suspension he sees profound psychological and stylistic ambivalences: see the final chapter of *Shelley's Style* (New York: Methuen, 1984).

Chapter 6. The Romance

1. The lectures, which were originally published in German in 1809, were translated by John Black and printed in two volumes by Baldwin, Cradock and Joy in 1815. The distinction between classic and romantic, though informing the entire series, is the specific subject of the first of the lectures. Anne K. Mellor, in the first chapter of *English Romantic Irony* (Cambridge: Harvard University Press, 1980), locates in the writings of August Wilhelm's brother, Friedrich Schlegel, the full intellectual underpinning of Romanticism's self-consciousness and self-critique, reinforcing the general tendency of modern criticism to find in Friedrich Schlegel's analysis of Romanticism a fuller awareness of its ramifications than his brother possessed. But the usual problem of transmission is crucial in this regard, since Friedrich was not translated into English until much later. The English translation of August Wilhelm's lectures is directly attributable to his being praised, largely on the basis of them, "as the first literary critic of Germany" in Madame de Staël's *De l'Allemagne*, published as *Germany* by John Murray in 1813 (II, 380). Her chapter "Of Classic and Romantic Poetry" (I, 304-312) is a facile reduction of A. W. Schlegel's argument, but it constitutes the first popular dissemination of the distinction in Great Britain.

2. On this collection see Arthur Johnston, *Enchanted Ground: The Study of Medieval Romance in the Eighteenth Century* (London: Athlone Press; New York: Oxford University Press, 1964), pp. 93-94. I am indebted throughout this discussion to Johnston's impressive survey, which focuses particularly on Percy, Thomas Warton, Joseph Ritson, George Ellis,

and Walter Scott, and in its learning, cultural perception, and readability is a fitting companion study to Friedman's *The Ballad Revival*.

3. Warton's only real sin among his manifest virtues was apparently recommitted by Ritson, a sin of omission in both cases. The two scholars, it appears, in their archival researches independently went through Nero X in the Cotton MSS, bypassing because of the calligraphy or the unfamiliar dialect the greatest of medieval English romances, *Sir Gawain and the Green Knight*, which was left to Richard Price to discover in preparing his 1824 edition of Warton's *History*. The standard account of Ritson, fittingly running to two volumes, is Bertrand Bronson's *Joseph Ritson: Scholar at Arms* (Berkeley: University of California Press, 1938).

4. They also had a powerful effect, not wholly salutary, on historiography. The entire culture adopted the argument of the celebrated medieval historian, Jean Baptiste de la Curne de Saint-Palaye, implicit in the title of the English edition of *Memoirs of Ancient Chivalry. To which are added, The Anecdotes of the Times from the Romance Writers and Historians of those Ages* [tr. Susannah Dobson] (London: J. Dodsley, 1784), that, as Mrs. Dobson wrote in her preface, "there requires little apology for classing the ancient romance writers with the historians of those times" (p. xvii). Mrs. Dobson also translated Saint-Palaye's *Literary History of the Troubadours* in 1807, providing the most extensive access thus far to Provençal poetry.

5. See, for instance, Walter Scott's joint review of Ellis and Ritson in the *Edinburgh Review*, 7 (1806), 387–413; or, as a complement to the increasing attention drawn to Italian romances, the monograph on "Narrative and Romantic Poems of the Italians" written by Ugo Foscolo as the concluding article in the *Quarterly Review*, 21 (1819).

6. See pp. 173–177 of the extensive Memoir by Sir Bartle Frere occupying the first volume of the three-volume *Works of the Right Honourable John Hookham Frere*, 2nd ed., issued by Pickering in 1874.

7. This is an overly simple demarcation between the genres, as the history of epic-romances from *The Odyssey* forward might suggest—or as I am continually reminded by having in this and the subsequent chapter arbitrarily to distinguish among major narrative poems by the same author, such as Southey, or to place Blake's wholly "improbable" sublime allegories with epic endeavors. But the distinction, if simple, was that observed in contemporary writing, for instance, in this schoolbook injunction: "The [epic] poet however should keep within the bounds of probability; otherwise his work becomes a romance"—[Joseph Robertson] *An Essay on the Nature of the English Verse, with Directions for Reading Poetry* (London: J. Walter, 1799), p. 109. On a greater level of sophistication is the Aristotelian analysis of N. A. Vigors [Frederick Nolan] in *An Inquiry into the Nature and Extent of Poetick Licence* (London: J. Mackinlay, 1810): "At the very opposite extreme of the historick epopee is placed . . . the epick romance; and this is so far the case, that the former appears the converse of the latter; what is incompatible in the one, is indispensable in the other. The historick epos, as its title imports, requires a foundation in historick facts; but the epick romance finds a sufficient support in legendary story" (p. 57).

8. See Marilyn Butler's comments on the social significance of this pagan revival in *Peacock Displayed: A Satirist in his Context* (London: Routledge & Kegan Paul, 1979), 106–109.

9. Jeffrey's antipathy to Southey increased with the years, especially as the latter's Tory sentiments became more prominent and more strident. Yet, in his attack on *The Curse of Kehama*, faint praise surfaces amid the damnation: "Every thing, in his pictures, is gaudy and glittering, and fantastically exaggerated and contrasted . . . soothing [us] . . . with the virtues and affections, as well as the marvels and legends of the nursery. . . . [H]e has come with his whistle, and his gilded book of fairy tales, into the assemblies of bearded men, and audibly undervalued all other instruments and studies. . . . The last unfortunate accompaniment of Mr. Southey's childishness, is the perpetual artifice and effort that is visible in every part of his performance . . . a determination to miss no opportunity of being fine and striking" (*Edinburgh Review*, 17 [1811], 433–435).

10. Southey, in reviewing Hayley's *Memoirs*, claimed: "A greater effect was produced

upon the rising generation of scholars, by the Notes to his Essay on Epic Poetry, than by any other contemporary work, the Relics of Ancient Poetry alone excepted" (*Quarterly Review*, 31 [1825], 283). Southey was also clearly influenced by the Egyptian epic-romance *Gebir*, published by his classmate at Oxford, Walter Savage Landor, in 1798. He reviewed it enthusiastically in the *Critical Review*, 3 (1799), 29–39, and took it with him on his trip to Portugal the following year. While the ship was becalmed for a week, he reported to his brother Thomas that he "read Gebir, and wrote half a book of Thalaba"—Southey, *Journals of a Residence in Portugal, 1800–1801, and a Visit to France, 1838, Supplemented by Extracts from his Correspondence*, ed. Adolfo Cabral (Oxford: Clarendon, 1960), p. 76.

11. All accounts of romance in this period must revert to Bloom's thoughtful exposition of the psychological transformation of generic standards in his essay, "The Internalization of Quest-Romance," most easily accessible in the collection edited by Bloom, *Romanticism and Consciousness: Essays in Criticism* (New York: Norton, 1970), pp. 3–24. The greatest exponent of the romance in modern criticism is, without question, Northrop Frye, most particularly in his *The Secular Scripture: A Study of the Structure of Romance* (Cambridge: Harvard University Press, 1976). Yet, Frye's synoptic view and archetypal approach belie historical exigencies and limit his applicability to the highly specific conditions of the Romantic period. Also, they beg the question of literary value. Of all Romantic poets the one best suited to Frye's approach is Robert Southey.

12. Anon., *Modern Poets. A Dialogue, in Verse* (London: White, Cochrane, & Co., 1813), p. 23. This 27-page pamphlet is a satire on contemporary metrical romances, and *The Curse of Kehama* is particularly emphasized. But it indicts the entire age for poetic degeneracy:

> Pale Learning, stedfast to her classic page,
> Unheeded toiling brands a trifling age;
> Moderns in Chronicles for wisdom seek,
> Odes yield to ballads, to black-letter Greek. (p. 4)

"Black-letter" here refers to the antique type used for printing romances in the sixteenth-century. The immediate point of this sneer may be the enormous prices realized for the early romances in the sale of the Duke of Roxburgh's library. Another anonymous satirist devoted six pages of annotations (110n–115n) to this folly of his culture, remarking "who is to believe Burke, 'that the age of Chivalry is past,' when the fortunes of Princes are expended in the purchase of descriptions of Tournaments?"—*Sortes Horatianae. A Poetical Review of Poetical Talent* (London: T. Hamilton, 1814), p. 113n.

13. If Southey had an influence on Blake, it was not reciprocated. Within the year of his Indian romance's publication, Southey visited Blake who "showed Southey a perfectly mad poem called *Jerusalem*—Oxford Street is in Jerusalem" (*Henry Crabb Robinson on Books and Their Writers*, ed. Edith J. Morley [London: Dent, 1938], I, 41). Southey's lack of belief in his own fictions evidently made him unable to fathom Blake's; and yet the fact that Blake would expose his epic-prophecy to Southey must suggest that he expected to find a kindred spirit in a poet who transposed whole mythologies into his narratives. More even than Southey, certainly more radically, Blake reveals the influence of Spenser. *The Four Zoas*, though never finished, would appear less fragmentary to its readers if it were seen in the light of Spenser's deliberate incompleteness, his episodic superimposition of narrative lines, his polysemous allegory, and his love of sheer invention. Though Robert Gleckner attends less to *The Four Zoas* than to earlier poems, his *Blake and Spenser* (Baltimore: Johns Hopkins University Press, 1985) is the fullest study of its subject to date.

14. The quest is also, of course, susceptible to politicization, which is truly to objectify it. But such an objective mode is more attuned to epic endeavors than to those of romance. The only poem of major pretensions that tries simultaneously both to internalize and objectify the quest is Shelley's *Revolt of Islam*, which strains uneasily between its romance and epic aspirations. It is heavily influenced by Southey.

15. *The Complete Poetical Works of Scott*, ed. Horace E. Scudder (Boston: Houghton Mifflin, 1900), p. 286. All references to Scott's poetry are taken from this edition simply because it is readily convenient. There is, however, no edition of Scott done on modern

scholarly principles that would allow readers to measure the growth of his texts and therefore conceptions through successive printings.

16. The importance of this figure for contemporary poetics cannot be too strongly emphasized: the minstrel becomes an archetype of creativity and an avatar of authorial self-reflexiveness. Though antiquarians such as Percy and Warton continually revert to the function of minstrels, Scott appears to have derived his conception of the figure more directly from his countrymen, particularly from the Ossianic bard of Macpherson and from Beattie's unfinished *Bildungsroman* in Spenserian stanzas, *The Minstrel; or the Progress of Genius* (1771-1774), and the nationalistic association is also reflected in the title of his ballad collection, *The Minstrelsy of the Scottish Border*. But the emphasis on the romancer within the romance, stemming directly from *The Lay of the Last Minstrel*, is Scott's contribution to the internalization of all romances in this period.

17. *Edinburgh Review*, 7 (1806), 496.

18. The sharpest critique, which was motivated by political animus more than the literary taste it presumed and which is also very careful not to upset nationalist loyalties by overstatement, was Francis Jeffrey's notice of *Marmion*, the leading article in the *Edinburgh Review* for April, 1808 (12, 1-35). Jeffrey's characterization of Scott's first two romances suggests both his classical biases and, unwittingly, how much these poems are imbued with and artfully exploit the conventions of medieval romance: "The characteristics of both [poems] . . . are evidently the same;—a broken narrative—a redundancy of minute description—bursts of unequal and energetic poetry—and a general tone of spirit and animation, unchecked by timidity or affectation, and unchastised by any great delicacy of taste, or elegance of fancy" (2-3).

19. George Ellis, because the anonymous publication of *The Bridal of Triermain* provided him an excuse, reflected in the *Quarterly Review* on the example Scott gave other poets, celebrating his careful sense of historical distinction—"he is profoundly acquainted with those circumstances that distinguished the ages of romance and chivalry, on one hand, from the classical times of antiquity, and on the other from the institutions and observances of modern days"—and then the oppositions he subsumed within his subject matter: a "mixture of ferocity and courtesy, of religion and barbarity, of rudeness and hospitality, of enthusiastic love, inflexible honour and extravagant enterprize . . ." (9 [1813], 483). The present argument has been influenced by the exemplary analysis of the dialectical complexity of Scott's fiction undertaken by Joseph Valente: "'Upon the Braes': History and Hermeneutics in *Waverley*," *Studies in Romanticism*, 24 (1986).

20. *Edinburgh Review*, 16 (1810), 263. Several years later, *Blackwood's* assessed Scott's impact on his era thus: "'The Lay' converted thousands, and 'Marmion' tens of thousands, and the *whole* world read poetry. . . . Mr Scott gave to the world a series of brilliant romances, and turned into this new-made channel all who ever in their lives read and relished fictitious compositions. All the poets, good and bad, forthwith wrote metrical romances . . ." (*Blackwood's*, 1 [1817], 516).

21. The fullest record of the history of this poem's composition and publication, pending a complete analysis in the Cornell Wordsworth series, is that provided by Mark L. Reed in Appendix VIII of *Wordsworth: The Chronology of the Middle Years, 1800-1815* (Cambridge: Harvard University Press, 1975), pp. 700-702. Clearly, there is much left unsaid behind the veil of Wordsworth's letter to Scott after his reading *Marmion*: "I think your end has been attained; that it is not in every respect the end which I should wish you to propose to yourself, you will be well aware from what you know of my notions of composition, both as to matter and manner" (*WLMY*, I [4 August 1808], 264). Earlier, while her brother was still undecided about pursuing publication of *The White Doe of Rylstone*, Dorothy Wordsworth had cited *The Lay of the Last Minstrel* as a standard against which to measure it (*WLMY*, I [28 March 1808], 203).

22. *Wordsworth's Poetry: 1787-1814* (New Haven: Yale University Press, 1964), pp. 327-329.

23. Wordsworth's staunch defense of his experiment deserves quotation as expressing the value he saw in an internalized narrative and his aversion to mere action (and its extension

in society as war): "As to the principal characters doing nothing it is false and too ridiculous to be dwelt on for a moment. When it is considered what has already been executed in Poetry, strange that a man cannot perceive, particularly when the present tendencies of society, good and bad, are observed, that this is the time when a man of genius may honourably take a station upon different ground. If he is to be a Dramatist, let him crowd his scene with gross and visible action; but if a narrative Poet, if the Poet is to be predominant over the Dramatist,—then let him see if there are no victories in the world of spirit, no changes, no commotions, no revolutions there, no fluxes and refluxes of the thoughts which may be made interesting by modest combination with the stiller actions of the bodily frame, or with the gentler movements and milder appearances of society and social intercourse, or the still more mild and gentle solicitations of irrational and inanimate nature" (*WLMY*, I [19 April 1808], 222-223).

24. The notion of "Oriental Tale" in Byron can be extended to a wide application, for both *Mazeppa* and *The Island*, though comparatively late and set in very different Eastern realms, practice variations on the essential themes broached in the Greco-Turkish tales. The same is true of the unspecified medieval realm of *Lara*, which is in fact the one of these poems most directly indebted to *Marmion*.

25. *Fiery Dust: Byron's Poetic Development* (Chicago: University of Chicago Press, 1968), pp. 141-164.

26. Medora pointedly compares herself with Ariosto's Olympia and with the forsaken Ariadne: *The Corsair* I.439-445.

27. Two minor romances published shortly after Moore's illustrate the tendency. Charles Dibdin's *Young Arthur; or, The Child of Mystery: A Metrical Romance* (London: Longman, Hurst, Rees, Orme and Brown, 1819) is continually broken by the author's instrusions and self-indulgent digressions, and its vernacular verse serves to force a modern sensibility on its ostensibly medieval subject. Thomas Lovell Beddoes's *The Improvisatore, in Three Fyttes* (Oxford: J. Vincent; London: G. and W. B. Whittaker, 1821) encloses the Gothic extremities we might expect from three tales by this poet within a highly domesticated medieval environment, where the minstrel wards off the boredom of a December evening.

28. *Observations on the Fairy Queen of Spenser*, 2nd ed. (London: 1762), p. 21.

29. See "Metaphor and Metamorphosis in Shelley's 'The Witch of Atlas'," *Studies in Romanticism*, 19 (1980), 327-353.

30. Wasserman's analysis is in *Shelley: A Critical Reading* (Baltimore: Johns Hopkins University Press, 1971), pp. 3-46. His stress on the role of nature, and thus on the impact of Wordsworth on Shelley's early ideas, has been equally influential, spawning a small and continuing debating society among critics. Yet, if we honor the claim that generic considerations are prior to thematic adjustments, or even that they simply deserve equal attention, then Byron's quest for an empowering ideal in his Eastern travels surely sets the stage for Shelley's even more extensive tour of the Orient and the impossible quest of his nameless hero. Moreover, the famous mystery surrounding the second paragraph of Shelley's prose introduction is immediately cleared up if we recognize that Shelley is distinguishing the quest of his driven visionary from that of the bored and barren Harold.

31. This is the perspective underlying Patricia Parker's *Inescapable Romance: Studies in the Poetics of a Mode* (Princeton: Princeton University Press, 1979), which treats Ariosto, Spenser, and Keats. An often insightful book, especially with Keats its phenomenological approach tends to convert all genres indiscriminately to the dynamics of this single mode, which in his case might simply be claimed to be that of Romanticism rather than of romance.

32. More explicitly, the pastoral world in which "A thing of beauty is a joy for ever" (I.1) has already proved inadequate to Endymion as we are introduced to him; Keats's celebration of tales of love is placed in sudden context by his turning to address the "Brain-sick shepherd prince" (II.43) made disconsolate by love; the meditation on the moon melds almost immediately into Endymion's prayer to the Moon (who is, of course, the goddess with whom he has fallen in love, Cynthia); and Keats's apostrophe to his native muse, his

sense of his lowliness as novice poet, and his attachment to his culture are suddenly contrasted with the prayer of the Indian maiden who has served in the train of Bacchus ("Ah, woe is me! that I should fondly part / From my dear native land!") and the hecatomb of Endymion to heaven that she interrupts.

33. *The Hoodwinking of Madeline, and Other Essays on Keats's Poems* (Urbana: University of Illinois Press, 1971); Rajan, *Dark Interpreter: The Discourse of Romanticism* (Ithaca: Cornell University Press, 1980), Chap. 3. Stillinger's title refers to a notable example of Keats's intrusion of a vernacular upon the language of romance, the description of Madeline as "Hoodwink'd with faery fancy" ("Eve of St. Agnes," 70). It is worth emphasizing that Leigh Hunt's *Story of Rimini* was influential among his circle in suggesting the inherent potentiality for romances in medieval Italian sources. "Isabella" was the first redaction of subjects from Boccaccio projected by Keats, in which he was to be joined by John Hamilton Reynolds. Reynolds mentions the failed collaboration in the "Advertisement" to *The Garden of Florence; and Other Poems* (London: John Warren, 1821), pp. [xi]-xiii. His title poem is taken from Boccaccio; the second in the collection, "The Romance of Youth," is an unfinished poem of 104 Spenserian stanzas influenced by *Endymion* and, generally perhaps, by Beattie's *Minstrel*. Neither Hunt nor Reynolds shares Keats's instinct for the antiromantic.

34. It is perhaps not misplaced to suggest that were Schlegel alive today, we would be confronted by the dichotomy between classical and deconstructive poetry.

35. As far as I am aware, no one has ever wondered about the implications of Byron's designating his protagonist a "Childe." In his preface to the first two cantos he alludes to the term as standard medieval nomenclature, citing figures (though without identifying his source) from Percy's *Reliques*. John Pinkerton—in a note to "Childe Maurice" in *Select Scottish Ballads* (London: J. Nichols, 1783), I, 138—remarks that the title is "applicable to a young nobleman when about the age of fifteen," which does not seem to be Byron's sense of the term (though it is possible that he meant to suggest a protracted adolescence in Harold). Percy in his headnote to "Childe Waters" likens its ancient usage to the term "prince," but then adds that "It ought to be observed, that the word *Child* or *Chield* is still used in North Britain to denominate a Man, commonly with some contemptuous character affixed to him . . ." (*Reliques*, ed. Henry Wheatley [London: Swan Sonnenshein, 1891], III, 58). It is also possible that Byron simply borrowed the title directly from Rose's translation of *Partenopex of Blois*, where it occurs so frequently to characterize the title character that the *Edinburgh Review* objected to it as a jarring archaism (13 [January 1809], 422). Were that the case, the very title might be meant as a further, if private, jibe at Francis Jeffrey.

36. *The Rise of Romance* (Oxford: Clarendon, 1971).

37. *The Idea of the Canterbury Tales* (Berkeley: University of California Press, 1976), pp. 326-332.

38. Surprisingly little has been written on the genre of this poem until very recently. Ronald A. Schroeder has shrewdly unraveled the complexity of Byron's response to George Ellis's review of the first two cantos in "Ellis, Sainte-Palaye, and Byron's 'Addition' to the 'Preface' of *Childe Harold's Pilgrimage* I–II" (*Keats-Shelley Journal*, 32 [1983], 25-30). The fine essay by my former student, Michael Vicario, constitutes the only substantial treatment of the poem's generic underpinnings, contrasting Byron with Thomson and Beattie on the purposes of poetic growth and arguing that the poet and Harold embody alternate approaches to the problems of romance: see "The Implications of Form in *Childe Harold's Pilgrimage*" (*Keats-Shelley Journal*, 33 [1984], 103-129).

39. In Canto IV, st. 153, Byron explicitly reminds his readers that he has taken them from Ephesus to Sophia to St. Peter's in his pilgrimage. That the eastern terminus of the quest in Canto II should be Haija Sophia is also a subtle rounding out of the canto itself, whose first line is an apostrophe to Athena, goddess of wisdom (Sophia). That she is not expected to answer his call is likewise balanced by the irony that Haija Sophia had become (and remained until very recently) a Muslim mosque. Today, appropriately enough to Byron's sense of the fate of shrines, it is a museum.

40. In his notes to the second edition Byron acknowledged that he had mistranslated the Spanish as "Our Lady of Punishment" (pena) for want of a tilde: the true name of the convent is "Madonna of the Rocks" (peña).

41. In fairness to other critics of this poem, I should simply note that this optimistic reading of *Childe Harold's Pilgrimage* is not universally shared. The most detailed examination of the poem ever conducted concludes that it is "an extraordinary imaginative journey into nothingness and despair"—Robert F. Gleckner, *Byron and the Ruins of Paradise* (Baltimore: Johns Hopkins University Press, 1967), p. 297. I would argue that it is precisely our awareness of the generic underpinnings of the poem that enforces an opposite conclusion.

Chapter 7. The Epic

1. Ellis, confessing himself uncertain whether Byron is contemplating an epic in *Childe Harold's Pilgrimage*, observes "that the subject is perfectly suited to such a purpose; that the foundation which he has laid is sufficiently solid, and his materials ample for the most magnificent superstructure" (*Quarterly Review*, 7 [1812], 191). The *Annual Review*, 4 (1805), gave *Madoc* a lengthy encomium, with this tribute occurring on p. 605.

2. John Milton, "The Reason of Church Government," in Don M. Wolfe et al., eds., *Complete Prose Works of John Milton* (New Haven: Yale University Press, 1953), I, 815. I have written previously on Milton's critical importance for Romantic epic: see *Shelley's Annus Mirabilis: The Maturing of an Epic Vision* (San Marino: Huntington Library Press, 1975), esp. pp. 6-12, and "The Mental Pinnacle: *Paradise Regained* and the Romantic Four-Book Epic" in *Calm of Mind*, ed. Joseph Wittreich (Cleveland: Case Western Reserve University Press, 1971), pp. 133-162. See also the introduction to Wittreich's *The Romantics on Milton* (Cleveland: Case Western Reserve University Press, 1970), and his *Angel of Apocalypse: Blake's Idea of Milton* (Madison: University of Wisconsin Press, 1975).

3. "Young Thelwall had now changed his residence, and his nominal profession [apprentice to a tailor]; but his pursuits were still the same. The shopboard, like the shop counter was a seat, not of business but of study. Plays (particularly tragedies) were perpetually in his hands and in his mouth. From thence he soared to epic poetry; devoured with insatiable avidity Pope's translation of Homer, and committed several hundred verses to memory; meditating the herculean labour of getting the whole Iliad by heart"—John Thelwall, "Prefatory Memoir" to *Poems chiefly written in Retirement . . . and Specimens of the Hope of Albion; or, Edwin of Northumbria: An Epic Poem* (Hereford: 1801), p. ix.

4. Le Bossu was the principal codifier of neoclassical epic rules in his *Traité du poëme épique* of 1675. His rigorous Aristotelian analysis elaborated his prescription that the epic was "a Discourse invented by Art, to form the Manners by such Instructions as are disguis'd under the Allegories of some one important Action, which is related in Verse, after a probable, diverting, and surprizing Manner" (*Le Bossu and Voltaire on the Epic*, ed. Stuart Curran [Gainesville: Scholars' Facsimiles, 1970], p. 6). As I observe in the introduction to this edition, Le Bossu's moralistic notion of the epic may be reductive, but his analysis of narrative methods was of great importance for the development of the eighteenth-century novel. Quotations from Hayley's *Essay on Epic Poetry* cite the Scholars' Facsimile edition prepared by Sister M. Celeste Williamson, SSJ (1968). On Hayley's reversal of conventional notions of epic in the eighteenth century, see the standard analysis of H. T. Swedenberg, *The Theory of the Epic in England: 1650-1800* (Berkeley and Los Angeles: University of California Press, 1944).

5. In 1800 six cantos (of the projected ten) were published in London by R. B. Scott, with a dedication to the king that is symptomatic of the political reversals that took place during the 1790s. It is possible that another contemporary epic on this subject also exists: the advertisement sheet included in Charles Crawford's *Liberty: A Pindaric Ode* (Tunbridge Wells: Jasper Sprange, [1789]) lists *The Revolution: An Epic Poem* among the author's works.

6. "Prefatory Memoir," *Poems chiefly written in Retirement*, p. xliii. Thelwall, whose treason trial of 1794 was a major national event, afterward seems deliberately to have tried to vindicate himself as a patriot, whether in this national epic or in the bombast of "The Trident of Albion, an Epic Effusion," published in 1805 to celebrate the Battle of Trafalgar and described by the author as "a hasty effusion, poured out, almost spontaneously, on the spur of the moment" (p. v). The posture is thus that of the inspired bard, even if the inflated rhetoric falls flat. It begins:

> Who first—who last thy Naval Thunder roll'd,
> And drove thy Water-Chariot o'er the deep
> Triumphant? trident-sceptred Albion, say— (p. 27)

7. Knight's comment on his generic designation is instructive: "Though constructed on a regular, connected, and unified plan, he hath not ventured to call his work an epic poem, lest its title should seem to challenge comparison with others of a more grave and exalted character; and thus cause it to be estimated by a scale taken from merits of a higher class." Knight is also well aware of the earlier epics on Alfred, suggesting that "should the author be deemed more successful, in treating his subject, than either of his predecessors, it will be owing to a free use" of fictional embellishment to history (*Alfred; a Romance in Rhyme* [London: Longman, Hurst, Rees, Orme, and Brown, 1823], pp. vi, xv).

8. The once burning issue of epic machinery was still very much alive at this time. Though Davenant had argued against it in the preface to *Gondibert* (1650), with the approbation of Thomas Hobbes, supernatural machinery was reintroduced in the eighteenth century, and it was defended by many, most lengthily by John Ogilvie in the "Critical Dissertation on Epic Machinery" he attached to *Brittania*. Southey's introduction of a panoply of supernatural agents in his Eastern romances contributed to its popularity. But, generally speaking, Milton supplies the *dramatis personae*, particularly among the Satanic legions. The accepted notion of piety among epic poets of the Romantic period is that you can scarcely touch the hem of God's garments, but you have utter license when it comes to a wardrobe for Satan and his crew. The ubiquitous employment of machinery is a further element making a strict separation between romance and epic during this period difficult. Although epic poetry is continually distinguished as representing the actual, there is not a single epic in English during this period—except for the very unconventional *Don Juan* that comes late and *The Prelude* that comes after—whose feet touch the same hard ground as *Marmion* or *Childe Harold's Pilgrimage*.

9. [Francis Palgrave,] *Edinburgh Review*, 25 (1815), 166. The diction here suggests that what is sauce for romance is not to be served with epic. The early pages of the review (146–151) argue the incongruity of pagan mythology in a modern poem.

10. The first edition of *Beowulf*, edited and translated into Latin by G. J. Thorkelin, was published in Copenhagen in 1815. It is another milestone in the recovery of medieval texts during the Romantic period, and Pennie's tribute to "That Saxon harp, touched by the wizard Scald, / Who th'Epic tale of Beowulf wildly sung" (p. 49), a full decade before John M. Kemble's English translation, is an indication of its rapid assimilation into the revised corpus of British literature. Pennie, who as far as I know here makes his debut in literary history, certainly did not wish it to come so late. In 1827 he published the rarest of all literary types, an anonymous autobiography, entitled *The Tale of a Modern Genius; or, the Miseries of Parnassus* (London: J. Andrews), in three volumes. Much of the third volume concerns the effort that went into his two epic poems, *The Royal Minstrel* and *Rogvald*, and the lack of taste that ensured their neglect. His portrayal of his driving ambition as epic poet (II, 324–334) offers insight into the climate in which he wrote. He certainly thought highly of his own epic achievements. In his school text, organized by genre, *The Harp of Parnassus* (London: G. and W. B. Whittaker, 1822), Pennie placed himself as the only epic poet in English after Milton.

11. *Letters on Literature, Taste, and Composition, Addressed to his Son*, 2 vols. (London: Richard Phillips, 1808), II, 294–295.

12. The connection with Milton's epic was obvious to contemporary readers. William

Mudford, in *The Contemplatist; a Series of Essays upon Morals and Literature* (London: Sherwood, Neely, & Jones, 1810), demurs from Southey's high estimate of *The Christiad* in these terms: "His editor says 'there is great power in the execution of this fragment': but I have sought in vain for it. I view it in no other light than as an unsuccessful attempt to put Milton's *Paradise Regain'd* into a Spenserian stanza: and how such a project is likely to succeed, the reader need not be informed by me . . . the whole appears so unequal, and so ludicrous, that I regret it should have been permitted to disfigure these posthumous volumes" (p. 253).

13. I have discussed this redaction at greater length as a means of understanding the conception of Milton's poem in *"Paradise Regained:* Implications of Epic," published in *Milton Studies*, 17 (1983)—*Composite Orders: The Genres of Milton's Last Poems*, ed. Richard S. Ide and Joseph Wittreich—209-224. An account of Ogden's life and writings can be found in Richard Wright Procter's *Literary Reminiscences and Gleanings* (Manchester: Thomas Dinham; and London: Simpkin, Marshall, and Co., 1860), pp. 29-40.

14. That the church was not of one mind in endorsing epic piety can be surmised from the Rev. C. Colton's sweeping denunciation of these efforts in *Hypocrisy. A Satire* (Tiverton: T. Smith; London: W. Button, 1812), p. 7:

> Now Southey's Madoc greets the groaning stall,
> To visit at the Grocer's, Sotheby's Saul;
> Now o'er this deluged land Exodiads bring
> A greater plague than all the plagues they sing;
> Wherein poor Pharaoh deems it sad to *sink*
> With Hoyle, drowned o'er again in seas of Ink.

15. We might simply note here the publication of Lucien Bonaparte's *Charlemagne; or the Church Delivered* (1815), dedicated to Pope Pius VII and translated by the Revs. S. Butler and Francis Hodgson, which is openly conceived as a defence of Christianity (I, xiii). A French and Catholic nationalistic, medieval epic to celebrate the restoration of the Bourbon monarchy would scarcely be expected to excite the British reader: Wordsworth could not get beyond the sixth canto (*WLMY*, II, 198).

16. The thesis of Joan Malory Webber's brilliant meditation on this genre, *Milton and His Epic Tradition* (Seattle: University of Washington Press, 1979), as noted in the first chapter, is that the epic line is one of continuing generic subversion, a history of counter-genres.

17. *The Poetical Works of Robert Southey* (London: Longman, Orme, Brown, Green, and Longmans, 1838), I, xxiii. The text of *Joan of Arc* presents a nearly insoluble problem for a modern commentator. The original edition of twelve books was pared to ten in the second by deletion of "The Vision of the Maid of Orleans," but numerous other changes were made then as well, including additions; and other changes were made as further editions were called for. In preparing his collected works in 1837, Southey again went through the poem to "correct" its youthful politics, which were, of course, directly contrary to those of the later reactionary. And yet, the first edition of the poem is certainly inferior to later ones, and its radicalism is actually made more explicit in subsequent early editions as Southey saw that he could get away with it. Since no modern edition of Southey has done more than reprint poems from Southey's final ten-volume collection, there is no convenient way of representing the stages of this poem. Southey does print the original preface in his 1838 edition. Quotations from the second edition (London: G. G. & J. Robinson, 1797) will be identified by date.

18. *Monthly Review*, 19 (1796), 361-368; in *Southey: The Critical Heritage*, ed. Lionel Madden (London: Routledge & Kegan Paul, 1972), p. 42.

19. The only extensive analysis of the Southey and Landor epic experiments is in Brian Wilkie's *Romantic Poets and Epic Tradition* (Madison: University of Wisconsin Press, 1965), Chap. 2. Wilkie also provides the one consideration of the epic claims of Shelley's *Revolt of Islam*. His recognition of the survival of conventions is often very insightful; at the same time, the extent to which Milton offered a direct alternative to heroic epic is underplayed.

20. The heroism of the British armies under Sir Sidney Smith provoked the one attempt in the period to create an epic directly out of contemporary events: Mrs. Hannah Cowley's *The Siege of Acre. An Epic Poem. In Six Books* (London: J. Debrett, 1801). For a second edition (London: G. Wilkie & J. Robinson, 1810) it was restructured in four books.

21. *Alfred*, Preface to the Second Edition (London: Longman and Rees, 1804), I, xxx [for xxxviii]–xxxix.

22. *Paradise Regained*, I.15. In the proem to Book IX of *Paradise Lost*, Milton claims an "argument / Not less but more Heroic than the wrath / Of stern Achilles . . ." (IX.13–15). The epic subversion of warfare in Cottle, Southey, and Blake has a direct basis in Hayley's *Life of Milton*, which in turn is influenced by Joel Barlow's notion of Homer as having "too great a tendency to nourish that sanguinary madness in mankind, which has continually made the earth a theatre of carnage. . . . [He was] accessary to the innumerable massacres with which men . . . have desolated the world" (p. 276).

23. The bibliographical record here is complex but exceedingly important. Barlow published his epic originally as *The Vision of Columbus: A Poem in Nine Books*, which was twice printed in Hartford in 1787, then reissued in London by C. Dilly and J. Stockdale that same year. A fourth edition (Barlow was under the apprehension that it was the fifth and so called it) was published by the English Press in Paris in 1793. After a significant career as a European representative of the young republic, Barlow retired to Philadelphia early in the 1800s and became obsessively preoccupied with the revision and reprinting of his epic as *The Columbiad*. The result was the finest book printed in America up to that point, an advertisement to the world of taste, elegance, and cultural vision. Published in Philadelphia by C. and A. Conrad and in Baltimore by Conrad, Lucas, and Co. in 1807, the sheets were then sent to England, where Richard Phillips set his imprint on them in 1809. Much of the substance of the revised epic is already present in the 1787 poem, including its prophetic vision of a federation of nations. The intriguing question is how well known was the original version of the epic, available in London well before the events of the 1790s constricted liberal sentiments. That Hayley read the poem is manifest from a note to him from Barlow, about to depart England in March 1792, asking him to return it with his criticisms: this is in the manuscript collections of the Huntington Library (HM 6568), and there are other letters from Hayley to Barlow housed in the Pequot Library (Southport, Connecticut) on deposit at Yale University. That Barlow by this point would have also known Hayley's *Essay on Epic Poetry* can be assumed, though the apostrophe to "Almighty Freedom" enters only with the retitled epic; clearly, Barlow shared and perhaps helped shape Hayley's views on the Homeric epic. It has been suggested that Blake knew *The Vision of Columbus*, since it is the only work to use the kind of machinery he adopted in *America*: see David V. Erdman, "Blake's Debt to Joel Barlow," *American Literature*, 26 (1954), 94–98, recast in *Blake: Prophet Against Empire*, rev. ed. (Princeton: Princeton University Press, 1969), pp. 23–26. John Howard's recent account of Blake's debt to Barlow inverts the perspective, concluding that "Blake's hero is the personified antithesis of all that Barlow believed in": *Infernal Poetics: Poetic Structures in Blake's Lambeth Prophecies* (Rutherford, N.J.: Fairleigh Dickinson University Press, 1984), p. 115. I am convinced that Shelley was strongly influenced by *The Columbiad*, as I argue later.

24. This is exactly where the bibliographical issue becomes so delicate. *The Vision of Columbus* lacks the epic grandeur overlaid by Barlow in *The Columbiad*; it also lacks the prefatory elucidation of underlying purpose. But the main sequence of episodes is already present, as is the ideological pressure, even if it does not call attention to itself. Its 1787 British imprint makes *The Vision of Columbus* the first epic to appear after Hayley's *Essay*, and, as it is the most direct extension of his principles, one might wish to argue that it established lines of thinking that other epics embodied from it. The evidence for this, however, is at best meager. The attention given *The Columbiad*, even when it was as condescending as Francis Jeffrey's notice in the *Edinburgh Review*, 15 (1809), 24–40, ensured a more widespread public reception.

25. By 1815 and clothed in piety, Cottle abandoned his earlier misgivings, expressed in the preface to the second edition of *Alfred*, that indicate how very common a device this had

become: "I have adopted an opinion . . . that all prophecies and anticipations of futurity, in an heroic poem, are defects of considerable magnitude. To ascribe predictions to a character, in which he traces a succession of subsequent, and, to the reader, familiar events, with all the accuracy of an historian, requires no imagination, little skill, and . . . to my feelings of propriety, has always been repugnant" (p. xxviii). With the visionary in epics thus threatening to become a tired cliché, we are perhaps better able to understand its conventions being openly assumed for the mere recital of history. William Lisle Bowles's epic history of ocean travel and exploration, *The Spirit of Discovery* (1805), is represented in such a visionary frame.

26. There can be little doubt that *The Columbiad* lies behind Samuel Rogers's brief epic of the next year (1810), *The Voyage of Columbus*, which is an experimental mixture of prose and poetry, overlaid with both the gods of the American natives and angelic messengers and ending in the customary vision. Though a curious work, its literary quality is unmistakeable. Two poems earlier in the decade embody something like Barlow's mode, though they were probably not influenced by him nor themselves influential. J. Sympson's anonymous *Science Revived, or the Vision of Alfred* (1802) is a versified history of European culture in which Alfred, praying to Science to disperse ignorance and bless England, is taken by her to the Palace of Genius and shown the progress of knowledge and liberty over seven cantos. George Sanon's *The Causes of the French Revolution; and the Science of Governing an Empire: An Epic and Philosophical Poem* (1806), dedicated to the ubiquitous Capel Lofft, has its hero awakened by the arrival of a beautiful maiden in a celestial chariot to instruct him. The poetical fustian is such that it is hard to discern what he learns. Still, there is manifest epic ambition: "The ancients left the three highest sciences in the rough, for posterity to bring to perfection: Newton has greatly improved one; and I have endeavoured to improve the other two, viz. The Science of the Human Mind (which will be published in November next), and the Moral Science" (Preface, p. vii). Since the author avows that this "work will be the unerring standard for the present and future generations" (p. xvi), the disregard for Romantic epics in later times may be assumed to have been a cause of general deprivation.

27. This is a scholarly assumption of very long duration, based on L. Kellner, "Shelley's *Queen Mab* and Volney's *Les Ruines*," *Englische Studien*, 22 (1896), 9-40. See also Kenneth Neill Cameron, "A Major Source of *The Revolt of Islam*," *PMLA*, 56 (1941), 175-206. Certainly, Shelley was familiar with Volney's revolutionary handbook, but it would be surprising if the adolescent son of a Whig M. P., who was of the liberal aristocratic faction, did not know Barlow's poem, either first-hand or through the notice it received, particularly in the *Edinburgh Review*. Barlow, it might be worth recalling, translated Volney's *Ruins* in 1802, and the edition appeared with Thomas Jefferson listed as coadjutor.

28. Stuart Sperry's reading of *Hyperion* as an allegory of the two generations of British Romanticism is so well argued that it has been generally persuasive: see *Keats the Poet* (Princeton: Princeton University Press, 1973), Chap. 7. I do not dispute his conclusions simply because Keats is never distant from his preoccupations with his vocation as poet. But I must agree with Morris Dickstein's observation in a paper delivered at the 1983 Modern Language Association convention that we have singularly blinkered ourselves from the contemporary implications of a poem celebrating a revolution.

29. *Lectures on Rhetoric and Belles-Lettres* (London: Strahan, Cadell, and Creech, 1783), II, 407, 409.

30. I am indebted to the single attempt to pursue this issue directly and without reproach, by Joseph Wittreich, "Domes of Mental Pleasure: Blake's Epics and Hayley's Epic Theory," *Studies in Philology*, 69 (1972), 201-229, substantially reprinted in *Angel of Apocalypse: Blake's Idea of Milton*, pp. 229-250.

31. The analogy with *Paradise Regained* seems to have been in Blake's mind, as he joins the final line of Milton's epic and the language of the prophecy of Daniel in a note inscribed on the back of a drawing for his own last plate: "Father & Mother I return from flames of fire tried & pure & white" (p. 730).

32. I refer to Vogler's study, *Preludes to Vision: The Epic Adventure in Blake, Words-*

worth, Keats, and Hart Crane (Berkeley: University of California Press, 1971). The treatment of *Milton* is particularly valuable.

33. I have dwelt at much greater length on principles of repetition and recurrence in this poem in "The Structures of *Jerusalem*," *Blake's Sublime Allegory: Essays on The Four Zoas, Milton, and Jerusalem*, ed. Stuart Curran and Joseph Wittreich (Madison: University of Wisconsin Press, 1973), pp. 329-346.

Chapter 8. Composite Orders

1. *Select Translations from Scaliger's Poetics*, ed. E. M. Padelford (New York: H. Holt, 1905), p. 54. On inclusiveness as the mark of the Homeric epics, see Rosalie Colie, *The Resources of Kind: Genre-Theory in the Renaissance* (Berkeley: University of California Press, 1973), pp. 22-23; and for Milton's untraditional and prosaic additions to epic inclusiveness, pp. 119-122. Milton's achievement is presented with unusual clarity and insight in Barbara K. Lewalski's prolegomenon to a full-scale study, "The Genres of *Paradise Lost*," *Composite Orders: The Genres of Milton's Last Poems*, ed. Richard S. Ide and Joseph Wittreich (*Milton Studies*, 17 [1983], 75-103).

2. *LSTC*, I, 320-321. Cottle, in publishing *Alfred* just two years later, obviously did not assume Coleridge's regimen. Just as clearly, neither did Coleridge, though he planned a number of epic ventures.

3. Joseph Cottle, citing Milton's example, argues for the value of an epic author's personal association with the reader in the preface to *The Fall of Cambria* (2nd ed., 1811), I, xxxvi-xxxviii.

4. The most direct considerations of the epic qualities of *The Prelude* are to be found in Herbert Lindenberger's *On Wordsworth's* Prelude (Princeton: Princeton University Press, 1963), Chap. 4, and Brian Wilkie's *Romantic Poets and Epic Tradition* (Madison: University of Wisconsin Press, 1965), Chap. 3.

5. Lindenberger remarks this fact: *On Wordsworth's* Prelude, p. 265. Once again the impact of Hayley is manifest.

6. Hartman's classic formulation is the focus of the second chapter of *Wordsworth's Poetry: 1787-1814* (New Haven: Yale University Press, 1964). Stuart Peterfreund offers another, more directly generic analysis in relating it to the Virgilian model for development: see "*The Prelude*: Wordsworth's Metamorphic Epic," *Genre*, 14 (1981), 441-472.

7. Wordsworth explicitly surrounds his shepherd with contraries. He is "A freeman, / wedded to his life of hope / And hazard, and hard labour interchanged / With that majestic indolence so dear / To native man" (1850: VIII.253-256).

8. Besides the incisive reading of Brian Wilkie's chapter, "The Epic of Negation," in *Romantic Poets and Epic Tradition*, see the opening pages of Jerome McGann's Don Juan *in Context* (Chicago: University of Chicago Press, 1976) and their critique and expansion in Donald H. Reiman's essay, "*Don Juan* in Epic Context," *Studies in Romanticism*, 16 (1977), 587-594.

9. *Romantic Poets and Epic Tradition*, p. 191.

10. McGann's contrast of Juvenalian and Horatian models of satire is useful for understanding stylistic nuance in the poem but unwittingly supports a generic stance that is for Byron at last untenable. My view here is more in accord with what Robert F. Gleckner, in his magisterial account of Byron's progress in this genre, has seen as his final position: see Don Juan *in Context*, principally Chaps. 5 and 6, and Gleckner, "From Selfish Spleen to Equanimity: Byron's Satires," *Studies in Romanticism*, 18 (1979), 173-205.

11. *Romantic Poets and Epic Tradition*, pp. 198-211.

12. *Romantic Poets and Epic Tradition*, p. 212.

13. Byron would almost certainly have been aware of the passage used as epigraph to this chapter, whether or not he had read Black's *Life of Tasso*, since, apart from his fluency in Italian, his deep knowledge of the culture and literature, and his several poetic tributes to Tasso, it is alluded to and partly quoted in Hobhouse's *Historical Illustrations of the Fourth Canto of Childe Harold* (London: 1818), p. 26.

14. The principal authority on this subject is Charles E. Robinson in Chap. 6 of *Shelley and Byron: The Snake and Eagle Wreathed in Fight* (Baltimore: Johns Hopkins University Press, 1976).

15. Among contemporary examples of this designation are William Richardson's *The Maid of Lochlin, a Lyrical Drama. with Legendary Odes and other Poems* (London: Vernor and Hood, 1801) and Cornelius Neale's *Lyrical Dramas, with Domestic Hours* (London: Pinnock and Maunder, 1819). For use of the term as a synonym for opera, consult *The New British Theatre* (London, 1814), III, 303. It is also not unknown for opera libretti to be published in volumes of miscellaneous poetry: for example, Mrs. J. T. [Olive] Serres added "The Castle of Avola, an Opera in Three Acts" to her *Flights of Fancy* (London: J. Ridgway, 1805), and "Theodore, an Opera" was published among John Henry Colls's *Poems* (Norwich: J. Payne, 1804).

16. With so much fine critical commentary accumulating on *Prometheus Unbound*, it is surprising to find this scene still occasionally misinterpreted as reflecting Shelley's urge to retreat from the political program implicit in his lyrical drama. What causes confusion is Shelley's reliance on traditional pastoral paradigms for establishing a frame of reference, paradigms immediately understandable to his own culture but unapparent if one attempts to read the poem independently of the multiple contexts it assumes.

17. Angus Fletcher represents the seventeenth-century masque as the quintessential mixed genre, allowing incorporation of elements beyond the traditional boundaries of any single genre: *The Transcendental Masque: An Essay on Milton's "Comus"* (Ithaca: Cornell University Press, 1971).

Chapter 9. Form and Freedom

1. Goethe's sonnet translates literally as follows: "Nature and Art—they appear to diverge, but before one even considers it turn out to be the same. For me their contention has disappeared; both seem to attract me equally. Only honest exertion has real value! And if, first having set time aside, we have bound ourselves in spirit and purpose to our art, then Nature will once again be able to stir the heart. So all things under formation are constituted. In vain will liberated spirits strive for a fulfillment of pure heights. Who desires great things must make great effort. Through restriction one proves oneself a master, and only law can give us freedom."

2. With all respect for the value of M. H. Abrams's *The Mirror and the Lamp: Romantic Theory and the Critical Tradition* (New York: Oxford University Press, 1953), its argument that Romanticism participated in a proto-Crocean expressionism, so strongly based on this evidence, has had a widespread and deleterious influence, especially as the putative evidence was gathered into a college handbook under the title of *Romantic Criticism: 1800–1850*, edited by R. A. Foakes (London: Edwin Arnold, 1968). Needless to assert, the evidence supporting the present argument is pointedly to the contrary and implies the need to rewire (or re-fuse) this as yet blazing Romantic lamp.

3. I refer to the scholarly controversy over "the Romantic ideology," a term that furnishes the title for Jerome McGann's refreshing critique of an earlier generation's willingness to raise to ideological certainties what are culturally determined and tentative celebrations of the imaginative propensities of an embattled humanity (*The Romantic Ideology* [Chicago: University of Chicago Press, 1983]). Such an antithetical statement, however, tends to reinforce a dialectic founded on erroneous assumptions, for, as McGann argues, there never existed an independent entity to be construed by this term.

4. Aside from numerous indigenous historical determinants, the way each culture defined its literary canon profoundly influenced its Romanticism. On this aspect one should consult Ernst Robert Curtius' magisterial and cautionary account, "Modern Canon Formation," in *European Literature and the Latin Middle Ages* (1948), tr. Willard B. Trask (New York: Harper and Row, 1953), pp. 264–272.

5. See Margaret Gilman, *The Idea of Poetry in France from Houdar de la Motte to*

Baudelaire (Cambridge: Harvard University Press, 1958), pp. 178–189, and Ruth E. Mulhauser, *Sainte-Beuve and Greco-Roman Antiquity* (Cleveland: Press of Case Western Reserve University, 1969).

6. Though Gilman (*The Idea of Poetry in France*, p. 162) argues that "Hugo with the ode, Lamartine with the elegy, Vigny with the 'poëme,' had created great poetry, because they had applied their talents to genres of which the French language offered either no examples or inadequate ones," at least with Hugo generic choices are also profoundly ideological. Laurence M. Porter rightly remarks that "Hugo's theoretical statements in his prefaces to the *Odes* clearly show that he associated the Ode form with the Ancien Régime. Progressively as he evolves from monarchical views towards liberalism, he experiences the ode as inadequate for his poetic vision"—*The Renaissance of the Lyric in French Romanticism: Elegy, "Poëme" and Ode* (Lexington, Kentucky: French Forum, 1978), p. 86.

7. For this history, with a chronological bibliography appended, consult Herbert J. Hunt, *The Epic in Nineteenth-Century France; a study in heroic and humanitarian poetry from* Les martyrs *to* Les siécles morts (Oxford: Blackwell, 1941).

8. The Jena circle of the 1790s, including Novalis, Wackenroder, and preeminently Friedrich Schlegel, from which we derive an Idealist Romantic poetics, represented their aesthetic of liberated poetry in the short-lived periodicals, *Atheneum* and *Lyceum*. Since contemporaneously Goethe and Schiller were developing their notions of a new classicism, it is perhaps natural for later historians to see in the *Atheneumsfragmente* the foundations of a Romantic aesthetics. But a meticulous historicism must paint a more complicated picture. Insofar as these figures were known outside Germany, they were represented by Madame de Staël's *De l'Allemagne* of 1810 in a suggestive but necessarily superficial fashion. Though her account spurred the classic-romantic debate, the ideas of the Jena circle were virtually ignored by Italian culture, generally disavowed by British empiricism and skepticism, and rather splendidly distorted the minute they crossed the borders into the France of the Bourbon Restoration. We might even infer that Schlegel's circle had a comparatively minor influence on the actual achievements of German Romanticism, since for all its energetic spirit of creative innovation, its pronouncements came a quarter of a century after Goethe's own fame was established, and he and Schiller dominated the European view of German Romanticism. Against those titanic presences the effusion of brilliant but gnomic ideas either in short-lived periodicals, through an extensive but unpublished correspondence, or in untranslated philosophical lectures could not compete on a European stage—nor, for that matter, among the general reading public of the German-speaking states. In order to avoid a serious distortion of the record in the interest of theoretical paradigms, the experimentation of the Schlegel circle needs to be grounded in this large pan-European perspective, rather than Romanticism be cut to the proportions of the circle—an enthusiastic avant-garde of a kind that the ensuing century would see recreated repeatedly in Paris. Even so, even at its most radically innovative, this circle was obsessed with the nature and uses of artistic form, and Schlegel himself, in his prescription for criticism, firmly acknowledged that "The determination of the genre and structure, of the general proportions and the limitations of a work of art is . . . one of the preparatory labors of actual critical evaluation." See Hans Eichner, "Friedrich Schlegel's Theory of Literary Criticism," in *Romanticism Today*, a collection of diverse essays without stipulated editor (Bonn-Bad Godesburg: Inter Nationes, 1973), p. 24.

9. *The Shape of German Romanticism* (Ithaca: Cornell University Press, 1979).

10. John Porter Houston, *The Demonic Imagination: Style and Theme in French Romantic Poetry* (Baton Rouge: Louisiana State University Press, 1969), pp. 51–53.

11. See Baudelaire, *Correspondance générale*, ed. Jacques Crepet (Paris: L. Conard, 1947–1953), III, 39.

Index

Abdiel, 174
Abrams, M. H., 232, 236, 250
Achilles, 169, 173
Ackermann's Poetical Magazine, 223
Actium, 153
Adam, 171, 174
Addington, Henry (Lord Sidmouth), 226
Addison, Joseph, 137, 229-230
Adonis, 149
Aeneas, 167, 173, 176. *See also* Virgil, *The Aeneid*
Aeschylus, 69, 199
Aesop, 174
Agamemnon, 153
Agg, John, 232
Aikin, John, 25-26, 167
Aikin, Lucy, 228
Akenside, Mark, 25, 58, 67-68, 231
Alcaeus, 63
Alexander the Great, 65-66, 169
Alexandria, 87
Alexandrine, 212, 213, 215, 220
Alfred, 161-162, 169, 178, 245, 248
Allegory, 25, 31, 60, 67, 87, 90, 149, 150, 166, 176
Alpers, Paul, 87-88, 113, 233
Alpheus, 149
Amadis of Gaul, 130
America, 80, 195. *See also* Revolution, American
Anacreon, 63, 70
Anderson, Robert, 19, 22, 83
Anne I, 91
Annual Review, 14, 159, 223, 244
Antiquarianism, 20, 21, 27, 30, 70, 131, 132, 136, 138, 210, 241
Aphrodite, 88, 121. *See also* Venus
Apollo, 12, 115, 173, 201, 218
Arabian Nights, 131
Arcadia, et ego in, 88-89
Archimago, 134
Arethusa, 149
Ariadne, 242
Ariosto, Ludovico, 130, 152, 153, 160, 242
Aristotle: literary form, 152; tripartite

classification, 5, 9, 221
Armstrong, John, 31, 225
Arnold, Matthew, 209
Arthur, King, 137
Ashburnham, William, 225
Atheism, 61, 63
Athena, 243
Atheneum, 251
Augustan literature, 20, 88
Austen, Jane, 7
Australia, 97-99
Austria, 81
Autobiography, 245

Babbitt, Irving, 128
Bacon, Francis, 175
Bakhtin, Mikhail, 222
Ballad, 12, 25, 31, 86, 99, 108, 129, 130, 141, 148, 182, 213, 217, 222, 236, 240; revival, 19, 21, 27
Bannerman, Anne, 31, 225
Barlow, Joel, 175; *Columbiad*, 170-172; influence, 247-248; *Vision of Columbus*, 171
Bate, Walter Jackson, 21
Batteux, Charles, 25, 70
Baudelaire, Charles, 216
Beattie, James, 241, 243
Beautiful, the, 185
Beauty, intellectual, 62-63
Beckford, William, 225-226
Beddoes, Thomas Lovell, 242
Belial, 162
Bell, John, 70-71, 83, 224
Beloe, Richard, 17
Beowulf, 5, 163, 245
Berkeley, George, 206
Bertrand, Aloysius, 214
Beulah, 113
Bion, 237, 238
Black, John, 238, 249
Blackmore, Richard, 165
Blackwood's, 14, 15, 20, 27, 50, 228, 230, 232, 241
Blair, Hugh, 25, 70, 100, 174

Gabriel, 164
Galahad, 134, 142, 148
Gay, John, 92-93, 206, 234
Genera mixta, 90. *See also* Composite
  orders
Generic signals, 9, 181
Genette, Gérard, 221
Genre: authority in, 27; breakdown of, 4-
  5, 21, 22, 207, 223; classification of, 24-
  26; continuities of, 4-5, 6, 11, 41, 48-49,
  50-51, 52, 67, 71, 83, 101, 107, 203, 208-
  209, 215, 223; conventions in, 24, 31, 53,
  219; definition of, 5-7; and evolution, 8;
  and freedom, 204, 208, 209, 213, 215,
  217, 219, 250; and gender, 9; hierarchies
  of, 70, 99-100, 104, 106-107, 116, 180-
  181, 185, 190, 202-203, 206, 213; and
  ideology, viii, 7-8, 10, 12, 24, 81, 181-
  182, 191, 195, 198, 203, 204, 206, 208;
  self-reflexive, 132-133, 144, 145, 146, 147,
  148, 150, 157, 176-177, 178, 183, 200-201,
  203, 206, 215-217, 218-219; theory of, 3-
  13, 221, 222, 223. *See also* Form; Self-
  reflexiveness, authorial; *specific genres*
Gentleman's Magazine, 18, 26, 27, 225
Geoffrey of Monmouth, 130
George III, 55
George IV (Prince of Wales), 165, 167, 232
Georgic, 86-87, 91, 94-95, 98, 106, 237,
  238; and pastoral, 7, 104
Gilfillan, George, 32, 226
Gilman, Margaret, 251
Girdlestone, J. L., 69
Gleckner, Robert, 240, 244, 249
Gloucester, 162
Goethe, Johann Wolfgang von, 204, 209-
  210, 215-216, 225, 250, 251; *Faust*, 124,
  125, 219-220
Goldsmith, Oliver, 86, 92-93, 232
Gothic: novel, 226; structure, 152
Gothicism, 145, 215, 242
Grahame, James, 237
Gray, Thomas, 17, 66, 67, 68, 69, 231;
  "The Bard," 68, 73, 74, 162, 171; "Hymn
  to Adversity," 77-78; "Ode on a Distant
  Prospect of Eton College," 68; "Ode to
  Spring," 68, 83; "Sonnet on the Death
  of Mr. Richard West," 30
Great Britain: imperialism, 14, 91, 96-97,
  98, 133-134, 167-168; nationalism, 14,
  15, 24; political repression, 14, 35, 46.
  See also Revolution, English
Gregory, George, 163
Guarini, Battista, 86, 233
Guillén, Claudio, 6-7, 222

Hadrian, Mole of, 156
Haija Sophia, 153, 243
Haiku, 6
Haiti, 47
Hardy, 9, 86
Harrington, James, 47
Hartman, Geoffrey, 185, 231, 249
Hatchard, John, 165
Hayley, William, 17, 34, 38, 159, 166, 168,
  175, 176, 179, 247, 248, 249; *Essay on
  Epic Poetry*, 133-134, 160-161, 170, 174,
  239-240, 244
Hazlitt, William, 12, 23, 115; *Lectures on
  the English Poets*, 21-22
Headley, Henry, 18, 22-23, 24
Heber, Reginald, 58, 69, 231
Hector, 173
Heine, Heinrich, 211, 215
Heinzelman, Kurt, 237
Helen of Troy, 177
Hellenistic poetry, 87
Hemans, Felicia Browne, 59, 230
Henderson, George, 29, 228
Herbert, George, 7
Herbert, William, 37, 131, 162, 225, 277
Heroic drama, 201
Herrick, Robert, 18, 224
Hesiod, 86, 211
Higgenbottom, Nehemiah. *See* Coleridge,
  Samuel Taylor
Historical poetry, 23, 184
Hobbes, Thomas, 95, 245
Hobhouse, John Cam, 153, 249
Hogg, James, 132, 237
Hogle, Jerrold, 147
Hölderlin, Friedrich, 210, 212
Hollander, John, 4, 221, 231
Holy Alliance, 17, 28, 50
Homer, 5, 6, 52-53, 158, 160, 167, 173, 174,
  180, 211, 219, 247, 249; *Hymns*, 58; *Iliad*,
  4, 164, 170, 177, 210, 223, 244; *Odyssey*,
  4, 7, 164, 171, 223, 239
Hopkins, Gerard Manley, 55, 56
Hoppner, John, 227
Horace, 211, 230, 249; odes, 63, 65, 67, 70;
  precepts, 77; unities, 199
Housman, Robert, 37-38, 228
Howard, Donald, 152
Howard, John, 247
Hoyle, Charles, 165, 246
Hugo, Victor, 210, 212, 214, 215, 251
Hulme, T. E., 128
Hume, David, 20, 206, 209
Hunt, James Henry Leigh, 23, 26, 27, 50-
  52, 54, 69, 224, 230; *The Examiner*, 50;

PR590 .C8 1986   CU-Main

Curran, Stuart./Poetic form and British romanticis

3 9371 00041 1918

PR 590 .C8 1986
Curran, Stuart.
Poetic form and British
 romanticism

DATE DUE			
MAR 1 7 1997			
APR 1 8 2000			

CONCORDIA UNIVERSITY LIBRARY
2811 NE Holman St.
Portland, OR 97211-6099